Reporting Public Affairs

Reporting Public Affairs

HENRY H. SCHULTE

The Ohio State University

MACMILLAN PUBLISHING CO., INC.

New York

Collier Macmillan Publishers

London

PRINTED IN THE UNITED STATES OF AMERICA

Macmillan Publishing Co., Inc.
866 Third Avenue, New York, New York 10022

Collier Macmillan Canada, Ltd.

Library of Congress Cataloging in Publication Data

Schulte, Henry H
Reporting public affairs.

Includes index.
1. Reporters and reporting. 2. Government and the press. I. Title.
PN4781.S39 1981 070.4'3 80-19306
ISBN 0-02-408040-3

Printing: 1 2 3 4 5 6 7 8 Year: 1 2 3 4 5 6 7 8

To Boo Boo,
who as a "newspaper wife"
has listened, loved, and inspired
for more than thirty years

The author
acknowledges major contributions
to his
understanding of the journalistic process
and
dedication to quality
by the
several newspapers that have left their mark
on a
former employee:
The St. Petersburg Times
The Louisville Times
The Nashville Tennessean
The Chicago Daily News

PREFACE
The Public Affairs Reporter

MORE than 40 years ago, Curtis D. MacDougall shaped the trend toward combining the function of interpreter with that of reporter, pointing to changing social conditions as the reason. Despite what he saw as an unmistakable trend, however, MacDougall reminded educators and professional journalists of the importance of the traditional role of straight reporting.

The old standards of news judgment have not crumbled and disappeared. They have merely been rendered far more complex by the society in which we live, and by an ever-shrinking world undergoing traumatic technological transformation. A new need has emerged: to explain ever more complicated processes, events and relationships among people and peoples.

But with these new conditions, the need to remain faithful to the basic reportorial approach remains: *What* happened? *When* and *why* did it happen? *How* did it happen and *who* is involved? *Where* did it happen and *when* did it begin? And equally important, *what* does it mean?

It has become clear that public issues, and that takes in nearly every aspect of today's complicated society, cannot be reduced to two-sided scenarios. They must be viewed as a complex equation, subject to dissection by the public affairs reporter in language that can easily be understood. The question becomes not only whether a public issue is relevant, but how best to present it.

Answering that question is only one of the purposes of this book, which is designed as a guide for the advanced journalism student as well as a handbook for the young professional. Public affairs reporting demands news judgment that comes only with experience. All the reading in the world serves only as preliminary preparation for the reporter's first assignment. He or she must actually *do* it.

The traditional reportorial process is unchanging, demanding persistence, care, accuracy, fairness and a knowledge of the process the reporter is covering.

—Politicians have *always* engaged in rhetoric designed to win election, whatever the facts.

—Holders of political office have *always* tried to put reporters in their pockets.

—Government agency officials have *always* attempted to handle what they consider "internal" problems without interference from the press.

—Sources have *always* dried up when a scandal is brewing.

These are the traditional journalistic realities, among many others. But while dealing with them, the public affairs reporter must also deal with new complexities.

—Confusing environmental and consumer protection regulations and their effect on many different segments of society;

—Scientific and technological advances with tremendous implications for the nation's work force that call for special expertise on the part of the reporter to explain them;

—A new awareness on the part of the public of the issues which deeply affect it, even though those issues may be emerging thousands of miles away.

So while the old standards of news judgment remain, they have become more complicated by new demands for sophisticated information. Today's reporter must be a political and social scientist, historian, mathematician, engineer, accountant and nutritionist—but first he or she must be a journalist. It is in this milieu that the public affairs reporter of today functions.

This book grew out of the fear of many professionals that the "new journalism" might ultimately displace the traditional legwork that is necessary for a solid news report. Some argue today that the age of the specialist is upon us and that reporters can no longer function as generalists. This ignores the reality that most newspapers and broadcast outlets cannot afford such specialists.

The public affairs reporter on most newspapers will continue to cover the police beat as well as city hall, the labor beat as well as the courts, and the county building as well as consumer affairs.

A basic grounding in the traditional assignments remains not only useful but imperative in fulfilling the reportorial function.

This book thus addresses the traditional press "beats" as well as newer, more sophisticated areas of inquiry. The old, often mechanical, method of covering government by attending its official sessions should be given an overdue burial. In its place should be a recognition by the public affairs reporter that many public and decision-making centers constitute the political governance process. Ignoring the interplay that precedes and follows official action totally ignores the reality of the process.

So while Part One of the text deals with the reporter's role in covering the traditional administrative and legislative affairs of government, a new task emerges: to focus on the authorities and other special district governments, whose unique quasi-public status has made such an impact on the communities in which they operate.

The overlapping jurisdictions and complex relationships among these old and new forms of government also point to a special responsibility for the public affairs reporter: sorting out the conflicting claims for effectiveness of the various political systems and explaining them to the reader or viewer.

The judicial process cannot be totally compartmentalized. Every public affairs beat leads ultimately to the courts in some way. But Part Two attempts to provide the beginning reporter with some sense of their form and function and the methods by which to report action inside the system for the benefit of the reader.

The role of the traditional private sector—business, industry, finance, labor, politics and the newly emerging field of consumer affairs—has received increasing attention in recent years. Its impact on the public interest is unquestioned, and Part Three focuses on the job of the public affairs reporter in this complex area.

Part Four is designed as an overview of some important by-products of press responsibility—the relationship between government and the media, the conflict between the traditional rights of privacy and of the public to know about affairs which affect it, and the continuing process of investigative reporting.

At the end of many chapters, suggested reading lists have been given that will provide other sources of good information for the aspiring journalism student.

This book is not designed as a political science or economics manual, and students are urged to acquire substantial background in those courses which serve as companions to journalism education. Change is everywhere, and the astute reporter recognizes and deals with this fact of life, adapting to the need for continuing education long after that first byline.

H.H.S.

CONTENTS

PART ONE
GOVERNMENT: Administrative and Legislative

CHAPTER
1 Covering Municipal Government 3

The Need for Municipal Government 5 / Creating Municipal Government 8 / Forms of City Government 10 / How Municipal Government Operates 16 / Complicating Factors for the Journalist 31 / Suggested Readings 37

2 County Government 38

Foundations of the Modern County 40 / Who Governs the County? 42 / The Cast of Characters 51 / Coping with Complications 60

3 Reporting State Government 62

The Powers of State Government 64 / The Legislative Branch 66 / The Executive Branch 80

4 Covering Federal Government 97

The Congressional Representative as Source 104 / Letting the "Strings" Work for You 105 / The Federal Regulators 107 / The Federal Structure 109 / Pressure Groups 120 / Suggested Readings 121

5 Reporting Education 122

Who Governs? 124 / Money Oils the Machinery 130 / A Trip into the School System 136 / Secrecy as a Problem 141 / Suggested Readings 142

6 Authorities and Other Special Districts 143

Origins of the Form 145 / Defining Their Functions 146 / Reporting Questionable Practices 154 / The Role of the Reporter 156 / Suggested Readings 159

PART TWO
THE COURTS AND LAW ENFORCEMENT

CHAPTER
7 The Judicial Process 163

A Basic Definition 169 / The Dual System of Courts 173 / Staffing the Courts 181 / Researching Court Cases 187 / Suggested Readings 189

8 Reporting Civil Actions 191

The Action Commences 193 / Dealing with the Complaint 194 / The Defendant Answers 196 / Discovery 200 / Remedies 201 / Final Pretrial Procedure 205 / The Trial 207

9 Law Enforcement 211

Complicating Factors for the Journalist 212 / The Enforcers of the Law 215 / Police Department Organization 217 / Covering the Police Beat 223 / Writing the Crime Story 226 / Police-Press Relationships 235 / State and Federal Agencies 241 / Suggested Readings 248

10 Reporting Criminal Actions 249

Arrest, Accusation and Pleading 258 / Criminal Trial 265 / Free Press vs. Fair Trial 271 / A Reporter's Guide to Legal Terms 272

PART THREE
THE PRIVATE SECTOR: People Make It "Public"

CHAPTER

11 Covering Politics 279

Political Party Structure 283 / Polishing the Ability to Solve Problems 288 / Monitoring Public Opinion 295 / Suggested Readings 300

12 Covering Labor 301

Balancing "Pluses" and "Minuses" 304 / The Labor Beat's Special Set of Problems 306 / From Agriculture to Industry . . . and Beyond 311 / Labor Organization 314 / State Government's Involvement 316 / Federal Government Involvement 318 / Labor Disputes: Strike or Lockout? 321 / A Labor Glossary 324

13 The Economics of the Private Sector 326

The Private Sector: Profit and Risk 330 / Monitoring the Community 335 / Government Involvement 342 / The Public Information Officer 350 / Generating Ideas 352 / A Reporter's Guide to Business-Financial Terms 354 / Suggested Readings 359

14 Consumer Affairs 360

Some Historical Dimensions 362 / Six Different Views 367 / Consumer Coverage: Reporter at Work 375

PART FOUR
PUBLIC AFFAIRS: An Overview

CHAPTER
15 Government and Media in Conflict 383

A Natural Tension 386 / The "Secrets" of Government 392 / The Dangers of Cronyism 395 / Booster or Watchdog? 398 / Suggested Readings 401

16 Investigative Reporting 402

Organizing for the Task 403 / Dealing with Sources 405 / Coping with the Task 407 / A Guide to Records 409 / Using the Freedom of Information Act 417 / Suggested Readings 418

17 Privacy and the Public's Right to Know 420

The Legal Limits 422 / Defenses for the Journalist 429 / The Ethical Limits 432 / Privacy Legislation 436 / Suggested Readings 437

Index 439

PART ONE

GOVERNMENT:
Administrative and Legislative

CHAPTER 1
Covering Municipal Government

THE American city, a complex geographical and social unit with a richly heterogenous cast of characters, represents the heart of public affairs reporting. Here at the local level lie the issues closest to the homeowner, the apartment dweller, the taxpayer, the parent, the student and the merchant.

Inside city hall itself, the real and sometimes imagined seat of local power, is another cast of characters who influence the course of nearly everyone's lives:

On the one side are the "ins," confident winners in the most recent election that has cast them, for a specified time at least, as power brokers with a temporary mandate to govern the community.

On the other side, and often with a power base inside city hall itself, are the traditional "outs," losers in the last election, whose philosophical goal is to constantly undermine the efforts of "that crowd at City Hall" and ultimately seize power themselves.

Trying to keep cool heads midway between these warring factions are the salaried professional managers who have been appointed to impartially administer the affairs of the city. They are trying, often unsuccessfully, to remain above the political arena.

And out along the streets and highways that typify the urban character of the community are the thousands of John Q. Publics, who require and are willing within limits to foot the bill for the costs of services they receive. To a large or small extent, they reach the electoral decisions that affect those in City Hall. Whether the city is a giant Chicago or a more modest Chillicothe or Chapmanville, the basic equation remains the same—although the character of the community or the system of governance may differ.

Into this mélange of people, politics and professional managers marches the public affairs reporter assigned to the municipal government beat. To do a competent job, he or she must successfully negotiate the intricate minefield of hoary tradition, legalistic rules, diverse personalities, special interests with axes to grind and an occasional lacing of fresh ideas.

To make the reporter's task even more complex, the readership to whom he or she reports ranges from total apathy to passionate involvement. This necessitates walking a fine line between far too detailed reporting that may satisfy the one and the merely superficial accounts that may satisfy the other.

Assessments Are Important

Despite wise counsel from supervising editors and sympathetic associates, the city hall reporter will approach the seat of local government for the first time experiencing a wide range of emotions. Anticipation of the new challenge will mix poorly with a natural fear of the unknown. This fear should pass quickly, and city hall will never seem quite so mysterious or forbidding to a reporter as it does on that first day.

Whatever the talents of the newcomer, one of the first important keys to successfully unlocking doors at city hall is the ability to be at ease in a new environment. It should not take long, but meanwhile the elected, the appointed and the hangers-on will keep their own counsel during those first days as they assess the newcomer "from the paper." It constitutes a waiting game as policy-makers and managers carefully attempt to answer what to them are the most important questions:

1. Will the reporter be willing to play by what they consider the traditional rules at city hall?

2. Is the reporter always going to be sniffing around for "sensational" stories, keeping low-profile managers in a continual uproar?

3. Will the reporter be understanding in his or her handling of the frequent, sensitive "personnel" matters with which city matters are often interwoven?

4. Can the newcomer be counted upon to provide a good press in return for cooperation?

Answers to these kinds of questions are important to people in city government, who are pragmatic men and women often honestly concerned with providing effective services and adequate protection to the citizens of the community for whom they work. Questions such as these are natural when a journalistic newcomer intrudes upon their turf.

While understanding this, the reporter will conduct his or her appraisal from a substantially different perspective and for a different purpose:

1. Just what are the traditional rules at city hall, and how much will the reporter have to give up in order to play by them? The stakes may simply be too high.

2. What kinds of "sensational" stories lie behind those closed doors, and how important are they to competent coverage of the beat? It may be that the managers' concerns are secondary to the demands of airing such information.

3. How much resistance will the reporter encounter in covering legitimate personnel matters that affect the public interest? They cannot all be lumped under the label of "sensitive" or "purely administrative," and the reporter's job will be to frequently unclog the drains in the city bureaucracy.

4. The reporter's focus should not be on whether he or she provides a good press or a bad press but, rather, on the extent of his or her cooperation with officials in order to assure an uninterrupted flow of information to the public.

Other nuts-and-bolts questions are important to the reporter too. Who of those in city hall will be most difficult to deal with? Who will provide the most help? What effect will they have on coverage? How can the reporter avoid the impending invitation and temptation to join the city hall "team" as a raiser of trial balloons for officials or as a highly selective story leaker? What levers will the reporter have to use to assure full and accurate answers to important questions, when some elements are uncooperative and unwilling for issues to be aired?

These two approaches may appear to be at odds, but they can be reconciled. The reporter will learn that quality coverage of city government calls for a measure of behavioral sensitivity, a give and take that allows room for the human element, yet does not at all impinge on the reporter's responsibility to fully and accurately cover the most important beat in the community.

It is simple: the reporter has a job to do, city officials have theirs. The jobs are not totally inimical to one another.

The Need for Municipal Government

Municipal government exists to provide services to an urban population and to establish regulations to assure order in the community.

Within the limits of what its residents are willing to pay for those services, a city maintains a police force, a fire department, crews to handle refuse removal, engineers to assure smooth traffic flow on the streets and highways, work crews to maintain those streets, parks and recreational facilities, and other such amenities of urban life as determined by the occasional mandate of the people.

There is a very important implication in this basic definition for the city government reporter. Since services are being provided, someone has to pay for them. Most municipal governments utilize a number of sources to obtain funds which pay for services, and the mechanics of collection and budgeting millions of dollars a year constitute one of the costs of doing business as a city.

Little is more important to a taxpayer than a demand upon his or her wallet or pocketbook, and the perceptive city government reporter recognizes this early and acts accordingly. An increase in the local rate of taxation or the other sources of city revenue, or a rarer decision to lower the tax rate is always near the top of the taxpayer's list of priorities. It should also be high on the reporter's list.

The Range of Services and Inherent Conflict

The modern municipal government offers an increasingly broad range of services. Aside from those already mentioned, it provides parking in business areas, collects garbage, inspects buildings, maintains public libraries, constructs arenas and civic centers, and provides any number of health services.

But municipal government also exists to regulate people's activity and assure an orderly community. Police officers and city judges do their share; so does a planning commission that promulgates and enforces zoning ordinances to ensure reasonable protection of property. In regulating many aspects of community life, however, government develops complicating factors because of the purely negative connotations:

—Residents may *not* burn trash or garbage within city limits; they may *not* maintain chicken or pigeon coops in their backyards which may offend neighbors; they *cannot* park in no-parking zones; they *cannot* erect a structure without a valid building permit; they *cannot* use the city parks after 10 p.m., to protect them from urban muggers.

Since such regulations are essentially negative, and since there is more inherent conflict in what people cannot do than in what they are allowed to do, restrictions are often what make news in a community.

An example:

—City council votes to close a major community park to vehicular traffic each weekend so that pedestrians and picnickers may benefit. Noisy traffic, including crowded vans with defective mufflers and souped-up motor bikes, had gradually supplanted the quiet, more pastoral scene.

A problem quite sticky by some community standards has arisen.

The council decision will restrict activities at the most popular gathering places in the city for young people, who in an urban environment tend to drive noisier cars and play their radios quite a bit louder. A basic conflict has developed because of city government's restrictions on traffic in the park.

The city hall reporter will tend to accumulate more of these "conflict" stories than other kinds of stories, and in the selection process he or she will have to evaluate story material so that less significant issues do not overwhelm others which take on greater importance. The reporter will have to evaluate material to assure that the more important issues are not lost in the shuffle.

Criteria for such evaluation include the number of persons affected by an issue, the impact of the issue on a group, the depth of feeling over the issue, whatever its importance, the setting in which the issue becomes public and the overall interest in it.

Hearing All Sides of An Issue

Closing the park to traffic offers another important lesson. In all stories dealing with such basic conflict between two groups or more, the public affairs reporter must take care to provide a hearing to all sides, not merely those most accessible.

In the park issue, young motorists have an interest in assuring that the facility remains open to traffic. City officials, however, have bowed to complaints of other park users who have demanded action. Still another group, nearby property owners, has an interest in the issue, since on-street parking in the area is affected by the council vote. The city hall reporter will anticipate these various "publics" and their points of view in developing stories that precede and follow council decision. Even such a simple issue as the park closing can have complex overtones.

A Basic Rationale for Coverage

The park example helps answer the question: Why is covering city government so important? There are a number of answers.

1. In contrast to state and federal government, city government is closer to those who are affected by its activities. For many, in fact, city hall is right around the corner, or at least only a few minutes away. A council member or other official may be a neighbor.

2. City government affects people more directly. Services provided are vital. Should a garbage truck neglect to service a neighborhood block, citizen response will be prompt and noisy. Should officials vote to change the traffic flow on a downtown street from two-way to one-way traffic for the sake of efficiency, merchants may roar with indignation. Because of this multitude of limited-interest issues, there will be a tendency for the city hall reporter to have a higher story

count than will other government beats, and the demands on the reporter will be greater.

3. In smaller communities, a neighborhood atmosphere creates a more basic interest in the activities of city government. A zoning issue might involve families who have ties to other neighborhoods or who feel threatened by the very fact that it is happening to someone across town. Police negotiations with city officials on salary increases may hold more interest for a neighborhood because a police officer is a neighbor.

4. Coverage is important because, as at other government levels, there is the constant implication of expenditures, which means that the public must ultimately pay for everything. The acquisition and disbursement of money is of universal interest.

Creating Municipal Government

In organizing a community to satisfy the need for services, citizens traditionally applied to state government for permission to carry on these functions. Cities and towns are creatures of the states, and municipal government power flows from the states under their reserved rights of sovereignty, based on the 10th Amendment to the U.S. Constitution:

> The powers not delegated to the United States by the Constitution, nor prohibited by it to the States, are reserved to the States respectively, or to the people.

While city government is designed to satisfy the needs and wants of a specific group of citizens who are willing to pay for the costs, the typical municipality derives its powers from state law and is generally subordinate to state authority in most of its activities. For example, final budget approval for a municipality must often be obtained from one of the state's fiscal agencies, and frequent state legislation influences the operation of local government.

The new city hall reporter should begin with a review of the municipality's charter, the basic document originally granted by the state for governing the community. Whether it was granted in 1880, 1920 or more recently, the charter details the powers and limitations of power upon those who govern, identifying what can and cannot be done at the local level.

For example, a city council may have the power to change the districts from which members are elected, or that power may specifically be vested in the hands of the electorate which must vote on any changes. The charter may specify that the city manager has the power to hire and fire city employees, yet be unclear on the role of the city clerk, who may be appointed by the council. The reporter should know the limitations imposed by the charter, as well as the powers specified by it.

Identifying Pressure Groups

The shape of the charter, with its powers and limits, was originally determined by pressure groups interested in forming the municipality. Those living within its borders were given the power to incorporate as a municipal body, with the city gaining legal status, generally "in perpetuity," to serve as agent for residents. While many charters call for non-partisan elections, the original pressure groups made them basic political documents, and they generally remain that way today. Whatever the charter's insistence on "non-partisan" elections, the fact remains that politics, through organized parties or otherwise, does play a dominant role in municipal governance.

Government is not neutral. It is the product of pressures from many groups, each of them at work to assure some kind of access to government or to some advantage. Many are working at cross-purposes.

One of the keys to effective coverage of municipal government is thorough identification of these pressure groups. Without necessarily stigmatizing these groups, the reporter must be sufficiently familiar with them to identify and be prepared to communicate their ideas and goals.

While this is not difficult, it requires a thought process that goes beyond merely identifying a public affairs issue and following it through to its conclusion. As an issue develops, the reporter must ask the question: Who is going to be most intimately involved in it and its resolution?

For example, an effort is under way to establish a halfway house for mentally retarded persons in an older neighborhood. While church organizations campaign actively for the facility, many in the neighborhood oppose it, possibly misunderstanding its intent. Elements on the campus of a nearby university hold strong views, both for and against location of the halfway house. The courts are asked to decide the issue, and a zoning board is intimately involved. Some professional organizations see the facility as a legitimate effort to solve the problem of endless incarceration in faceless mental institutions, and still other pressure groups bear in on the issue. It is easy to see the role of the reporter in this sensitive issue. Providing access to the larger public so that each group's interests may be fully aired is essential to the honest resolution of the issue.

Other pressure groups have become a traditional part of the scene. The business community usually possesses influence that far exceeds the size of its membership. Labor groups, because of their size and composition, form an important pressure group. Other organizations such as civic clubs, women's clubs, church and ministerial organizations, and neighborhood clubs all influence municipal government.

At the outset, the reporter will identify the groups that have a particular interest in the outcome of an issue, discussing with their leadership the pressures that are being exerted, either in favor of or in opposition to it. But care must be taken to assure that the reporter does not become part of the issue itself through the reporting of it and that the stories produced mirror only the effort to illuminate the issue.

Forms of City Government

Municipal government in this country generally takes four forms: the mayor-council form, the city commission, the council-manager form and the fairly recent metropolitan form of government. Because the urban scene is in a constant state of change and presents so many problems, the city government reporter should be familiar with all the forms. While city charters have been traditionally subjected to little or no change, they are not written in concrete, and there is some change as the recent developments in metropolitan areas attest.

The Mayor-Council Plan

The mayor-council form of city government is the oldest, growing out of the 19th century. It is a product of Jacksonian democracy, and it continues to reflect the spirit of the frontier with a skepticism of politicians and, indeed, of government itself. The form developed when the functions of city government were fewer, when local officials were "coordinated" through powerful political parties, and when people were reluctant to assign too much power to an individual or group. Their philosophy was simple: allow an office-holder few powers and saddle him with many checks and balances, with the result that he could commit little damage on the public purse.

In this way, a weak mayor-council form developed, with both the mayor and council elected to office and all sharing legislative and administrative power. Council serves as both a legislative and executive branch of government. In addition to setting policy through legislative action, the council appoints administrative officers such as a city attorney, city clerk, city engineer and police court judge. A committee of council often is responsible for preparing an annual budget. Some power accrues to the mayor because he or she presides at council meetings, but the mayor is considered to be merely first among equals. As such, the power of the office is limited.

The mayor is not weak because he or she lacks policy-making power but, rather, because he or she lacks administrative power. The potential problems in this form of municipal government are quite visible: no single individual is responsible for seeing to it that ordinances and other rules are carried out. There is a tendency for weak administration to develop, no matter what the intent of a city council.

The reporter operating in this environment may find many officials willing to discuss the issues, but few with actual power to dispose of them. The result will be that many long-winded discussions of issues will develop and remain in the news for lengthy periods of time.

Strong Mayor-Council Form

Because of these deficiencies, the strong mayor-council form of municipal government began to develop at the end of the 19th century, differing from the weak mayor form only in degree.

Administrative responsibility is concentrated in the hands of an elected mayor, and the policy-making responsibility becomes a joint effort of both the mayor and the council. Thus, council takes a sublimated role. The mayor exerts strong administrative leadership, appointing and dismissing department heads, making all kinds of decisions that affect the running of a city. He or she usually prepares the annual budget, and the burden is on council to alter it.

In sharing power with the mayor, the council is limited in function to legislative policy-making, and even this function must often be shared with the mayor. An additional and important factor must be considered: the mayor's position allows him or her to exert strong political leadership, further enhancing the mayor's role as the city's administrator. This is important to the mayor who as an elected official must regularly renew his or her mandate from the public, but it also offers the opportunity to further exert leverage over a sometimes politically divided council.

Because of its provisions for vigorous political leadership, the strong mayor form has proved effective in large cities, where complexities of government and varied ethnic concentrations call for firm leadership and direction. Its major advantage lies in the ability of the system to pinpoint responsibility and to plan overall city policy. And since it somewhat separates the legislative and executive functions, the strong mayor form offers a system of checks and balances not quite so clear with other forms of municipal government.

However, some disadvantages have been noted. The form appears to expect too much of a mayor, because few persons combine the talent of an adroit politician who can be elected and an expert administrator. There is a vast difference between the ability to draw sufficient votes to remain in office, yet make the difficult and often unpopular decisions expected of the administrator of a large city. The late Mayor Richard Daley of Chicago seemed to combine these qualities to create a powerful office. So did the late Mayor Fiorello LaGuardia of New York.

The reporter's coverage in this form of government will focus on the administrative end, with a natural tendency to more fully illuminate the mayor's position. With all its power, a diffuse council—sometimes with more than two dozen members—does not offer the reporter the opportunity to focus on points of view.

Deadlocks are likely to develop between the mayor and council, and the reporter will find himself or herself a key element in communicating the arguments to the electorate. Care must be taken that the power of the press, with its capacity for focusing on specific political personalities, is not abused by them.

The Commission Plan

The commission form of government grew out of an emergency that gripped Galveston, Texas, in 1900. Following a hurricane and tidal wave that devastated the community, the State of Texas suspended local government in Galveston and substituted a temporary government of five local businessmen—the Galveston Commission.

So successful was the work of the commission that this form was retained in the city and attracted wide attention as a "businessman's government." Within 10 years after its creation, the new form was in use in more than 100 U.S. cities, and by 1920 more than 500 cities had shifted to the commission form. Growth continued at a much slower pace to World War II.

The outstanding characteristic of the commission plan is the dual role of the commissioners, each acting individually as the administrative head of a city department while collectively acting as policy-makers for the city. There is no real separation of powers, since commissioners perform both legislative and executive functions. It should be noted that the commission plan has evolved in different ways and that in some cities the commissioners do not run departments.

This form of local government has fallen into decline because of some basic disadvantages. It is difficult to find citizens of professional caliber to operate city departments while overseeing their own affairs. Successful business executives are reluctant to give up their jobs or to take time from their businesses to accept a city job at less pay.

Other weaknesses were apparent. A small (generally five-person) commission allowed little room for the important function of criticism and a fraternity of tolerance was likely to result. Just as important, each commissioner tended to jealously guard his or her territory, and the top of the administrative pyramid was effectively sawed off. Overall planning in the city was apt to suffer, despite the avowed intention of the commission to act together in legislative matters.

The City Manager Form

At the outset of his or her career, the young reporter is more likely to encounter the city manager form of government. It prevails in many middle-sized cities where journalists often get their start. This form began to evolve early in this century following a proposal that there should be a "distinct profession of municipal managers." The growth and complexity of the city dictated evolution of these experts trained specifically to direct its affairs.

Nearly 2,500 U.S. cities operate with this form of government today, with most of the growth occurring after World War II. The characteristics are fairly uniform, although wide variations exist in specific situations.

An elected council or commission, composed of laypersons, is responsible for setting policy through ordinances and resolutions. This body hires a professional administrator to carry out its policies and oversee direction of the city, with the administrator answerable to council. The manager serves at the pleasure of council, and dismissal is generally in the hands of that body.

A mayor is usually elected from among the members of the council to serve as presiding officer and represent the city at official functions. Thus, the mayor is merely first among equals, having the same vote in policy-making decisions as council peers. However, the role of presiding officer and heightened ceremonial visibility offer somewhat greater power for the mayor.

The powers and duties of the city manager are clearly outlined in the city charter, pointing to a purely administrative role in overseeing affairs. He or she appoints and, when necessary for the good of the city, dismisses employees; prepares an annual budget and submits it to council with a complete report on finances and administrative activities; submits monthly statements to council of all receipts, disbursements and unpaid accounts; and keeps council advised of the future needs of the city, making recommendations on them.

In this manner a council entrusts to a professional administrator responsibility for the day-to-day operation of municipal government. The city manager form generally includes a merit plan to attract persons who are technically competent, but the manager is exempt, often serving without even a contract. Some employees of the city are often excluded from the city manager's jurisdiction, among them a city clerk who answers to the council or commission and a city attorney who advises council as well as the city manager.

As a result, the reporter will often find the lines of responsibility confused and unclear, with a formal organization chart failing to completely clear up the confusion.

EMPHASIS ON TECHNICAL COMPETENCE

The socio-economic character of a community often determines whether it adopts the council-manager form of government. Rapidly growing cities are likely to experiment with this form, and it has also proven popular in cities with heavy concentrations of young families or with mobile, middle-class populations. The bigger cities with major elements of working-class populations or heavy concentrations of ethnic groupings have traditionally endorsed the mayor-council form of government.

While most city planners praise the city manager form, some complicating factors are important to the journalist who reports on its activities.

While the system places heavy emphasis on technical competence, council or commission members, as elected officials, continue to suffer pressure from elements of their constituencies to act in their behalf. So while a professional manager is deciding priorities in an impartial manner, citizen groups are putting pressure on the policy-maker in a different way to influence the final decision. The reporter is often faced with two points of view: the professional may not always be the primary source of the decision, the elected official playing the major role. Such a diffusion in the decision-making process calls for a knowledge of personalities and the sources of real power.

The council-manager system is often misunderstood. Some critics call it "dictatorial," because the city manager, not being an elected official, answers only to the council or commission that appointed him or her. Supporters of the system respond that there is adequate access through the elected officials.

City managers, like the elected officials who hire them, come and go, with policy and politics playing a role in the arrival and departure. In this respect, the city manager system is not unlike the other forms of local government. A change in administration often foreshadows further changes down the line, and the city hall reporter will be alert to such long-range shakeups.

> Stephen Weeks, the city's director of public works and perhaps the last vestige of the James Stillman administration, announced his resignation this morning, effective immediately.
>
> Weeks weathered the turmoil at City Hall for more than a year after the resignation of Stillman, the city manager who hired him in 1977.
>
> Weeks declined to discuss the turmoil of the past year. "I don't think any more discussion about the problems at City Hall is necessary," he said. "Enough has been said."
>
> Nearly 20 other department heads and professional city employees have left since Stillman's departure—some by resignation, others by elimination of jobs from the budget, and still others by outright dismissal by new City Manager Robert Barton.

Metropolitan Government

More than likely, the young journalist reporting for work at a metropolitan newspaper or broadcast outlet will be shunted to the far suburbs to cover one of the smaller governments ringing the larger city. Even more likely, the reporter will find one of the traditional forms of municipal government awaiting him or her.

Increasingly, however, new general-purpose governments are being created in metropolitan areas to cope with their problems, and the public affairs reporter today can expect assignment to one of the new umbrella governments.

Most U.S. municipalities are encountering major financial difficulties, caused partly by the increasing cost of providing adequate services to burgeoning urban populations. As the demand for such services has grown, so has the financial burden on taxpayers. The problem has been exacerbated by the fragmentation of government—the rush to the suburbs and decline of the central city.

The older governments, with their built-in restrictions and traditional biases, have often been unable to cope with the pressures brought about by these changes. The problems have intensified—congested highways, a rising crime rate, unemployment, inadequate public transportation, pollution and environmental neglect, and deteriorating services. The standard approach was to increase taxes. However, as taxes increased, homeowners began fleeing the central city to the suburbs, creating a further drain on the city's tax base.

Those who fled found new sets of problems awaiting them in their new locations: lack of public facilities, which were expensive to duplicate and maintain; even more congested highways and far less adequate public transportation; and a tax problem caused by greater dependence on residential taxpayers who had left industrial, financial and business communities behind in the city.

Suburban taxpayers found that many of the old problems had simply followed them to their new homes, and the older central city found itself surrounded by many square miles of crowded suburbs, all with their own local governments.

DIRECTIONS OF REORGANIZATION

While the press tries to cope with reporting on the complex municipal maze, some government reformers have experienced success in restructuring urban government, in an attempt to make it more capable of coping with the problems of the metropolis.

Three types of general-purpose governments have been most closely studied:

1. The central city government has been consolidated with the existing county government.

2. Reorganization of the county has been proposed on an internal basis to create a more effective form of government.

3. Creation of a two-tier instrument of government has been effected, with one tier responsible for areawide services, the other covering purely local functions.

There were early notable examples of consolidation—New Orleans in 1805, Boston in 1822, Philadelphia in 1854 and New York in 1898—but the movement languished until after World War II. Since that time, consolidation has experienced some success: Baton Rouge, Louisiana (1947), Nashville, Tennessee (1962), Jacksonville, Florida (1967), and Indianapolis, Indiana (1969). Other urban areas are considering city-county consolidation.

Under the two-tier concept of metropolitan government adopted by Miami and Dade County in 1957, the restructured county government assumed responsibility for areawide functions—mass transit, public health, some central police and fire services, and planning. Other more purely local functions were left to the 26 municipalities, school districts and other special districts in the county—police patrol, public education and control of local land use through zoning. The two-tier system applies only to incorporated areas. The 43 percent of the population not incorporated depends on county government to handle both local and areawide functions.

Most other proposals for metropolitan government tend to bypass consolidation and deal with creation of an executive office to centralize control of dispensing services and regulating affairs of the urban area. The reporter can see that actual change has been somewhat limited in scope, but the future certainly forecasts continued pressure for alterations.

How Municipal Government Operates

When the sharp rap of a gavel signifies passage or rejection of an important proposal at a city council meeting, it is often merely the final curtain to what may have become a long-running drama. During the process, the city hall reporter has probed dozens of sets of raw nerves in interviewing the actors in presenting the various acts to the readers and viewers of the community. While it is important that the final act be reported, the arguments, discussions and sparring that accompany acceptance or rejection of an issue are the stuff from which useful news reports are created.

While the heart of municipal news coverage lies in the council chambers, the preliminary deliberations often cover weeks, even months, and take place in offices far removed from city hall. An informal meeting leading to a key decision may take place in someone's home, an attorney's office, the quarters of a city planner, or even in an upstairs hallway. While it is impractical to assume that the reporter will be a participant in all these informal decision-making sessions, he or she will try to follow the issues wherever they lead. It is the responsibility of the reporter to mirror the development of these issues rather than to cover only the final act of the drama.

How Council Operates

A city council or commission is composed of a group of elected citizens, with regular meetings scheduled to conduct the policy-making aspects of municipal business. Only at these official meetings are ordinances enacted and resolutions passed expressing the intent of the members. A preliminary meeting or "work session" is often conducted to prepare for the official meeting, although sunshine legislation in some states has inhibited the practice. Often this preliminary session is the more productive of the two sessions, because the reporter will find a more informal give and take among members. The argument over a controversy may be resolved at the work session after some negotiation, and an ordinance may breeze through the official meeting with little or no discussion. Without benefit of the work session argument and compromise, the story is only half complete.

> An ordinance requiring registration of all charitable fund-raising drives in the city flew through Council last night after two members withdrew their opposition in an acrimonious work session earlier in the day.
>
> The ordinance, passed by a 5-0 vote on final reading, will go into effect immediately.
>
> "We're satisfied the ordinance will be enforced fairly," Councilman John Prudy said. Prudy and Councilman Charles Coors had objected to a clause requiring annual resubmittal of a request for registration by such agencies as the Salvation Army and Volunteers of America.

Most municipal councils operate through the traditional committee system, with standing committees studying proposals on public safety, finance, public works, transportation, civil service, recreation and health. As with the preliminary work session, the reporter will find that many key decisions are reached in committee meetings, often not attended by members of the press. Sometimes what appears to be a popular proposal dies quietly but firmly after a committee meeting is held on it.

Councils take official action through passage of *ordinances,* which are municipal regulations with the force of law, and *resolutions,* which merely express the intent, permission or opinion of the council. Often a resolution, however, may be more important than a vote on a routine ordinance because it indicates policy direction taken by the governing body.

A resolution directing the city manager to execute a contract to construct a multimillion-dollar sewer and water project that presages development of a major industrial park carries many economic implications for the growth of the community. Meanwhile, an ordinance changing the method of applying reserve funds may be much less vital to the average reader. The new reporter will quickly learn to distinguish between items of substance and those which are only housekeeping measures.

An ordinance is usually introduced in an official session, read by the city clerk and assigned to an appropriate committee for study and further action. The committee recommendation is often important. The proposal is brought up for discussion and a second reading at a subsequent council meeting. Some municipalities provide for a third and final reading. Many councils can suspend the rules on an emergency basis and vote on two readings at the same session, resulting in quick enactment of an ordinance. After passage, the ordinance becomes law, sometimes immediately, but often 30 days following passage.

Resolutions and other actions by the body, such as appointments to boards and agencies, usually require only one reading before council.

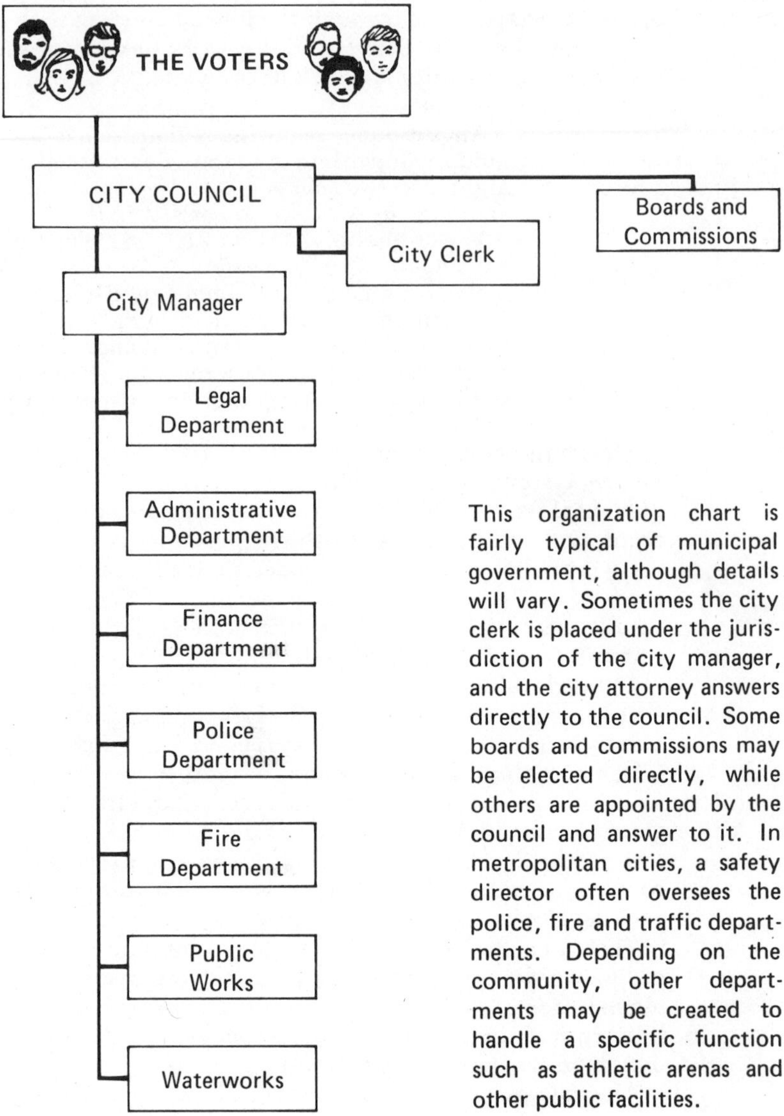

This organization chart is fairly typical of municipal government, although details will vary. Sometimes the city clerk is placed under the jurisdiction of the city manager, and the city attorney answers directly to the council. Some boards and commissions may be elected directly, while others are appointed by the council and answer to it. In metropolitan cities, a safety director often oversees the police, fire and traffic departments. Depending on the community, other departments may be created to handle a specific function such as athletic arenas and other public facilities.

FIGURE 1–1. *Organizational chart of a typical municipal organization.*

A TYPICAL COUNCIL SESSION

In advance of the official meeting, the city clerk has published and distributed an agenda, a document that begins with roll call and synopsis of the previous session. Some agendas provide little more than a mere listing of the topics; others give pages of detail. The agenda offers the reporter assurance that an item will be up for discussion and provides an excellent opportunity to check issues that he or she may have overlooked in the press of other city hall coverage.

Here is a typical rundown of a council meeting:

—The city manager reports on contract bids, such as new police cars, office supplies, and equipment for the streets department. A preliminary check often uncovers newsworthy items in seemingly routine contract discussions. Re-award of liability insurance for city employees offers an opportunity to explore the cost, effectiveness and usefulness of the insurance. Bids on supply of street salt for winter enables the reporter to look ahead at plans to cope with the winter snow and ice that is certain to come.

—Council hears a second and final reading of an ordinance to modify parking along a neighborhood street. Members approve the ordinance, which had received a unanimous aye vote at the previous meeting. That vote had indicated agreement on the issue, and this vote is routine.

—Council approves another ordinance on second reading, this one to amend a zoning ordinance to allow two-family dwellings in a changing neighborhood formerly restricted to one-family dwellings. Like the last council session, there are no objections.

—A member of council introduces an ordinance to more closely regulate taverns, following complaints by residents of objectionable noise and activity outside some of them. With little discussion, the ordinance is referred to council's legal committee for study. (The reporter had reported the residents' complaints earlier.) Lack of discussion at a council meeting does not impute a lack of importance to an issue. At this stage, the reporter's obligation is to obtain a copy of the proposed ordinance and report its contents, while seeking follow-up comment from the council member who sponsored the ordinance and persons who will be affected by its passage.

—A resolution is proposed, calling for a moratorium on construction of new downtown parking facilities until a traffic study has been completed. Several persons in the sparse audience have asked for permission to address the council on the resolution, and it is apparent that conflict has developed over the issue. Several persons explain why they favor the resolution, while others express opposition to its passage.

Council temporarily sidesteps the issue by tabling the resolution until it receives further study by the city traffic engineering department. While no vote has been taken on final resolution, the arguments offer the reporter the opportunity to produce a detailed story on the issue. Comments of those addressing council will be noted, and names and identifications double-checked. Why they are involved is an important question to answer.

The issue will surface at a subsequent council meeting, but the competent reporter will pursue its progress between sessions, because publication of the divergent points of view is important to resolution of the issue.

—Following a series of routine requests for a parade permit and a donation to a local charity, the session is adjourned.

Official council meetings such as these require specific activity by the city hall reporter, who will arrive at council chambers early to better determine the composition of that day's audience. Who are they? What issue or issues are they interested in following? What interests are they representing? Such preliminary effort eliminates some of the risks of misspelled names and improper identification, as well as a better perception of what the issue involves. A precouncil discussion with members of the audience often leads to other facets of the specific issue.

The reporter should always research the agenda before the official session to discover pertinent information that may be important to an issue. A copy of an old ordinance should be obtained and in hand when the reporter realizes that an attempt is going to be made to amend it. The process of selecting a new municipal judge should be reviewed carefully by the reporter *before* officials begin the discussions that will lead to appointment. Preliminary work like this can also be priceless at deadline time.

Avoiding the Label of "Routine"

Difficult as it may seem, the label of "routine" should be avoided in coverage of municipal government. The reporter's first step should be to try to drop the word from his or her vocabulary. To help accomplish that, the reporter should begin asking questions that will pull any issue out of the "routine" category.

Often what seem to be routine appointments to boards and agencies carry possibilities of major policy changes or initiatives. A new member on a 12-person Human Relations Commission may not materially affect the makeup of the commission, but consider the new member of the three-person Parking Authority, whose basic philosophy may be to take all parking off the downtown streets and into high-rise multimillion-dollar parking garages. A new board lineup could substantially affect the policy of the governing body.

Politics is often involved in such appointments. Council is aware of the implications of a specific appointment; the reporter should also be aware and communicate his or her knowledge to the public.

Some Do's And Don't's for the Reporter

The reporter will usually enjoy good rapport with a council and with a cooperative city clerk, but the relationships with the citizens who attend the council meetings can be difficult. A sparsely attended session or a full house can pose the same problems for a reporter on deadline. Input at a council meeting can be abnormally heavy in a short amount of time, and confusion often exists. To cut through some of it, here is some advice for the city hall reporter:

—Citizens addressing council are generally asked to identify themselves, but exact identification is often difficult at the moment. Familiarity with the agenda permits the reporter to briefly leave his or her place at the press table to obtain further details from those persons.

—Many persons attending a council meeting are interested only in a single issue. They will tend to quietly depart the session after that issue is disposed of. Reporters should be careful that a vital element of a story is not allowed to escape, then later be unavailable. The reporter may have a person's telephone number for a later question, but the person may be elsewhere in the city and totally unavailable.

—When the identity of someone making a significant point at a session is unavoidably lost, there is a temptation to gloss over the point, and even to delete it from the story. Every effort should be made to identify the source, and it should be remembered that the point may be too important to eliminate.

—A reporter will encounter frequent problems with the accuracy of citizen information at a council meeting. A complainant may cite 10 business establishments which support his contentions, and the reporter's check will indicate that only six are actually involved. Committing time to tracking down and verifying such facts is a major problem for the council reporter, but it is time that often must be spent. Making a practice of asking for verification on the spot is helpful.

—Reporters should always ask for copies of printed agreements, which council usually makes for its own use but which it does not always circulate. There should be no hesitancy in asking for all the public documents with which municipal government deals.

—The city clerk is a valuable source for verifying information, generally tape recording or otherwise collecting a verbatim record of the proceedings. While transcripts are not usually available immediately, confusing points can be cleared up with the clerk.

—Reporters should always be on the alert for "telegraphed information," the informal kind that indicates that something is in the wind. An aside by one official to another that a "short meeting" is being held in the mayor's office after the council meeting is a sufficient signal to determine the reason for it. A fine line exists between an informal meeting and an official executive session. While either may not produce newsworthy material, they can indicate important future developments.

—Why is a council member missing? He or she may be ill, merely indisposed or conducting some specific business for the body. The reporter should be careful in dealing with specific votes when someone is absent. A "unanimous 6–0 vote" on an ordinance is not really unanimous when the seventh member is absent. The missing council member should be so identified.

Pursuing the Story

The importance of pursuing budding issues before council begins deliberating them cannot be overemphasized. Not every official will be happy with this approach, but it offers the best to the reader or viewer.

How often the reporter will hear from an official, "Why don't we just wait till council looks at it?"

A city hall reporter has heard through the grapevine that a new tax is being considered to raise funds for the financially pressed municipal government. It could involve expansion of fees currently being collected from local businesses. These are some of the steps that a reporter might take to produce a complete story before council takes up the issue:

1. Whose idea is it? Such proposals rarely spring spontaneously from the woodwork, yet many persons are unwilling to publicly commit themselves as sponsors of a project. Every effort should be made to discuss the proposal with the sponsor.

2. When was it proposed to other officials in city government? How did they react to it? How did they become convinced that it should be considered? What alternatives were or are being considered?

3. What are the chances for the proposal's adoption? What will passage mean in terms of estimated revenue? What will passage mean in terms of the average taxpayer? Will the tax be passed on by business operators?

4. What is the reaction of business?

5. What created the need for the increased revenue? Is there really a need? How will such a proposal affect other possible tax measures?

The sources are plentiful: the city manager and other officials surrounding that office, council members, the treasurer or finance office, organizations interested in the proposal, citizen reaction.

Success turns on the reporter's persistence in following the story, which will get to the reader long before it is presented as an "official package" at a meeting.

The Budget: Income and Outgo

Cyril Thornburg thumped the thick document on the desk in front of him.

"Solid as the Rock of Gibraltar," the Rockmont council president proclaimed of the newly proposed $29,570,500 municipal budget for next year.

"No sir, there's no fat here," he announced proudly to three reporters in his city hall office. "It's lean but it does the job."

Kevin Lockerby was not impressed.

Down the hall in his office later, the lone Democrat on City Council bitterly denounced what he called "the Thornburg crowd's insensitivity to the need for greater human services at the local level."

"Every year," Lockerby complained, "they trim the help for the needier segments of the community, and add the money to those who support them at election time."

Then he flipped open his copy of the new budget to offer an example.

Within this developing economic story, which will affect thousands in a community, lies a host of charges and countercharges. The job of the public affairs reporter is not to start a controversy, but to help lay it to rest by publishing the issues involved.

In reporting the financial affairs of municipal government and the budgeting process, these questions are basic to the reporter's effectiveness:

1. How much does it cost?

2. Who is paying for it?

3. What are the residents getting for their money?

4. Do they really want it?

How the city hall reporter responds to these questions dictates the quality of coverage. The budget is the single most important document issued by local government, and it constitutes a major policy statement by those in power. It indicates the bottom line on what services will be expanded or cut back during the coming year, and how individuals and groups will be affected.

Although politics certainly does play a major role in preparation of the budget, the reporter should take care not to treat it primarily as a political document. The political aspects should be balanced against the financial details of how millions of dollars will be spent during the coming year.

Just what does the city do with its $28.1 million annual budget? For one thing, a chunk of the money goes to agencies and services which aren't even controlled from City Hall.

About $2.6 million of it is distributed to two dozen agencies that range from the Regional Transit Authority, which receives $600,000, to the Kiwanis Day Nursery, which gets $1,500 to spend as it chooses.

Most of the agencies have been receiving money for years. Some are funded solely through contributions from the city and county. But all of them are finding themselves in the same budget crunch that is causing city officials to comb the budget these days looking for money to cover employee pay raises.

One of the keys to effective coverage of a municipality's financial affairs lies in the changes a budget produces. Who is going to win and who will lose in the budgeting process? The pressures for new fire stations may be outweighed by minicrime waves that have forced priorities in the police department to the top. And a department such as streets and highways may find itself caught in the middle.

The reporter needs patience to deal with what seem to be interminable preliminary sessions which often indicate the directions that officials are taking. The discussions of items, line by line, provide excellent guideposts to readers through preliminary coverage that points to final decisions.

Much important budget news occurs after the initial presentation. The reporter then has time to document a case history on the funds for a specific project. He or she can explore the project's current funding—what is being accomplished—and determine how the new money will be used. Media spotlights such as these often shine on projects that otherwise rarely see the light of day.

The reporter should possess the ability to digest technical financial information and have a knowledge of the budget process. It has become a continuing process, worth attention all year. The reporter can create interest in it by writing about budgets in terms of people—those who prepare it, those who are served by it, and of course those who are paying for it.

At the other end of the spectrum is another important document—the audit. The budget directs spending for a specified period, the audit assesses and evaluates the expenditures. Both documents are important in covering municipal government. Most government units require audits, and they are available to reporters as public record. The city hall reporter should be aware of their dates of issuance and the agents who conduct them. State and county units most often are responsible for conducting such audits.

Some of the audits cover broad areas of government, while others are much more limited in scope. All of them indicate the detailed record of expenditures: what, how and why.

Depending upon whose figures one uses, the city's new

Civic Center either made $60,000 or lost $130,000 during its first nine months of operation.

Last summer, former civic center director William B. Leal displayed records which concluded the center had earned $60,000 during that period. A new audit released yesterday, however, concludes the facility lost $130,000 during the same time.

The $190,000 difference apparently is the result of a difference in how the depreciation "life" of the civic center is measured.

Leal's "profit" was based on measurement of depreciation over a 100-year period, while the new audit used a 40-year depreciation figure.

Special audits are much more visible than are those required routinely by state law, and they are usually triggered by internal financial or personnel problems.

A special audit of the city's financial records reveals "numerous violations" of the City Charter requirement for competitive bidding on purchases over $2,500, City Manager Richard Bloom said yesterday.

Although the State Tax Department auditors completed their work yesterday, the report must be forwarded to the city through the state tax commissioner's office.

The audit was prompted by the dismissal last week of city purchasing agent Lawrence Snow. A dispute had developed last month over purchase of a $33,000 insurance policy bought without the approval of council.

The city hall reporter does not have to await an official audit by financial experts to check municipal spending, however. The documents reviewed by outside auditors are on file in most city offices. It is a matter of the reporter's knowing where to look. He or she may not win a popularity contest in asking to review them, but the rewards are often worth the cost of popularity.

City officials have spent more than $35,000 since July 1 to "boost" the city through civic promotions, and have also spent $28,000 to join a variety of organizations, according to Finance Department documents.

A review of canceled checks on file at City Hall indicates that thousands of dollars were spent in the last four months on Hershey "kisses," banners promoting athletic events, Christmas lights and keys to the city costing about $20 each.

The "organizational dues" spent by officials range from $28 on behalf of City Manager Dick Scanlan to the American Academy of Political and Social Science to $11,460.50 for annual dues to the State Municipal League.

With eight months remaining in the budget year, the current city budget lists total appropriations of $33,500 for civic promotion and $18,250 for organizational dues. Both budget items have already been exceeded, the records indicate.

A Sample Municipal Budget

Summary of Revenue and Resources

Revenue and Resources	Last year's	Proposed
TAXES		
Business and occupational	$ 4,525,000	$ 5,045,000
Property, current	264,589	360,706
Property, prior years	35,000	35,000
City franchise	68,699	70,000
Liquor, 1%	165,000	170,000
Utility, 2%	640,000	650,000
On domestic animals	3,303	3,500
Amusement	11,958	12,500
Hotel-motel	28,916	30,000
LICENSES		
General business	87,032	87,000
Special	2,025	2,000
Bicycle	2,921	3,500
FEES AND PERMITS		
Parking meter collection	90,869	94,000
Parking meter fines	49,964	55,000
Police court fines	162,661	165,000
Building permits	49,043	53,000
Sign permits	887	1,000
Street and sewer permits	3,800	4,000
Electrical inspection	15,070	16,000
Plumbing inspection	1,651	1,500
Health inspection	1,385	1,500
Fire service fee	1,606,838	1,600,000
Refuse removal fee	440,548	485,000
Animal control fee	8,974	9,000
Federal revenue sharing	2,449,000	2,477,000
Interest income	30,112	32,000
Miscellaneous	65,632	78,000
TOTAL REVENUE AND RESOURCES	$10,810,877	$11,541,206

Sources of Operating Funds

A typical municipality obtains operating and capital improvement funds in a variety of ways. They include a business and occupational tax, property tax, a franchise tax on some businesses, a tax on utility bills, an amusement tax on theaters and other places of entertainment, a hotel-motel tax, parking meters, police court fines, building permits and refuse removal fees.

Based on sales of gasoline, cigarettes, alcohol and automobile licenses within the city, the municipality may also receive substantial tax money from the state. Fees for bicycles and dog licenses are not overlooked, and many cities have begun collecting a local income tax.

Summary of General Fund Expenditures

Purpose	Last year's	Proposed
Mayor	$ 2,400	$ 2,400
City manager	56,015	59,765
City council	7,433	7,500
City clerk	23,582	25,207
Police court judge	23,657	25,715
Legal department	55,556	57,128
Finance department	367,481	378,420
Human resources	20,229	21,725
City hall and other buildings	619,766	637,512
Police department	2,460,589	2,639,600
Fire department	2,187,949	2,427,117
Health department	164,904	179,904
Refuse removal	947,679	1,016,376
Sewer maintenance	255,765	272,885
Street department	563,272	604,510
Engineering	146,437	156,894
Building inspection	123,849	134,332
Street cleaning	223,374	205,295
Signs and signals	157,092	162,246
Equipment maintenance and operation	355,097	373,348
Construction division	393,573	446,212
Parks and recreation	108,705	138,014
Parking lots and meters	32,015	33,525
Public library share	15,000	20,000
Civil preparedness share	8,000	8,000
Planning commission	67,357	73,945
Animal control	39,528	42,962
Employee benefits	774,140	814,032
Attorney fees and court costs	12,507	12,000
Travel and training	10,158	10,000
Boards and commissions	316,900	318,792
Construction and improvements	236,639	205,845
Civic promotions	14,453	15,000
Contingencies	19,776	15,000
TOTAL EXPENDITURES	$10,810,877	$11,541,206

A good grasp of these sources and their effect on municipal spending is helpful to the city hall reporter who will be a familiar face in the finance office.

Substantial funds are also received from the federal government through revenue sharing, some of it earmarked for specific projects such as minority housing and education projects. In recent years these federal grants have become a major source of revenue for cities, and many municipalities employ special offices to deal exclusively with these federal grants.

> Nearly $7 million in federal community development grants to the city have been approved by the Department of Housing and Urban Development.
>
> Among the projects approved were loans for housing

> rehabilitation, revitalization of the East End community, sanitary sewers along the Anley Turnpike, three new day-care centers and a training center for the handicapped.
>
> City Manager Warren Bonner also said city officials are preparing an application for an additional $1 million Urban Development Action grant that would provide sewers to sites outside the city.

Municipalities are constantly experiencing problems of adequate funding and searching for new sources. A proposal for a new tax or fee calls for reportorial legwork to determine the potential success or failure of the measure. The reporter may be the one who raises questions about the effectiveness of the proposal.

> Your neighbor sneaks out in the middle of the night and stuffs his garbage into your trash can.
>
> Or he just allows his garbage to pile up on his front lawn, or simply dumps it on the steps of City Hall.
>
> If City Council goes ahead with a plan to impose garbage collection fees of $36 a year, and require stickers on or near cans to indicate payment, how is the city going to deal with those who won't pay?

Officials and experts often raise such questions, and citizen groups are generally not shy about questioning such proposals. But the fact remains that the alert city hall reporter is one of the most effective questioners of municipal practices.

Income is only half the financial equation. Expenditures qualify as the other essential element in the city hall reporter's mandate to supply coverage of financial affairs.

Typical expenditures include operation of city hall itself, the police and fire departments, maintenance of streets and highways, parks and recreation, the finance department, public health and welfare, operation of a court system, garbage removal and a host of minor services.

A municipality often subsidizes associated agencies that depend on it for operating funds, without taking a direct part in their operation. Or it may join with a county government in assisting a metropolitan transit system or an areawide health services program. It may also contribute to the operation of a community library system or a civil defense office. The relationships between the municipality and these other agencies are important to the city hall reporter.

> A $50 million bond issue to generate a "pool" for low-interest mortgage loans channeled through local banks has been agreed to in principle by officials of the city and county.
>
> "We're hammering out the details," Mayor Kevin Stanley said this morning. "The money should be available in 90 days."
>
> The 30-year bond issue is designed to produce 30-year home loans with interest rates of 9-10 percent, substantially below current bank rates.

An individual or family with a gross income level of under $30,000 can apply for the loans, Stanley said. "The county and city agreed on that level because it includes a broad majority of middle-income families," Stanley added.

The City Hall "Team"

The organization of municipal government is important to the reporter who must deal with personnel in many departments far removed from the policy-making council or commission.

The best summaries of organization are found in the annual budget, where the reporter can determine allotment of funds and personnel, which offers further insight into breadth of services and importance of the various departments. Many of the departments are technically co-equal, with their directors reporting to a city manager or other key official, but some certainly wield more power and influence than others on the chart.

A typical municipal government includes the police department, fire department, finance department, health department, legal department, administrative office and public works department. Public works is the agency with the most personnel and the one that carries the most implications for the average resident. Included are subdepartments for traffic control, engineering, street maintenance, construction of new public facilities, inspection bureaus, sanitation control and refuse removal, and maintenance of public facilities.

Because of their intrinsic importance and the extensive personnel, the police and fire departments always constitute major divisions. The legal department, on the other hand, may include only a city attorney, several aides, and a few office workers. The finance department is somewhat broader, encompassing a purchasing department, controller and auditors, a data processing department to handle city records and employees to handle other fiscal affairs.

The growth of federal funding to cities has also resulted in establishment of special departments to apply for, collect and administer federal funds. A community development department might include housing inspection and housing rehabilitation. A human resources department might oversee minority recruitment and selection of city employees on a merit basis, employee relations and safety.

A child of city government, the Human Relations Commission, is investigating the employment practices of its own parent.

The commission will meet with city council today at 4 p.m. to discuss the city's own affirmative action practices.

At issue, Commission Chairman James Hesson explained, is what he calls the "questionable hirings" of

> several city employees in recent months before the official advertising deadlines had expired.

It should be pointed out that the official organization chart often differs somewhat from the unofficial lines of communication and authority, complicating reporting of municipal government.

An official organization chart may show the city clerk as answering to city council and subject to dismissal by that body, but a large measure of the clerk's duties center on the city manager's office. That official may have no control over the city clerk. The director of an industrial development office may officially answer to the city administrator, but often deal directly with the policy-making council or commission.

These unofficial "lines of authority" should be part of the reporter's arsenal of pertinent information because he or she will often have to follow them in tracking down a story.

The mayor, fearing that a financial crisis is brewing, calls a press conference after conferring with the finance director. Here is how the story was handled:

> City layoffs ranging from 130 to 190 persons and freezes on hiring were recommended yesterday by Mayor Isaac Solomon, who said he fears a "budget crisis" because of the city's loss of revenue during the current recession.
>
> Solomon called a news conference and issued a statement after consulting with Finance Director Gary White.
>
> Solomon said his statement was sparked by a substantial drop in the city's business and occupation tax collections, its biggest revenue source.

Finance Director White nominally reports to the city manager, and is in fact subject to dismissal by that official, yet the normal chain of command is frequently disrupted by such developments as these. The city manager later told reporters he was not briefed by the mayor before the news conference, but noted that he is in basic agreement with his proposals.

However, the mayor's associates on the council may not agree with him on the emergency proposals and insist on detailing their own side of the story.

> Mayor Isaac Solomon's recommendations for layoffs of city employees and freezes on hiring during what he calls the city's "budget crisis" received a cool reception from other members of city council today.
>
> Solomon suggested the measures in light of a 2.1 percent drop in business and occupation tax revenues.
>
> Councilmen Dean Storm and Robert Bailes objected to the proposal. "No matter if he says 10 percent," Storm said, "there are six others of us on council, and what we collectively decide goes. I don't see any reason for absolute panic."
>
> Bailes agreed. He said he considers layoffs "a last

resort. We have a long way to go before we reach that point," he added.

Similar disruptions in the chain of command can arise with citizen access to the council in matters involving strong personal interest, although the director of that department answers to the city administrator. Members of boards and commissions may also answer to city council but in practice deal directly with the administrator.

A safety director may exercise authority over the police and fire departments, yet actually retain little or no control over those departments. The legal department may answer to the city manager but find itself frequently questioned by council and asked to provide specific information to that body. These unofficial lines of authority may in fact be more effective and useful in the practical governance of the municipality. The reporter must be aware of these sometimes unorthodox lines.

Complicating Factors for the Journalist

Long after the reporter has passed the first hurdle at city hall, learning to be comfortable in the role of information gatherer in strange and often hostile territory, other factors intrude to complicate coverage. Some are merely mechanical problems, such as how to organize a story with several important facets. Others carry deeper significance, such as the necessity of balancing coverage among the various pressure groups in the community. The effective reporter learns how to deal with all these problems.

Pressure Groups

The political complexion of the municipality varies from city to city, and its power structure shows immense variety. Paralleling the need for a background in government itself is still a further requirement for the reporter: he or she must possess a practical knowledge of the socio-political system in the community.

Many municipal governments include the traditional political parties in their formation, while others officially label themselves non-partisan. In some cities, for example, the elections are specifically non-partisan, and a candidate for council cannot be a member of a political executive committee.

Whatever the designation and practice, however, alliances do form, and many of them are politically inspired and long standing. Candidates find others with similar philosophical views toward government and run as a "slate," opposing other organized groups with divergent viewpoints. While some of these alliances are no longer visible in the traditional political sense, the city hall reporter must be aware of them, familiar with their makeup and impact on local government.

As already noted, government is not neutral, serving instead as a means of access or advantage to selected groups. While municipal government can be said to operate for the greater good of all, in practice political decisions stem from a working union of interests, ideas, institutions and individuals. The competent journalist understands, accepts and operates within this framework. As much as any social scientist, the reporter recognizes that local governments are not monolithic entities.

Government is actually a complex of decision-making islands, from which flow decisions and actions carrying the stakes and prizes of politics. These clusters of participants in the process are especially concerned with the decisions that issue from that particular island.

> "Your right to defend the value of your property is in jeopardy," is the headline on an unsigned flyer being distributed in several city neighborhoods.
>
> The mimeographed sheet discusses a proposed amendment to an ordinance which would allow developers to construct "multifamily dwellings" in R-4 zones without a public hearing.
>
> Under current city ordinance, a hearing is now required. Planning Director Gary Bunn favors the amendment as one method for equalizing requirements for developers.

Implicit in this report is the pressure being exerted on resolution of an issue by some individual or group, usually the latter. It is important for the reporter to know that each cluster does not wield the same amount of influence and that participants' strength varies from issue to issue. For example, the business community may act as a unit in discouraging a decision to permit a huge shopping mall on the edge of the city, yet take little or no interest in major extension of sewer lines to an as yet undeveloped section of the city. However, that issue becomes substantially more important to an organized group of developers who require the lines to construct new housing or to nearby homeowners who also want the sewer lines.

These clusters of pressure groups may simply be a ministerial organization, civic clubs, labor councils or other organized groups. Just as likely, they will be neighborhoods which frequently band together when their interests are threatened.

> Some people in the Highlawn area believe the city is trying to pull a fast one.
>
> Their leaders say the city's Board of Zoning Appeals didn't notify residents about a public hearing on a proposal to establish a private club in the area, and now they are petitioning to protest the move.
>
> Planning Director Amy Melvin argues that the city has done everything it is required to do—and more. A public hearing on the proposal to establish a restaurant and private club at 1400 Eastmoor St. is scheduled for 7 p.m. today in City Hall.

> "We think they tried to sneak it in on us," said Mrs. John Sallivant, 2700 Highlawn Ave., who initiated a petition she says contains 360 names.

These clusters and their participants call for sensitivity on the part of the city hall reporter to their interests and constitutes one of the complicating factors of local government.

Policy-Making vs. Administration

Where does policy-making end and administration of that policy begin? This question poses special problems for the journalist who covers the council-manager form of government, but it can also be a factor in reporting other forms of government as well. While most city charters spell out the policy-makers, it is more difficult to draw the line in practice. And some administrators tend to draw the line much tighter than others to serve their own particular interests.

"I can't answer that question," the administrator informs the reporter. "That involves policy and you'll have to go to council for the answer to that." The administrator has quite possibly drawn a sharper line than council would have him or her draw, creating "dead space" in which neither an administrator nor a policy-maker cares to venture. Yet this "dead-space" area may be important to the reporter's story—and to the public.

An example:

—A major industry is preparing to locate within a municipality, and execution of an agreement may lie solely within the hands of an administrator to provide sewer service, upon which acquisition of the industry turns. As a practical matter, however, the final decision lies in the hands of council as policy-maker. Someone will have to address the issue, but if it is controversial, no one may be willing.

As a practical matter, the professional administrator plays an important role in setting municipal policy. However, the apolitical position generally assigned to the manager in the city manager form of government frequently obscures and often inhibits the manager's contribution to the local policy-making process. And the legal constraints usually written into city charters emphasize the division of work between members of council as policy-makers and city administrators as just that—administrators.

The result is that the reporter often finds it difficult to draw the line of demarcation. The lead to this story makes the point quite clearly:

> City Manager Barry R. Evans is apparently bowing to City Council's order that he not release information to the news media before presenting that information to Council members.
>
> "Council's the boss," Evans said today when he was asked about the reprimand.

> Mayor William Schiller had sent Evans a letter yesterday reproaching him for telling reporters he will recommend to Council that downtown traffic patterns be drastically changed.
>
> Evans had discussed with a reporter what he sees as ineffective traffic patterns.

The professional administrator cannot remain completely aloof from politics, and many of them recognize and deal with this fact of life. As one well-known city manager put it,

> Some people have criticized me for attending a Republican dinner or a Democratic ladies' tea. I'm officially non-partisan, but I'm going to get to know the candidates who are running and what they're going to do for the city. You've got your head in the sand if you don't think there's politics at city hall. A city manager ought to stay out of city politics though, as far as who's running and what area they come from.

What a city manager does is often seen as politics by the policy-makers, and there are few managers who won't privately admit that the policy-makers too often poke their noses in the purely administrative aspects of local government.

> Commissioner Jean Blackmon failed to dismiss City Manager Kenneth Blake Tuesday, her motion to fire him losing by a 4-1 vote.
>
> Her motion, seconded by Commissioner Al Kirkland for reasons of discussion, followed Blackmon's lengthy criticism of Blake's alleged threat to fire any city employee found discussing city business with a commissioner.
>
> "His threat is a flagrant violation of the First Amendment to our Constitution," Blackmon charged. "Now that he (Blake) has told our employees with whom they can speak, will he next tell them where they must buy their clothing and groceries?"

Relationships with Other Governments

Involvement of municipal government with other agencies and governments also complicates the reporting process. There are long-standing associations, not only with other local governments but with the parent state and federal systems.

The direct grants of funds flowing from the federal government to the city have created a new layer of officials charged with administering the programs produced by the money. Much of the funds is funneled directly to a grant official who receives his or her salary from a federal grant. Thus, city council action is effectively bypassed and the funds are channeled into local projects without official local action. It requires additional legwork on the part of the reporter to follow the progress of the programs.

State involvement adds a different perspective. Approval of many local projects, even a final annual budget, often must be obtained from state agencies. While a good part of the approval is only a formality, the relationship adds another layer of officialdom with which the reporter must deal.

Other local governments, however, often overlapping in jurisdiction, provide a greater complication in the city hall reporter's work. The two governments are generally co-equal and secure in their belief that theirs is the more important part of the equation.

A city and a county government are negotiating to construct and jointly operate an animal shelter for the area. Negotiations are characterized by on-again, off-again discussions, but the need is clear: both sides require the facility. The reporter's job is rather sensitive in dealing with two units such as these. Both sides are working to specific advantages. How will the costs be met? Whose job will it be to construct the facility? Who will exercise control of it?

Reporting is always made more complex with the addition of another unit of government to the issue.

> The County Commission has postponed for 30 days any decision to allow Columbus to annex seven parcels of land northwest of the city.
>
> The postponement was decided after Westerville City Manager Maynard Peek appealed to the commission to delay the annexation until Westerville is given an opportunity to annex the property.

Such an annexation proposal by a larger city is complicated by the smaller city's decision to seek annexation of the property. The parcels are adjacent to both communities. The decision is complicated by the role of the county, which must decide who will annex the land.

Important questions must be answered. What is the county's role in the process? What are the political implications in the decision? What do the property owners prefer, and do they have a choice? Why does either municipality want to annex the land? What are its potential valuations on the tax rolls? What city services would either city have to provide and how much would they cost? Who has analyzed the dispute for potential benefits to the total community? Such disputes among governments complicate the city hall reporter's job.

Reporting in the "Public Interest"

How much should the journalist report in municipal government personnel matters? When is an internal personnel matter of legitimate public interest, and when should it be ignored as merely an "internal" matter?

None of these questions is simply answered, and further complicate the city hall reporter's job.

A city commission occasionally closes a portion of its meeting, declaring an executive session to discuss a "personnel matter." Is such closure really necessary?

The line drawn between those questions bearing legitimate public importance and those not attaching such importance is a fine one. Is confidentiality necessary in interviewing candidates for an important city position? The prospect and searchers may claim unwillingness to expose the job search to current employers, but doesn't the community conducting the search have a right to know who is being interviewed? The tendency in recent years has been to keep such searches under wraps, but that may not benefit the community.

Public affairs reporting implies that full and accurate news coverage better serves the reader. While sensitivity on the part of the reporter and his or her editor is always desirable, the final decision in "personnel matters" should always remain with the journalist.

An official being considered as city manager is plagued by a 25-year-old bankruptcy he endured as a young man. Should the information be made public by the city hall reporter? The answer lies in the importance of the position to those in the community. Since the candidate's qualifications are being pointed out in detail, shouldn't any negative connotations be aired also? Fairness to the public dictates that the other side be aired too.

The most important argument for leaning in the direction of publication of all sensitive personnel matters is that those involved are on the public payroll and influence public policy in some manner. Rarely can this legitimate argument be refuted.

How Much Is Too Much?

The broad range of issues covered by a municipal governing body at its official meetings creates a further problem for the reporter. How much of the material should be covered, and how should it be packaged? The answer, of course, depends on the policy of the publication, its editors and their perception of community needs, and the reporter who must organize and produce a competent report on the meeting and all preceding it. A council session may produce half a dozen major news stories and a dozen other reportable items, all with a need to be covered in some detail. A good rule is better too much than too little, and the stories that were developed days before the official session spread the material through a series of days rather than waiting for the session itself.

Constructing a preliminary story with all the pertinent information lessens the need to fully develop it after a council meeting, although the official action should be so noted.

Some reporters break down the important material into separate news stories, for display purposes as well as for ease in reading. They should be carefully organized, with one of the stories being used as a catchall roundup for less important items.

Equal care should be taken to assure that the routine items are not dropped.

> In other action, Council:
> —Enacted an ordinance extending to 10 p.m. the operating hours of parking meters on downtown streets.

—Approved requests for bicycle parades on city streets July 11 and 18.
—Awarded a $10,980 contract to East End Cycle Sales for three Kawasaki motorcycles for the police department. There were no other bidders.

Good news judgment demands that council stories be packaged in such a way that their close relationship is immediately recognized to the reader or viewer.

The size of the city itself, with its attendant complexity, places a final burden on the reporter in attempting to determine what must be reported and in what depth. An ordinance closing a minor street in a residential area may carry more weight in a small city and be ignored in a metropolitan area because of limited interest.

Relationships between the journalist and sources are also complicating factors. The one-to-one city hall relationship in a small city gives way to different relationships in bigger cities. It is often more difficult for a reporter in a smaller city to be as objective as a big-city counterpart, whereas the metropolitan reporter tends to be more insensitive to issues close to people.

All these complications are relative, placing upon the journalist the burden of sorting out the pieces and placing them correctly in the jigsaw puzzle that is local government.

Suggested Readings

BANOVETZ, JAMES M., editor, *Managing the Modern City* (Published by the International City Management Assn., 1971, as part of the Municipal Management Series). Chapter 15, "Public Relations." A discussion of the public relations process as it relates to municipal administration. The student will find these other chapters useful: Chapter 4, "The Environment and Role of the Administrator"; Chapter 5, "Leadership Styles and Strategies"; Chapter 12, "City Planning."

STILLMAN, RICHARD, *Rise of the City Manager* (Albuquerque, NM: Univer. of New Mexico Press, 1974). Introduction and Chapter 6, "Some Perspectives on the Present Dilemmas and Future Directions of the Profession."

ROYKO, MIKE, *Boss: Richard J. Daley of Chicago* (New York: Dutton, 1971). Chapter I, "Daley's Day; a Day in the Life of an Urban Mayor" and Chapter IV, "The Machine and How it Works in the Big City."

CHAPTER 2
County Government

Overall, county governments are a mixed bag. They show signs of adaptability and inflexibility, of innovativeness and sluggishness, of being the most important local government of the future and of becoming practically lifeless.

So wrote political scientist John C. Bollens in evaluating research into this venerable form of local government that stretches from sea to sea and exists in so many rich variations.

Although restricted to only half a dozen basic forms, county government reveals all the shades of difference that an independent pioneer population could conjure up as it swept out to found what was to become a union of quite diverse people. Its diversity creates difficulty in providing a single meaningful model of county government for the public affairs reporter.

First at the Scene

Counties were there first—authorized by newly formed state governments to serve as their instruments—and, give or take a few, the number has changed little since the last wave of settlers rolled west. Other forms of local government have proliferated, but they have merely been superimposed on the existing county structures, providing different services and enforcing other regulations. The very permanency of the county structure points to the political implications of officeholders long in power and backed by solid tradition.

This permanency itself places a subtle burden on the public affairs reporter who would ingratiate himself or herself with the "courthouse crowd" to more effectively cover county affairs. Most have been on the scene longer, either as hangers-on and whittlers in the courthouse square or as courtly county commissioners in the habit of doing business "in the same old way." Times are changing in the county courthouse—the old brass spittoons have all but disappeared—but many of the ancient traditions remain.

Furthermore, size of governmental expenditures is not always a good indicator of the relative importance of governments in a community. The reporter may find that a municipal budget is five times larger than is that of county government, but the totals can be quite misleading. Many functions of county government, notably subsidization of the court system and collection of taxes, strike more closely at the average citizen than do some of the services provided by town and city government.

Some Subtle Differences

It is important at the outset to note the subtle differences between the older counties and the more modern municipal corporations that have been superimposed over them. While both were created by state government, the courts consider municipalities legal corporations. The courts recognize counties as quasi-corporations, utilized primarily as instruments of state government. They consider counties as having always "been there"; cities are created at the instigation of citizens who reside within their proposed borders, who tailor the powers and functions of municipal government to suit their own purposes.

A charter authorized by the state makes a municipality a corporation. The county has no such charter; it is subject to the action of that state—executive, legislative and judicial. Thus, cities and other municipalities often serve proprietary interests, while the original counties serve a basic governmental function.

These municipal proprietary services include refuse removal, water service, fire and police protection, parks and recreation, and other amenities demanded by residents of an urban community. The cost of nearly all these is prorated among those residents as service charges.

The county too provides some services, but it serves another and subtly different function. The state has traditionally directed county government to perform such functions as tax collection, construction and maintenance of highways, law enforcement, educational services and record-keeping. Counties also serve as convenient subdivisions of the state in operating the courts, conducting elections, dispensing auto licenses and collecting a number of state fees.

Some New Functions—and Problems

Increasingly, however, counties are being called upon to broaden their role as mere administrative functionaries by providing services and enforcing regulations normally under the purview of municipalities that overlap them. Counties have responded by providing such services themselves or by creating new subgovernments that do so.

This modern tendency to create new arms of government to

dispense specific services has further fragmented local government, and the county finds itself overlapped by an older metropolitan city, a series of newer municipal suburbs and a multitude of special districts. Direct revenue sharing by the federal government to all these units has exacerbated the problem.

Thus, the sheer antiquity of the county structure, its basic subservience to the state government as an administrative arm and its increasingly complex relationship with its fellow local governments all pose a challenge to the public affairs reporter assigned to the county beat. As with other forms of local government, the first rule for the journalist is to carefully determine the character of the government that he or she is to cover.

Foundations of the Modern County

U.S. counties are a product of the colonial period, originally developed from the English county form to administer rural areas under pioneer conditions. Some of their functions appear outmoded today, but they continue to thrive and to serve citizens across the country.

Many of the old titles and offices also continue to flourish, albeit with somewhat different functions. The office of sheriff has an unbroken continuity back to the English; the justice of the peace, the coroner and the grand jury date to the 12th century in England. Although it might seem foolish to cling to outmoded political institutions, political scientist Paul W. Wager suggests that it is not wholly without purpose:

> Americans are rightfully proud of their political inheritance from England—representative government, the Bill of Rights, trial by jury, the common law—and something precious might be lost if we severed the visible ties that bind us to the past. We see no inconsistency in furnishing a modern home wholly or in part with antiques, or in retaining a fireplace in a steam-heated house. So it is with the courthouse. We retain the ancient shire-reeve, provide him with an automobile and a two-way radio set and then transfer his police functions to the state police. We set up courts of record to meet the needs of a complex society but cannot bring ourselves to dispense with the six-hundred-year-old justice of the peace. The coroner, though universally recognized as an anachronism, remains in most states.

It is important to note, however, that while the system was borrowed from England, it was generously adapted to pioneer and near-pioneer conditions in the new land. Modifications were made based on the needs of early settlers and further modified as Americans migrated west—out of New England and the Middle Atlantic states and toward the Pacific Ocean. By the time the Far Western states were colonized, county government was a practical mixture of what had become four basic regional plans.

The New England Towns

The New England town form evolved to accommodate the compact settlements in that section of the new country and performed the same functions as did English counties. The popular assembly was most democratic; residents chose selectmen to administer the affairs of the county, constables to enforce the law, tax assessors and others. (Counties do exist in New England, but they serve merely as judicial districts.)

The form, characterized by strong self-government, proved effective because of the closely bound nature of people in the region. Town meetings continue to flourish today and even play an occasional role in influencing broader political events. Those held during the Watergate scandal may have been instrumental in events leading to President Richard M. Nixon's resignation from office. With the president under fire for his involvement in the Watergate cover-up, the subject of impeachment arose in at least 13 of the annual town meetings held in Vermont in 1974. Resolutions calling for Nixon's impeachment were approved at eight of the town meetings and were quite visible through the national news media at the time.

In a similar fashion, the national debate over U.S. involvement in faraway Vietnam was escalated by the vigorous debate in the New England town meetings.

The Southern County Form

While New England was producing its special form of local government, the South was more faithfully reproducing the English version of the county. A more scattered settlement of that region and the different character of the settlers created a county government with authority in the hands of a court composed of justices of the peace transacting the administrative, fiscal and judicial business of the community. Smaller political subdivisions, such as the town or township, were non-existent in the Southern counties.

Townships and Supervisors

The township-supervisor form of county government, which originated in New York, was a compromise between the New England town and the Southern county, built on the principle of representation rather than on the direct town meeting format.

Supervisors elected in their own towns served collectively as a county governing board while continuing to hold administrative power in their respective towns. Justices of the peace faded from the scene, and the county board of supervisors exercised administrative and fiscal responsibility in managing affairs of the county.

Borrowing from the Southern plan, New York limited the range of countywide functions, leaving control over roads, public welfare and other functions in the hands of town boards. The relatively stronger position of the county ultimately led to the demise of the town meeting, with the county board settling questions of policy and electing its officers by ballot.

The Commissioner Form

Both counties and townships existed in Pennsylvania, but the influence of the towns was much less pronounced. As a result, town government never became established, and the Southern system, with its centralized administration, was not favored either.

In the system developed in Pennsylvania, county commissioners were elected at large and produced a strong but responsive county government. Counties were divided into townships for administrative purposes, but the townships never acquired the status of those in New York. The township was made subordinate to the county board and was not represented on it.

Further Compromises

As the nation grew westward, the states created in the Great Plains, the Rocky Mountains and the Far West evolved further compromises in the original four plans. As in the Southern plan, there were no towns or townships, but most areas adopted the commission form of Pennsylvania.

The 3,049 counties represent the vast bulk of these basic forms of government, but a few areas have either no county government or have wholly or partly consolidated with municipal governments. Most of them are metropolitan areas, such as New York City, New Orleans, Boston, Philadelphia, San Francisco and Denver. The state of Rhode Island has no organized county government, and it is not present in the cities of Virginia.

In recent years, further efforts have been made to modernize the structure. Many counties have established a form of government similar to the city manager plan, with a specialist hired to administer county government who answers to a board of commissioners, which continues to establish policy.

Who Governs the County?

The portly county commissioner adjusted himself more comfortably in his seat, chewed on his cigar for a moment, then responded carefully to an angry constituent: "I know it's what you folks want, and I'd really like to help," he assured his visitor. "But our hands are tied. The state calls the shots on this and we have to go along."

This is best known as "passing the buck," and the constituent is left little choice: drop the matter or take it to another level of government.

An uncommon response at the county level? Not at all. Historically, the primary function of the county has been to serve as a convenient subdivision of the state government, administering state activities at the "local level." Furthermore, counties have increasingly taken on a similar role for the federal government, serving still another jurisdiction which provides the funds and calls on county government to administer them. Funding sometimes calls for a major multimillion-dollar public development, but more often a much smaller project.

> Additional federal manpower funds totaling $68,000 have been received by Johnson County, Supervisor Tod James said yesterday.
>
> The funds, which must be disbursed according to Department of Human Resources guidelines, will be used to supplement summer employment in local areas of high joblessness, James said.

Within these basic limitations, which also serve as a political check and balance system, counties enjoy a considerable measure of self-government. County officials are popularly elected and as part of the electoral process must fulfill the needs of the voters as far as possible. The commissioner's response to the angry constituent was tempered by the realization that such negative responses have to be limited in number in order to assure successful re-election campaigns.

At the same time, state constitutions and legislatures have attached strings to counties that limit their ability to always act unilaterally in fiscal matters. The county reporter will anticipate these attachments to the parent government, partly because of the potential for conflict inherent in the relationship.

> State Tax Commissioner David Hardesty has warned the Marshall County Commission he will not approve the county's new budget if it includes $38,500 in raises for the county's elected officials.
>
> The commissioners included the increases because state law provides for them when a county's tax base reaches $600 million.
>
> Although Marshall's tax base has topped that figure this year, the state constitution prohibits alteration of county officials' salaries during their terms of office, Hardesty pointed out.

The reporter will note a further subtle difference between the county and municipal government. With its responsibility for administering state affairs at the local level, the county tends to be somewhat more administrative and judicial. Municipalities, with their ordinance-writing powers, tend to be more legislative. With increasing latitude from states in recent years, however, counties have been acquiring greater powers to enact ordinances. The practical effect has been to allow officials to respond more positively to the demands of their constituents.

This has been effective in counties with substantial growth, but that growth has led to new challenges for the older county

FIGURE 2–1. *Nowhere is the U.S. system of political governance more complicated than in a county with many divergent interests—urban, suburban and rural problems. The reporting problem becomes similarly complex.*

government. Demands are often made upon it by three very diverse groups of citizens—the traditional rural population, urban residents and the mushrooming suburban citizenry.

The net effect often creates conflict which is difficult to adjudicate. Citizens of purely rural areas may seek services very different from those sought by residents of more highly developed urban areas. And the interests of the suburban residents may be at even further variance with those of the others. The effect on the county reporter is to create a logistical problem in obtaining feedback from these diverse sets of interests.

> The Earl County Commission voted yesterday to limit commercial growth on Western Highway by zoning the area for two-family residences.
>
> The effect, according to Commission Chairman John C. Wilson, will be to prohibit developers from constructing a 70-store shopping center along the highway.
>
> "It's far more important that we keep traffic moving along this stretch than allowing new stores which will only jam up our roads," Wilson said.

For the suburbanite who must travel additional miles to the nearest shopping, the decision may have a negative effect. For the urban resident who is trying to get to a job in the area each day, the effect may be positive. The same pressure groups that operate within a municipality also influence decisions in the county environment.

The Practical Exercises of Power

Contrary to popular belief, newly elected officeholders do not always dismiss their predecessors' entire staffs after a hotly contested election. It is undeniable that some displacement takes place, but overall there is considerable continuity in county government from election to election—usually a four-year span. Partisan politics is generally an integral component of the scene, becoming much more pronounced as election day nears. But the clerks who routinely handle the public's business are coming increasingly under merit systems, providing considerably more stability.

The county also acquires stability because of its quasi-corporate character. It can acquire and possess property, enter into contracts, borrow money within limitations imposed by the state, and enjoy other privileges of a true corporation.

Whatever the designation for the county governing board, and there are more than two dozen in use today,* it generally organizes or reorganizes after each election, selecting a chairperson or president from its ranks to preside at regular meetings.

Governing boards vary in size from three to as many as 100 members, but three to seven members on a board are most common. A tendency on the part of the board to close ranks in the face of the press makes it somewhat more difficult for a reporter to cover a three-person county commission.

Even when the board is split by party affiliation, the county reporter often finds little disunity among members, who usually find common ground for practical agreement outside the official sessions. The effect is to make the job of reporting the why of a decision more complicated.

* Aside from the more prosaic designations of county commission and board of supervisors, names of county governing units include fiscal court, levy court, county court, board of chosen freeholders, board of revenue, quarterly court and police jury.

Boards with larger memberships offer the opportunity for the reporter to locate dissenting and sometimes vocal minorities. However, these boards become unwieldy for the reporter to cover. The bigger boards permit broader representation but create administrative problems, resulting in reliance on the work of committees. The reporter's efforts, therefore, must be directed toward the work of these many subunits; final action by the full board is often a mere formality.

Whatever the size of the board, it meets regularly at a specified location to conduct its business. As with other governmental beats, however, the county reporter will soon learn that he or she cannot rely on official meetings for up-to-date and total coverage. Major decisions, and a host of minor ones that affect the readership, are often thrashed out between sessions, and the reporter who is content to wait for the regular meeting to collect information will usually listen to the chair's gavel banging a *fait accompli*.

> Without discussion last night, the Blount County Commission approved guidelines tightening restrictions on admittance to the Aid for Senior Citizens program.
>
> "We've decided that there must be real need before a person is enrolled," said Commissioner Redmond Stone.

Long before this official decision was reached, the matter had been thrashed out at informal meetings, telephone conversations and hallway conferences. A study may have preceded the decision. The place for the reporter, of course, was in the middle of these preliminary negotiations that led to the decision.

Collecting: A Complicated Process

One of the county's indispensable functions is to serve as a collecting and disbursing agency for the funds that provide services. Salaries, maintenance of public buildings and highways, special programs and costs of education are all funded from a variety of sources. Whatever the source—taxes, grants from other governments and agencies, and use fees—and whatever the use, the money flows into and out of the county treasury. The county sometimes serves as collecting agency for other governmental units within its borders, such as towns, cities and school districts.

Under authority conferred by the state, the county assesses property, levies and collects taxes based on those assessments, decides upon appropriations, incurs indebtedness and makes arrangements to repay it, awards contracts and manages county property.

The money-collecting process begins with a listing of all property in the county by the tax assessor, an office that is usually elective. The assessor places a value on all property and assesses it for tax purposes. Many counties make a distinction between real and personal property for tax purposes, taxing separately. Real property, essentially real estate, includes land and the buildings or other improvements on it. Personal property judged taxable often includes automobiles, boats, trailers, jewelry and other movable possessions.

Based on state restrictions or the policy of the county governing board, the assessment ranges from 25 percent to 100 percent of true value. The key to the total the homeowner must pay is the county's current tax rate, which determines the tax. The rate is usually expressed in terms of $X.xx per $100 of assessed valuation. If the tax rate is $3, for example, the owner of a $90,000 home valued by the assessor at $45,000 will owe a tax of $1,350 on the property.

In covering these tax matters, the reporter should always try to relate the decisions reached by officials directly to the reader, explaining how a specific increase or other change will affect an individual.

> Faced with rising salary costs, the board of supervisors increased the county's general tax rate 10 percent yesterday.
>
> "We've opted for a continuation of services, rather than cutting what we believe is an irreducible minimum of services," said Supervisor Roy Williamson.
>
> The board added 32 cents to the current tax rate of $3.20 per $100 of assessed valuation, with rates for special districts to be decided later.
>
> Under the new general rate, the owner of a $60,000 home assessed at 50 percent of that figure will pay $1,056 next year.

All county property is reassessed at infrequent intervals, often by outside specialists hired for that specific purpose. Improvements, additions to property and rising values will thus be reflected in the tax totals. Some counties have adopted the practice of reassessing property each time it changes hands, maintaining a truer picture of property values in an expanding or growing market.

> To maintain a more up-to-date figure on county property values, Assessor Bert T. Stark said yesterday his office will begin checking property transfers.
>
> Here is how Stark said the procedure will work:
>
> Each week Stark's office will study transfers, the price paid and the new owner or owners. The price will be checked against the current value of the property on the county rolls.
>
> "If the price paid is 15 percent more than current valuation, we will adjust the assessment and it will be reflected on the next tax bill," Stark said.

After the assessor has officially set the figures, a board of equalization meets to hear complaints from taxpayers who believe their assessment is too high. The board usually has the power to adjust the assessment upward or downward. Often a county commission sits as a board of equalization or board of adjustment, reviewing assessments itself.

> A downward reassessment in the value of a residence owned by J. C. Tonley at 1600 Broad St. was granted yesterday by the Equalization Commission. It was the commission's only adjustment this year.
>
> The Tonley assessment now more closely parallels adjacent property for tax purposes, Commissioner William Hands said. Six other requests for downward reassessment were denied by the commission.

Commercial property values, and their substantial effect on tax assessments, should be closely monitored by either the business reporter or the county beat person. Property assessed for millions of dollars may be sold for much less than its value on the tax rolls and trigger major changes in final totals. Many appraisals are far too high on older downtown properties, whereas formerly rural land on the fringes of the city is appraised at much less than its real worth.

After assessments are completed, the county governing board draws up a budget and then sets the tax rate designed to produce the revenue which will balance it. The rate determines whether the taxpayer will owe $200 or $2,000. All these continuing revenue processes require continuing coverage, with explanations of the effect each will have on the taxpayer's wallet or pocketbook.

The final step is to determine the amount of each bill and to send the bills to the taxpayers. In some counties, the sheriff serves as tax collector; in others a county treasurer fills this function.

Disbursing: Who Gets the Money

—The sheriff wants funding for four more deputies, citing the increased pressures of process serving and an increase in rural crime calls.

—The three circuit court judges want their courtrooms and offices painted and a modern jury room installed in the courthouse.

—County clerical workers, banded together in an informal "association" in lieu of an official union, have demanded an across-the-board pay increase of 12 percent.

—The cost of gasoline has skyrocketed, and the county garage supervisor is asking for more money to meet the expense.

—The county clerk, always anxious to satisfy a demanding electorate in an election year, wants desperately to computerize his operations and run on that record.

Each of these hypothetical requests, and many others, will be pondered by the county governing board before the budget is made final. And while the board ponders, the reporter writes—about all the requests, their impact on county services, which ones are merely frivolous and which appear to be legitimate. Some officials prefer to air their needs publicly through the press; others work quietly behind the scenes for funds which they believe will enable their offices to function smoothly.

So with the public watching through the eyes of the reporter, the budgeting and spending process in county government hinges on practical politics. Before a final budget is adopted, trade-offs will take place, new political alliances may be effected (and some rudely shattered), disappointments will occur among some, and taxes may even be raised to accommodate the major requests for funds.

> Franklin County commissioners adopted a hard line yesterday on a supplemental appropriation request made by Prosecutor George C. Allen.
>
> In deferring action on Allen's plea for an additional $85,000 to pay staff salaries and to cover costs of three major criminal trials this year, the commissioners indicated they will not honor the request.
>
> "The only way to hold back government spending is to say no," said Commissioner Michael Dorrian. "I'm not in favor of giving any more money unless we open the supplemental door to every officeholder."

With a convoluted budgeting and spending process that affects so many elected officials and their offices, the county reporter cannot afford to merely await the outcome of the negotiations. In analyzing the proposals, the reporter should also be prepared to assess the current levels of services and spending.

Are needy agencies receiving their fair share of county funds? Are favored agencies top-heavy with personnel? Are the proposals overlapping with each other or with other units of government? Is the county overextending itself with new programs that offer the potential for substantial tax increases when they are finally put in place?

The reporter can pursue many avenues in these kinds of analyses. County and state auditors are often useful sources. Subordinates in the affected offices are often willing to discuss the effectiveness of the agency. Experts outside county government can often be counted on to provide a balanced opinion, and heads of other agencies should not be overlooked, although their opinions must be weighed carefully for possible bias.

A Sharing of Revenues

County governments accumulate operating funds from a variety of sources other than direct taxes. Fees are collected from users of county-operated facilities, such as civic centers, field houses and recreation complexes. Fees are often collected for documents filed with the county clerk and for handling the state's business in the courthouse. Most of the funds are returned to the county treasury to carry out the specific programs from which they were obtained.

A more recent substantial source of funds has been revenue sharing by state and federal governments, particularly the latter. A typical state grant might include matching money to assist in purchasing or developing new facilities that would be operated by the county.

> Charleston—Gov. John Rockefeller yesterday approved a $150,000 allocation of state funds to purchase a small airport in Cabell County.
>
> The money, with $50,000 provided by the Cabell County Commission, will be used to purchase Kyle Field on Highway 22. Commission Chairman William L. Dundee said the county will develop the property as a public general aviation facility.

Federal contributions to local governments have been equally substantial. A typical list of federal grants to counties includes funds for judicial purposes, health and safety, law enforcement and jail facilities, and manpower training. Some counties employ experts to study federal regulations and determine new sources of possible funding. These grants range from multimillion-dollar projects to more modest $1,500 matching grants for purchase of a van to transport the elderly.

Reporters should be aware that most of these federal grants programs require a careful accounting of funds spent at the local level. A county "monitor" is often appointed to investigate the efficacy of the programs.

> Following allegations of misconduct by county ambulance personnel, the County Commission yesterday transferred the Emergency Medical Service from the sheriff's office to a newly formed Department of Emergency Services.
>
> The report of misconduct was prepared by James C. Wesson, a county monitor for programs funded by the federal Comprehensive Employment and Training Act. The ambulance service is funded by the program.

Many county governments prepare two separate budgets, one based on local tax revenue and another detailing disbursement of up to 25 percent of the total which flows from federal sources. Breakdowns might be quite specific, showing local revenue for operation of the sheriff's department of $420,000 and federal funds of $115,000. The "local funds" budget might show no money for fire protection, whereas the federal funding would indicate $140,000 for volunteer fire departments throughout the county.

Revenue sharing is not a one-way street, however. County governments often earmark substantial grants to other local agencies for services deemed essential to the economic health of the area. A grant may be provided for regional bus service operated by a special district that draws funds from the federal government, several affected municipalities and the state as well as the county. The county governing board may participate in other programs such as regional airport facilities, public library systems and sewage disposal.

The relationships among these sponsoring government units

become more important to the county reporter. One of his or her roles will be to closely monitor the movement of funds from one "jurisdiction" to another, for evaluative as well as for political reasons. No one is more knowledgeable or better prepared to smoke out unnecessary "sweetheart arrangements" among officeholders than a perceptive reporter. The best rule is always to "follow the money."

Even more often, politics plays a part in decisions to provide grants or withhold them from other agencies.

> The Seymour County Commission has decided to cut its $400,000 donation to the Regional Airport Commission in half next year, citing as its reason "major budgeting problems."
>
> However, the commission, which drastically changed its political complexion in the recent general elections, has been engaged in a running and often visible debate with the airport commission over selection of a director.

The Cast of Characters

No structure houses so many public officials with such widely dissimilar functions as the county building. The county surveyor may be only a few feet down the hall from the county prosecutor, but the difference in jobs is worlds apart. A magistrate has little in common with the county agricultural agent.

Not only are the functions of the offices different, but the manner in which each official reaches the job varies from state to state and even from county to county. The health officer may be appointed by the county commission as a practicing professional, whereas the assessor or treasurer must stand for election.

Nowhere is the old and ingrained suspicion of politicians more apparent than in the county building. Built into the system is the election process that enables the public to toss out officials in whom it has lost confidence, and most county officials continue to be elected. As a practical matter, however, election to office is somewhat more secure than it sounds, particularly if the candidate possesses some expertise, few skeletons in the closet, many friends and an effective campaign organization.

With all these dissimilarities, one constant remains—the jockeying for position and power that accompanies most units of government. It is a fact of life, and the reporter must learn to deal with it at the county level. Personalities of these officeholders and the jobs they hold play a major part in how the reporter covers the beat.

Non-Judicial County Officers

Depending upon the region, tradition or legislation, county officers function either directly under supervision of the governing board or under separate agencies or boards with varying degrees of autonomy. These officials may be dependent on the board for

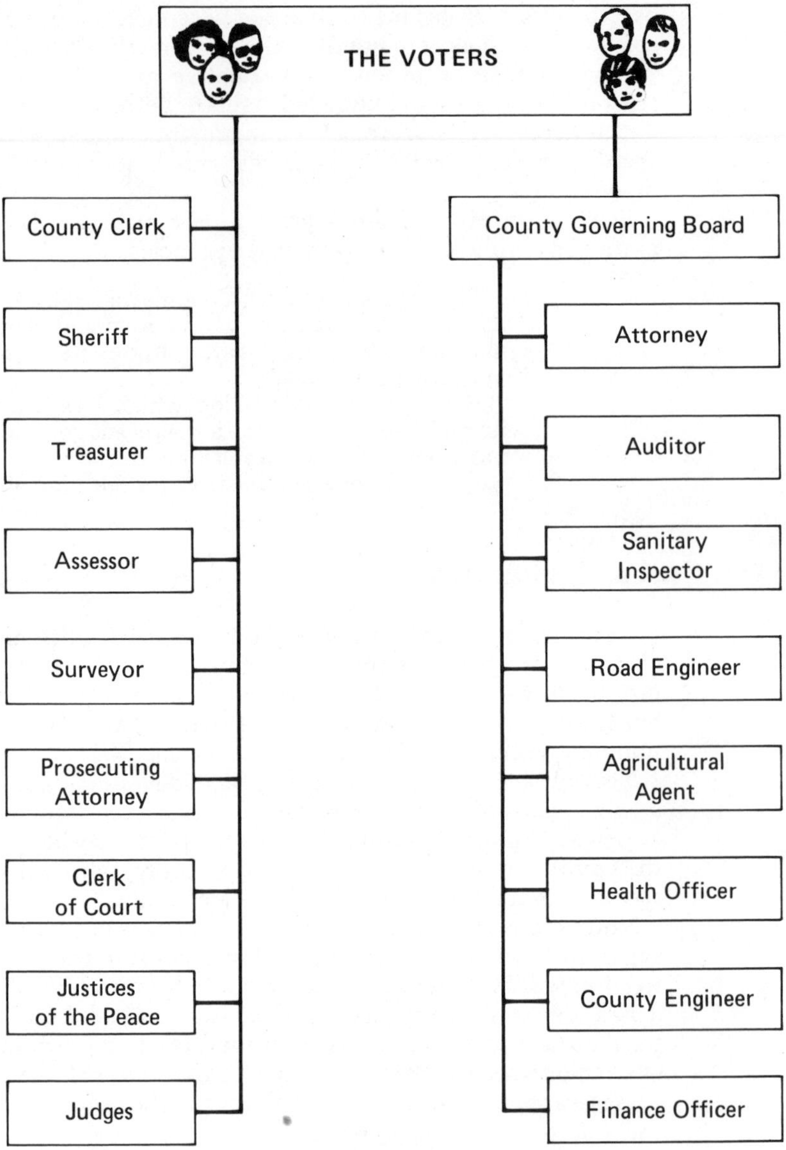

FIGURE 2–2. *The organizational chart of a traditional county government.*

salaries and other financing, subject to regular audit or other controls imposed by legislative action.

For instance, a county board may employ a school superintendent and staff or may delegate that responsibility to an entirely separate collateral agency such as a board of education. A popularly elected county assessor may have no ties to the county commission aside from dependence on it for funding. A county commission may elect to abrogate its responsibilities and appoint an entirely separate advisory council to oversee a sensitive area of service.

> The first step to create a countywide public service district to handle all water and sewer service was taken by the County Commission yesterday.
>
> Commissioners voted 3-0 to abolish the Office of Water Supply, which now operates under direct supervision of the commission and services 60 percent of the county, and establish the new agency. Service would be expanded to the 40 percent of the county not being served.
>
> Reaction was favorable from members of the Planning Commission, but Water Commissioner Christopher Schwab expressed surprise that a separate agency is being planned.
>
> "The water office is in place," he said, "and only needs to be upgraded with funding to get that other 40 percent of the county."
>
> Commissioners refused to comment on Schwab's future or disposition of the other 11 current employees of the water office.

The county reporter should have a clear picture of the fiscal and legal lines of authority. One way to get this is to construct an organization chart if one is not available, looking at both the official lines as well as the unofficial ones.

THE COUNTY CLERK

The office of county clerk is nearly universal in some form. The clerk is popularly elected in some states and appointed in others, and the reporter will find this official one of the most important on the county beat.

As the principal recording officer, the clerk supervises the recordkeeping of legal instruments such as deeds, mortgages, leases, property transfers, wills and trusts, often births and deaths, and results of elections.

The office may handle licensing for state agencies, such as drivers' licenses or vehicular tags. The clerk or a deputy generally serves as recorder for the county governing board, preparing the board's agenda and maintaining records of meetings. A cooperative clerk or assistant in the office can provide unending assistance to a busy reporter as a source for all kinds of potential stories.

In many states, however, some of these functions are handled by a register of deeds or county recorder.

> The Cautious Jenkins home, built in 1833 and considered one of the area's oldest landmarks, has been sold to a restaurant chain for $320,000, property transfer records in the County Clerk's office show.
>
> Officials of the chain, Cattle Rustlers Delight, refused to comment on the transaction, but Mrs. Nell Dwight, 84-year-old former owner, said the 21-room mansion at 700 Front St. would be restored as a period restaurant.

Transactions of this kind and other records are readily accessible in the clerk's office.

THE COUNTY ATTORNEY

Most often appointed, the county attorney is an important official whose major duties are to advise the county governing board and represent the county in legal actions. The attorney also draws up contracts, interprets board actions and assists in drawing up the annual budget. Sometimes the county attorney acts as prosecutor, filing informations and assisting law enforcement officials in investigations.

Like the more visible county prosecutor, the attorney's position is often a stepping stone to higher elective office. It is frequently filled by political appointment, with the party in power exercising control over the process.

> The Potomac County Commission appointed a new county attorney this morning, but not without a dispute that ended when Commissioner William Schultz walked out of the meeting.
>
> Republican Commissioners Ted C. Johnson and Raymond L. Adams voted to employ George A. Mills, a 33-year-old Republican and partner in the law firm of Greene, Ketchum and Mills. Schultz, a Democrat, had objected to Mills' appointment. After the vote, Schultz stalked from the room.
>
> "What Potomac County needs is someone with experience in government, not someone with political connections," Schultz said later.

COUNTY TREASURER

The county treasurer serves as tax collector in many states, sending the tax bills after rates have been set and acting as custodian of all public funds. Often the treasurer is popularly elected. Details of county expenditures, maintained in that office, are available to the reporter as part of the public record.

Beyond this detail, however, the treasurer is often available as the reporter's source for impending changes in funding and should be cultivated for other developments. As a reasonably independent officeholder, the treasurer may not be as reluctant as other county officials to discuss controversial and negative developments.

> A "major crisis" in public service employment—the loss of up to 120 jobs—may befall the county by January, County Treasurer Barnett Ross warned yesterday.
>
> The loss of federal money will mean budget problems for the county, Ross said. "It's going to affect us quite drastically, particularly in the job area."
>
> Ross said his office had received notification of federal program changes from officials of CETA (Comprehensive Employment and Training Act) yesterday. He cited a change in the federal formula.
>
> "We've got too many people on board," Ross said. "But we're not the only ones in this boat. It's happening all over."

COUNTY ASSESSOR

Assessment of property for tax purposes is a nearly universal function at the county level, and a popularly elected assessor fills that job in more than half the states. Where townships exist as a subdivision of the county, assessors at that level handle the function. Some states place assessment of property in the hands of a board of tax assessors.

The reporter should not wait for the annual assessment time to come around to look for news stories in this office. Changes in property values, in methods of assessing valuation and in general economic outlook often generate news through the assessor. The reporter should consider this official an expert in the real estate field and look to him or her as a valuable source of information. The assessor knows the community as well or better than anyone else and can spot trends a mile away. Usually he or she has the facts and figures to back them up.

> The eastern—and much older—half of the county is more than pulling its weight in tax income.
>
> That's the assessment of one county official who has studied the trend and has the figures to back them up.
>
> "If you draw a line down Bull Street, the older half of the county is supplying 62 percent of the money," says Assessor Warren Shelton. That amounts to $4.3 million of the $7 million collected by the county in property taxes.
>
> Shelton was responding to criticism by the Taxpayers Association that the recent revaluation tended to favor the older half of the city.

COUNTY AUDITOR

Many states authorize a county auditor or comptroller who functions as chief budget officer or accountant. The designation is misleading because outside audits, often by the state itself, are conducted on county government every year. In some areas the auditor serves as clerk to the county governing board.

In some states, the auditor serves as a county clerk, handling collection of personal property taxes, maintaining financial records for county agencies and disbursing county bills. Sometimes the auditor serves as one of the members of a county budget commission, which mediates disputes among the various agencies.

OTHER COUNTY OFFICIALS

Many counties elect *surveyors,* whose offices maintain detailed county maps and determine boundaries in dispute. *County engineers,* usually required to be registered professionals, are authorized to perform the duties of a civil engineer, responsible for construction, maintenance and repair of roads and bridges. The engineer, sometimes elected and often appointed, prepares plans and specifications prior to public bidding on projects under that office's jurisdiction and prepares tax maps for other officials.

A *health officer*, usually a physician, is generally employed by the county, and the work is diagnostic or preventive. Selection of a chief health officer is often placed in the hands of a separate Board of Health, which develops services and conducts educational campaigns.

> The Graham County Commission appointed a new health officer yesterday, concluding a six-month search for a successor to retiring Dr. James L. Partin.
>
> Dr. William G. Giles, a general practicioner, will give up his private practice to take the $36,000 a year position. "The county deserves a full-time diagnostician," he said, "and that's what I intend to be."

Some county governments place sanitation and enforcement of pollution regulations in the health office, while others employ a *sanitary engineer* to oversee refuse regulations.

The larger counties appoint a *finance director* to provide fiscal control and coordinate operating and capital fund activity. This official may also assist in drawing up the annual budget. Creation of a central purchasing department often calls for appointment of a county *purchasing agent*.

Another office often funded by county, state and federal money is that of the *agricultural agent*, which serves as a source of information on agricultural activities. As with other little-cultivated county offices, the persistent reporter will find a broad range of news material, some of it important as well as interesting.

> Walter and Lona Hayes have lost more than $2,000 worth of cattle this year on their small East Lynn farm because packs of dogs—not necessarily wild—have literally run their livestock to death.
>
> "This has been going on for several years," said County Agricultural Agent Mary Crawford. "The Hayes are losing feeder calves along with some others in that section of the county."
>
> The agent said the dogs run the calves until they are exhausted. "Older and larger cattle can usually take care of themselves," Crawford said. "It's the young calves that are killed."

Some counties make provisions for an animal control department, which enforces laws requiring control and licensing of dogs and other animals. The board collects license fees and revenue-sharing funds to operate.

Officials of the Judiciary

The courts play a prominent role in the business of the county, and a substantial share of the budget is earmarked for housing and operating them. Some states arrange for payment of judges' salaries, while the remainder of the court operations is the responsibility of the county.

The operation of the courts and the work of those who staff them are discussed in detail in later chapters. County funding provides a wide variety of judicial officials.

CLERK OF COURT

A trial court of general jurisdiction is nearly always attached to the county courthouse. The clerk of court is its official record-keeper, with a staff to assist in expediting the judicial process and in maintaining records. The office is most often elective, and the clerk sometimes has duties other than those involving court recording, such as issuance of notary public commissions, real estate brokers' licenses and vehicular titles.

SHERIFF

The office of sheriff is the most universal of all county offices, although the duties vary widely. The office is immensely visible and carries great power and influence. The sheriff is generally elected, usually for a four-year term, and like the prosecuting attorney's position is often a stepping stone to higher office.

As court officials, the sheriff and deputized employees assist in its operations, serving papers, swearing in witnesses, acting as bailiffs during trials and following instructions from the bench. In some states, the sheriff also serves as county tax collector.

The sheriff is traditionally the county's chief law enforcement officer, although growth of state police agencies has tended to limit this function. Most sheriffs, however, continue to maintain responsibility for enforcing the law in unincorporated areas of the county.

Criticism of the office usually centers on the wide range of responsibilities that may impinge on quality of work produced. Often the answer to this criticism centers on the argument that a lack of funding is the problem.

> To have someone arrested, a warrant is needed and a law enforcement officer to serve it.
>
> Having that warrant served in Clay County, however, is easier said than done.
>
> The backlog of unserved warrants on file totals 2,800, according to records in the Sheriff's Department, and appears to be increasing every month.
>
> The reason, officials say, is an insufficient number of deputies. "We don't have the manpower, and the men on the job don't have time to do it," said Lawrence Stephens, chief deputy.
>
> Stephens said a deputy requires at least 90 minutes to serve a warrant, take the suspect before a magistrate and complete the paperwork.
>
> "That's if the deputy has no problems locating the suspect," Stephens pointed out.

While the sheriff's law enforcement function has been somewhat minimized, the official continues to serve as custodian of prisoners, maintaining jail facilities. In many areas, the facilities to incarcerate municipal, state and federal prisoners have been combined and the keys given to the sheriff.

With this range of responsibilities, and with a finger on nearly every pulse in the county, the sheriff becomes a much more important source to the reporter than most other officials.

PROSECUTING ATTORNEY

Depending on the state, the attorney who conducts investigations and criminal prosecutions in the trial courts is identified as prosecuting attorney, solicitor, state's attorney or district attorney. It is an elective office in most states, and the occupant exercises considerable political power because of the visibility of the office. Successful prosecution in criminal cases often enhances this official's career and usually assures re-election.

Conversely, failure in very visible criminal prosecutions often creates problems of tenancy in this office. Political organizations, seeing a negative effect developing prior to election time, have been known to withdraw their support for a candidate whose success has been questionable.

JUSTICE OF THE PEACE

Often elected, justices of the peace are still found in most states, serving mainly as judges of small claims courts and issuers of warrants. Increasingly, state legislatures are modernizing their functions, even to the extent of abolishing them and transferring their functions to other offices.

CORONER

The primary duty of the coroner is to determine the exact cause, method and manner of death. As the county's medical examiner, the coroner conducts autopsies and hearings to determine whether a crime has been committed. This office too is being modernized, often changing from an elective to an appointive office. For the sake of efficiency, some states have created state medical examiners in central locations.

Collateral Boards and Agencies

Nearly every county governing board authorizes some form of independent board or agency that functions separately from the board itself. Sometimes they are composed of substantial citizens who give their time as a public service, and as such they exist to take essential county services "out of politics." In other cases, the boards are quite political. Sometimes these collateral boards are used in an effort to circumvent state restrictions.

The reporter must determine the relationship between the governing board and these independent agencies, learning what strings are attached and how much power the agencies actually possess.

Membership on the various boards is often determined by the governing board through appointment, although some boards are elective. In either case, political friction is often created because of jurisdictional problems, sometimes culminating in court action.

> Legal suits pending between the Haskell County Commission and the County Parks Board were dismissed yesterday by Circuit Court Judge Robert Dutton.
>
> Under terms of the dismissal, operation of the county field house will revert to the County Commission, and the Parks Board will continue to administer the adjacent playing fields.
>
> "I believe this is an equitable solution to the problem," County Commission Chairman Ted Durant said after the decision was announced.

Two other agencies often separated from jurisdiction of the county governing board are the county planning board and the county zoning board, although they are sometimes combined. A county commission may exercise veto power over the actions of these boards, as a check on their powers.

Sometimes a county's building and zoning director has dual responsibility for enforcing county and state building codes, as well as county zoning laws. The director inspects facilities, notes deficiencies and files appropriate action with the county prosecutor.

Many counties allow only a rudimentary zoning power, responding to the will of unincorporated areas that a person be allowed to do what he or she wishes in those areas.

> The tool shed you're building in your back yard may be a little illegal, says Robert Drinnon, county director of water, sewer and building permits.
>
> Although anyone erecting a structure containing more than 100 square feet in the unincorporated sections of Harrison County must purchase a building permit, many residents ignore the regulation, according to Drinnon.
>
> County commissioners want to rely on "education and persuasion," he said, and do not want to enforce the $25 to $100 a day penalties for noncompliance.
>
> "We want to assure people that these permits are not a step into zoning," Drinnon said. "We want to stay away from enforcement. We don't like that concept."
>
> The permits are required as part of the county's compliance with the federal Flood Insurance Program, which provides low-cost flood insurance and other grants to the county.

Frequently the same zoning issues that make news in municipalities appear on the county scene and work their way into court. Residents may not object to a henhouse full of chickens in someone's backyard, but they protest vehemently a proposed trailer court half a mile away.

Other agencies most often separated from direct control of the county governing board include a county health board, a board of education, a public welfare board, an elections commission and often a parks and recreation board.

Coping with Complications

Three requirements are indispensible in competently covering county government:

1. A total familiarity with the system itself, the functions and powers of the various officials and their offices, and the relationships among them. The layered nature of government at the local level, both physical and fiscal, complicates straightforward reporting of the facts.

To further complicate matters, the state legislature is constantly imposing itself on county agencies through its actions, and the reporter must be alert to actions affecting county government.

> Reimbursement to counties for handling juvenile offenders would be drastically altered under a $32 million bill introduced yesterday in the State Senate.
>
> The bill, introduced by Peter Crossland (D-Mansfield), would require each county to set up a local review board to outline a plan for handling youthful offenders.
>
> Each county plan would have to include specific procedures for contracting foster home care, sheltered care services, group homes and home advocacy services. The bill mandates that juveniles not be jailed with adults.

The reporter must also understand and deal with the occasional anachronistic practices that he or she will encounter, submerging the frustration almost certain to be felt. "We've always done it that way," is not an uncommon statement in the county courthouse, and the reporter will quickly learn to work around the obstacle.

2. The absolute necessity of understanding practical politics at the county level.

The crusty old courthouse regular knows that he or she cannot stick his or her head in the sand, because politics exists at every level and in every office. Even the walls have ears where ambitious political figures are concerned, and nearly every action will be weighed for its implications. Like the politicians, the reporter will learn to carefully weigh them too.

No one knows the skeletons in the courthouse closets better than the oldtimers, but the reporter should be forewarned: their views are often colored by ancient friendships, old family alliances and always shifting opportunities. The reporter should keep his or her own counsel and carefully weigh all "inside information." It is often unbalanced and sometimes "unbelievable."

3. An understanding of the character of the community in which the reporter is operating.

Such an understanding will help place information in better perspective. The county may be predominantly rural or may contain strong agricultural elements that will color the complexion of the governing power structure and affect the importance of some of the agencies.

Knowing these elements and understanding their interests, the reporter will find it easier to deal comfortably with all of them. A commissioner may have a responsibility toward a special constituency and thus has a dual role: representing that constituency and serving the county at large. Sometimes these responsibilities are divergent.

A county board may include a representative from a citrus-producing section and another with different interests in a phosphate-producing area.

> A few months after William L. King took office as a Marlin County commissioner in January, he found himself sitting between frequent antagonists President Loren Slack and Commissioner Harry Sling.
>
> King won the votes of both men yesterday to take office as commission president for the coming year and said he hopes to tone down the arguments between the two men.
>
> "It has gotten better," King observed. "They are a long way from agreeing on everything, but we're losing some of those personality clashes. I think we'll have a productive year."

Such problems are more likely to occur within counties that contain strong elements of different types of constituencies—rural, urban and suburban.

CHAPTER 3
Reporting State Government

WITH usual terseness, the editor's memo is right to the point.

> John: the gov. has skedded press confab for noon today. Some kind of announcement in the wind. Drive up and see what's on his mind.

The order sets in motion a chain of events that results in often typical news coverage of the state's chief executive. In this case, the editor and his newspaper staff have been depending on wire service coverage of the governor's office for several months. The opportunity to staff an event in the capital—and to provide the reporter with several additional hours in which to re-establish personal contacts—has found favor with the editor.

The news conference is carefully staged in a small auditorium adjacent to the governor's office. Present are two wire service reporters who normally cover the capital for the newspapers of the state, a reporter for a group that owns and operates four newspapers in the state, three television camera crews cognizant of the visual impact of the event, half a dozen reporters from around the state specifically in the city to cover the conference, the governor's press secretary and two other aides.

Of these, only the wire service reporters, the group representative and two other reporters regularly cover the governor's office. The last two represent the newspapers publishing in the state capital itself.

The governor's announcement is brief—a new $4 million program to provide home repair grants for low-income and elderly residents, with the funding coming from the federal Department of Housing and Urban Development. Eligible applicants will be served through county offices throughout the state. The governor answers several questions on the subject, then responds to a series of questions from reporters on non-related issues. The press conference concludes with the governor's thanks and the participants disperse.

With a few changes in personnel, timing and the issues involved, this scenario is repeated regularly in many states. Depending upon the resources of a newspaper or broadcast outlet and the impulses of editors or news directors, state government is covered far more solidly than this, in similar fashion or not at all.

The average newspaper and television station, not to mention the radio outlet, depends primarily on wire services to monitor the state's activities, whether that state is the nation's biggest or smallest. Only during sessions of the legislature is coverage expanded, and even then a newspaper may dispatch a staff reporter to ferret out material with a "local angle," mainly seeking out representatives from its home area and continuing to depend on wire services for general legislative coverage. Only occasionally will the staff reporter submit material of statewide importance.

Even during the legislative session, the newspaper with full-time coverage of state government is the exception rather than the rule.

Thus, a vast array of state agencies, institutions and constitutional offices, staffed by thousands and operated with billion-dollar budgets, is often covered on a catch-as-catch-can basis. Even when conscious efforts are instituted to obtain the news, only the most visible offices and agencies are selected for coverage.

However slim the capital press corps may be, state governments are covered in countless ways by reporters at the "local level." If it were not for this, news of state government would be scarce indeed. The long arm of state government reaches into every county and municipality, attaching strings to them by the very fact that they are the offspring of the state. Cities obtain their charters from the legislature, and counties serve as workhorses for state government, dispensing services mandated and often funded at the state level.

The local reporter, with an understanding and awareness of these strings, a knowledge of their controllers and the issues involved, is in effect covering state government at the local level.

—A state board of education checks a county school system's funding for construction, asking a lot of pertinent questions.

—A city government institutes efforts to enact a local income tax and seeks approval of the state legislature.

—A county and its sheriff work on a plan to improve its outdated jail facilities, with the help of additional state funding.

—An investigative reporter digs into local pharmaceutical firms' questionable relationships with the State Board of Pharmacy.

All these are examples of "local" stories that have another focus at the state level. At whatever end of the string the reporter begins unraveling, the state-level story will still be told.

Similarities In Systems

Journalists who have covered state government in more than one state can easily recognize the stereotyped similarities in systems and personalities. Every state has its share of orthodox and unorthodox political figures: the wealthy business executive who offers "new, responsive and businesslike" government in expensive election campaigns, the folksy candidate who always appeals to the rural interests, and the elder "statesman" who is always unbeatable at election time.

There are other similarities. State legislatures are usually composed of part-time citizen-legislators, heavily laced with men and women who practice law as a profession and who can afford to leave their practices for several months while the legislature is in session in a distant city. Although one finds farmers, teachers, people from business, physicians and even journalists serving in the legislature, an intimate knowledge of the law binds lawyers together. Experts in that field abound in the statehouse.

The reporter covering and interpreting state government must sort out a complex mix of professional politicians, expert and inexpert administrators, and part-time citizen-legislators.

However, the powers and functions of state government must first be understood in order to competently report on the issues and personalities.

The Powers of State Government

State government is organized much the same as its federal counterpart, assuming basic powers from a constitution, and promulgating laws or statutes to carry out the various functions demanded or implied by the document.

Under the early constitutions, state government functions were limited to preserving order and establishing a judiciary to protect the rights of its citizens. With the passage of time, however, state functions have proliferated. Only about 20 states continue to operate under original constitutions. Some in other states have been revised as many as 100 times.

Like their federal counterpart, the states have developed three distinct branches of government, with a legislative branch prescribing the law, an executive branch administering it, and a judiciary interpreting the statutes as well as the original constitution.

Like its federal counterpart, state government has evolved into a complex institution, with a variety of overlapping authorities and functions often leading to fuzzy jurisdictions and the inevitable political arguments that accompany them. Nowhere is this truer than in the relationships between state government and its various offspring—counties, cities, towns, special districts and new single-purpose authorities that dot the landscape.

With these relationships in a constant state of flux because of the flow of power among and between these government units, the reporter covering the statehouse will find politics the order of the day no less than at the local level.

The Framers' Mandate and the "Partnership"

The framers of the federal Constitution delegated to the fledgling states a broad mandate, articulated in the 10th Amendment. While this original 1791 mandate provided a broad range in which to operate, the federal government since that time has steadily encroached upon the state's domain, providing it with increased financial and other assistance, while insisting on extensive guidelines and restraints which have created an interlocking federal-state partnership.

This has been accomplished through federal legislation providing grants-in-aid and revenue-sharing programs for the states. The interstate highway system, with funding by the Federal Highway Administration, offers an excellent example. The federal government underwrites 90 percent of the cost of the system, with the states providing the remainder. However, the states must follow federal guidelines in constructing, maintaining, policing and even beautifying the highways. When the federal government mandated a 55-mile-an-hour speed limit on the highways, the states were bound to enforce it, under threat of losing federal funding.

The States' Own Powers

Despite a federal-state partnership that is still emerging, states retain the power to raise extensive taxes for many purposes and may borrow money to promote long-range projects. States also administer a vast body of civil and criminal laws, much more far reaching than the legal powers reserved to the federal government.

Except for the inevitable federal taxes, much of the legislation that affects the average citizen is state law. Each year state legislatures argue, process and pass on to their governors hundreds of new statutes, all dealing with specific measures regulating safety, health, education, law enforcement, welfare and transportation and all affecting the lives of everyone in every city, hamlet and rural area.

Billion-dollar budgets balanced through taxes and other revenue sources provide for operation of colleges and universities, highway maintenance and construction, facilities for the ill and handicapped, the election process and control of commerce within the state. Public facilities are expanded, new recreation areas established, agencies set up to promote industrial development and new programs established to further mental health. The list of programs is nearly endless.

Powers of the state do not end there. The average citizen is followed from beginning to end. Birth statistics are recorded (often in county offices by direction of state officials), education records are maintained, marriages are consummated with state approval, drivers licenses are issued to qualified motorists (following tests and inspection), a state certificate is issued to a college-trained pharmacologist or to a new medical practicioner, and a death certificate is recorded in the state archives. The final burial permit and adjudication of the deceased person's estate through a probate court concludes the cycle.

With local government often acting as agent, the state's activities are all pervasive. Whether a citizen wishes to hunt, fish, practice law, lease or purchase property, or operate a commercial enterprise, the state is the unseen arbiter through the state code which permits the activity. While these regulatory activities are administered by the executive branch, they are constantly under scrutiny by the legislative branch, with the judiciary interpreting points of law.

Each of these strikes closely at the average citizen. So is it any wonder why this accumulation of state-inspired do's and don't's is so difficult for the statehouse reporter to cover?

The Legislative Branch

Of the three branches of state government, the legislative element is closest to the will of people. The present bicameral system evolved after the American Revolution, when most of the colonies established two houses. The lower house, with a larger membership, is generally called the house of representatives, although some states distinguish it as the house of delegates, the assembly or the general assembly. The upper house, the senate, often has powers similar to its federal counterpart—confirmation of executive appointments and the power to impeach. Longer terms of office in the senate bring considerably more stability in membership. Many constitutions require that measures involving financial appropriations originate in the lower house.

Proponents of the two-house system, which is in effect in all but one state, cite the "checks and balances" as improving the legislative quality, but political scientists argue that other factors have intruded to obscure the issue. Today's process, they suggest, allows legislatures to evade their responsibilities by making it difficult to enact wise or appropriate legislation.

Only Nebraska employs a unicameral legislature, although other states have explored the possibility. Students of government agree that the Nebraska system has stifled "buck passing" between two houses and cut down on end-of-the-session logjams, as much a hindrance to good reporting as to effective legislation.

Sizes of the houses vary across the United States, with the upper chamber ranging from 18 members in Delaware to 67 in Minnesota. The lower house varies in size from 35 in Delaware to 400 in New Hampshire.

Although population has long served as a yardstick for apportioning representation in state legislatures, the rule was loosely applied in many states until 1964 when the U.S. Supreme Court fixed population as the sole basis for apportionment. Significant shifts in population had led to wide discrepancies, and the court's one-person, one-vote ruling created broad reapportionment.

As with their federal counterpart, state legislatures are chosen through the traditional political process, with participation in political party affairs usually a prerequisite for party nomination.

Most states have fixed the term of office for members of the upper house at four years, but a two-year term is popular in some states. All but four states have fixed the term of office for lower houses at two years, requiring those legislators to return to the voters for a more frequent mandate.

Seniority usually decides key leadership positions in the legislature, and members with lengthy tenure assume the chairmanships of the committees. Compensation fluctuates widely, with more populous states paying legislators up to $50,000 annually and others paying as little as $3,000. Poor compensation has often been blamed for high turnover and poor quality of public officials, but studies have not always borne this out. The traditional practice of compensating legislators on a per diem basis has given way to annual salaries and in some cases full-time legislative responsibility.

Length of legislative sessions varies, but most states have adopted the annual session. A few states continue to meet biennially, despite the observation that annual sessions contribute to political stability. Nearly all legislatures begin their sessions in January, but the lengths vary considerably. There are 40- and 60-day time limits, and some bodies meet throughout the year.

Legislative Organization

Organization of the state legislature is dependent on its political complexion. The majority party controls the leadership positions, committee assignments and other organizational affairs. Decisions are made at party caucuses, which are not always open to the press, and reporters must often rely on secondhand information.

Leadership in the legislature is determined by tenure, the power of a legislator's constituency, the legislator's ability to negotiate from positions of strength, his or her friends in powerful places and personality. An awareness of these factors will help the statehouse reporter identify and keep tabs on those at the top.

Party caucuses held regularly throughout the session continue to guide the political direction of the lawmakers, particularly during election years. The state chairman of the majority party may not even be serving in the legislature, yet possesses considerable power to influence key votes that may help swing elections.

The executive branch, with its mandate to prepare and "sell" the state budget to the legislative branch, often exerts influence on the makeup of the legislative leadership. With power playing an important role, the governor is often able to effect selection of cooperative allies. Extensive behind-the-scenes maneuvering often takes place, little of it visible to the public. The reporter may see the refusal of a key legislator to cooperate with the governor as a sign that shifts in alliances are being made and that the power has shifted to another area.

When party discipline is strong, political leaders can bring weight to bear on the legislators. Their word on a controversial measure often carries weight with legislators.

A leader's power may also be enhanced by the role of a presiding officer. The lower house selects a speaker, the upper house is presided over by the state's lieutenant governor or by a president selected by the senate membership. Other key positions include the majority and minority leaders who direct party activities on the floors of both houses. In some states, party "whips" enforce discipline and encourage attendance.

Committee assignments also determine the power structure in the legislature. A position on a powerful rules committee, a steering committee, or a committee on committees is often more important than is the chairmanship of a minor committee.

> The faces at the top remain the same.
>
> The only State Senate committees with new chairmen in the 94th Legislature will be two whose leaders were election casualties.
>
> Appointments to 16 standing committees were announced yesterday by Senate President George T. Arnold, with key judiciary, finance and education posts unchanged.

Some of these decisions are reached between sessions, and the reporter should remain sufficiently close to sources to signal them to the reader. Legislatures appoint interim committees between sessions to take up special problems, or appoint legislative councils that function as permanent joint committees. Regular meetings offer members high visibility during non-legislative periods.

Many states require legislative audits, and important stories are often developed through this office. Auditors conduct regular visits to institutions and agencies, filing information with the legislature. The auditor's office should be a regular stop on the statehouse reporter's beat.

> A legislative auditor's report has cited the State Tax Department for irregular mileage reimbursements.
>
> Assistant Tax Commissioner Anne Schwartz said the money has since been repaid. One member of the department, the audit showed, had been charging mileage of 75 miles between the capital and Williamson. The actual distance is 35 miles.

Such minor ensnarements are routine, but often more important details are disclosed through the auditing process. An audit may find improper bidding procedures by the State Highway Department or questionable expenditures by a state institution. The reporter's persistence will assure that these kinds of stories are not left uncovered.

How a Bill Becomes Law

While the procedure varies from state to state, the law-making process embodies several principal stages, which the reporter will recognize as checkpoints on the long road to passage. A bill moves ponderously from wind-testing discussion to formal introduction, on through a committee (often a burial ground for legislation), through the complexities of debate and approval in each house, on to a conference committee for approval, back to each house for final passage and finally to the governor's desk for signature—or possible veto.

Hundreds and even thousands of proposals are submitted each session, but relatively few survive the rigors of scrutiny and debate to become law. The origin of proposals is important to the reporter, who can use the information to better judge their importance.

Some bills originate with individual legislators, others in committees or legislative councils after much study. Still others are proposed by the governor or an agency official. Some come from special-interest groups such as teacher organizations, labor unions, environmental groups or business councils.

Legislators do not have to support a measure philosophically to introduce it. Many offer bills proposed to them by persistent constituents, even though they know the bill will get nowhere in the legislative process.

Organized labor constitutes one of the most important pressure groups, and the reporter should be alert to its interests as the session approaches. Sympathetic legislators can be counted on to introduce proposals backed by such groups and also to serve as the reporter's source for advance information.

> The incoming legislature will quickly see introduction of labor-backed legislation to increase unemployment compensation benefits and raise the ceiling on workmen's compensation benefits.
>
> Passage of the proposals is being sought by the leadership of the 230,000-member State Federation of Labor, headed by Walter C. Mears.

Legislators whose constituencies contain important elements of such organized pressure groups are those most likely to introduce and support such legislation. Often the size of the pressure group is less important than its visibility or activism. Law enforcement agencies, with active blocks of voters, constitute such pressure and would be likely to lobby for changes in laws expediting their efforts in containing crime or criminal elements.

> Two bills stiffening penalties for violent crimes were introduced in the House yesterday by Rep. Charles E. Wilson (D-Logan).
>
> One bill would restore the death penalty, abolished by the state in 1967. The other would require a mandatory five-year prison term for anyone convicted of a crime in which a firearm was used.
>
> Both measures are supported by the state Fraternal

> Order of Police, whose leadership has been vocal in its calls for tough enforcement measures.

The major bill producer is often the governor, who may deliver a message to the legislature summing up proposals for the upcoming session. Supporters of the chief executive in both houses introduce the proposals and lobby for their approval, often with the expectation that the governor can improve their political prospects and give them a greater voice in filling appointive offices.

> An administration-backed proposal to create a new agency to deal with state energy matters was introduced by five co-sponsoring senators yesterday.
>
> One of them, Wilson Armstrong (D-Canton), said the groundswell for the legislation is strong enough to assure early passage in the Senate.

The five sponsors may or may not be enamored of the proposal, but they certainly won't hurt their relationships with the chief executive by their action.

Advice to legislators—and often proposed bills—also comes from dozens of lobbyists who represent special-interest groups. Retail merchants, physicians, lawyers, teachers, beauticians, osteopaths, publishers, farmers, public utilities and other can be counted upon to send experts to plead their causes in the capital during a session.

The identity of lobbyists is often important to legislation. Former state and local officials frequently represent special interests because of their expertise or connections. Many legislatures require official registration of lobbyists.

> Former House Speaker Julius R. Swain and former Welfare Commissioner Lee Winfrey were among 26 lobbyists who signed identification papers yesterday with the Senate clerk's office.
>
> Swain, a Democrat from Morgan, said he is representing the Mining Operators Association. Winfrey, a Republican from Scottsburg, said he is representing the state County Commissioners Association.

Identity of the other 24 lobbyists, also important to the story, included such disparate interests as utility firms, savings and loan associations, insurance boards, parent-teacher associations, state medical associations and a pharmaceutical group. The reporter should not only be familiar with identity of the lobbyists, but should be able to reach them on short notice, since their views on pending legislation are often important to a story. While lobbyists often try to use reporters as sounding boards, their major thrust is toward influencing legislators, and they are generally open in their relationships with the press.

In recent years new types of lobbyists have descended on the halls adjacent to the floors of the legislatures. They include college students, senior citizens and others who lobby for a much broader constituency. Citizen action groups have sprung up, "people's lobby" groups have proliferated, and other citizen organizations have formed new special-interest lobbies. Such groups often represent a number of statewide organizations—the League of Women Voters, the State Abortion League, Common Cause, the Izaak Walton League and others.

Although it is generally difficult to identify illegal or unethical practices in the horse-trading and maneuvering that takes place during a session, the reporter should be alert to them, noting the heavy pressures that may have been placed on specific legislators in an effort to carry a vote.

Sometimes legislators themselves "blow the whistle" on free-wheeling lobbyists.

> A member of the House said yesterday that a lobbyist for a Columbia small loan firm handed him a $100 bill as he left the chamber during a recess.
>
> In a speech on the House floor, Jerard Tighe (D-Canton) said he later returned the money. A bill raising limits on loans such firms can make was at amendment stage in the House. The bill was tabled later in the day.
>
> Tighe said James T. Bailey, a registered lobbyist for Capitol Financial Services, was the person who handed him an envelope containing the money. Bailey could not be reached for comment. An official at the Capitol Hotel said he had checked out of the hotel yesterday.

Conflicts of interest also appear in the legislature in other forms. The roster of a legislative insurance and banking committee may include members who have close associations with banks or insurance companies, information that is important to the reporter and to the public.

Individual financial interests or occupations should always be clear to the reporter because these factors affect the legislative process. Members of a legislative subcommittee may be studying the issue of splitting retail gasoline outlets from their parent oil companies. Some of the members may have interests or even stock in oil companies, creating at the very least the question of conflict of interest in any decision reached.

THE COMMITTEE SYSTEM

Legislative committees constitute the "proving ground" for laws that are finally enacted, and the effective reporter stalks their meetings like a predator. Proposals are strengthened or weakened in committee meetings, die quietly, survive opposition attempts to table them indefinitely and head for the floor on the heels of noisy public hearings.

Following introduction in the legislature, a bill is given first reading and is referred to an appropriate committee by the presiding officer of the house or senate. The reporter observes another key decision which lies in the hands of the leadership—the ability to direct a proposal to a sympathetic committee or to one that will effectively kill the bill by simply ignoring it.

Although details differ from state to state, a bill must be placed on the committee calendar, sometimes successfully survive public hearings and be favorably reported out to the main legislative body. Most legislatures have the authority to bring up a bill that is bottled up in committee, but the effort is seldom undertaken. The matter must be of sufficient importance to risk offending the committee membership and the legislative leadership.

The reporter carefully follows movement of legislation in committees, making sure that he or she is present for key meetings. Opposition and support surface at the frequent public hearings, and the reporter's early arrival for these help sort out the people who have a part in them and who have power to influence the legislation through testimony.

Tactics used by legislators to influence legislation should also be clear to the reporter.

> A bill weakening the open meetings law narrowly survived a motion to table it permanently in the Senate Judiciary Committee yesterday, and was sent to a subcommittee for further consideration.
>
> "It's hurt but it's not dead," commented the leader of the effort to weaken the law, Sen. Sylvester Powers (R-Mingo).
>
> Powers and others are seeking to remove the present requirement that governing bodies must notify the public of meetings by paid advertisements in the media.

A legislator may realize that he or she does not have the votes to move a bill out of committee and fail to appear when the vote on the proposal is scheduled. A courtesy move would temporarily sidetrack the bill, allowing the legislator time to corral the necessary support for passage. Awareness of this reason for the legislator's absence, rather than merely indifference, is important to the reporter's news account of the delay.

Committee hearings are also the center of citizen involvement in the legislative process. Such public hearings may be the vehicle for an impassioned plea for more school transportation funding by a parent-teacher group. Representatives of an association of apartment owners may vigorously oppose legislation strengthening tenants' rights in disputes with landlords. The reporter armed with on-the-scene testimony will write a much more accurate and compelling story than one who is not present.

Personal committee coverage also enables a reporter to ask pertinent questions at the scene, rather than being forced to later track down pivotal figures in an issue.

THE CALENDAR

When a committee favorably reports a bill to the floor of the house or senate, it is placed on the calendar, which is already heavily laden with similar legislation awaiting action. It is not uncommon for a bill to languish on the calendar until adjournment, effectively relegating it to permanent limbo.

The leadership must be persuaded by the bill's proponents that the measure deserves consideration, which is where much horse-trading takes place. Power to obtain positive action on legislation in its course through the process is essential for the effective officeholder.

As the session nears its end, a special calendar becomes the springboard to success of a proposal reaching the floor. The leadership often constitutes itself as a special committee to determine what bills will be acted upon during the final hectic weeks, meeting each day to decide what will receive priority. Without this priority, bills are usually given little chance of passage. While rules may differ, this power to consider the order of bills nearly always lies in the hands of a few legislative leaders.

FLOOR DEBATE

For all its reputation as an exciting part of the process, floor debate and action on legislation are generally routine. The reporter, however, will find coverage a necessary part of his or her schedule and must be knowledgeable regarding formal parliamentary procedure.

The senate or house may only meet formally an hour or so each day, taking long weekend recesses, but the possibility of argument erupting over an issue is always present during these brief official sessions.

Successful passage of a bill through committee sends it to the floor of one of the houses for a second reading after it is scheduled. Efforts may be made at that time to amend the bill, sometimes amounting to a redrafting of the legislation. If the bill survives, it is placed on the calendar for a third and final reading. Special limitations often apply to final readings, such as consideration of it without the privilege of amending.

Approval through the final reading moves the bill into the other house where it must run a similar gauntlet. Frequently, however, a companion bill has been introduced in the other chamber, and agreement between the two houses is only a formality.

When amendments are added and the bills differ, the bill is referred to a conference committee composed of members of both houses that tries to reconcile the differences. Nowhere is this reconciliation more important than in dealing with the state's annual budget. Upper and lower houses have each approved their version, and compromises are usually necessary to secure passage.

Funding for a new health program may die, or be emasculated; pet school projects may be put aside for a year; money for new state parks may suddenly disappear as powerful conference committee members maneuver to keep their chamber's favorite projects. In the struggles that ensue, the most powerful emerge winners, and political scars often remain. Budget compromises are always effected, allowing the legislation to become effective. Other legislation may not be so fortunate. When agreement is impossible in conference committee, the proposal dies.

TO THE GOVERNOR'S DESK

Of hundreds of original proposals, the fortunate few pieces of successful legislation make their way to the desk of the governor where they encounter a final hurdle—the veto. This power, while essentially negative, assumes significant proportions at the end of the legislative session.

In most states, the governor is allowed from three to 15 days to decide whether to sign a measure into law. He or she may sign or veto it, which returns the bill to the legislature for further consideration if it is still in session. The houses must vote to override the veto, generally by a two-thirds majority. Some states allow the governor to disallow specific items in an appropriation bill, and in other states the chief executive is allowed to reduce some budget items.

Covering the Legislature

The size and scope of activity by a state legislature during its brief or extended annual existence requires the statehouse reporter to undertake massive preparations. Simply keeping track of daily developments calls for careful organization. Furthermore, whatever textbooks may assert about legislative coverage constituting a "seasonal" effort, the far-reaching actions of that body reach into every community to become a 12-month responsibility.

The process is not only legislative but political, as this typical example shows:

—The leaders of the city's police and firemen's fraternal organizations have successfully appealed to area legislators to introduce a bill raising pensions for retired members of the two departments. But since the municipal government must absorb the $900,000 increase in its annual budget, the proposal arouses vigorous protest from municipal officials.

A compromise is effected, with the total increase trimmed to a more modest $250,000. No one is really satisfied, however, and the compromise proposal dies in the final stages of the legislative session. From adjournment through reconvening of the legislature the following year, the pension increases and their effect on the municipal budget become a major community issue.

When the legislature convenes, municipal officials persuade another area legislator to introduce a bill that would transfer the power to regulate pensions from the legislature to municipal officials, who argue that their lack of control over the fund runs counter to community interest.

How is such a story covered? As completely as possible—from the legislative maneuvering in the state capital, through the police and fire officials who have insistently demanded changes, through the municipal officials who have their own ideas about how to balance a budget, and on to the pensioners themselves and the community in which the issue has been raised.

In this case, and in many similar ones, the issue spills outside the legislative chambers and into different political and social arenas, creating the need for much broader coverage. Such issues cannot be capsulized within the boundaries of a legislative session.

THE JOURNALIST'S CHECKLIST

Unless the legislative reporter organizes well, such community controversies will create massive logistical bottlenecks before a session even begins, and the result will be superficial coverage.

Particularly for the reporter about to be drawn into the maelstrom of a legislative session for the first time, the task is clear: some absolutely vital preliminary work must be done. The best way to begin is to compile a checklist. Whether it is all completed, the list at least guarantees that bases have been covered.

These should constitute the minimum preliminaries:

1. Area legislators should be contacted, identifying their plans for introducing potential legislation. The reporter should obtain assurance that he or she will be able to contact them on short notice.

Some members of a local delegation rarely submit legislative proposals, involving themselves instead in their favorite statewide issues; others are active in submitting local bills. Preliminary stories provide readers with advance information on pending activity.

> A new legislative session usually brings with it a shower of new proposals, and tomorrow's opening is no exception.
>
> Harrison County's all-Republican delegation promises a range of activity from "a great number of bills" to virtually none.
>
> Sen. Charles Palumbo says he plans to introduce a great number of bills, because "they are nothing more than concepts or ideas whose time may or may not have come."
>
> At the other extreme, Rep. Patricia Hart says she plans to introduce no bills. "Virtually everything worthy of merit will be introduced by someone else," Hart says.

Potential legislation that has important local implications should be identified early, through the area legislators and other community officials. The process through which purely local legislation is enacted should also be reviewed.

Relationships with area legislators are important, and sometimes become sensitive, because of the reporter's insistence upon closely following critical issues. While both journalist and legislator may perceive themselves as serving the public, the estrangement sometimes takes strange forms. The reporter should be prepared for them.

> A state legislator, miffed at a reporter's story that he claimed cost him 1,000 votes in the last election, suggested yesterday that his House colleagues restrict access to reporters in House chambers.
>
> But after his resolution was read on the floor, Rep. John Clyde (D-Mason) said he would carry the issue no further. He said the resolution was "merely a demonstration of my unhappiness with a member of the media."

2. The reporter should become familiar with legislators in leadership roles, especially those who have been selected to those roles for the first time, and with the key members of the house and senate committees.

Potential major legislation should be researched, with special attention to the lines that will be drawn in the issues.

It is helpful to re-establish a familiarity with the rules of the two houses, and a physical visit to the scene prior to actual convening of the legislature can be beneficial to the newcomer. Offices are often shifted between sessions, and information services may be relocated and new procedures established. For the new reporter, a review of the sections of the state constitution dealing with the legislature can be helpful.

3. A good backgrounding in the current relationship between the legislature and the executive branch is essential to competent legislative reporting. What legislators will be considered crucial to passage of the governor's program? Who are expected to be most inimical to the executive branch's requests for funds? What state agencies will be making special requests?

Officials from state agencies are often called to testify on legislative proposals that affect their operations. The state commissioner of finance may be quizzed on mushrooming operating losses in the state parks system. The state banking commissioner may be asked to tell the House Banking Committee why some banks are obtaining short-term loans to circumvent investment laws, then selling the loans after they are checked by the State Banking Commission. Conflict between counties and the state for a bigger share of the auto license fee may require testimony before a finance committee by the state motor vehicles commissioner.

Many state officials request an appearance before committees that are considering legislation, mainly because they have an interest in the outcome.

> The seal of a notary public on a legal document is intended as proof that the signatures on it have been witnessed and verified. But state law does not make that as clear as Secretary of State James A. Mandell would like it to be stated.
>
> Mandell appeared before the Senate Legal Committee

> yesterday to explain why stronger legislation covering notaries public is needed.

Conflicting testimony from state officials often leads to a series of appearances by members of the executive branch, particularly when more than one agency is involved in the legislation.

> State Beer Commissioner Jack T. Baldini said yesterday he initiated the proposal to dismantle the State Beer Commission and merge it with the Alcoholic Beverage Control Board.
>
> Baldini told the Senate Finance Committee that he believes the present system of beer and liquor commissions constitutes a duplication of effort. Baldini was the fourth state official to testify on the issue this week.

4. The reporter should enter the new session with a working knowledge of the previous session's business. What important bills were passed? What are the prospects of the bills that died in the previous session? How did the governor and others fare in passage of programs, and who was responsible? What new political alliances were made at the last session, and what are the prospects of their continuance? Out of the past often come the answers to future action. The competent legislative reporter possesses a long and reasonably accurate memory.

Knowledge of the routine in the statehouse is also important. Contact should be made with personnel who handle legislative services, processing new bills and amendments. A knowledge of committee meeting locations can make or break a reporter's day, particularly if the site has not been publicly announced. Most capitols are overcrowded mazes, and a 30-minute search for an important committee hearing can be fatal to on-the-scene reporting. When the issue is a popular one, advance notice helps a reporter to arrive early to identify and question participants who plan to testify.

Most legislatures employ specialists to assist members in dealing with complex fiscal matters. The reporter should become acquainted with them. Clerks are employed around the clock to follow legislation, furnishing copies of the bills introduced, the journal covering the previous day's activity and agendas for the houses. Like the legislator, the reporter has access to these services, which eases the task of covering the detail.

Much of the reporter's time will be spent checking new proposals, chasing down legislators, state officials and lobbyists for comment, monitoring floor debate, sitting in on important committee hearings and staying abreast of behind-the-scenes maneuvering. Often the last activity constitutes the most important part of the reporter's efforts. An issue may die in this manner and never reach a committee room hearing or a floor argument. It is the responsibility of the reporter to try to accurately portray the death of such issues.

> The lobbyist for the State Pharmaceutical Association wore a broad smile in the hallway. A senate bill calling for posting of all medicinal prices, opposed by Tom T. Broadmoor and his organization, was dead.
>
> No one wanted to be quoted on the issue, but the consensus was that the proposal was killed by agreement among the legislative leadership to support a House measure requiring only posting of life-supporting drugs.

Liaison with the reporter's home office is essential. Absence of the city manager from his office may occasion little or no notice at home, but that official may in fact be attending a committee hearing at the capital in which the city has a strong interest. Such attendance often goes unreported in a busy and crowded statehouse.

The city manager may be pressing for legislation taking control of the city's water system rates away from State Public Service Commission jurisdiction. County officials may be visiting their legislators to promote a bill allowing them to establish a planning and zoning board. A public service district official may be seeking legislation raising the district's bonding capacity.

Close cooperation between the legislative reporter and those back home is necessary to track down the movements of such figures.

Facilities for the press in statehouses range from spacious quarters with the latest electronic hookups with the home office to cramped basement quarters containing a typewriter and a telephone. Most legislatures reserve press tables in the main chambers and provide access to reference material.

As the session progresses, its tempo increases. What seemed to be a leisurely pace during the first weeks, with brief afternoon floor sessions, suddenly becomes more of a rat race, with floor sessions beginning at 9 a.m. and lengthening perceptibly. Night and weekend sessions replace the three- and four-day weekend adjournments to allow members time for visits home.

"LOCAL" LEGISLATION

The legislative reporter will be concerned with two distinct levels of legislative activity: the "local" bills that affect only the home community and the more important statewide proposals. Both of these must be addressed in some manner, despite the tendency of many newspapers to leave the general legislation to the wire services.

Legislation that applies to a particular area sometimes proceeds quite differently. In some states, local bills are passed as a courtesy to local legislators unless those officials are divided on the issue. When there is a conflict among the delegation, the proposal usually dies unless a compromise is found. The reporter must take care that such local proposals are not lost in the shuffle of more general issues affecting the entire state.

These levels of legislation also create a subtle problem for the reporter—the frequently conflicting responsibilities of the legislators themselves:

1. They must represent the interests of the constituents of the county or district that elect them to office.

2. They are also charged with voting conscientiously in the best interest of all the people in the state.

These interests may not always coincide, and the attentive reporter reflects this in news accounts whenever possible. One such method is to publish the "shopping list" of a local legislator, asking him or her to reconcile the needs of the constituency with those of the state at large.

Easing environmental standards on burning of coal might be beneficial to the legislator's industrial area but not in the best interests of the state. Cognizance of the dichotomy of these dual constituencies can clarify the reporter's coverage.

Problems also exist in two other important areas of coverage closely related to the legislative process:

1. Far from the debate in the legislative chambers, someone must gauge the reaction of public officials and others who have a direct interest in the outcome of an issue. The busy statehouse reporter may be half a state away from such reaction, so the responsibility falls on reporters at the scene. Care must be taken that such material does not go unreported.

2. Someone must be responsible for assessing the workability of new legislation. Passage of a new law is only the beginning. How it finally affects people is the element of reporting that logically follows. There is a tendency on the part of public officials and the press to ignore the past and look to the future.

Is a law actually working? Is it unreasonable? Is it doing the job it was designed to do? Is it more costly than its proponents argued it would be? Has it had the effect of merely giving people jobs, without any other justification for existence?

Who is going to answer these questions?

Two years after establishment of a state Commission on the Spanish Speaking, for example, it is time to assess its impact. The task falls to the statehouse reporter rather than to those who are on the payroll of the commission. The following are some of the reporter's logical sources:

—Those who originally supported the legislation, those who opposed it, the officials who set up the commission, the people who are most closely affected by it and experts who have no axes to grind whatever the findings.

Because of the broad range of legislation, the task of assessment will also fall to the municipal government, county, education or police reporter, and this is why it is essential that reporters on all beats have a sound knowledge of legislative action and its possible effects.

> Has the two-year-old County Commission on the Aging been a worthwhile community investment?
>
> The verdict is still in doubt, but its original opponents contend the $130,000 a year it costs could have been much better spent.
>
> "The commission has only served to fragment services to the elderly," Will F. Spearman, president of the Taxpayers Association, said.
>
> But its supporters, including the leadership of the local chapter of the American Association of Retired Persons, argue that the commission's accomplishments have outweighed its frequent problems.

The reporter has the responsibility of covering legislative action that brings new priorities and new programs to a state. The further responsibility is evaluation of those programs, bringing into play a fairness and balance not always equaled elsewhere.

INTERPRETING AND ANALYZING EVENTS

Special care must be taken by the reporter in interpreting and analyzing the course of legislation, particularly in predicting what may or may not occur. Careful analysis of an issue, clearly labeled, does have a place in legislative reporting. It cannot replace, however, the straight reporting necessary to public knowledge, but only enhances the light thrown on an issue.

Interpretation of a complex proposal, with a discussion of its chances of passage, may often be necessary to public understanding. Like analyses, it should be undertaken carefully and with the awareness that balanced coverage lies almost solely in the motives of the reporter.

The safest course is to clearly label analysis and interpretation and to avoid it entirely if publication threatens even a hint of misunderstanding of the reporter's motives.

Relationships between journalist and legislator are also important to proper functioning of the press as a neutral observer. Studies suggest that reporters and legislators, who are cast in adversary roles, possess similar views in their perceptions of the public's interests and its need to know about legislative affairs.

Reporters and legislators work out relationships based on mutual dependence, while trying at the same time to alter the situation. Like other beats, the game is the same: Reporters work to conform to their self-image as independent, uninvolved observers. Officials work to assimilate reporters into their world as disseminators of authorized information.

Keeping this in mind, the reporter must be armed with a permanent and special neutrality to assure a final balanced legislative report, despite frequent dependence on mutual "self-help" in disseminating the news.

The Executive Branch

The size and scope of state government today, combined with fractionalization of its functions and powers, create a formidable obstacle to thorough coverage. The reporter must rely on a combination of effective sources, knowledge of agencies and issues, aggressive instincts and a dash of luck to do the job well.

The problem: What stories have priority? Even a team of capital reporters has to wrestle with the problem.

The Agriculture Department announces important changes in its million-dollar meat inspection program; the governor makes a hurried visit to a flood-ravaged community; the Alcoholic Beverage Commission schedules an important meeting; the State Education Commission plans a special hearing on textbook purchases. On any given day in the capital, these and dozens of other legitimate news stories compete for coverage.

The tendency is to report on the most visible personalities and agencies in state government, but they are not always the most important.

The typical executive branch will include dozens of different agencies, boards, commissions or departments. Some are gold mines of information; others yield little of interest to the reader. Some agencies are nearly invisible because their activities are so routine; others work deliberately to maintain a low profile.

Some agencies are important to the reporter because they extend long arms of control into local communities, such as a board of higher education which oversees colleges and universities throughout the state. Some agencies are nearly independent of the executive branch; others are highly political in character.

The reporter's challenge is to sort out the multitude of possibilities and carefully organize coverage to take cognizance of the most important as well as the most interesting. The task can never be complete, no matter how extensive the staffing, but it can be acceptable.

Roadblocks to Effective Coverage

Aside from the pure size of state government and the limits to reportorial personnel, other factors create roadblocks to effective coverage of the executive branch. Archaic procedures and outmoded offices are preserved in some constitutions, creating an administrative nightmare with political overtones. An anachronistic state highway commission may possess many overlapping functions with a more modern public works commission. There are also many pressures for agency autonomy, with long-term officials jealous of their sinecure. Powerful political allies support their position.

Disputes between agencies are not uncommon, and often the governor must act as mediator, as well as the legislature.

> State Finance Director Miles Sinnet says he can't figure out what the Commission on Mental Retardation does and is trying to abolish it.
>
> But the commission has survived at least two other attempts on its life, both foiled by legislative action. "Its function as a grantsman agency as well as a lobbying unit should hardly be financed by the state," Sinnet said yesterday.

> With a current budget of $337,000 and a $36,500-a-year directorship, the commission coordinates federal grants to communities and state mental retardation services.

Relationships between the executive and legislative branches also complicate news coverage. Many basic decisions of the executive are subject to review by the legislature, and the reporter should be able to identify the political ramifications brought about by legislative review of executive decisions.

Despite the increasing tendency toward professionalism in public service, the "spoils system" continues to exist and even thrive in many states.

> A key state senator said yesterday he would oppose confirmation of a mental health expert as director of the State Health Department.
>
> Committee hearings on confirmation of Dr. John C. Oskenhirt, who was appointed acting director of the department by the governor Nov. 1, are nearing an end.
>
> "Too many questions remain concerning his background in diagnostic health services," said Sen. Sam Gillian (D-Lowery), who announced he would vote against confirmation.

Pressures of many special interest groups also intrude on operation of state agencies, and the reporter should be able to identify to the public the origin of such pressures.

Pressure may be exerted on a highway department by trucking firms to allow heavier loads through special permits. The permits may not be in the best interests of the motoring public.

Antiquated facilities in the state mental health system may be kept open despite recommendations of a study commission that they be closed. Pressures to keep them open come from a community which says it cannot afford the loss of jobs.

The "clients" of many state agencies also constitute a major element in operation and policies of the offices. Welfare recipients, while individually appearing to have little voice in policy-making, in fact may constitute a formidable pressure group. The journalist should be familiar with the leaders of such "client" organizations and understanding of the pressures they exert on agencies. News accounts may ultimately reflect the fact that the "clients" forced an important policy change rather than a political figure.

> A farm leader threatened to organize a march on the state capital next week to press for changes in the system of figuring tax credits for using land for agricultural purposes.
>
> "It's outdated and costly, and needs to be revised," said Thurman Whitley, president of the State Grange.
>
> The Agriculture Department maintains it cannot change the rules without legislative approval.

The reporter operates in a climate where often there is widespread feeling that some agencies should be "above politics," with the effect of creating closed doors for the reporter where none should normally exist. Especially susceptible to this problem are such areas as education, prisons, correction and parole procedure, promotion of fair employment practices, law enforcement, management of state resources and many purely personnel matters.

These areas are no more non-political than others, but the effect of this attitude makes the task of covering the agencies subtly more difficult.

> The Parole Commission yesterday rejected a newspaper's request for records of parole violators, despite assurances that the publication is interested in total figures rather than individual involvement.

Education is especially subject to this tendency. Officials feel they qualify as experts who know what is best for the public school system and don't always want to be bothered by the press. Their approach sometimes is: "Don't call us, we'll call you."

It is not an attitude easily overcome.

The newly emerging partnership between state government and the federal government's grants-in-aid programs is another obstacle for the reporter. The need to monitor and report upon two different levels of government create a different kind of problem.

> A new Congressional proposal to limit funds supplied to state governments for secondary highway construction has drawn criticism from the director of the State Highway Commission.
>
> "A cut in matching funds will endanger our whole program. It's already five years behind our neighboring states," John T. Blasik said yesterday.

The reporter must reconcile the response of an angry state official with the actual federal proposal under scrutiny, which first means double-checking the proposal at the federal level. How much is the reduction? When will it be scheduled? What are its chances of passing through Congress in the first place? What areas are actually threatened? What is the response of the state's congressional delegation?

Lots of levels need to be contacted, against the word of only one state official.

The Governor and the Office

The pivotal and commanding figure in the executive branch is the governor—ceremonial, legal and political chief of state government.

A peculiar overlay of personalities and functions is embodied in the one official. As the state's chief administrative officer, mandated to supply efficient yet sensitive government to a broad constituency, the governor exudes confidence that these responsibilities will be successfully met.

But a seemingly contradictory personality emerges from the same official—the cautious politician staging a "media event" at just the right time, often unwilling to commit himself or herself to a direct answer and always hedging a little to avoid alienation of any segment of the electorate.

To the reporter, who realizes that public office is part of the recurring pattern of politics, election and re-election, it is one of the realities of covering the statehouse.

The governorship is the state's chief political prize, arising partly from the power of the office to influence public policy and the role of the governor as spokesperson for the state in its relationships with the federal government and with other states. It also stems from the governor's role as head of his or her political party, which adds additional strength to the office. The governor also has the capability of diluting somewhat the power and prerogatives of the legislative branch and assuring that the executive's initiatives have some chance for success. The sheer visibility of the office is an important factor.

It should also be pointed out that several factors intrude to minimize full use of these powers. Most states operate under constitutions that limit power and responsibility. Some diffusion of responsibility and power occurs because of the political need to make contradictory campaign promises. A gubernatorial candidate may promise tax relief on the one hand, yet assure that a proposed new highway program will solve all transportation difficulties. The two promises may be wholly incompatible, threatened in part by the reporter's insistence upon pointing out such contradictions.

Diffusion of power also exists because the governor must share it with other elected officials—a lieutenant governor, attorney general, a secretary of state, a treasurer and/or a comptroller. To add to such diffusion are independent agencies, directed by appointees from past gubernatorial officeholders, that also decentralize authority.

It is within this framework of complex bureaucracy that the reporter must operate, and knowledge of the complexities will assure more thorough coverage.

So while the governor may propose, the legislature may finally dispose—and in a manner quite contrary to the way in which the chief executive sees the problem. The legislative leadership may indeed have its own priorities in the decision-making process.

> The Senate's president and Finance Committee chairman took off in a different direction today from Gov. Will Hochman on proposed tax relief.
>
> President Bruce Angelo, R-Fanning, and Chairman Patrick Donovan, R-Cayman, introduced a bill to raise the personal exemption on the state income tax from $750 to $1,000, the same level as the federal exemption.
>
> In his state of the state address Monday, Hochman had requested removal of food from the 4 percent current tax, a move that would cost the state $118 million a year.

But the governor also receives help from friends and political appointees, who can be counted upon to put pressure on the legislature to enact the chief executive's programs.

> Gov. Will Hochman's tax relief plan is superior because

> only it can provide a tax cut to all 3.7 million residents of the state, Tax Commissioner David C. Hardy Jr. said yesterday.
>
> Hardy commented during an extensive briefing with reporters on Hochman's proposal, an indication of the administration's resolve to remove food from the 4 percent state sales tax during the current legislative session.

Despite the limitations imposed by the constitution, however, the governor wields extensive administrative authority, appointing and removing many state officials, and conducting the day-to-day business of the state. He or she is responsible for law enforcement and acts as commander of the state militia or National Guard except when it is called into federal service.

The reporter's regular access to the governor will be determined mainly by those around the chief executive. The ability of the journalist to penetrate the sometimes formidable barriers of press secretary, personal secretary and/or any number of other aides depends upon a number of factors—persistence and personality of the reporter, openness of the chief executive, and willingness on the part of aides to encourage such openness.

Information from the top "through channels" is rarely as effective as firsthand material, and every effort should be made to create regular dialogue with the person in charge.

Lacking that direct access to the governor which is most desirable, the reporter must turn to aides for needed information and acceptable detail for stories. The most helpful will be those with direct access to the governor. It will be necessary to identify the mere errand-runners and the real decision-makers around the chief executive.

Other State Officials

One of the major factors that influences the governor's full use of the powers spelled out by the state constitution is the other popularly elected officials over whom the chief executive has little or no control.

The *secretary of state,* popularly elected to a constitutional office in 37 states, rival the governor in prestige if not in power, directing a state department that reaches into every community.

As the state's chief election officer, the secretary registers political parties and determines ballot eligibility, files nominating papers, assumes responsibility for referenda and initiative petitions, decides on the form of the ballot, files candidates' expense papers and publishes election results. Even outside election years, the secretary of state's office yields regular news material for the statehouse reporter. The secretary rules on irregularities in the election process or takes them to court and oversees local election laws as well as those involving statewide contests.

> The three unlocked ballot boxes in Wayne County's First Precinct did not constitute a deliberate fraud, and

> won't affect the county's school bond levy election, Secretary of State James A. Manchin ruled yesterday.
>
> "I am convinced it was wholly accidental," Manchin said after his office completed an investigation of the incident. The $7.5 million levy passed by a wide margin last week.

Licensing and registration constitute another area of responsibility. Depending upon the state, the secretary registers automobiles, licenses business and professional enterprises, supervises banking and securities legislation, commissions notaries public, registers trademarks and prepares extradition papers.

Custodial duties include maintaining records of state lands, filing articles of incorporation and issuing charters. The office is a constant source of news.

Because of its high visibility, the office is often a stepping stone to other important political offices. Depending on the demands placed upon him or her by the constitution or by the legislative process, the secretary of state requires performance by local government officials, such as city and county clerks, creating a need for reporters to check at the local level as well for news developments.

> Secretary of State Wilson M. Morris ruled today that the city's effort to obtain property adjacent to City Hall for parking lots had to go through the condemnation process, whatever the willingness of property owners to sell to the city.
>
> In a letter to City Clerk Mary L. Neeley, Morris stated that City Council's agreement to buy the land must be taken to Circuit Court.

The secretary of state also maintains the state archives and collects extensive vital statistics data from other agencies, making that office a prime collection point for the reporter.

The watchdog function of the office occasionally intrudes on the prerogatives of other state agencies.

> With his usual flair, Secretary of State Sam (Slim) Black announced today that his office will investigate a country music promoter accused of deceiving singing star Marty Robbins, which resulted in cancellation of a concert in Arlington last week.
>
> The investigation stems from Robbins' complaint that he was lied to about weather conditions in the state, causing him to make a decision to abandon the trip to Arlington.

The secretary of state also serves as an ex officio member of various state boards and commissions.

The *attorney general*, popularly elected in most states, is another important constitutional figure. As the state's chief law officer, the attorney general issues official advice to the governor and other agencies, interprets statutes or regulations, prepares or reviews legal documents and represents the public before state agencies. In some states, the official exercises supervisory authority over local prosecuting attorneys.

Providing opinions on issues gives the attorney general's office considerable prestige as well as power. While the opinions can be overturned by judicial action, the rulings often take on the force of law. As a constitutional officer, the attorney general operates apart from the governor and frequently issues decisions that foreclose a particular course of action on the part of the chief executive.

In recent years, legislation has allowed the attorney general wide latitude in the field of consumer protection. In many states, the attorney general can commence civil or criminal proceedings in consumer protection cases, administer consumer protection programs and handle consumer complaints. Many of these officials now possess the power to prosecute complaints against merchants in the courts.

> Attorney General Chauncy D. Browning yesterday filed suit against the Ford Motor Co. and a local auto dealer, charging that they had defrauded customers by selling vehicles without proper warranties.

An aura of financial wizardry and a measure of public trust are ingredients that characterize the office of *state treasurer*. The office, filled by popular election in 38 states, is the custodian of state funds, disbursing them as authorized by law.

Wise investment of idle funds, which may sit in banks for months or more, constitutes a significant source of state revenue. The treasurer is often guided by state depository legislation requiring a board to designate banks for depositing such funds.

With millions of dollars at stake in deposits, politics often plays a role in determining where the funds will be deposited. The alert reporter who carefully checks depository agencies may find favored banking institutions with the lion's share of state deposits, sometimes under questionable circumstances. An investigation of political contributors sometimes will yield similar dividends.

Only about half the states continue to elect a *state auditor*, whose duties are to periodically audit the accounts of the treasurer and other state officials. The auditor also acts as a check on the treasurer, authorizing disbursements from the treasury through a pre-audit.

State Agencies and Departments: A Logistical Nightmare

Without a working knowledge of the specific functions of the various government agencies and the staff which directs them, the reporter will always be playing catch-up in the competition for news.

Who regulates activities and administers the broad range of services? In any state, a long list of agencies, which are often cumbersome and headed by officials generally appointed by the governor, must first be identified. Other activities are directed by multimember boards or commissions. Their operations become more complex with the addition of local or regional offices, often with substantial autonomy.

Thus, the pure bulk of the bureaucracy, despite efforts to reorganize and modernize in recent years, creates a logistical nightmare for the reporter trying to competently cover state government.

The first step is to identify the functions and the personnel. What are the basic services provided by a department? How is it organized? Who are the key personnel? What is the best way to efficiently cover its activities? Who are the people who can most effectively provide information?

Similar questions apply to regulatory agencies. Who are the regulators? What are the rules under which they operate? At what levels does the reporter most efficiently obtain information? In answering specific questions such as these, the reporter will more quickly solve the problems of time, red tape and resistance to pursuit of information.

Although degree and direction vary considerably, these are the major services provided at the state level: education, health and welfare programs, public protection, transportation, protection of natural resources, housing and development, labor relations and a revenue and taxation unit to collect funds to provide for those services.

Added to these are agencies to facilitate administration of the growing federal grants-in-aid and revenue-sharing programs to local governments.

EDUCATION

The perceptive education reporter often detects an undercurrent of anxiety in local school board offices, not necessarily connected with the day-to-day administration of purely local school affairs. The reason is not complex: while delegating responsibility for education to local governmental units, a "higher" authority, the state legislature, enacts the basic laws governing the public school system.

The legislature determines how local units will be organized, who will govern them and how they will be selected, and what avenues of revenue will be available to officials. These statutes are enforced by a state board of education, which may account for the undercurrent of anxiety. If local school officials sometimes feel that a higher authority is looking over their collective shoulders, they are not far wrong.

Whatever authority local school boards possess, the statehouse reporter must recognize that a state-level school board or commission has assumed important responsibilities. At this level, teacher certification may be fixed, subjects to be taught in the classroom prescribed, textbooks to be used, compulsory attendance laws promulgated and salary standards established. No matter what the state, some educational policies are determined at the state level.

A familiarity with the authority held by the state governing board and "strings" it attaches to local school systems are essential if the reporter is to coordinate coverage at both levels of government.

> State Board of Education Chairman Robert C. Myer charged yesterday that the Warren County Board of Education failed to comply with state standards in spending school construction funds.
>
> Myer appointed a three-member committee to review procedures used by the Department of Education to assure that school boards are spending funds in compliance with the law.
>
> In a report issued to other board members, Myer stated that the Warren board had failed to show in its budget proposed sources of income to complete construction projects at seven schools in the system.

On the surface the dispute appears to center around reporting policies of local school units, but the persistent reporter may find that other factors are involved, sometimes including the personalities of officials themselves.

> Controversies in Warren and Lincoln counties appear to have been factors in the sudden resignation yesterday of State School Superintendent James C. Wilson from his $45,000-a-year position.
>
> Wilson, who has been superintendent for nine years, announced his resignation effective June 1.
>
> Handling of a Warren school construction controversy and a Lincoln tax dispute which poses a threat to the state's educational funding formula led to Wilson's differences with some Board of Education members, including Chairman Robert C. Myer.

Strings of a different nature bind institutions of higher education to special state boards which govern them. Increasingly, such boards are insulated from legislative and executive branch demands, decreasing the likelihood of political interference upon the boards.

While operating control resides at the level of the institution, a board of regents or education commissioners develop general guidelines and enforce statutory demands. These demands often include a role in the budgeting process for the institutions.

Duties and selection of these boards vary, with some established by constitution, others by legislation. But whatever the composition of the boards, the pragmatic reporter recognizes once again that politics often plays a part in the decision-making process, even at the college or university level.

> "Politics," observed Board of Regents Chairman Rogers Thornby yesterday, "is the art of people working together or not working together."
>
> With that observation, Thornby dodged a direct question on whether the board's Higher Education Resources Fund has become a political football.
>
> At its monthly meeting in the capital today, the board will discuss the fate of the $34 million fund, collected as

> student fees and used for athletic equipment, team travel and other current expenses.
>
> State Tax Commissioner Warren C. Still has criticized the regents' handling of the fund.

While the regents' chairman dodged the question, others directly involved might be willing to discuss the issue: the state tax commissioner, other regents, legislative officials interested in the outcome of the argument, university officials charged with disbursing the funds and even the students from whom the funds are collected.

HEALTH AND WELFARE

The elderly pensioner clutched his robe more tightly about his thin shoulders and responded slowly to the reporter's question:

Yes, he said, the new facility for the elderly and disabled seems "just fine." The nurses are efficient, the food is adequate, proper medication is always available, television and radio sets are nearby. But, the pensioner sighed, something is lacking. Despite all its controlled activity, the place seems lonely, he said.

The reporter was questioning an aid recipient in depth, which is a familiar device to illustrate how a state welfare agency is performing its function. In covering human services, the effective reporter works both at the administrative level and at the client level. An interview with the state welfare commissioner is only half the story. The response at the other end is equally important—if somewhat more demanding.

Health and welfare programs affect nearly everyone, so they must be considered an integral part of state coverage. Cost of human services may not match that of public education, but substantial funds are required to provide health care, aid to indigent persons not fully covered by federal programs, and special services for the handicapped and aging. As with other service agencies, department types vary from state to state, but they can be quickly categorized.

Total funds budgeted are not always a factor in intrinsic news value. A modest department designed to ease the burdens on the elderly may possess only vague powers, but still yield important story material.

> Half the pharmacies in the state are ignoring a new law requiring substitution of cheaper generic drugs for brand-name prescriptions, the director of the State Commission on Aging said today.
>
> Louis C. Gerrard said the commission had completed a spot check this week indicating implementation problems with the law, which went into effect July 1.

Public health has increasingly become the responsibility of all levels of government, contributing to the difficulty of news coverage. Health care was traditionally the responsibility of the states, with diagnostics rather than specific care the original goal. The federal government, with a cabinet-level Department of

Health and Human Services, has deeply involved itself in many programs, among them extensive grants-in-aid to states for investigating maternity and child health, industrial health, communicable diseases, heart disease and cancer.

Early emphasis at the state level centered on medical care for the indigent and control of epidemics. Today's services are a far cry from those limited programs and now include mental as well as physical well-being. A study by the Public Health Service lists 36 different health services performed by the various states, including disease control, sanitation, collection of vital statistics, operation of state hospitals, health insurance and many specific hygiene programs.

The list includes some type of authority over local health units, including private hospitals and other facilities. Local health departments turn to state units in policy matters, while maintaining the freedom to handle their own administrative affairs.

> The State Board of Health announced yesterday the Wheeling Hospital will be permitted to proceed with construction of a four-floor addition without delay.
>
> The board had withheld certification while considering whether a new maternity ward was warranted in the community of 80,000.

Welfare services have also expanded beyond their original scope. Services for certain disadvantaged groups now embrace dependent as well as underprivileged children, handicapped persons and delinquents through a broad range of public services, including institutional care, public assistance and other welfare programs.

A state welfare department also coordinates federal funding and provides guidance to local agencies. The substantial nature of the funding calls for coverage from a technical as well as a human standpoint.

> The State Welfare Department yesterday revised its standards for supplying minimum payments to the indigent, to conform to new federal guidelines.
>
> The effect of the action, Director Yvonne Salinger said, would be to increase the monthly payment by $11 to $147, effective in July. Half the annual $27 million cost will be borne by federal revenue sharing, she said.

A host of new programs, many of them controversial and more newsworthy than traditional services, has cropped up in recent years. Identification of the programs is sometimes difficult because they are federally funded and no accounting needs to be made to state legislatures.

> Family planning has become big business for the state, which dispenses more than $7 million a year in federal funds to hold down its population.
>
> The State Department of Health's project pays for a male's vasectomy, a female's tubal ligation, and dispenses free birth control pills and other contraceptives, according to department literature.

A Health Department spokesman said the line is drawn at providing free abortions, but callers to the project's toll-free hotline number are told where they can obtain abortions at little or no cost.

PUBLIC PROTECTION

The trooper carefully backed his black-and-white squad car, with radar pointed at the long curve on the interstate highway, onto the median and turned off the ignition. Passing motorists carefully checked their speedometers, then breathed sighs of relief. While he represents state law enforcement in its more visible form, the trooper is only the tip of the public protection iceberg.

The range of agencies assuming responsibility for protecting the public is far more extensive, ranging from the state highway patrol, state police forces and National Guard contingents to regulation of public utilities, licensing of medical and dental practitioners and consumer protection agencies.

The Public Utilities Commission Friday issued orders to keep the San Francisco Bay mass transit tunnel closed pending correction of problems that led to a fatal, terror-filled fire during the rush hour Wednesday.

Bay Area Rapid Transit General Manager Keith Bernard told the commission at a hearing that the fire, which claimed one life and injured 45, "could happen again." He said the precise cause of the accident was not known.

Under a mandate to protect the public, states prescribe general qualifications that must be met by applicants who wish to practice most of the professions, as well as other occupational callings. In most states these include accountants, architects, attorneys, chiropodists, engineers, nurses, pharmacists, physicians, teachers and veterinarians.

Some states include barbers, beauticians, insurance and real estate brokers and surveyors. Licensing boards or commissioners, composed wholly or partly of members of the profession, examine and approve applicants. The boards also consider revocation or suspension of licenses for specified reasons such as incompetency, malpractice or unprofessional conduct.

The State Medical Licensing Board has agreed to hear a petition by Dr. David Johnson of Forest Hills, which asks the agency to reverse its decision to revoke Johnson's medical license.

The board revoked Johnson's license Jan. 13 as a result of his conviction last year on charges of possessing marijuana with intent to deliver it. The physician served six months at the prison camp at Ravenswood.

Because public utilities generally enjoy monopolies, they are regulated by states in the public interest. The complex decisions involving these enterprises are among the most difficult to report in state government. Some technical and financial expertise is desirable in reporting on such essential and widely used services as electricity, gas, water and sewage facilities, telephone and telegraph services, and transportation services.

State utility commissions, with staffs of experts, regulate rates to ensure a fair return to private investors, issue certificates of convenience and necessity for expansion of services and approve corporate actions construed as affecting the public interest.

TRANSPORTATION

Nowhere is the multilevel structure of government more evident than in the field of transportation, particularly in construction and maintenance of highways and roads.

The reporter leaves home and backs the car out of the driveway onto a city street, purely the responsibility of the municipality in which the reporter resides. The route to work leads through an unincorporated area, with county maintenance of roads, and along a highway constructed and maintained by the state. Before parking the car in still another municipality with its own street responsibilities, the reporter has traveled a brief stretch of interstate highway, constructed mainly with federal funds but maintained by the state.

Traffic bottlenecks, ice and snow removal, and even road repair call for a large measure of cooperation and interdependence among the governmental units described.

The journalist is reporting on transportation for a nation on wheels. And despite their negative impact, unrepaired potholes and mile-long traffic snarls rank among most reported stories.

There are many others, however, and reportorial awareness of the technicalities of highway construction and traffic control ranks high in importance. Why is the state's interstate system composed mainly of concrete, while a neighboring state sports macadam surfacing? Politics or good highway construction? What percentage of the cost does the State Highway Department pay for farm-to-market county roads? How are road funds apportioned among counties? What's the formula? Is politics involved in the sudden transfer of district road supervisors in the area? What will the governor's highway reorganization mean to the public?

These are the kinds of questions that must be answered for readers. The transportation beat wends a winding course from the legislature, which appropriates funds for highways and ups gasoline taxes for that purpose from time to time, to the executive branch, which administers the roads at the state level.

The pothole repairs, in fact, may be the simplest story of all. A knowledge of classes of roads is important—generally designated as primary and secondary highways, farm-to-market roads and city streets. But, more important, the reporter should know who has the responsibility for maintenance and traffic control.

States have increasingly become involved in mass transportation projects, with many supporting bus and rail systems. Such systems cross county and even state lines, necessitating special governing units to administer such programs. Federal funds often provide the bulk of the financial assistance, with help from state and local units.

> The state will assist in underwriting the cost of a regional bus system in the Johnson City area, Transportation Commissioner Wilson Everhardt said yesterday.
> Everhardt said the state would assume 20 percent of the first year's operating costs, estimated at about $3.5 million. Johnson City and Wilmer County have each agreed to underwrite 10 percent of the cost, while the federal government's share will be 60 percent, or about $2.1 million.
> "Next year's state share will be the responsibility of the legislature," Everhardt warned. A special contingency fund for mass transportation makes the first year's funding possible, he said.

NATURAL RESOURCES

The tree-lined bluff overlooking the blue waters of the sound was crowded with people of all ages. The group carried a sign that proclaimed "SAVE OUR STATE'S WATERFRONT!" Representing various conservation organizations, they were protesting the decision of state officials to allow an industrial plant to locate nearby on the sound.

Urban or rural? Mountainous terrain or flatland? Agricultural economy or industrial heartland? Mile after mile of timber or rich mineral deposits? Open prairie or ocean vistas? The mix of natural resources a state possesses dictates the direction a state government reporter follows in covering their development. Every state has a mix of such resources, but the importance of each varies widely.

An Agriculture Department takes on less importance in the industrial East, whereas environmental regulation and pollution control assume a more vital role. Whatever the locale, natural resources are regulated through basically similar boards, agencies and commissions.

For generations, the nation's resources have been treated as an inexhaustible fountain, but in recent decades the public has come to realize that regulation is necessary if each state's natural wealth is to be preserved for future generations.

Some states provide an umbrella agency, a Department of Natural Resources, to cope with the complex problems of forest management, soil and wildlife conservation, flood control, state parks and other recreation facilities, and agriculture.

Others have allowed a number of separate administrative agencies to develop, often with overlapping jurisdiction, and sometimes with conflicting roles in protection of resources.

> Two state agencies are arguing over disposition of federal funds for conservation, and the governor says he'll mediate the dispute.
> The Agriculture Department has earmarked the $11 million windfall for soil conservation purposes, but the

Forestry Service claims that a share of the funds belongs in its forest management account.

The new importance of energy conservation has led to creation of departments addressing themselves specifically to energy in some states, often with overlapping responsibilities with Departments of Conservation and Public Utility Commissions.

A new emphasis on recreation has fostered important State Parks Departments, which operate extensive lodging and recreational facilities. Since income from use of the facilities rarely covers the cost, such agencies are dependent on the state legislature for additional funding.

The parks system is again running into financial difficulties, and Parks Commissioner Sylvester Freed warned today that the legislature must face up to the problem.

"Our income simply won't cover the difference between what the legislature provides and what it takes to assure a first-class system," Freed said.

He estimated that the deficit will approach more than a million dollars by the end of the fiscal year.

BUSINESS AND LABOR

Responsibility for regulatory action in the fields of private enterprise and labor, often with those groups in conflict, lies with state government.

A Department or Bureau of Labor, headed by a director appointed by the governor, deals with health and safety standards, liability of employers, unemployment and disability compensation, and compilation of labor statistics. The department also interprets and executes state laws relating to labor, including state mediation and arbitration services.

An increasing emphasis on business and industrial development as aids in protecting and expanding the state's economy has also led to creation of special agencies to deal with the issue.

Aiming at new employment opportunities for citizens and new sources of tax revenue, departments of Industrial Development send representatives to other regions, enticing industrial firms to establish plants within the state. Some states offer lucrative tax write-offs; others offer to underwrite bond issues to remain competitive. Reporters will find agencies such as these secretive about their affairs, since the field is so competitive. With tax shelters a part of the negotiations, however, the public interest is involved, and the statehouse reporter should remain close to the story.

State Planning Commissions sometimes assume these recruiting functions and go farther, assisting private industry and business in securing outside contracts for state-produced goods.

The governor and six officials of the Industrial Development Board flew to Hong Kong yesterday on the first leg of their trip to the Far East to drum up new business for the state.

THE INSTITUTIONS

The state's institutions, many located in inaccessible rural areas, pose a special problem for the state government reporter.

The problem: day-to-day activities of the facility are carried on far from the scene of the policy-making activities, which normally occur in the agency offices in the state capital. Meanwhile, many of the financial functions may be carried out in still another office, and the auditing process may be located in still another office.

Many newspapers tend to leave the reporting of state institutions to the statehouse reporter, who is far from the physical facilities. As a result, coverage of institutional affairs is fragmented and generally minimal, with only those possessing great public visibility enjoying substantial coverage.

Dozens of such facilities are scattered around most states—educational, correctional and vocational institutions, and facilities for the indigent and handicapped. Educational centers are often the best covered, while mental institutions and health care facilities are among those with the poorest coverage.

Editors and reporters should maintain an effective checking system to assure that such institutions do not become totally invisible to the public except during emergencies. Access to these institutions often pose the biggest problems of coverage by reporters.

> Washington—Warning that "we must not confuse the role of the media with that of government," the Supreme Court ruled yesterday that the press has no "constitutional right of access" to jails and other government facilities beyond the access permitted to the public at large.

Decisions like these create further problems of coverage by newspapers and broadcast outlets seeking to enlarge public knowledge of these institutions.

CHAPTER 4
Covering Federal Government

THE word is out, and the city room of the Midwest newspaper is rampant with speculation. There's an opening in the staff of the Washington bureau.

Who's going to get the job?

Thousands of budding young journalists cherish a secret ambition. Their dream is to cover the nation's capital, asking probing questions at televised presidential news conferences, interviewing powerful and charismatic figures in congressional cloakrooms, and poring over federal documents to break the "big story" that shocks the nation's readership.

It is only a dream for most of them. Only a small percentage of those thousands of print and broadcast newspersons will ever wend their way to Washington, D.C. to regularly report on the operations of the vast bureaucracy that is the federal government.

However, most of those ambitious reporters will find solace in another important fact: Most of them working at the local level will regularly cross countless thresholds of federal offices to dig out stories with a "federal" angle as genuine as the Washington article. More than that, they can rest assured that *their* news coverage equals the importance of their more visible counterparts in the nation's capital. For instance,

—The Commerce Department's decision to sharply restrict imports of foreign-produced automobiles will affect a Midwest city's job market, which has been weakening for many months. The decision promises to affect half a dozen other economic segments of the community. The roundup story, which touches on both the Washington and local angles, belongs to the reporter at the local level.

—A major local industry, whose efforts to solve its pollution problems along the region's major river have not proved entirely successful, is directed by an office of the Environmental Protection Agency to place a timetable on its efforts. A local reporter with the right contacts will be the likely recipient of this particular news break.

—A catchall spending proposal has moved ponderously through the Congress, with an $870 million price tag attached. Buried deep within the several hundred pages of local projects is a provision for a modern $14 million library facility, replacing the community's 1930s vintage Carnegie library. Successful passage of the bill will assure construction of the facility, and the alert reporter at the local level is likely to have the story.

—The White House has proposed a cutback in funding for a federally assisted summer work program in urban communities. A two-paragraph Washington report cannot communicate the implications for the home folks who must find alternate solutions for funding. The local reporter will again tie the story together, utilizing sources in the community as well as Washington.

However, stories like these will not fall to the reporter who merely observes the routine, but to the alert journalist who works at identifying the various federal agencies, their functions and their impact on the local community.

Covering at the "Local Level"

Before successfully solving the problem of covering the federal beat at the local level, the reporter must answer three basic questions:

What agency am I looking for? The alert reporter is always asking, What's the federal angle? Is it a transportation development? Perhaps a discussion of funding for a regional mass transit system? What will the involvement of the federal government be? A basic reassessment of the city's postal facilities? As a courtesy, will federal officials inform local government leaders? Is rehabilitation of the local jail facilities going to involve federal assistance?

Where do I go for the answers? Good questions demand good answers. Many of them will be developed in the local offices of federal agencies, particularly those that have the closest relationship with the public. How will new social security regulations affect retired people here? The Social Security Administration maintains offices in most communities, and its employees are alert to new federal initiatives involving the elderly and handicapped. Who has the answers to how the new jobs program will work? A city with unemployment and low-family-income problems is likely to be involved with the Economic Development Administration, a Commerce Department agency that assists in creating new jobs and development of public facilities. Many important federal agencies staff only regional offices, and the reporter should possess a working familiarity with those as well.

Who do I see for the answers? The clerk in a local federal office may be able to answer one question for the reporter and have to refer others to a superior. While one of the first stops on the road to a federally related story may be the local office, the reporter should be prepared to be sent elsewhere. The Agriculture Department maintains a local office, but its staff may refer policy questions to other officials. The reporter should remember that, while questions may not always elicit specific answers, there is always a "higher-up" to whom he or she can turn for more decisive responses. A good case can also be made for starting in Washington and working down to the local level. The nation's capital is as close as the reporter's telephone.

A typical problem: A local industrial firm with a substantial payroll is polluting the coastal sound, not only at the point of discharge but in other water areas as well. Officials of the firm are naturally reluctant to comment, although an effective public relations staff has previously pointed out that the sound's status as an "industrial area" is a legitimate excuse for the pollution.

The political power exercised by the industrial firm is such that local government officials refuse to be drawn into the controversy, which leaves the federal agencies involved as the "enforcers" in the dispute. The issue is joined: Many jobs depend upon the financial solvency of the industry, but new federal regulations limiting pollution into the nation's coastal waters are costly and difficult to implement. Because of the trade-offs in financial and economic advantages, the story is more sensitive than it appears.

With few willing sources at the local level, the reporter turns to federal agencies issuing the orders, in this case the Environmental Protection Agency's regional center, which says it represents "the commitment to the development of strong local programs for pollution abatement."

Federal officials are not as reluctant to provide information, some in the form of official documents, and so it is at this level that the reporter obtains the basic facts in the issue, generally sufficient to shake loose reaction comment at home.

The reporter's route to the answers, however, is not always direct. Responsibility for these new programs is in a constant state of change, because of action by Congress and the executive branch. For example, administration of the water pollution program has shifted through a number of agencies and offices before finally settling under the aegis of the EPA.

In 1965, it was called the Federal Water Pollution Control

Administration, answering to the secretary of health, education and welfare. A year later the agency was transferred to a completely different department, the Department of the Interior. In 1970, the pollution designation was dropped from the name, and the agency became the Water Quality Administration. Soon after that, the entire agency was abolished by a federal reorganization, and its functions were transferred to the EPA. It now comes under direction of the assistant administrator for water and waste management.

Not every federal enforcement program undergoes this kind of metamorphosis, but enough of them do to make coverage more complex for the inquiring reporter.

The Answers to "Where to Go"

The indispensible element in successfully collecting accurate and useful information from the vast federal bureaucracy is knowing where to begin. No freedom of information act can assist a reporter who is knocking at the wrong door. This simple quiz will prove instructive. Check the answer you believe to be correct, then read on to determine whether you have the answer:

1. The *U.S. Botanic Garden's* purpose is to collect and cultivate various vegetable productions for exhibit and study. Who supervises the Botanic Gardens?
   a. Commerce Department
   b. Agriculture Department
   c. The Congress
   d. Interior Department
   e. It is independent

2. Who oversees the *Government Printing Office*, which prints all government documents?
   a. Treasury Department
   b. The Congress
   c. Commerce Department
   d. Interior Department
   e. The executive branch

3. The *Forest Service* manages federal forest reserves throughout the United States. To whom does it answer?
   a. Bureau of Land Management
   b. Commerce Department
   c. Agriculture Department
   d. Interior Department
   e. None of these

4. To whom does the *U.S. Court of Military Appeals* answer?
   a. Supreme Court
   b. Administrative Office of the U.S. Courts
   c. Defense Department

d. Department of the Army
e. It is independent

5. The *Federal Aviation Administration* is charged with regulating air commerce to foster aviation safety. Under whose jurisdiction does it lie?
   a. Civil Aeronautics Board
   b. Commerce Department
   c. Department of Transportation
   d. Interstate Commerce Commission
   e. It is independent

Five perfect responses indicate an extensive knowledge of the federal bureaucracy; most reporters will come up with less.

1. The Botanic Gardens, founded in 1820, is under the control of the Joint Committee of Congress on the Library, which funds it directly from congressional appropriations. Garden officials will most likely respond to a reporter's question concerning a rare, unidentified plant specimen, whatever the region.

2. The Government Printing Office is controlled by the Congress and executes orders for printing and binding of all establishments of the federal government.

3. The Forest Service is under the jurisdiction of the Agriculture Department, since being transferred there from the Interior Department in 1905. One of the sources for a news story on the spread of a tree parasite through a region would include the field office for the Forest Service.

4. The U.S. Court of Military Appeals is judicially independent, although it operates administratively out of the Defense Department. Problems at a nearby military installation which lead to disciplinary action might conclude with the need for a reporter to contact the appeals court clerk in Washington.

5. The Federal Aviation Administration, formerly an independent agency, became a part of the Department of Transportation in 1967. In researching a story on the air controllers who operate the city's flight control towers, the reporter's path might lead to the regional office of the FAA.

The reporter whose beat includes any of hundreds of such diverse "federal angles" will discover that things are often not at all what they seem. Talking to the right official in the right department can save much time and effort, particularly at deadline time. Whether plotting a course to get federal reaction to a local airplane crash or checking a report that tobacco subsidies are being adjusted sharply downward, the reporter's goal is the same—getting to the source quickly and efficiently.

The reporter should acquire some sense of the kinds of questions likely to be answered at the local level, as well as those that probably will be "bucked up" to the district or regional office.

The list of federal offices in a community depends on its size, location in the region and the characteristics of the people who live there. A river port in the Midwest will house an extensive Coast Guard operation, directed by a captain of the port. Therefore, a knowledge of the agency's functions is important, both for routine coverage and during infrequent emergencies on the river or in the port.

As these functions make clear, the duties of the Coast Guard transcend a single beat: It engages in search and rescue operations on navigable waters of the United States (police reporter); maintains aids to navigation (outdoor editor); enforces rules involving security of ports within its jurisdiction (financial reporter); supervises loading and unloading of dangerous cargoes (labor reporter); operates a program of prevention, detection and control of pollution in all navigable waters (environmental reporter); operates boating safety programs (education writer). Many different reporters may be in contact with such a federal agency, which will be the source for all kinds of stories at the local level.

In non-river communities, other agencies might be more visible. A city in the Sun Belt with many elderly retirees would provide more extensive services from the Department of Health and Human Services or the Social Security Administration. A Farm Belt city's Agriculture Department offices would be more extensive than would be most other federal agency offices in that region. And a metropolitan area would be the focus of extensive offices for the Department of Housing and Urban Development.

The Nearly Universal Federal Arm

While a Coast Guard facility does not exist in every community, all cities of any size include a basic complex of federal offices, all of them serving the public and many of them a regular source of information for the press.

A nearby airport facility? It is almost certain to include offices for the National Weather Service, an arm of the Commerce Department. Air control personnel on the scene are employed by the Federal Aviation Administration.

The universal mail carrier? The independent U.S. Postal Service handles 100 billion pieces of mail annually, a portion of that eagerly awaited by thousands in the reporter's hometown each day. The postmaster and subordinates are a source of local news—new postal regulations, changes in routes and in type of service, issuance of new stamps and even registration of aliens in the U.S.

Taxes? That universal function, operated by officials of the Internal Revenue Service, the tax-collecting arm of the Treasury Department, is nearly everywhere. The decentralized nature of the agency allows reporters better access to much information of public interest. Collection of income taxes, only a part of the IRS responsibilities, and general information on audits create informative and interesting news stories. Regular reports are also available involving statistical information—filing on returns, refunds and total number of returns.

As with other agencies, an IRS announcement in Washington often generates local stories. Easing restrictions on granting tax exemptions to private schools, for example, will bring response from many segments of the public at the local level, including education officials and local tax administrators.

Law enforcement responsibilities offer still another area of news coverage. Federal wagering stamps are sold by the IRS, and professional gamblers can be identified through agency records.

Nearly every action taken in Washington invites reaction of some kind at the local level, but successful execution requires alertness to the daily flow of national news and the ability to translate it quickly into questions that will generate a worthwhile local news story.

The opportunities are endless:

—Congress takes action on a program to improve counseling services for veterans of the war in Vietnam. At the local level, the reporter will discuss the changes with counselors for the Veterans Administration, who explain how counseling is handled locally and how the changes might affect older veterans.

—The Department of Energy proposes to create wage-price information centers in cities around the United States. Who will staff them? What information will they provide specifically? How soon could they be placed in operation? Has anything similar ever been done before? What are examples of kinds of questions to be answered?

Federal officials at the local level may be charged with carrying out directives from Washington, but many local offices do not publicize their activities. Regular checks of offices are often necessary to collect information which becomes a significant news story. Decisions of the Labor Department's Wage and Hour Division, for example, may affect dozens of local businesses and industries, but the reporter may have to make personal contact to obtain the information.

> Six area industries have been ordered to revise their application to minimum wage regulations, and 11 others are under investigation for similar problems, the local office of the Labor Department's Wage and Hour Division reported yesterday.

Not every local federal office has identical news value. Some agencies empower their offices to release substantial quantities of useful information on the public, others authorize little. But even contact with the latter agencies is not entirely fruitless, since the net effect is closer identification of sources up the line in the federal hierarchy.

The Congressional Representative as Source

The congressman answered the phone himself. After the usual pleasantries, he got down to business. Yes, he told the reporter calling from one of the cities in his district, he had heard that federal funding for the new health services facility was in danger. Clearing his throat, the representative expounded, "The battle has just begun to save that facility. I don't care what the other problems are. The people of this district are my first priority."

A quotable quote, and certainly part of the story the reporter was pursuing. But it was not the entire story, and that is the key to the reporter's relationship with his or her congressional delegation.

As a practical matter, the pivotal offices for many such stories are occupied by the congressional member representing the district in the nation's capital and the senators representing the state. It is through these offices that many announcements affecting the interests of the community or region are deliberately funneled. Officials of federal agencies learn quickly to allow representatives and senators the privilege of formally announcing programs and decisions that tend to enhance a political image.

—New medical facilities, including a psychiatric wing, have been approved for the Veterans Administration hospital in the district, and the representative duly announces the details, albeit somewhat sketchily.

—The Office of Personnel Management, formerly the Civil Service Commission, is planning a new job information service, with a full-time office staff in the city, and the representative's office leads with the announcement.

—A federal committee is planning a fact-finding agricultural tour to assess the district's potential, and the representative hurries to make the announcement.

Meanwhile, the same federal officials learn to make the "problem" announcement themselves when it is necessary, such as plans to close a small postal facility, trim back the personnel of a nearby army installation for reasons of efficiency, or cut funds for agricultural research in the area.

Elected officials are jealous of their prerogatives and often put pressure on agencies to give endangered projects another look. Part of the strategy may include a very visible news story in the media.

> WASHINGTON—Senate Majority Leader Robert C. Byrd, D-W.V., yesterday said James McIntyre, director of the Office of Management and Budget, has assured him that the $800 million coal liquefaction plant proposed at Morgantown will be "objectively and fairly reviewed" alongside a similar Kentucky project.
>
> "Each project will be reviewed on its individual mer-

> its, economic competitiveness and future impact on our energy markets," Byrd said.

While the congressional press conference announcing such matters is inescapable, the impact of press release journalism at the federal level can be minimized if the reporter maintains sufficient contact with other federal officials involved. Often agencies themselves provide much more pertinent detail than the representative's office hands out in a press release. The political figure often seeks only high visibility; the reporter seeks details of an important decision affecting his or her community.

This is not to suggest that a close relationship between the office of representatives and senators and the reporter on the federal beat is not desirable. The representative's office is usually the first to know about developments affecting the reporter's community, and close ties with that office are very useful. The reporter should be able to put the informational expertise of the representative and his or her staff to good use. Usually the office is eager to help.

The reporter's strategy should be to successfully trigger important news stories by anticipating them through good contact and then by digging beyond the representative's planned but brief conference.

Letting the "Strings" Work for You

The long arm of the federal government reaches into each community in many different ways. The reporter, realizing that "strings" are attached by Washington to his or her hometown, seeks ways to ensure that no opportunity is missed for a significant story.

The legislative branch initiates hundreds of measures during each session that affect various segments of the community. A typical session of Congress will create these kinds of potential stories:

—Authorization for a pilot project for a new mineral extraction process near a community can create an instant business boom.

—More funds can be provided for the needy through a new program aimed at community block development.

—A new foreign trade program, which includes duty-free ports of entry, can affect the economy of an entire region.

Such information is often visible because of the national news media's interest in it, requiring only an enterprising reporter who follows the news closely to come up with local angles. However, many other developments of purely local interest may be buried in catchall legislation, stagnating for months in agency offices until an official acts to implement a particular project.

A $5 million grant allowing a city to extend sewer service to an adjacent area will create new jobs, additional housing and the potential for new industrial development, yet the enabling legislation may have been approved by Congress several years before. Responsibility for applying for the funds lies in the hands of local officials; informing the public that the funds are available is up to the reporter.

By monitoring the "strings" that tie local government to the federal establishment, the reporter can often obtain both ends of a story rather than merely one end.

> The federal government has $3.1 million to loan, and Mayor William L. Anderson said he wants the city to apply. "The money is there for the asking," Anderson said.
>
> However, R. J. Gibson, regional service officer for the Department of Housing and Urban Development, said the city will be competing with agencies from nine other counties for the funds, which must be used to construct 200 units of multifamily housing.

Federal grants are also available to many non-profit organizations in a community, some of them organized specifically to implement federally funded projects. Identification of these organizations is essential to effectively cover the federal-local spectrum.

> The Southern Community Action Council has been awarded a grant for $317,000 for a major new program to help preschool children acquire basic skills.
>
> Funds will be provided to the private agency by the Department of Health and Human Services, Council Director Jane Bevin said yesterday.
>
> The project, which will be conducted with help from the Board of Education, "will provide continuity in programming basic skills as children move from development centers to the elementary school classrooms," Bevin said.

Whether the reporter who handled the original story follows up the program or leaves that job to the education reporter, a later assessment of the value of the project is also important. Follow-up stories are all too often ignored in favor of exciting new projects.

While federal grants center around education, health, housing and employment, other fields receive funding too, affecting communities and the people living in them. Arts centers receive funds for cultural purposes, and historic preservation has become an important federal item.

> The city's Heritage Village will receive the lion's share of a federal grant available to the state for historic preservation projects.
>
> Marla Cerveris, Village director, said the restored railroad station on Eaton Street will get $49,000 of the $73,000 available from the Department of the Interior.

The funds, to be matched with $49,000 from private sources, will be used to install outdoor lighting, construction of ramps for wheelchair visitors and landscaping, Cerveris said.

The Federal Regulators

They decide that factory stairways must be at least 22 inches wide, and they protect bank depositors from losing billions of dollars in savings.

They won't allow cut-rate, $135-a-person airline service between New York and London, and they make commercial broadcasting feasible.

They bungle, and drive a toymaker to the edge of bankruptcy. They succeed, and save motorists' lives.

They have a voice in what Americans eat, breathe, wear and drive.

"They" are the unelected federal regulators, a growing band that now makes more rules directly affecting the people than do the elected members of Congress.

That's how the Associated Press characterized the reach and power of the federal regulatory process which continues to expand each year.

More than two dozen major agencies currently set the rules for millions of Americans, at a cost of more than $4 billion a year. Critics, numerous and vociferous, point to the cost and to examples of delays, bungles, overzealous regulation and conflicting rules. Proponents counter that regulation has been a factor in improving the quality of life in many areas. Even the auto manufacturers concede that federal auto safety regulations have resulted in saving thousands of motorists' lives. And America's air is measurably cleaner since regulators began regulating.

As the arguments swirl about the combatants, amid efforts to mount reform of regulatory agencies, the need continues to report on them. Whatever the outcome of the reform effort, the reporter's role remains: to report on new rules and their effects and to assess old ones.

The regulators have become a sea of alphabet soup, with the reporter and his or her readers awash in it. Still, abbreviations such as FDA, FTC, EPA, CAB, FCC, ICC and SEC have legitimately become household fixtures, along with those not so well known: National Transportation Safety Board, Nuclear Regulatory Commission, Equal Employment Opportunity Commission, Occupation Safety and Health Review Commission, and the Consumer Product Safety Commission. Most actions of these agencies create a ripple effect, with the demand placed upon the reporter to explain action and effect to the reader.

The wire services report that the Food and Drug Administration is "working very hard" to eliminate methapyrilene, a cancer-causing antihistamine, from over-the-counter sleep aids and other drugs. What are the implications of this unpronounceable substance for the reader? And what is the reaction of the pharmaceutical community? No development such as this would be completely covered without checking pharmacies. The time element in federal recalls is also very important.

Inspection procedures followed by the federal government to assure successful completion of local projects also lead to investigation of questionable practices, followed by court action. The reporter should always be alert to such possibilities. A knowledge of the standard under which projects are evaluated is often helpful in explaining action to the reader.

> A federal investigator researching the scaffold collapse which left 11 men dead at Oak Hill April 12 says the concrete supplier should have known there were problems the day before the disaster.
>
> In a report submitted to the Occupational Safety and Health Administration, investigator Tillman C. Moody said tests indicated numerous air pockets in the concrete used on the Midwest Power Co.'s Mississippi River project.

Federal agencies often take their cases to court to protect what they perceive to be the public's interest and sometimes to protect themselves in the process.

> A federal judge yesterday issued a restraining order, halting FMC Corp. production of carbon tetrachloride and emission of the chemical into the Soloway River.
>
> Judge Charles V. Kelley acted after the Environmental Protection Agency filed suit earlier in the week to prevent what it termed "the repeated history" of FMC spills into the river.
>
> An EPA spokesman said the action was taken under the emergency provisions of the Safe Drinking Water Act and the Federal Water Pollution Control Act.

Local law enforcement agencies are often involved in investigating practices carried on through federally funded programs. The Federal Bureau of Investigation, which is nominally responsible for enforcement in such areas, may be only casually involved.

> Armed with 23 payroll fraud arrest warrants, city police took into custody 19 workers and administrators of the federally funded Reading Application and Practice Center yesterday.
>
> Conviction on charges of public payroll fraud carries a maximum sentence of 10 years in prison.

In this case, the reading program was under the direction of the State Department of Education, but most of its local employees were being compensated through the federal Comprehensive Education and Training Act, known as CETA. Sometimes an alert reporter, assessing the quality of such programs in search of a story, will ask the right questions and stumble across the information before the auditors get to it.

Private institutions are often involved in agency actions. Efforts by a local hospital to acquire federal funds for expansion may require special reviews to determine whether there is a real need for the expansion. The reviews, in fact, may be triggered by competing area hospitals or by a state health agency which questions the necessity to expand.

Airline routes are important to a community's transportation needs, and despite deregulation of the airline industry, the federal government continues to be a part of the decision-making process. The Air Transport Deregulation Act of 1978 introduced more competition among airlines and eliminated some of the regulatory procedures. While the legislation simplified proceedings with the Civil Aeronautics Board, it eliminated CAB authority over domestic airline routes.

Federal subsidies affect routing, however, and the reporter should be alert to CAB action in cases involving airlines serving the community.

> U.S. Air's inability to regain its federal subsidy is seriously limiting its ability to serve small cities, including Lincoln, Edwin T. Baker, president of U.S. Air, told a congressional hearing yesterday.
>
> Despite skyrocketing fuel costs and other problems, Baker said, the airline has been unable to persuade the Civil Aeronautics Board to restore the subsidy dropped last year.

Whether the agency is regulating overtime pay (Labor Department), poisoning of coyotes in the Rockies (EPA), or use of antibiotics to treat cattle (FDA), the alert reporter far from the Washington scene is the handler of the best part of the story—how those rules affect people in his or her world.

The Federal Structure

To even categorize, much less fully cover, the vast bureaucracy that is the federal establishment is a Herculean task. To make sense out of the interminable maze of offices, duties, relationships and often conflicting functions, the reporter must begin with basic guidelines that will expedite the process of selecting what departments to cover and the kind of information that will be sought.

At least in part, some pattern is necessary to exercise vigilance against a natural tendency to allow the bureaucracy to set the agenda for the reporter, instead of the reverse. It must be remembered that the reporter is seeking *useful* information; officials are not always interested in that criterion, preferring instead to promote successful projects and ignore those with more questionable status. This is why guidelines are so important.

In assessing the role of communicator of federal affairs, and setting his or her own agenda for coverage, the reporter must ask these basic questions:

1. What agencies, programs and developments among the thousands affect the greatest number of people, and why?

2. Which ones are considered important in terms of public policy?

3. Does the information have current interest to the reader, and in what way?

4. Are major changes being effected, new programs being developed or new facilities being added?

Armed with the answers to such basic questions, the reporter is in a far better position to set an agenda for coverage more closely attuned to the needs of readers.

The important place to begin is with the function and makeup of the departments and agencies. Every reporter, whether stationed in Washington or elsewhere, should be on familiar terms with them. While there are frequent changes in the makeup of federal agencies, some mandated by Congress and others within the executive branch, the majority of offices remains stable and without significant realignment from year to year. With only a few exceptions, the basic departments of the executive branch have remained unchanged.

A Department of Energy has been added to the traditional Agriculture, Commerce, Defense, Housing and Urban Development, Interior, Justice, Labor, State, Transportation and Treasury departments at the cabinet level. And the giant Department of Health, Education and Welfare has been separated into two departments—Health and Human Services, and Education.

Every reporter should have close at hand the most recent edition of the *U.S. Government Manual*, which offers specific information and easy access to location and personnel of all government departments and agencies. The 900-page manual, available in paperback from the Superintendent of Documents, provides superior references by subject, agency and personnel identification. The reporter can quickly determine the functions of an agency, regional office location, source of information and even telephone numbers to obtain specific public information. Included are detailed listings of the legislative and judicial branches, as well as the executive.

These are some of the departments with which the local reporter should be familiar in covering the federal beat.

Department of Defense

Few federal departments are so all-encompassing at the local level as the Department of Defense. Growth of military installations, along with their occasional demise, with their attendant importance on the economic well-being of the communities in which they are located, create a regular and potent news source.

While the reporter should be alert to major developments in the secretary of defense's office in the Pentagon, subsidiary departments of this giant umbrella agency are more often the sources of information—the Air Force, Army, Navy and Marine Corps. Whatever the installation, the reporter should be familiar with the chain of command, the exact nature of the units at the base, and the public information officers and their availability.

Movement of personnel, shifts in housing practices, changes in purchasing procedures and many other military activities affect a community and even an entire region. Too often this information gets lost in the shuffle of other assignments. The reporter who is sensitive to such changes and to the impact of the military units will find this beat a gold mine of information.

> Shifting a 400-person maintenance unit from Hunter Air Force Base to the Midwest will cost the community 200 civilian jobs with an annual payroll of more than $3 million a year.
>
> Chamber of Commerce Director Ben C. Stack used those figures in estimating the economic loss to the area.
>
> Defense Department officials in Washington confirmed the maximum loss in civilian jobs, but a public information officer said there is a possibility that as many as half of those could be absorbed into other units on the base.

Political officeholders are often finely tuned to developments affecting their constituents, and major developments affecting military installations in their districts frequently receive their initial airing through their offices.

Sometimes other agencies will be involved in military affairs and trigger news developments. The General Accounting Office, the investigative arm of Congress, may question the need to continue commissary activities at an Air Force base that is closing. Military officials, backed by pressure from retired service personnel in the area, may seek to continue the commissary, which operates at a loss but which is subsidized by federal taxes.

Another major source of news flowing out of Defense is the Corps of Engineers, a traditional part of the military structure. Functioning under the Department of the Army, the corps maintains offices in many cities along rivers, the ocean coasts and lakes.

As its military function, the corps plans and carries out construction and maintenance of military facilities, such as harbor and waterway work. But the civilian activities of the corps have become an important part of community growth and activity. Acting to prevent and control flooding along the nation's waterways, the corps constructs dams, bridges, locks, reservoirs and levees, assuring vehicular passage by both commercial and pleasure craft.

An indication of the magnitude of the agency's functions, and its importance to the federal beat reporter, can be seen in the official delineation of its duties:

> These (engineering) works provide flood protection for cities and major river valleys, reduce the cost of transportation, supply water for municipal

and industrial use, generate hydroelectric power, provide recreational activities, regulate the rivers for many purposes, including the improvement of water quality and the enhancement of fish and wildlife, and protect the shores of the oceans and lakes.

Activities of the corps affect water transportation, the economic character of the communities along the waterways, and even the lives of individuals residing along them. The complex of locks and dams that enable giant barges to move smoothly along the nation's rivers directly influence the growth and decline of nearby communities.

> New high-lift dams along the Ohio River are creating major soil erosion problems for hundreds of farmers and homeowners whose land abuts the river bank, a private agency charges.
>
> In a 26-page memorandum to the Corps of Engineers, the Taxpayers Council details specific instances of acreage being lost to the river because of channel changes along a 120-mile stretch of the waterway.

Consider the sources which must be contacted by a reporter pursuing this story: personal visits to the affected farmers and homeowners, the corps itself, county agricultural agents who may be involved, local tax officials whose books are being affected by the loss of property, and legislators whose constituency includes both the landowners and the barge operators who are benefiting from the high-level dams. Geological experts will also be useful.

Dams are established primarily for flood control, but they have an additional effect of providing recreation for those living nearby and enhancing the potential for tourism in an area. Relationships between the Corps of Engineers and local government units become important when financial agreements are concluded for each to share in completion of a complex that will encompass elements of protection and recreation.

> The State Parks Commission and the U.S. Corps of Engineers have reached agreement on financing the new Mill Run Dam recreation project, which will cost about $8 million when it is completed next year.
>
> Access roads and boat ramps to the 17-square mile lake will be provided by the federal government. A 300-site camping area and public facilities to accommodate the thousands of visitors will be financed by the state.

District offices of the corps are excellent sources of information for continuing flood prevention activities. Area surveys are often available, and the office serves as a coordinating center in time of natural disaster.

> As many as 3,000 persons would be affected by straightening a two-mile stretch of the Menlo River as it leaves the flood-prone Menlo Valley, a preliminary study by the Corps of Engineers indicates.

A military area often overlooked are the reserve units scattered around the country. Their size and visibility usually dictate considerable general interest, and often stories emerge from their activities, including activation and deactivation of units, training programs and maneuvers, and personnel changes.

The reporter should not overlook the many recruiting offices operated by the military in cities across the country, which provide periodic statistics on enlistment and sometimes offer social implications of military changes. If allowances are made for the public relations aspects of these offices, they can be a fruitful source of information.

Commerce Department

Cold or warm? Wet or dry? Windy or calm? The public may laud the weather reporter or curse him or her for reporting nature's whims, but the federal forecaster is one of the most important sources of information for the media. A routine but necessary part of the daily news budget, weather stories remind us that this most visible agency of the Commerce Department—the National Weather Service—is on the job 24 hours a day.

The Commerce Department's mission, however, is more far reaching. It promotes the nation's economic development and technological advancement through its nearly 40,000 employees and $4.4 billion budget. The department approaches its role in a variety of ways—through business development and links with other nations; the Maritime Administration, which oversees the merchant fleet; an Office of Minority Business Enterprise, which aids ethnic minorities throughout the nation; U.S. Travel Service, which stimulates travel to other countries; the National Bureau of Standards, which sets weights and measurements; and an Office of Telecommunications, which develops new systems and services for communication.

The department is continually expanding. Recent additions to its responsibilities include a Fire Prevention and Control Administration, whose function is to reduce loss of life and property through improved fire prevention procedures.

At the local level, the Economic Development Administration aids areas with severe unemployment and low-family-income problems. The EDA is active in cooperating with local governments to provide employment opportunities by financing needed public projects.

> A $3.7 million grant from the Economic Development Administration will enable the city to proceed with plans for an expanded sewage treatment plant in the south end.
>
> The city's share of the project will bring the total cost to around $5.5 million, Mayor Ralph Waite said yesterday.

The "whys" of such actions are also important to the reporter, and contact with officials of the federal agency will often disclose the reasoning behind award of substantial grants of funds to cities.

> An unemployment rate of nearly 9 percent, caused by plant closings, was a significant factor in the Economic Development Administration's decision to grant funds to expand the city's sewage treatment facilities.
>
> The effect, according to R. C. Hobbs, regional director, will be to add construction jobs over a year-long period. He cited other factors which led to the EDA decision:
>
> —Surveys by the EDA indicated continuing economic problems in the region.
>
> —Average income per household in the city had dropped substantially during the past 24 months.
>
> "The need for infusion of new jobs, even on a temporary basis, was implicit in these statistics," Hobbs said.

Another visible reminder of the Commerce Department is its practice of taking the census every 10 years to collect a vast amount of social, economic and other data. The Bureau of Census continues to operate, but as a component of the Social and Economic Statistics Administration. The agency serves as a center for collection, compilation and analysis of a broad range of information, most of it readily available to the news media.

The reporter interested in analyzing long-range trends in his or her community will find a wealth of data available on housing, income levels, age factors in the population, job opportunities and many other specific answers to population demographics. The statistics are as readily available to the public as they are to business, industry, government officials and the press, but it is often the reporter who puts the material in perspective for readers and viewers.

> Statistics being analyzed from the new census will show a dramatic change in the community's way of life, a census official predicted yesterday.
>
> "Preliminary compilation indicates that three of every 10 dwelling units in the city contain no married persons," Rodney White, field supervisor for the regional office, said.
>
> He suggested that research into issuance of marriage licenses, coupled with new demographic figures on residences, will yield important implications in the city's changing lifestyles.

Department of Health and Human Services

Even without its former education component, the Department of Health and Human Services surpasses most of the other cabinet departments in size and scope. The importance of its services dictates a need for regular, comprehensive and often sensitive coverage of its activities. While federal legislation assuring privacy for individuals inhibits some reporting, the arms of HHS reaches out with monetary assistance and a multitude of programs providing for old-age and survivors' insurance, child welfare and aid to disabled and dependent persons.

No federal agency touches the lives of so many so often, yet much of its activities goes unreported:

—A new senior citizens center is dedicated, after being constructed with joint funding from local and federal sources. Staffing and other services are also provided through federal grants. Who is using the facility, and how is it affecting the lives of those who do?

—An added provision in federal law brings new recipients under supplemental funding providing assistance to families with emotional problems. How will it be administered, what kinds of problems will it be expected to solve, and what will be local and federal government's roles?

—A new federal grant changes and expands the foster home program in the city. What are its implications, and how will it affect present local efforts to find homes for abandoned children?

While many local organizations, some of them private, exist to carry out HHS programs, the agency often provides another dimension to what might appear to be purely a local project. The Public Health Service, another agency of HHS, operates public hospitals, collects vital statistics, helps local health planning and offers grants for a wide variety of health protection.

Because of the emphasis on research, several elements of the service are often useful to the press. The National Institutes of Health, which include research agencies in cancer, heart and lung disease, allergies and infectious diseases, child health and environmental health, are an important source of information to reporters, even those who are not near the institutes. They are scattered about the country, but their expertise is available to the media.

HHS also provides a wide range of financial and technical assistance to local and state governments in the field of education. The key to covering the Office of Education lies in an awareness of the "strings" it attaches to its numerous grants at the local levels. Study of the school board's annual budget will uncover the important areas of federal assistance.

HHS provides other facilities in communities, including resources of the Office of Equal Employment Opportunity, an intergovernmental and congressional affairs office, an administrative services center, budget and accounting offices, and facilities for hearings and appeals of federal decisions.

Department of Transportation

Whether you board a flight to Los Angeles, wheel your auto out onto Interstate 10, barely miss a subway train in New York City, step aboard a Canada-bound ferry on Lake Erie, or board an intercity passenger train for Chicago, the Department of Transportation is looking over your shoulder.

To the reporter, it is further evidence of the federal government's basic involvement at the local level. The Transportation Department, established in 1966, coordinates the nation's transportation programs. Depending on the subsidiary agency, the department is either intimately or only peripherally involved at the local level.

—A community's bus service is near collapse, mainly because of the defection of riders to the ubiquitous automobile. The role of the Urban Mass Transportation Administration is to assist in development of an efficient and successful system. It supplies techniques, equipment and financial assistance, with federal experts becoming deeply involved. Increasing costs of energy are sending local officials to the federal level for help in meeting the transportation crisis in urban areas.

—The final phase of the interstate highway network nears completion at one end of the city, with only a few miles remaining to be opened to traffic. Financing has been arranged through a 90 percent grant from the Federal Highway Administration, and the other 10 percent through the state. In the middle are local officials who want desperately to complete the link. The story of the holdup lies in the priorities established by the state—and this particular interstate linkup is obviously not one of them.

Evidence of the Federal Highway Administration's presence is everywhere: its funding is used to eliminate road hazards and initiate safety improvments; the natural beauty of the countryside may be preserved with its funds. The program of matching funding is complicated, and federal officials are often helpful in explaining its intricacies.

Regulation of air transportation is in the hands of another subsidiary agency, the Federal Aviation Administration, although an independent federal agency, the Civil Aeronautics Board, has the responsibility for authorizing service in and out of cities. With much of the activity of airlines documented with the CAB and on public record, it is comparatively easy for the reporter to follow a paper trail to important information. Whatever the origin of the assignment, the financial desk or the federal beat, air transportation is a vital component of a community's well-being and should be so covered.

The day of the steam locomotive puffing 'round the bend with scores of passengers may be gone forever, replaced by a few sleek diesel engines pulling a handful of aluminum cars to and from a selected few cities. The Federal Railroad Administration consolidates federal support of rail transportation, enforces safety regulations and provides financial assistance to some railroads in need of help.

But the national passenger system today is administered by a quasi-official agency, the National Railroad Passenger Corporation (Amtrak), which operates independently of the Transportation Department. Amtrak was conceived on a for-profit basis, with operating losses currently made up with federal financing. The agency provides 90 percent of intercity rail passenger service, operating its own trains between points designated by the secretary of transportation.

With Amtrak's ever-shrinking rail service in doubt, despite rising fuel and other energy costs, reporters in cities along its routes will find frequent newsworthy developments in the system's future.

Department of Interior

Formerly general housekeeper for the federal government, the Department of Interior has become custodian of the nation's natural resources. The department administers half a billion acres of federal land and 50 million more acres of native Indian reservations, oversees conservation and development of mineral and water resources, and is responsible for conservation of fish and wildlife resources. Whatever the outdoor area of the nation, Interior helps formulate policy. Other functions include Job Corps Conservation Centers and Youth Corps programs and preservation of scenic and historic sites.

Common news sources in the western parts of the United States include the Bureau of Indian Affairs and the Bureau of Reclamation. The National Park Service and the Bureau of Land Management are more widely known agencies in other sections of the country. The reporter should also be familiar with the functions of some of the other agencies under direction of Interior—the Geological Survey, the Bureau of Outdoor Recreation, the Bureau of Mines, the Mining and Enforcement Administration and the various hydroelectric projects.

Various reorganization plans involving natural resources are occasionally proposed by the executive branch, then shelved by congressional opposition, but the journalist should be aware of them.

> Within an hour of the president's proposal today to create a new Department of Natural Resources, the chairmen of the congressional committees most affected by the plan came out against it.
>
> The major element in the reorganization would be transfer of the Forest Service from Agriculture Department and the National Oceanic and Atmospheric Administration from the Commerce Department to the new department.

The new department would absorb the Department of Interior, with the interior secretary becoming head of the new agency.

Department of Agriculture

No industry in the United States has a greater federal involvement in a variety of ways than does agriculture. It is the nation's biggest, and more people are affected by its economic well-being and its collective problems than is any other segment of the economy.

Whether the reporter's beat encompasses a Farm Belt community or an Eastern metropolitan city dependent upon a constant supply of produce, there is news in "agriculture." And the federal agency that coordinates programs to assure stability and a constant food supply is the giant Agriculture Department. Preceding the first planting, through the growing process and the harvesting, and on through marketing, some type of federal agency is involved.

With the objective of aiding the producer and stabilizing the complex process of putting food on the table for nearly 230 million people, these agencies operate around the clock and throughout the year. Whether reporting in the Farm Belt or elsewhere, the reporter should be familiar with the following agencies:

Research, education and conservation are carried on through the *Agricultural Research Service*, which provides information to help farmers produce efficiently, while conserving the environment.

A nearly universal local office is the *Extension Service*, the education agency of the Agriculture Department. Area and county agents work with individuals, families and larger groups in supplying the technology for effective agricultural production. The service has been broadened in recent years to include home economics and nutrition for its primary audience—non-metropolitan families.

A national soil and water conservation program is carried out through the *Soil Conservation Service*, another agency with nearly universal local ties. Cooperating with landowner, land user and developer, the service offers technical assistance to more than 3,000 conservation districts throughout the United States, developing watershed projects and flood control plans.

At planting time, the *Farmers Home Administration* provides financial credit to rural Americans who have difficulty obtaining it from other sources. Areas that suffer natural disasters are also eligible for such credit from the agency, which has nearly 2,000 local offices.

Other agencies within the department offer assistance in other forms. The *Rural Electrification Administration* helps to finance electric and telephone service; the *Rural Development Service* coordinates a program with emphasis on community development. (An independent agency, the *Farm Credit Administration*, was originally capitalized by the federal government to provide credit through a system of federal land banks. The system, now owned by its users, is a nationwide network of boards that provides various types of credit to those in agriculture.)

In efforts to stabilize production and coordinate it with demand, the *Agricultural Stabilization and Conservation Service* administers programs for wheat, corn, cotton, peanuts, rice, tobacco, sugar, milk and other products that are grown in every area of the country. Often little noticed, this "coordination" affects the prices that consumers pay. Local farmer members assist in directing programs in which they are involved.

A drop in price supports for a major commodity can create powerful and emotional copy for the reporter. Nothing is closer to the farmer's pocketbook than federal assistance that stabilizes the agricultural economy. The *Commodity Credit Corporation* administers the federal government's price support policies, purchasing excess production and disposing of it through domestic and international sales. The *Federal Crop Insurance Corporation* provides crop insurance against loss from unavoidable causes, such as weather, insects and disease.

Assistance in marketing of farm products comes from the *Agricultural Marketing Service*, which offers current, unbiased market information to producers, processors, distributors and consumers to assure orderly marketing of products. The service establishes grade standards for produce and administers regulatory programs. Changes in these standards often are newsworthy, both to farmers and consumers.

An important recent addition to the department's list of agencies is the *Food and Nutrition Service*, which administers federal food assistance programs, including the Food Stamp Program and the National School Lunch Program. Both these areas are high on the list of newsworthy priorities, with millions of recipients involved. The strengths and weaknesses of both programs have been widely publicized, and they continue to provoke broad public response. The reporter, whether in an urban or rural setting, should monitor them closely.

Another important agency that should not be overlooked is the *Forest Service*, an unlikely Agriculture Department offspring, which manages federal forest reserves. The service administers 155 national forests and 19 additional grasslands in 41 states and cooperates with state and local governments in protection, reforestation and utilization of forests. Public interest in this area, both as recreation and for construction resources, dictates substantial coverage.

General Services Administration

The federal housekeeper, the General Services Administration, constructs, maintains and protects federal buildings and other properties. The GSA is active in the local community, distributing supplies, operating motor pools, disposing of surplus property and stockpiling strategic materials.

Its service contracts locally often constitute a significant portion of a community's economy. Contact with GSA officials often provides the reporter with information on federal spending at the local level, forthcoming changes and the implications.

Veterans Administration

Few federal agencies reach more extensively into local communities than does the Veterans Administration, which administers a wide range of benefits for former members and beneficiaries of former members of the armed forces. Its health care system includes 171 hospitals, 213 clinics and 84 nursing homes throughout the United States. Communites are also affected by the broad programs in medical research and education and training of health workers. Its cooperation with state and local communities has resulted in extensive assistance in establishing new medical schools in many areas. Nearly every city has a VA office to handle veterans' claims for disability compensation and pensions, auto allowances and special adaptive equipment.

Changes in programs, development of new facilities and new procedures for filing claims create news stories of interest to a substantial segment of the community.

Pressure Groups

The reporter cannot lose sight of the special interest groups, both in Washington and at the local level, that influence actions of the federal bureaucracy. Such individuals and groups affect not only the decisions themselves, but the process through which the reporter covers the federal beat. At nearly every turn, the reporter will find that a thrust brings a counterthrust, a charge calls for a countercharge, and a preliminary decision often brings a later decision overturning that decision. It is part of the process of governing.

The reality of special interest groups was made clearer by Donald Kennedy, former commissioner of the Food and Drug Administration. Asked about the power of special interests in Washington, he admitted they are competitive and effective: "I think that they can delay legislation, but I don't think they can delay a good piece of legislation indefinitely," Kennedy said. "I would say they are strong, they try to get their way, but that they don't win all the time."

How might this affect a reporter working on a story?

—A federal highway agency makes a preliminary decision to toughen standards governing weights of trucks on interstate highways. What pressures are going to be generated and from what direction will they come? The work is cut out for this reporter.

He or she heads for the trucking associations, who are certain to growl that they are being discriminated against, and to others known to favor the trucking industry. The truckers on the highway deserve equal time, and consumer activists concerned with safety and highway maintenance spring up to do battle. State officials, who are often subject to similar pressures, may exert pressure themselves.

So, while the decision is purely "preliminary," possibly only being advertised in the *Federal Register* pending any final approval, it passes through a period of great uncertainty. How public and how visible this argument becomes depends on the ability of the reporter to cover the substantial areas of disagreement.

The federal beat, as much as any, demands that the reporter be aware of the pressures exerted because of their effect on the final decision. This awareness will help the reporter to file more accurate and complete stories.

Suggested Readings

MAYHEW, DAVID, *Congress: The Electoral Connection* (New Haven, CT: Yale University Press, 1974).

REAGAN, MICHAEL D., *The New Federalism* (New York: Oxford University Press, 1972). Federal funding is discussed in Chapter 3, "Grants-in-Aid: The Cutting Edge of Intergovernmental Relations."

LEACACOS, JOHN P., *Fires in the In-Basket* (Cleveland, O.: World Publishing, 1968). The media role in federal coverage is reviewed in Chapter III, "The Mass Media: Sieve, Mirror or Mirage."

PETERS, CHARLES, *How Washington Really Works* (Reading, MA: Addison-Wesley, 1980). An anecdotal account of how various institutions in Washington operate, as viewed by a veteran reporter.

DEAKIN, JAMES, *The Lobbyists* (Washington: Public Affairs Press, 1967). Chapter 1, "Billions" and Chapter 2, "Pressures" offer an overview of lobbyists' operations in the nation's capital.

BLANCHARD, ROBERT O., editor, *Congress and the News Media* (New York: Hastings House, 1974). A collection of helpful readings discussing how Congress and the news media interact in the legislative and plicy-making process.

HEIBERT, RAY E., editor, *The Voice of Government* (New York: Wiley, 1968). Useful pointers in these articles, including Chapter 10, "Telling the Congressman's Story," Chapter 7, "Information and the Law," and Chapter 9, "Opening the Door on Foreign Affairs."

HERBERS, JOHN, *No Thank You, Mr. President* (New York: Norton, 1976). A White House reporter discusses the beat. Especially helpful are Chapter 3, "A Beat Without Sources" and Chapter 4, "Down on the Plantation."

CHAPTER 5
Reporting Education

A GREAT silence engulfs the newsroom of the *Gazette*. It is the last gasp of summer—the long Labor Day weekend. A lone reporter pecks out an accident roundup on a video display terminal as the city editor wrestles with beat assignments for the coming week.

"Vacation's over," he grumbles to himself. "Johnson's got to get back on schools Tuesday." As the final holiday of summer nears an end, thousands of children will troop back to the classrooms, making most parents happy and offering mixed emotions for the teachers who are concluding a nearly three-month holiday. The machinery that operates the education pipeline is creakily returning to action.

The summer has been good to the *Gazette* city editor; he hasn't had to concern himself with schools. Ostensibly they've been in recess, and so—in a sense—has this particular newspaper.

But the hiatus has not extended into the administrative offices of the school system. Administrators and other non-teaching personnel employed on a 12-month basis have put the summer to good use:

—They have evaluated and made major adjustments to the school system's new resource room program (A story here?).

—They have completed a year-long pupil survey that will have far-reaching effects on the districting of the school system (Another story here?).

—They have completed work on an innovative program to integrate the vocational program into the school day rather than to continue the traditional night classes (Still another story here?).

So, while an education reporter and his or her editors may be snoozing during the long hot summer, school machinery continues the process that affects thousands of students and their families.

The school reporter can ill afford this "summer mentality," just as he or she can ill afford to merely cover the Board of Education's official meetings without probing further into the operations of the school system. The education beat is one of the most important in the community, yet newspapers and broadcast outlets tend to overlook the bulk beneath the tip of the iceberg.

The "Whys" of Coverage

Education systems siphon off far more money from citizens than does any other form of local government. In a typical county with a population of 130,000, the county budget will total nearly $5 million. The municipal budget for the 75,000 persons residing in its principal city may total $15 million for services. The budget to educate the county's children during the same year will reach more than $32 million.

Thus, the sheer weight of dollars alone, most of it raised through local taxes, creates the need to determine how and why the money is being spent.

The other "whys" of education coverage are similarly easy to explain:

1. Nearly everyone in the community is involved in the education process or affected by it in some way—as parent, teacher, student, taxpayer or employer.

2. Most parents are concerned about what is happening to their children. Education is often a complicated process, with input from a wide range of publics, and it is important to translate developments into understandable and readable language.

3. Capital construction, maintenance of buildings, operation of fleets of vehicles, and employment of a substantial segment of the population in the education "industry" all play an important part in the economic life of the community.

For these reasons the public affairs reporter must prepare carefully when an editor or news director summons him or her to handle the education assignment, a challenge that demands more than merely a superficial approach. To be done well, it must be done thoroughly.

Who Governs?

When the presiding officer of the Board of Education bangs the gaval and announces the board's vote, the action symbolizes the conclusion of a special decision-making process. Despite the seemingly routine ballot by the board, governance in a school system is somewhat different and more complex than are other forms of local government.

The sheer size of the system, and its various "publics" who range from parents and taxpayers to an inordinately large number of employees (some of whom work nine months while others work 12 months) to the composition of the school population itself create the need for an authoritative governing board. Yet that board must be responsive to the thousands affected by its sometimes complex decisions.

Each decision often affects people in different ways. Can the school district really afford a multilevel approach, preparing children for college and vocational training at the same time? What should be done about violence in the schools and the increasing problem of truancy? Is competency testing fair, and should it be made obligatory in the school system?

The School District

The vehicle that has evolved to respond to these complex, growing needs is the independent school district. Most states provide for these governmental units that respond to education needs at the local level.

School districts are characterized by substantial legal and financial autonomy, not usually having to submit their budgets or other decisions to general local governments for possible alteration. They function as direct suppliers of education, their policy-making board generally answerable to the public during regularly scheduled popular elections. In some matters, however, they are increasingly answerable to state school boards. State legislation may set maximum class loads for teachers, specific hours of instruction, or mandate certain financial procedures, subject to state board approval. Despite this tendency, most decisions continue to be made at the local level.

While most states utilize independent school districts in providing education below the college level, some states authorize other local governments to provide educational services. A municipal government may have the basic responsibility for financing and administering the education system.

School district lines generally follow those of other local units, usually city or county lines, but many rural areas do not follow this rule. Size of the districts varies—from a few square miles to as many as 5,000. Responsibilities range from purely elementary education to the full range—kindergarten through junior college.

Districts are often separated into attendance districts, which serve the school population of a particular geographical area. Larger school districts may encompass as many as 50 attendance units, a form of education subgovernment that simplifies administration and reporting procedures.

The long-term trend toward consolidation of school districts continues, with most of the changes being made through legislative action at the state level. Although some states have adopted procedures for making consolidation mandatory, most often it is accomplished through local initiation and majority approval.

The decline in school districts has been dramatic—from 127,000 in 1932, dropping to 67,346 in 1952 and to only 15,781 in 1972, according to the Census of Governments.

Several reasons have been given for this development, but the decline in farm population—and the resultant movement of people to urban and suburban areas—and the outmoded and inadequate facilities of many smaller districts played a part.

Professionals saw consolidation as a means of providing better education in terms of instruction, curricula, improved equipment and better recreational facilities. Increased efficiency and the resultant savings to taxpayers helped "sell" consolidation.

The Governing Boards

School districts operate under the guidance of a governing board that sets basic policy and employs an administrator to carry it out. Designated as a board of education, a board of school trustees or some similar title, the policy-makers are usually elected by popular vote at intervals of three to seven years. When non-elective procedures are used, the appointing individuals or groups include grand juries, the governing board of a county, the mayor or council of a municipality, the governor or higher board of education.

While less overt, the political character of the governing process remains to some extent. Who serves in these policy-making positions that normally carry little salary and even fewer other emoluments?

A retired schoolteacher oftens runs for office, urged on by his or her friends and many still in the school system. The principal of a junior high school decides that he can set policy better than it is currently being set and files for candidacy. A parent who has been active in parent-teacher associations and who has high recognition in the district is encouraged to seek a seat. A successful business executive is asked by a minority of board members to run for election, with the expectation that the minority will enjoy the presence of a kindred philosophy on the board.

As these examples show, politics is subtly different at the education level, but it can be highly emotional. The reporter should be forewarned: In some areas the campaigns are fiercely waged, with many sore losers and often court battles in the aftermath.

Upon election, board members will find their powers defined by the state constitution and legislative action, with members retaining ultimate responsibility for the quality, extent and cost of primary education in their district.

The board usually determines the education tax rate after preparing and adopting a budget. It has the power to raise revenue for capital construction by issuing bonds, often after approval of voters in a referendum. It selects building sites and authorizes new construction, sometimes after bitter arguments over details. It selects new textbook series for the district, often after concurrence of special parent-teacher committees that have studied the alternatives. It employs, dismisses and transfers teachers, usually within the framework of a well-defined tenure program, and employs, discharges and transfers non-teaching personnel, who may include principals and custodians. It is easy for the reporter to see the potential conflict in these decisions.

It is not always so easy to resolve the issue of how to cover them, as these two examples show:

—The textbook committee for the Board of Education, which includes teachers and administrators, has completed its selection work for the coming year. The action seems routine, but the reporter learns privately that some of the selections have created friction among members of the committee. However, the vote has been cast, and the Board of Education has given its approval in official session without public comment. The issue apparently is closed. Does the reporter pass on to other assignments, or begin the job of determining what the problem was?

—The waiting list for teaching jobs in the district is quite long, and there is little turnover. A reporter learns that one of the waitees, No. 13 on the list, has been given an available opening because she has the "requisite background." Many of the waitees with lower numbers are unhappy but are unwilling to jeopardize their places on the list by complaining publicly. The Board of Education says it is a "personnel matter" and declines to discuss it.

These are the kind of administrative matters with which the governing board and the education reporter must grapple. While dealing with multimillion-dollar budgets, school boards also wield the power to make all reasonable rules and regulations within the district, disciplining both students and teachers, and admitting and excluding children for sufficient cause.

While some of these actions are increasingly concluding in judicial action, school board decisions are usually final, subject to the later expression of the electorate at the polls.

Covering the School Board

As noted, the nature of the education beat dictates a far more thorough approach to coverage than merely reporting the decisions of the governing board at official sessions. However, the importance of the official actions should not be underestimated. And, as with other local governments, the reporter will discover that major issues have often been thrashed out at any number of "informal" meetings in advance of the official session.

Like so many other administrators, school officials do not like "waves" and much prefer smoothly functioning machinery in government. Issues discussed at length in public have a way of making "waves."

The ambivalent attitude adopted on the part of a substantial segment of the public makes the task of the reporter more difficult in identifying education issues and writing about them. Many parents, as newspaper readers and television news viewers, express a desire for news of education, yet they approach the reality of it in an inconsistent manner. "We should leave the job of teaching our children to the professionals," they assert, and often take the side of education officials who call for key decisions on school issues to be worked out privately.

> Members of the Wilkes Board of Education met yesterday in an unannounced session that ended abruptly when a reporter for the *News-Dispatch* appeared.
>
> President Clarence Tooey said the meeting did not end because the reporter appeared. "It was simply time for the meeting to be over," he said.
>
> School Superintendent William Cryce said later that the informal meeting was called to discuss the federally ordered realignment in the school district to bring about better racial balance.

While such meetings may be illegal under some states' open meeting laws, their nature is often disguised as informal. Yet the issues discussed and often reconciled affect thousands of people in the school district.

The reporter should remember that one of the functions of official meetings is to provide a forum for the public. Feedback on issues that arise from time to time is important in a system the size of most school districts. Unless issues are properly identified beforehand, however, citizens must rely only on informal community grapevines for information.

The board of education's agenda, and the reporter's ability to identify issues preliminary to official discussion and action, form an important part of the communications equation. Preliminary stories set the stage for discussion and often outweigh actual coverage of the event itself.

> The Younts County Board of Education will decide tomorrow whether to continue to provide bus transportation to students who live between one and two miles of schools they attend.
>
> State law mandates bus service only to students living two miles or more from school, but the Younts board has regularly reduced that figure to one mile.
>
> "Transportation funding is short," Board President T. S. Hite said yesterday, "and we can't decide where to cut costs. We'll just have to vote tomorrow and hope we're doing the right thing."

THE SCHOOL BOARD AGENDA

There is no typical school board agenda. One district's policy may be to prepare a detailed 40-page agenda which lists every ream of paper to be purchased on bids and every can of paint to be bought. Another agenda might be as superficial as this:

BORDEN COUNTY AGENDA, APRIL 20

1. Reading and approval of minutes from previous meetings.
2. Reports from the superintendent.
3. Transfers of nontenured teaching personnel.
4. Report from budget committee on new federal grants.
5. School calendar adoption for coming year.

Such agendas tend to disguise the important elements. The transfer of non-tenured personnel may involve key athletic coaches and prove to be a major issue. Or the system of transfers itself may be undergoing a major metamorphosis. The new federal grants may involve major construction possibilities or, worse, an indication that the pipeline from Washington is being closed. The school calendar may also be undergoing some major changes, with abrupt shifts in snow-day scheduling and spring vacation shuffling.

This is not to suggest that the longer, 40-page agenda will offer fewer disguises. The tendency for the longer agendas is also to disguise important elements, merely because of their length.

The longer agendas suggest that a policy-making board has allowed itself to become bogged down in nitpicking details, with the effect of sometimes turning the policy-making function over to administrators. By the time the board gets through detailed pages of minor bids to be awarded and requests for use of school facilities, it has little time to discuss more major issues that confront it.

A 30-page school board agenda in a Southern community listed these decisions which the board had to make during its twice-monthly meeting:

—Request for out-of-state travel by a guidance counselor; employment of two substitute teachers during a partial school year; employment of substitute cooks for cafeterias in several schools; acceptance of resignation of a teacher who was leaving the district; a request for verbal support for a summer camp program designed for superior science students; a request for bus service to transport a class to the science and cultural center in a nearby city; a change order in a plumbing contract at a junior high school; and so on.

Lost in the shuffle and still on the desk of the superintendent were the major issues of truancy, the problem of what to do with the elementary school to be permanently closed in the spring, and whether to allow city police to search students' lockers for drugs and alcohol.

The reporter who is close to the scene will cut through the extraneous routine and focus on other issues—including those which do not offer apparent importance. A routine listing of medical expenses might not, for instance, tell the whole story. What physicians were paid by the school system last year, who is on the payroll this year, how were they chosen, how much are they being paid and why?

Who are the major firms doing business with the school system, what do they supply and how much? The unanswered questions and story possibilities at the administrative level are endless.

REPORTING PERSONNEL MATTERS

Because many school decisions involve personnel matters, the education reporter must develop a sensitivity that will enable him or her to identify and report personnel matters that legitimately call for public exposure and to reject those that may not fall into the "public" domain.

A fine line exists between the public's right to know and the right of a public employee to a modicum of privacy. It is too simplistic to use the argument that, because the teacher is on the public payroll, his or her affairs are public. The question instead is whether it is in the interests of the public to pursue and publish. The competent education reporter, with advice from editors, should be part of the decision-making process in whether to communicate questionable material.

> The Cale County Board of Education approved certification of 11 teachers yesterday, but held up action on one because the teacher's application for state approval is still pending.
>
> Certification of Sally Ann Hager, who is the daughter of Assistant School Superintendent Wilson Hager, will be delayed until the state acts, the board decided.
>
> "It is a minor point," Board President Watson Sims said, "but we should be correct about it."

In this instance, the reporter must decide whether a minor point on a personnal matter becomes a public issue because the teacher in question is the daughter of a school administrator.

School officials will sometimes reprimand a teacher or other school official and refuse to make details public. The effect is to raise more questions than are resolved by the refusal. The reporter will encounter situations like these in every school system and will have to develop persistence if he or she is to play a role in deciding how far to go.

Some educators tend to draw the line more sharply in revealing potentially sensitive personnel matters to the public through the press, often resulting in suppression of stories that should otherwise be legitimate public information. The following story was deliberately withheld from the press on the grounds that the employee in question had resigned and thus the matter was settled. A persistent reporter ultimately uncovered the pertinent facts and wrote the story.

> Charles C. Sites, former director of the County Vo-

> cational Center, repaid more than $1,450 to the Board of Education after the board determined that certain purchases were "improper and illegal."
> The information was obtained from a board audit obtained by the *News-Dispatch*.
> Sites resigned last week, but the Board of Education members have refused to reveal reasons for his sudden resignation.

Education officials reasoned that no purpose would be served by publicizing the fact that the employee had resigned after returning the funds in question. An alert reporter, deciding that the affair should properly have been made public, confirmed the facts and published them.

Personnel matters do not constitute the only area of sensitivity for school officials. Others include transportation of students for purposes of racial integration and sex education in the schools. The reporter's job is to address such emotional issues in a dispassionate manner, without inflaming them.

> Richard Branch began to discuss the sex education class he teaches and the 50 assembled parents grew still. Suddenly the silence was shattered by a man in the rear of the room who tried to shout down Branch.
> Margaret Wilson, chairman of the committee on sex education for Middleton County, immediately told the man he was out of order, but his comments prompted lengthy committee debate.
> Could the committee, members asked, ever debate the sex education issue if it allowed parents at its meetings? The committee finally agreed that parents should play a role.
> The incident points up the highly emotional atmosphere surrounding the sex education issue in Middleton County.

An equally sensitive issue emerging is competency testing, which would require passing standardized tests to move from one grade to another or to graduate with a high school diploma. Many educators support such a plan, but substantial segments of the public oppose it. As with the issue of sex education, the reporter has an obligation to write about the issue while recognizing its emotional aspects.

A solid professional relationship between the education writer and school officials, teachers and parents will help solve the problem.

Money Oils the Machinery

An education system is merely a sophisticated pipeline. Uneducated youngsters and money are plugged into the system, and educated students march out the other end. Between the two ends of the pipeline lies complicated machinery, much of it human, that converts the money into teaching salaries, quality educational facilities, funding for special programs—a multitude of equipment and services designed to enhance the probability of success at the end of the pipeline.

The Budgeting Process

In a nutshell, the role of the education reporter is to audit the entire process—from "laying the levy," a fiscal term for deciding upon the rate at which citizens will be taxed to pay for the schools, to the graduation exercises and beyond.

Partly because of the fiscal complexities, it is often suggested that education coverage demands a "specialist" who can concentrate on problems, trends and developments. This argument can be refuted for at least two valid reasons:

1. Any competent journalist, confident of his or her abilities and unafraid to ask for explanation of technical points, is fully capable of handling the education beat. If a little more sensitivity is required than for dealing with politicians at City Hall, so be it. As in the case of other beats, people make up the bulk of the reporting process, and the reporter with a "nose for news" will quickly succeed.

2. As a practical matter, many newspapers and broadcast outlets cannot afford a full-time education specialist, no matter what the need. The school beat must share the personnel necessary for competent coverage.

These generalists, however, must learn to translate specialized legal and fiscal language for the average reader or viewer. The broadcast reporter faces special problems because of the limits imposed by time restraints. Two minutes of air time leave little room for a detailed explanation of a multimillion-dollar school budget. Broadcast reporters, as well as print journalists, must be able to translate a tax decision into lay terms.

When a board of education decides upon a tax levy of 91.8 cents the reporter must be able to explain:

> The school board's rate is 91.8 cents on each $100 of assessed property valuation, which is one half the appraised value of the property. For example, if a home is appraised at $60,000, its assessed value is one half or $30,000. The homeowner can figure the tax by dividing the assessment by 100 and then multiplying by .918. The tax bill will be $275.40.

There are other methods for determining the citizen's tax rate and tax bill, and the reporter need only to explain any of them simply and clearly.

The bulk of the education budget is spent for "personnel services," basically salaries and other employee benefits. Details of a proposed budget, often published as legal advertisements, provide the reporter with the opportunity to check salary ranges and many specific expenditures. Some line items, for example, will list "contracted services." What specifically are they, and how do they fit into the system's other services? A line item of $315,000 for "consultants" will raise the question of why the consultants. The capital outlay should be studied closely and questions should be raised about its purposes.

Knowledge of the fiscal setup, officials and the way in which breakdowns are made in the budget is necessary. Armed with these, the reporter can question, for example, expenditures listed to "C. I. Thornburg Co. ($903), Claud Thornburg ($532.24) and Thornburg Insurance Agency ($1,513) to determine the relationship of Board of Education President Claud Thornburg to the other expenditures. The journalist's role in reporting fiscal activity in education affairs is often investigative. It is worthwhile to develop skill in checking such budget or audit figures.

It is not uncommon for a prominent businessman such as Claud Thornburg to serve on a board of education, placing his business in the hands of relatives, and allowing them to bid on school insurance contracts. Such personal information is often pertinent to the reporter.

Publication of huge outlays of funds for education are made much more meaningful if the writer breaks down the figures and tries to tell the reader what they mean. For example, a school's budget may total $28 million, a minimal increase over the previous year. Where is the increase going to be spent? Here is how one reporter addressed the question.

> School officials call it "holding the line."
>
> Of the $2 million increase in the Roane County school budget, $1.7 million will be used for salaries and fringe benefits, an analysis of the $28.8 million proposed budget shows. The school board will vote on the bůdget tomorrow.
>
> Nearly 81 percent (more than $23 million) of next year's budget total will be spent on personnel. Surveys indicate the national average percentage ranges from 77 percent to 84 percent, Treasurer Will McCabe said.
>
> The Roane system employes 1,861 full-time personnel and 200 part-time workers, including substitute teachers, records show.

A schedule of disbursements offers the best opportunity for the reporter to compare categories of school expenditures. The typical legal advertisement shown in Table 5–1 indicates general breakdowns in the budgeting process. More detailed breakdowns are generally available from school fiscal officers.

Each of these categories will yield to the right questions from the reporter. What substantial changes are being made and why? How does a category differ from that in the previous year? What are the "contracted services" and why? How much of the budget comes from sources other than local taxes? What efforts are being made to build efficiency into each category?

Table 5–1. Board of Education—Estimated Disbursements

ADMINISTRATION	
Salaries	$ 422,500
Contracted services	31,000
Other current expense	58,350
Total administration	$ 511,850
INSTRUCTION	
Salaries	
Principals	$ 1,075,000
Consultants or supervisors	315,000
Teachers	10,826,200
Other instructional staff	641,000
Secretarial and clerical	460,000
Other salaries, non-professional	240,000
Other current expense	
Textbooks	$ 130,000
Libraries, audiovisual materials	102,000
Teaching supplies	277,771
Other expenses	146,400
Total instruction	$ 14,213,371
ATTENDANCE SERVICES	
Salaries	65,000
Other expense	3,000
Total attendance services	$ 68,000
HEALTH SERVICES	
Salaries	73,500
Contracted services	5,000
Other current expense	12,100
Total health services	$ 90,600
FOOD SERVICES	
Salaries	26,000
Other expense	64,850
Total food services	$ 90,850
PUPIL TRANSPORTATION SERVICES	
Salaries	520,500
Contracted services and public carriers	50,000
Replacement of vehicles	120,000
Public transportation insurance	21,500
Expenditures in lieu of transport	2,000
Operation and maintenance	195,700
Total transportation	$ 909,700

Table 5–1 (*Continued*)

OPERATION OF FACILITIES	
Salaries	1,060,500
Contracted services	6,000
Heat for buildings	377,000
Utilities, except heat for bldgs.	530,000
Supplies	82,100
Other expense	500
Total operation of facilities	$ 2,056,100
MAINTENANCE OF FACILITIES	
Salaries	257,870
Contracted services	114,700
Replacement of equipment	19,400
Other expense	182,000
Total maintenance of facilities	$ 573,970
FIXED CHARGES	
Contribution to employee retirement	1,016,893
Insurance and judgments	134,135
Rent of land and buildings	15,000
Other fixed charges	28,000
Total fixed charges	$ 1,194,028
CAPITAL OUTLAY	
Sites	100,000
Buildings	600,000
Equipment	72,402
Total capital outlay	$ 772,402
SPECIAL ACCOUNTS	
Food services	1,386,000
Student body activities	11,660
Total special accounts	$ 1,397,660
TOTAL ESTIMATED DISBURSEMENTS	$22,132,186

Relationships with Other Governments

The mere fact that a traditional physical overlap exists between school districts and other, more political forms of local government complicates the relationships among them. Personalities of individuals play a part as do different philosophies of governing. The reporter must remember that all these local governments are appealing to the electorate for operating funds and that education needs are generally paramount. The occasional disputes among local leaders are very real and often point to divergent views of priorities.

When school officials must appeal to county or municipal boards for some type of funding approval, conflicts tend to arise. Legislation often requires joint sharing of fiscal responsibility for such facilities as libraries and recreation areas. And while it is usually a formality, state auditors will likely study school-spending procedures at regular intervals.

Increasingly, a broad range of federal spending will be found at the local school level, and frequent accountings are necessary. Much of the federal spending is earmarked for special programs, such as lunches for needy students, aid to handicapped students and funds for special instructional materials. The whys of such funding are important. Often a computer printout will provide the education reporter with a breakdown of federal funding areas. Because federal funding generally constitutes a large percentage of the total budget, the reporter is well advised to follow implemention of the programs and to provide a periodic assessment of their effectiveness.

> Cook County teachers have found the federally funded slow-learners program difficult to administer but effective for most of the students.
>
> "The paperwork is terrible. It takes all our time," moaned Neal Workman, coordinator for the select group of 35 teachers who have been organizing the program with a $780,000 grant from the Department of Health and Human Services.
>
> "But it's working for most of our slow learners," Workman emphasized. Under the program, special classrooms are being set up in 35 schools.

School systems receive funds from the Department of Education, the newest cabinet-level department in the federal structure, as well as enforcement in the form of its Office of Civil Rights. Automatic formulas embodied in programs such as Title I of the Elementary and Secondary Education Act allocate funds to systems based on a broad poverty index.

Relationships between school districts and other governments often reach beyond fiscal matters. Library services are integrated in some areas, and there is regular involvement with recreation, adult education and vocational education. Law enforcement often creates a need for sharing of responsibilities.

> A Rockford Police Department detective has been assigned to each of Stiles County's public schools in an effort to deal more effectively with juvenile problems.
>
> The detectives will not patrol the 13 schools, Superintendent John Stinson said, but will be on call to the principal of their assigned school.
>
> "The whole idea is for schools and police to have better communications with each other," Stinson said.

After innovative programs such as these have been put into effect, it is the responsibility of the education reporter to assess the reaction of students and teachers to them and, most important, help to evaluate them for the public after a reasonable period of time.

A reminder file is helpful in keeping track of such developing stories, not trusting to memory to update them many months later. After a program has been publicly launched, for example, the reporter will later trigger a "success story" or at least a progress report.

> The six-month-old plan to deal with juvenile crime in Stiles County schools has not been effective, Superintendent John Stinson admitted yesterday.
>
> "It's been too complicated to work smoothly," he said. Each school had been assigned a Rockford Police Department detective, who has been on call when needed.
>
> Stinson and police officials will meet next week to discuss ways to improve the program.

A Trip into the School System

Whatever the distance from the central school offices to the individual schools, whether a few blocks or several miles, the reporter will cross the threshold into a self-contained world of its own in each school. The authoritarian impression one often gets at the Board of Education level does not disappear; it merely crops up in a more parochial form.

School systems tend to be authoritarian in approach, and nowhere is this feeling more pronounced than inside individual schools. A familiar figure figuratively guards the front door—the principal. Whether stern-visaged or kindly in demeanor, the principal is ruler of his or her domain and the point of initial confrontation for the reporter.

Through establishment of confidence, coercion or other means, the reporter must first breach this battlement to gain access and have any hope of competently covering the system from the inside. Access to the offices of school buildings always precedes the freedom to freely roam halls and classrooms where "people" stories are found, and school officials are increasingly cognizant of the visibility that news stories offer their particular school, both positive and negative.

Human nature being what it is, the principal is apt to be far more supportive of a warm feature about a spelling champion than of the publication of an ugly racial development that has created policing problems at his or her school. Doing the first and doing it well often opens the door to the more sensitive stories that must be mined.

At a somewhat different level, the teacher is "policy-maker" in his or her classroom. He or she can help to produce a good story or effectively kill one, so the reporter must establish a working relationship with teacher as well as supervisor.

> Students about to become "two-time losers" sit down

> with Eileen Jennings at 8 o'clock every morning in Santa Rosa High School.
>
> Jennings, a teacher at SRHS for six years, tries to help students who are about to fail a course for the second time.
>
> "It's a tough challenge," she admits, but says some potential dropouts seem to be helped by the program.

The effective education reporter cannot fully cover a system unless he or she gets down into it. The size of the system dictates the need to physically spend time inside it, listening to officials, teachers, guidance counselors, custodians and students. Covering the system from the outside through frequent press releases as news tips will not work. A prime example follows.

—The press release noted that a prominent circuit court judge and the county prosecutor would address a parent-student meeting at the junior high school, discussing the problems of alcohol and drug use. An advance story was duly published, and a reporter was assigned to cover the meeting. It was well attended, and it provided substantial quotes, including the comment from the principal that the session was merely a preventive measure. "We have no problems here, of course," he said.

If the reporter had acted on the principle that "where there's smoke, there's fire," he or she would have learned that indeed the school did have problems. A serious case of alcohol poisoning during a class excursion had sent one student to a hospital in a nearby city, and all out-of-city class trips had been canceled for the remainder of the year. Suspensions had been numerous for alcohol consumption inside the school.

There is no doubt that the story would have been written somewhat differently if the reporter had gotten inside the system.

No administrator or public information officer can provide the personal view of the school system that teacher and student can. The reporter who earns the confidence of administrators and others at the front door will be better able to penetrate the red tape that often ambushes easy access to the schools, both rural and urban.

A Wide Range of "Publics"

To effectively cover the education beat, the reporter must address many publics, all of them with different interests in school affairs. Separately, they constitute special-interest groups, often with a unique response of their own toward decisions reached in the school system. At the same time, the reporter must remember that collectively they represent the community. Consider the following different publics.

THE TEACHERS

As a part of the school system itself, the teachers are an important element. When combined with relatives, friends and neighbors, they become even more so.

Furthermore, teachers are becoming increasingly better organized, through associations and labor unions. They constitute a powerful voice in the community, and the education reporter must take care to note their actions and reactions to current issues.

> A newly formed teachers' political action committee will consider endorsing candidates for two Board of Election seats in the May 9 election.
>
> Questionnaires will be mailed to the seven candidates, Fran Sellers, chairman of the County Classroom Teachers Association, said yesterday.
>
> "People who run for the school board affect all of us—teachers, children, schools," Sellers said. "We have a responsibility to take a position in politics."
>
> About 350 teachers are members of the association, she said.

Teachers are interested in new programs but perceive them somewhat differently than do administrators or parents. The parent asks the question, How will the program affect my child? The teacher asks, How will the program affect me? The reporter must answer questions for both.

With their safety at stake, teachers have similar concerns with the problem of violence in the schools. What legal rights do they have in protecting themselves from unruly students? How are their roles changing in the classroom? How do they perceive outside influences, such as television, as affecting their jobs? Many of the major education issues directly affect teachers, who are one of the education reporter's key sources in effectively covering the beat.

PARENTS AND TAXPAYERS

Because their interests may sometimes be divergent, the reporter will often treat taxpayers and parents as two separate publics. The parent might be willing to accept higher taxes to assure continuance of quality education and, in fact, might be downright adamant about it. As a taxpayer, however, another parent might strongly resist a proposed increase to maintain current programs.

In recognizing this problem, the education reporter must fulfill the information needs accurately, portraying this dichotomy as clearly and as objectively as possible.

> The mushrooming student population in suburban Wilkes County means higher taxes if the school system is to maintain its high standards, Cheryl Whitten, president of the Parent-Teacher Association warned yesterday.
>
> "Parents are going to have to choose between higher costs and reduced services—and soon," she said.

> Whitten called on the Board of Education to provide the public with a "balance sheet" so that it can study alternatives and make an informed decision.
>
> "The PTA has in it both taxpayer and parent," she said, "and the roles don't always coincide."

In addressing taxpayers and parents, the reporter should keep two objectives in mind:

1. New developments in education must be quickly and accurately reported and fairly interpreted.

2. The potential costs must be accurately assessed. It is important to obtain such assessment from objective school officials and experts who do not have a vested interest in seeing a program adopted.

The manner in which the reporter portrays such programs and their costs will often have a bearing on whether they are finally adopted. It is an important responsibility. The reporter should be studying issues such as these:

—Is the middle school concept workable in the school system? What's to be done with the 11 vacant buildings when the system finally shifts to the concept next year? How will the cost of educating gifted students be borne? Is the system doing enough for culturally deprived children?

These and dozens of other issues affecting parent and taxpayer are legitimate subjects for pen or camera.

THE STUDENTS

If for no other reason than lack of an organized spokesperson, the student population should be considered one of the education reporter's important publics. In part, the school beat exists to inform the "educatees" as to what the educators are thinking and doing that affects the classroom itself. A school "grapevine" is a poor substitute for the work of an informed reporter.

No matter that students at the lower grade levels are not the most avid newspaper readers in the community. It is for this public that the reporter must pursue information into the schools themselves rather than relying on the occasional public relations release on scholarship winners.

At graduation time, the reporter will seek more than merely the valedictorian's comments and the graduation lists, looking for trends that bespeak future issues and problems in the system.

> The number of graduates at Washington County's four public high schools has dropped below 1,600 for the first time since 1968, statistics from the superintendent's office show.

> A decreasing birth rate, both locally and nationwide, was cited by administrators as the major reason for the drop, but residential movement to the far suburbs was also mentioned as a factor.

What are the issues that interest as well as affect students? Quality of the school lunch programs, basic changes in length of the school day, new truancy regulations, police searches of school lockers for suspected contraband, and special areas for smoking on the school grounds.

The answer for the reporter lies in a balanced news report that touches on issues such as these as well as on more basic ones. The alert reporter will not leave athletics solely to the sports department. Funding, changes in coaching personnel and the more basic changes in the sports ethic itself are more important to many readers and viewers than who won or lost a game.

OTHER PUBLICS

Other special-interest groups are often neglected by school reporters. Business and industrial firms have a special stake in the quantity and quality of graduates from the system, and not merely because of the taxes they pay. As employers, such corporations have a vested interest in the quality of young adults that emerge from the educational pipeline. How many and which ones will go on to college? Who will constitute the job pool right out of high school? What skills are being taught to those who will enter the job market immediately after graduation? Such questions are important to business and industrial firms and individuals.

> Nearly 75 percent of the 2,650 Duchess County high school graduates will go on to college in the fall, affecting the job market here next year.
>
> "That seems to be an accurate reading," Schools Superintendent Joseph Slash commented on a survey conducted by the *News-Dispatch* this week.
>
> "The rush to college is certainly going to affect employment practices in Duchess during the coming year or more," he added.

As with other taxpayers, members of the business community are sensitive to financial matters, and changes in the community's tax base affect them more deeply than they do individual homeowners. Tax abatements to bring new industry and business to a city are often hotly debated among the public.

> The Board of Education decided Tuesday it will not support future tax abatements for businesses and industry unless the school system is reimbursed for the loss of tax revenue.
>
> The city has offered tax abatements to lure business and industry, but the policy has been criticized because it weakens the tax base that supports the school system.

> "Tax abatement is not an innocuous tool that stimulates the economy," said board member Gary T. Holland after the 5-1 vote against abatements. "It is detrimental to the schools and the community."

The alumni in the school system are another public often overlooked by the education reporter. While graduates ultimately become taxpayers and parents themselves, alumni status confers a requirement for addressing this group in a special way. What's happening in their schools will be of long-term interest to graduates.

The journalism student should not be misled into believing that he or she must consciously write for a particular audience every time the video display terminal is addressed. Most education stories will interest wider segments of the community. But an awareness of these various publics will assure more thorough coverage of education.

Secrecy as a Problem

In analyzing the key points of coverage in the system, the school reporter should study the levels that yield the most important results for the reader. At whatever level, people will play the most important role. Their creativity or lack of it, their innovativeness or failure to study new ideas and approaches to education will all affect the reporter's approach.

But one of the problems in many school systems is a tendency by some officials toward secretiveness. It is a fact of life with which the reporter must deal.

> The Orange County Board of Education, embroiled in a controversy which resulted in resignation of Superintendent James Lang last week, met privately last night to discuss the problem.
>
> Four of the five members refused to discuss the unannounced meeting, but the fifth member confirmed it was held. R. C. McCoy said the board discussed the qualifications which would be sought in Lang's successor.

To combat this problem of secrecy, which may be rare or common depending on the community and its attitude toward employees of its school system, the reporter has a number of options:

1. He or she must prove through ability that an accurate portrayal of the system's actions is possible. This is important to breaking down barriers to better and more open relationships.

2. Whatever the problem, the reporter must aggressively pursue the story if he or she determines that it is legitimately public affairs. Nothing helps to open closed doors shielding secret

conferences as much as accurate accounts of the meetings. Officials often decide to allow reporters access to information in self-defense, reasoning that it will be at least more accurate that way. Maintaining an even disposition is important too. An even temper and a good humor can often cool the worst-tempered public official.

3. Most states have enacted legislation prohibiting closed meetings by public officials and have also enacted open records legislation. While the laws are often cumbersome and ambiguous, they can often be effective in gaining access to information through judicial action.

> Citing the right of the public to know how tax dollars are being spent, the publisher of the *News* yesterday filed a legal action to obtain details of an audit performed for the Sutton County Board of Education.
>
> Attorneys for Publisher Harold Burton filed for a writ of mandamus in circuit court to compel the board to release the information. Reporters have been denied access to the audit since it was completed last week.

The education beat is as susceptible to problems of secrecy as are other areas of local government, and the reporter should be aware of his or her rights of access.

Suggested Readings

BOLLENS, JOHN C., *Special District Government in the United States* (Berkeley, CA: University of California, (1957). Chapter 6, "School Districts."

WYNNE, EDWARD, *The Politics of School Accountability: Public Information About Public Schools* (Berkeley, CA: McCutchan, 1972). Fact-finding in the school system, with a chapter beamed to education reporters.

CHAPTER 6
Authorities and Other Special Districts

LAUGHTER echoed behind the closed door, then dropped to a hum of conversation as the small group of men got down to business.

Their leader brought the meeting to order, asked the executive director for a financial report, heard briefings on committee activity, then called for discussion of the major topic of the meeting: expanding the scope of operations and increasing fees to meet increases in operating costs.

A consensus was apparent, and the group voted in the affirmative. The meeting concluded, and the group adjourned to a nearby restaurant for lunch and return to each member's private affairs.

No illegalities had occurred, and the public had not been bilked. It had merely not been consulted on a matter that would deeply affect it at a later date. This was one public body's method of doing business. Although a public body, the group had not announced date, time and place of the meeting. As a matter of fact, the press hadn't asked and may not even have been aware of it.

Thousands of meetings are being conducted all over the United States each month by such groups that have been legally constituted as a little-known type of public agency—special district government.

In 1917, H. S. Gilbertson had labeled county government, which up to that time had been subjected to little study or analysis by political scientists, as "the dark continent of American politics." Forty years and two world wars later, political scientist John C. Bollens respectfully disagreed. He contended that the term could be much more accurately applied to the special district governments that have proliferated during this century.

These new units, frequently called "phantom governments" because of their low visibility, are now more numerous than are municipal and county governments combined. In studying them, Bollens reported, "People who receive services from them often do not know they exist or exactly where they function. Although most districts have definite areas and boundaries which limit their jurisdication, there is seldom visible evidence of these facts."

Few public affairs reporters will work in a community in which at least one of the special districts or "authorities" do not function. And while it may take considerable research, the reporter will unearth units of government providing a vast range of services. The spectrum reaches from public education, the best known and most visible of these special district governments, to public transportation, sewage disposal, recreation facilities, cultural arts complexes and industrial development zones.

Most familiar to the public are the traditional school districts, which were conceived to provide funds for and administer public education. Such districts formerly outnumbered other types of special districts, but consolidation has drastically cut the number during the past 30 years. Meanwhile, new limited-purpose special districts have experienced dramatic growth.

The passage of time has helped outline the distinction between the terms "special district" and the more recently popular "authority." Twenty-five years ago special districts were generally defined as being independent government units; authorities were characterized as being dependent on another governmental unit, either fiscally or administratively. Growth of these authorities and the broad range of the functions they perform has caused a major change in this distinction.

Today, special districts are considered those units relying primarily on special taxes to fulfill their function. Public authorities are considered those units relying primarily on borrowed funds, raised through revenue bonds, to handle a specific function. The borrowed money is paid off through collection of fees or charges upon the users. The distinction is not all-encompassing, however, because many of these special units of government rely upon both sources of revenue.

Whatever their revenue sources, special districts and authorities operate outside the regular or traditional structure of government. It is easy to confuse them because many combine functions and names, which vary from state to state.

Futhermore, many are tied in some manner to other local governments, either as dependent children tied to apron strings or as grown-up children subject to little or no scrutiny.

So many have been created in the last 40 years that it is nearly impossible to classify them, except in a very general way. Further, their numbers—and functions—continue to expand, along with arguments for and against their existence.

A preliminary examination of these units will help the public affairs reporter prepare for an inevitable confrontation with one of them. One of the greatest challenges in covering local government lies in this area.

Origins of the Form

While the origins of these special units of government reach back into the 18th century, the term authority is fairly recent. When a Port of London special district was created in England in 1908, the problem of labeling it arose. David Lloyd George, then chancellor of the exchequer, found himself unable to decide on a name for this nontraditional mold of government. The story may be apocryphal, but a reporter for the *London Observer* suggested the solution: With so much repetition of the term "authority" in the enabling legislation, the new unit should simply be called an authority. The name stuck.

These special district forms, however, date back to 1790 in the United States, when the City of Philadelphia established a new governmental unit to combine administration of city and suburban prisons. Then, as now, the intractable nature of political boundaries created jurisdictional problems, solved in the case of Philadelphia with a totally new overlapping government fulfilling only one specific function.

So effective was this new method of coping with the problem that others followed in Philadelphia—a board of port wardens with jurisdiction over the waterfront district along the Delaware River, an areawide board of health, a consolidated school district and a special metropolitan police district.

By 1900 half a dozen other metropolitan special districts had been established, with various functions and powers. They included a sewage and water district in Boston, sewage districts in Chicago, New York and northern New Jersey, a levee district in New Orleans to protect the city from the frequent excesses of the Mississippi River, and a port district in Portland, Ore.

These original metropolitan units were given powers similar to those bestowed by states on authorities and special districts today: the right to borrow money by issuing long-term revenue bonds, to spend the money in operations, and a certain degree of autonomy in fulfilling special functions.

A new interstate dimension to the growth of these new forms of government was added in 1921 with formation of the New York Port Authority, created through agreement between the states of New York and New Jersey to develop the commerce of the port of New York.

Seven years earlier, the *American Political Science Review* had begun reporting on "special municipal corporations." In one of the early reports, Charles Kettleborough wrote, "In the past few years there has been a significant increase in the number and diversity of municipal corporations, and the creation and development of interesting political units seems to be only in its infancy."

In retrospect, Kettleborough's modest prediction was an understatement. The 1972 Census of Governments reported that the number of special districts has risen to 23,885 (not including the 15,781 school districts in the United States) as compared with 18,517 municipalities and 3,044 counties.

Defining Their Functions

The reporter asks a legitimate question: Why would a community need yet another government to clutter the landscape? Doesn't it have enough now to do the job?

The answer is complex and lies at least partly in the growing pressures by the public in the last generation for more services. Another answer lies in a story told by Julius Cohen, general counsel for the New York Port Authority, many years ago:

—An executive for the authority once conducted a seminar in the Middle West for municipal administrators. After the official concluded his talk, a fiscal officer from a nearby community approached him and said, "Mr. Speaker, what you just said about the Port Authority hits the nail on the head in my town. We have been wanting to build a playground in my city, but the taxpayers have opposed it because they don't want to spend any money and raise taxes. But I told the mayor, 'Why don't we have a Playground Authority? The taxpayers have heard all about the wonders of the Tennessee Valley Authority and the New York Port Authority. And if we just call this project the Playground Authority, the taxpayers will fall for it like a ton of bricks.'"

An "unpublic" approach perhaps, but the story exemplifies to some degree the basic function of an authority: it is generally created to accomplish some public or quasi-public purpose that cannot be accomplished through traditional government units.

Residents of a growing area, for example, want a new airport that will serve a multicounty range. Through their elected officials, they petition the state legislature to enact a law permitting formation of such a facility. It will function outside the regular structure of government because it overlaps so many of the traditional units. The sole purpose of the authority will be to finance, construct, dedicate and operate the regional airport.

The enabling legislation may have been passed by the legislature years before and is now a part of the state code. Only an affirmative vote of the electorate may be needed to bring the government unit into being.

The reporter may pick up the story through the legislative proposal, but more than likely the issue will have been argued at length at the local level and will be highly visible through the mass media.

The legislation gives the authority corporate form in an effort to make it more businesslike, assure greater efficiency and create a climate in which lending institutions will be more likely to provide the capital for construction of the facilities. Those same lending institutions see the new government unit as serving a strictly public function; thus, it obtains funds at a more reasonable rate, backed by its public status.

To protect the other governmental units which are unable or unwilling to finance the proposed facility because of limited resources, the state legislature limits their liability. Thus the new government agency cannot impinge on the credit of the older governments.

All these powers, with their concurrent limitations, create a working definition for these authorities:

> A limited legislative agency of corporate form intended to accomplish specific purposes calling for long-range financing of specific public facilities without legally impinging on the credit of the state or local governing unit in which it operates.

The functions performed by these authorities have become so numerous that they have been grouped into basic categories:

—Health and sanitation; protection to persons and property; road transportation facilities and aids; other transportation facilities and aids; utilities; housing; natural resource and agricultural assistance; education; parks and recreation; and cemeteries. Efforts to foster industrial growth in some communities have led to proliferation of authorities specifically designed for this one purpose. So have recreation facilities, such as civic centers, designed to enhance the tourist industry in communities.

The lack of ability by traditional government units to legally finance the major capital improvements wanted by the public is only one of the reasons for the growth of these special districts. Another is the overlapping jurisdictions of local governments, including growth of populations across state as well as county borders. Intercity transportation facilities are feasible because the cities and counties involved can turn to a new umbrella unit of government to handle the operation.

Municipalities in two different states, separated only by a major river, discuss establishment of a port facility that will enhance the industrial growth of the entire region. New industry and increased river traffic is the goal. However, there is a problem: two states and two state legislatures are involved. Action will have to be taken on both sides of the river to establish the authority that can construct, find the financing and ultimately operate the facility.

A reporter covering this complex story must find the answers to these questions:

—What kinds of present legislation does each state possess that will allow such cooperation to take place? What are the limitations imposed by each? Will one or both of the communities have to go to the legislature for special legislation? How will the proposed unit of government be set up? How will it be financed on a preliminary basis? What will its permanent financing be, and who will ultimately pay off the bonds that will be floated to finance the construction? What ties will the new unit have with present governments, and to whom will it be responsible—if to anyone?

The unit created often takes on a special life of its own. Its governing board will probably be appointed by the traditional governments which were reponsible for creating the new unit, or it may be elected through popular referendum, as is frequently the case with school districts, or appointment by state officials. So the relationships between the new unit and its "parent" governing bodies have the potential for becoming fairly complex.

In covering creation of the new port authority, the reporter will discover a wide range of methods through which it may be funded. Grants may be obtained from the federal and/or state governments, contributions solicited from the local "parent" units, funds obtained by floating long-term revenue bonds which must be repaid, and in some cases even private contributions are made.

The new umbrella government has the capability to tie together these various revenue sources, cut across traditional political boundaries and provide a specific facility or service to communities that might not otherwise be feasible.

Claims for their Effectiveness

The rapid growth of these special units of government is only one manifestation of their effectiveness. The sheer volume of physical facilities they have engendered is another. But every government has its advocates and its detractors. These are some of the claims of proponents of special districts and authorities:

—These new governmental units make possible the financing of desperately needed capital construction which otherwise would be impossible under the restrictive debt ceilings in some states. This is done by floating bonds in the name of the authority, usually without obligation to existing governments. Facilities constructed revert to traditional governments when the bonded indebtedness has been paid off. A toll highway constructed in this manner would revert to the state after money from highway users retired the long-term bonds.

—Since these authorities are engaged in only one important function in the community, there is a greater attraction to professional people to associate themselves with it, with a parallel diminution of politicians. Proponents argue that governance of the unit is enhanced because of this ability to draw "better and more informed citizens" to serve on its board and in other capacities.

—Authorities must be businesslike because of the fact that they do not rely normally on direct taxation, but instead must finance themselves through sale of revenue bonds. A businesslike approach assures a good bond rating, which means that interest on the loans is reduced. Proponents argue that, while the authorities' functions are quasi-public, others take on the cast of the private sector, enhancing the businesslike approach.

—By establishing a new unit of government, free of the traditional restraints and relationships of the old, its operators take the functions of the new unit out of politics. By bringing in citizens with successful records of community service and allowing them to operate in a businesslike manner, a nonpolitical cast is placed on the authority, promising greater effectiveness.

—Through their flexibility, authorities make possible the formation of more logical lines of jurisdiction, no longer tied to intractable political boundaries established in another century. Cities, counties and states can cooperate to establish joint ventures not possible in the past.

Opponents Argue the Deficiencies

Not everyone is in agreement on the effectiveness of these governmental units. Critics counter that the special districts and authorities possess the potential for creating more problems than they solve. Here are some of their arguments:

ACCOUNTABILITY

After these authorities are established to perform a specific function, critics argue, they are not sufficiently accountable to the public for their actions. Yet those actions, which often involve the social and economic development of the community, have a direct effect on the lives of the people residing under the umbrella of the unit.

The reporter, as a representative of the public, may find officials of authorities reluctant to provide any information beyond the most superficial. Administrative operations, particularly the financial aspects, lie just a little beyond a closed door. Reportorial persistence, moreover, does not always pay off, and even a trip into the courts for relief may not bring results.

After the *New York Post* filed suit to inspect contract records of New York City's Triborough Bridge Authority, the courts ruled that the authority did not have to provide the records or other information to the newspaper. It ruled that body "is a legal entity, separate and apart from the state which created it, and the city and counties which it serves."

But while the press was denied access, the courts did suggest the authority was not totally immune to scrutiny, noting these other avenues of accountability:

—New York's State Investigation Commission could investigate and audit the authority. So could the comptrollers of New York State and New York City.

—The authority was required to submit an annual detailed report of its operations to the governor of New York.

—The bank which was serving as trustee of the bonds for the bridge authority had the right to investigate the authority's financial operations if it chose to do so.

—The bondholders themselves held special powers to investigate the authority if they desired to do so.

The problem with "investigations" by these officeholders would be the political implications that might come out of them, something that could not be imputed to an impartial reporter asking pertinent questions. The result of the court ruling: the public is involved in this authority's accountability process only in a very peripheral manner.

Critics also contend that members of governing boards of authorities are generally appointed and serve for longer periods of time than do other officeholders. Thus, they are not as accountable to the public as other officeholders who must frequently return to the electorate for a mandate to continue. Governing board members tend to be more insulated from the public and its representatives—the press—and from parent governing bodies. Some authorities, in fact, are given the power to perpetuate themselves by selecting members to vacancies on the board themselves.

The function of an authority is sometimes given as the reason for refusing to make its records available for public inspection. A mental health program, set up to provide privacy to its clients, may have the concurrent effect of closing its financial operations to the press and the public. It defends its accountability to the public by pointing to independent audits that may be scrutinized by other public agencies but not by the press.

The answer is not always easy for the reporter trying to cover these government units, and it often involves subterfuges, such as obtaining fragmentary information from dissident employees or secondhand information from another public agency. At least a part of the answer is maintaining constant pressure on officials, with as much of it in public view as possible, depending on public pressure to build against continued secrecy.

REALLY MORE "BUSINESSLIKE"?

Many observers, including journalists, concede that these special governments possess the potential for a more efficient and businesslike approach to their functions. However, political scientist Kirk Porter complains, "The prime evil of the special district is that it grossly decentralizes administration. It tends to exalt each little service, and tends to make those in charge lose their sense of proportion."

A Southern community, which had created an authority to capture new industry, bringing more jobs to the area and enhancing economic growth, offers an example. After months of maneuvering in secrecy, the authority announced with much fanfare that a "major outside industry" would acquire and construct facilities on prime riverfront property. The public euphoria was short-lived, however, since the "major" firm was finally identified as a cement storage plant that would employ only 17 persons when the facilities were completed.

This poses a further problem for the reporter, who may have sniffed out the information being closely held by officials. Does he or she hold it until the deal is consummated or pass it along to the public and allow inevitable public discussion? In the case of the cement storage plant, public discussion might have been highly beneficial. But, in other cases, the reporter could be blamed if a story is published and the negotiations fall through.

Other critics argue that the single-function approach can be inimical to a community's interests. Says Luther Gulick,

> When you set up a function in a single authority, that single authority knows it was designated by God to do a certain job—and its work is the most important in the world. Nothing can stand in the way of what the authority is planning to accomplish. They don't care if they bankrupt the town—they're going to get their job done because it's the only job they have to do.

Journalists also cite as one of the complicating factors the ability of authorities to shift into and out of the public and private sectors whenever they wish. When a reporter asks to check their records, they are a "private" agency. When they submit an annual budget request to a parent government unit, they become a "public" agency serving the public.

UNDUE BONDHOLDER INFLUENCE

There is always a possibility that the influence of bondholders on the operation of an authority will be disproportionate to that held by other individuals and groups.

Holders of the bonds which must be repaid by the authority out of revenues collected have a right to assurance they will get their money. But critics argue that their influence is not always in the public interest.

Robert Moses, former chairman of the Triborough Bridge

Authority, used investors as an excuse for withholding information on the authority from the press and public. Moses vigorously opposed legislation to have all records of public authorities declared public records, open to inspection by reporters at all times subject to reasonable regulations. He argued, "The general dissemination of information, alleged to be culled from authority files, which distorts and twists the facts in the interests of sensationalism, would necessarily erode investor confidence in authority operations."

From the beginning, the investor gains a pre-eminent role in the operation of an authority. Critics contend that he or she is a far distant but useful tool which authority officials can cite in maintaining secrecy of operation.

FRACTIONALIZATION OF EFFORT

While proponents argue that more logical lines of jurisdiction are possible through these new units of government, critics assert that the majority of the new districts have the same boundary lines as existing governments. They point out that the lines are merely superimposed over those of traditional governments, resulting in a "disguised" government.

These superimpositions may be one reason for public ignorance of these special governments and for lack of coverage by reporters. A county government decides to seek establishment of a water and sewer district that will serve the unincorporated area of the county. The district will not overlap into adjacent counties or the municipalities presently in the county, serving merely as an administrative device for the county commissioners. Over a period of time, the district takes on a life of its own, establishing special relationships with other local governments and with its parent.

Creation of such authorities has resulted in awkward relationships with existing governments, and the cumulative effect may further serve to fractionalize planning and cooperative efforts at the very time that coordination may be a major concern. Carl H. Chatters, a planning expert, argued that "Freezing a single function or activity into an authority may prevent the unification of all government. A careful look ahead is needed in any metropolitan area before the 'fractionating' is frozen even more thoroughly into the governmental structure."

Two researchers, Tina V. Weintraub and James D. Patterson, concluded after a study of Pennsylvania authorities that: "There is virtually nothing an authority can do which could not be done by a regular unit of government, except where the need exists to unify functions and services across municipal or state boundaries."

The reporter may even find that this fractionalizing of effort has a tendency to engender competitive relationships among the government units involved, a far cry from cooperation.

It may be merely a case of personality conflict, or much more seriously, a feeling by two different agencies that their mandate is the more important. A housing authority may be seeking federal funds for a major project and realize that another local government unit is vying for the same money. It will take an arbitrator with uncommon ability to find a solution to this problem, much less sell it to the disputants.

TAKING AUTHORITIES "OUT OF POLITICS"

The boards of many authorities stress their non-political composition, selling themselves to the public as uncorruptible units acting only in the public interest. These units of government do offer a certain insulation between the boards and the pressures of the public which sometimes places a political cast on the proceedings.

Quality of the insulation, however, depends on the locale. One New Jersey county established an authority to handle a single countywide function and then appointed itself as the new unit's governing body. The all-Republican board immediately established itself as a highly political entity, a designation it never relinquished.

As the reporter knows, practical politics continues to play a part in the relationships between the old and the new government units. Citizens who serve on such boards are often political amateurs, who are unaware of this fact. This danger was cited by Dennis O'Harrow, director of the American Society of Planning Officials.

O'Harrow warned that, by use of special districts or authorities, a city "exchanged one set of intelligent politicians, sensitive to the citizens' wishes, for a group of inept politicians who, because of their amateur standing, didn't give a damn about the citizens."

The policy-making board of an authority may in fact be ignorant of day-to-day affairs, meeting only occasionally to put a routine stamp of approval on actions of its administrators. An Eastern newspaper exposed major corruption in a sewage authority and found the governing board unaware of the problems: falsified records, double billing, retroactive bids, misuse of county and state funds, faulty materials used in construction, phony tests and illegal payoffs.

As a practical matter, the idea that creation of a semiautonomous unit of government automatically "takes it out of politics" is far too disarming. Politics and special-interest pressures are much too pervasive.

UNREPRESENTATIVE BOARDS

Many well-informed citizens constitute the boards governing some of this country's authorities, but the question of representation remains.

Research into the characteristics of members of authority boards in Pennsylvania found that members did not mirror the characteristics of the people they were supposed to represent. The comparison, by Paul A. Pfretzchner of Lafayette College, "firmly establishes that Pennsylvania authority members are thoroughly unrepresentative of their communities in terms of their age, education, income, occupation, politics and race."

A further restrictive element in adequate representation lies in the built-in requirements that some members of governing boards be selected from certain groups. Often the enabling legislation for an authority calls for appointments from structured lists: a member of a board of trade or chamber of commerce, a merchant, a banker, an industrialist with specific expertise, or even a tugboat captain in the case of a port authority.

The authority in one Southern community charged with the single function of acquiring new industry for the community listed on its governing board the managers of two of the city's biggest industries, the presidents of the gas and electric companies and two bankers representing the major financial institutions of the city. The mayor of the city served on the board—but merely ex officio. It took years for the local press to work up the courage to point out that the board appeared unrepresentative of the community, but the result was far-reaching changes in the composition of the authority.

ULTIMATE USEFULNESS

A final criticism of authorities is that they have a tendency to self-perpetuate themselves. Because of the decades necessary to retire long-term money obligations, it is difficult to fully assess this criticism.

It is a fact, however, that few authorities have gone out of business. One of the exceptions was a New Jersey city's parking authority which was created in 1953. After conducting business for nine years, board members realized that they could eliminate awkward relationships with the city and save nearly $100,000 in future interest payments by dissolving themselves and turning the authority's functions over to the city. So the assets were given to the parent government and the authority went out of business.

The tendency toward self-perpetuation is epitomized in actions of the New Jersey Highway Authority, which operates the Garden State Parkway. Its original function was to construct and maintain a toll highway parallel to the coast. So successful was the facility that substantial funds were generated by the users, much of which were plowed back into expansion of the highway. However, the authority decided to expand even further to construct a major arts center, accessible only from the toll road. Amid much public controversy generated by this new function, the arts center became a reality in 1968.

Reporting Questionable Practices

Authorities have often been the subject of controversial investigations. Prestigious journalism prizes have been awarded to reporters and their newspapers for uncovering and reporting questionable practices of these units of government.

George Bliss of *The Chicago Tribune* won a Pulitzer Prize in 1962 for his accounts of scandal in the Metropolitan Sanitary District of Greater Chicago, which resulted in discharge of more than 100 employees. The Pulitzer Prize for public service was awarded to *The St. Petersburg* (Florida) *Times* in 1964 for its investigation of spending by the Florida State Turnpike Authority.

In a series of 1975 reports, *The Newark* (N.J.) *Star-Ledger* detailed many abuses in operations in a patchwork of local authorities in northern New Jersey. The *Star-Ledger* reported

> New Jersey's freewheeling system of independent authorities is a jungle of confusion and red tape that has bred and fostered the mismanagement of millions in taxpayers' money.
>
> The authorities were created profusely in the last five years, mainly to finance sewage treatment projects that became too expensive for municipal and county governments.
>
> One high-ranking law enforcement official described the system as a "grab bag" for unscrupulous and sometimes incompetent—but politically well-connected—administrators, lawyers, engineers and contractors, whose fees and salaries often bear little relation to their abilities and performance.
>
> One lawyer, who admitted developing an expertise in sewer authority-related matters because it was a lucrative field, collected $500,000 in fees during a five-year period from sewer authorities he represents. He also collected an additional $370,000 during a four-year period from the municipality which he serves as town attorney, doing much the same legal work as he did for the authorities.

The newspaper's investigation raised further questions about the validity of superimposed government on others, even in such a key area of waste disposal in an urban area.

Individual instances of wrongdoing often surface, despite the essential secrecy provided in authority operation, and court action is sometimes involved. *The New York Times* accounts of questionable activity by officials of the Port Authority of New York offer a good example:

> John Tillman, former director of public affairs for the Port Authority of New York and New Jersey, who admitted last year that he had systematically padded his expense account, was indicted yesterday on criminal charges of defrauding the authority of more than $1,500.
>
> In an 80-count indictment brought by Manhattan District Attorney Robert M. Morgenthau, Mr. Tillman, 61, was accused of grand larceny and falsifying business records. If found guilty, he could face a sentence of seven years in jail.
>
> Malcolm P. Levy, deputy director for physical facilities at the World Trade Center, was also charged with grand larceny of more than $1,500 from the authority in an 86-count indictment. Both men pleaded not guilty to all charges in an arraignment yesterday.

Despite such court action, authorities often continue to treat such matters on a unilateral basis. Without access to their records, reporters must rely on law enforcement officials for information. In this case, the *Times* did obtain some information from spokespersons for the authority.

> Last summer Mr. Tillman was suspended for six weeks from his $55,000-a-year job as director of public affairs after he admitted padding his expense account. He was reinstated as an assistant director on Oct. 17 after he repaid the Port Authority $1,619.91.
>
> Mr. Tillman now earns $49,504 in another public relations post at the Port Authority. A spokesman said neither Mr. Tillman nor Mr. Levy, who earns $52,780, would be suspended from his job, despite the indictments.

Six months later, on Nov. 6, 1978, Tillman was fined $1,000 after he pleaded guilty to reduced charges of petit larceny, official misconduct and offering a false instrument for filing, which are all misdemeanors. The *Times* reported that, after he repaid the Port Authority $1,619.91, Tillman was demoted to the job of director for radio-television-film, with a salary of $49,504 a year.

Tillman's attorney told the court that his client was accused of "something which thousands of businessmen do every day." Tillman maintained that, in falsifying his expenses, he was merely following the accepted practice of colleagues and predecessors. Despite this stated defense, the information will have a sobering effect on the journalist as well as on the public to whom he or she reports.

The Role of the Reporter

A study of the arguments favoring creation of these units of government and the objections to them indicates the complexities which the public affairs reporter faces in dealing with authorities. Because of their unique role as quasi-public institutions, it is substantially more difficult to cover their activities, and reporters often find it nearly impossible to cover official meetings, despite the growth of sunshine laws in many states.

Many boards are secretive about their financial condition and personnel matters. Sometimes it is difficult to determine even routine facts such as how many persons are actually employed by the authority.

Asked for details of an authority's operation by a reporter, one administrator declined to reply except for one cryptic comment: "We simply engage in sound business practices. The public will have to trust us to do a professional job." A response such as this should only inspire any good reporter to insist on digging further into operations which are legitimate public business.

A Midwest newspaper routinely reported the "resignation" of the general manager of an area transit authority. Only after the police reported that the official was later hospitalized for an overdose of sleeping pills did reporters discover that the resignation was more than merely routine. It took persistent pressure on the part of the press to uncover the details of an audit of the authority's operations. Following the audit, the official had been asked to repay more than $2,000 in unauthorized personal expenses, then allowed to "resign" his job. Many authorities tend to operate in similar secrecy.

There is much that is newsworthy about these special units of government, including of course their birth. The opening of a new facility may be marked with great fanfare, while creation of a new authority in another community may occasion little or no notice.

One extreme is illustrated by *The New York Times* account Aug. 30, 1962 of ceremonies opening the second deck of the Port Authority's George Washington Bridge.

> The hour-long ceremony ended with the cutting by the governors of two traditional red-white-and-blue ribbons, one for each state. As the tapes dropped, gold-covered curtains parted and the states' seals, with "Welcome" at the top, were unveiled to 3,000 invited guests. . . . As Governor Hughes' car moved east toward the speakers' platform, Governor Rockefeller was moving west in another 1931 touring car . . . the Coast Guard cutter *Campbell*, at anchor below the bridge, roared a nineteen-gun salute, and harbor craft blasted foghorns.

At the other extreme is the report of the establishment of the Onondaga, N.Y. County Water Authority. "It is significant to note," reported Roscoe C. Martin, "that, except for a brief news story dealing with the original recommendation to the Board of Supervisors by the study committee, practically no publicity attended the creation of the authority. The water authority slipped by without dissent and virtually no notice."

The reporter whose beat includes these authorities should have a working knowledge of their reasons for existence, which takes in the manner in which they were created. That in itself will tell a reporter much about the unit. There are also other "must" questions:

—What are their powers and limitations? What checks and balances keep them responsive to the public? What are the relationships with their parent government? Whom does it employ, and how many? What are the roles of the employees?

The reporter should also be aware of the means employed by the authority to keep its parent government informed of its activities, for this may be one of the keys to important information. If it takes the form of annual reports, the reporter should maintain permanent files to compare them from year to year, researching possibly changing functions in the unit or its operations that may never be publicly announced.

Because of funding requirements, audits may be regularly sought by state and federal governments. The reporter should consider these a means of monitoring the local authority. This may be particularly true of housing authorities which deal in substantial federal funds.

> Open conflict has erupted between the Metropolitan Housing Authority and the U.S. Department of Housing and Urban Development over a HUD report criticizing MHA management.
>
> The report states that the MHA has too many vacant housing units and is not using its financial resources to best advantage.
>
> It also questions the competence of MHA's property management staff, policies regarding staff travel, the use of MHA cars and executives' salaries.
>
> MHA Executive Director Stephen J. Bollinger is bitter about the report: "It fails to acknowledge the tremendous progress we've made here in the last two years."
>
> When he became director two years ago, Bollinger said, MHA was more than $1.2 million in debt. When the books were closed last month, however, MHA was in the black by $1.1, Bollinger argued.
>
> "HUD calls that 'marginal' improvement," Bollinger said disgustedly. "I call it a miracle. No other housing authority in the country has been able to make that kind of turnaround."

Methods should be taken to exert leverage to regularly obtain hard-to-get information on operations of the authority. In this case, cultivation of personnel inside the agency might have offered advance clues as to the problems being encountered. Another area which should be cultivated by the reporter is the client-agency relationship. Sometimes, merely driving into the housing areas themselves and talking to tenants reveal problems that will only surface much later in official audits.

The reporter should never allow the authority to get "too far away from him," always creating the impression for authorities that he or she is totally aware of its activities. Authority sources often dry up in direct proportion to lack of contact with authority officials. Many of them would infinitely prefer for reporters to busy themselves on other beats far removed from their activities.

The reporter should keep superiors informed about the problems of covering such a secretive unit of government. Authority executives often have a healthy respect for power, and knowledge that the editors are especially interested in operations can be helpful in opening some doors.

Because of the sometimes secretive nature of authority operations, information is not always totally accurate. Nothing injures the reporter's effectiveness quite so much as providing officials with an excuse to tell the community, "See, reporters can't get our complex and sensitive information correct and cause us problems in operating in a businesslike manner."

Whatever their amateur or professional status, authority officials often play pressure politics in attempting to operate by their own rules. It is the job of the public affairs reporter to assure that those officials play by the public's rules.

Gaining Needed Familiarity

Preliminary research can be helpful in learning more about these units of government. The following are some methods for becoming more familiar with them:

1. Identify one or more authorities or other special districts in the community and study them to determine their functions and methods of operation. Compare the enabling legislation of one of these authorities with the charter granted to more traditional governmental units, such as a city or town.

2. Plan to cover a regular meeting of an authority, compiling a full report. If the sessions are closed to the public, determine what information is actually made public through the media.

3. After researching the enabling legislation for an authority, interview officials of that agency's "parent" government to get their perceptions of the relationship.

4. Conduct an unscientific but careful survey of average citizens in the community, asking key questions to determine their awareness or knowledge of these special units of government.

Suggested Readings

WALSH, ANNMARIE HAUCK, *The Public's Business* (Cambridge, MA: MIT Press, 1978). The first definitive publication on special district government in many years. Chapter 12, "Reappraisal," should have special interest for the young reporter.

CARO, ROBERT A., *The Power Broker* (New York: Knopf, 1974). Chapter 28, "The Warp on the Loom" and Chapter 43, "Late Arrival" offer insight into the operations and administration of special district government in a metroplitan area.

PART TWO

THE COURTS AND LAW ENFORCEMENT

CHAPTER 7
The Judicial Process

—A small loan company files suit in court to recover more than $13,000 in funds it charges were misappropriated by one of its employees.

—A city in the Midwest files suit to force a firm that has contracted to collect the community's garbage to fulfill its contract obligations.

—A mother files suit to regain custody of her two children, asking the court for an order to force her former husband to produce the children in court.

—The Food and Drug Administration files suit to force a drug manufacturer to conform to new regulations involving a recently marketed drug.

—A pedestrian, who claims he had the right-of-way in a crosswalk, sues the motorist who struck him.

All these claimants are making use of the judicial process to obtain redress for what they consider is a wrong that has been inflicted upon them. The courts constitute the machinery that functions to right or prevent a wrong committed by one person against another.

The same system also functions to punish persons who commit acts deemed injurious to society, instituting criminal action to formally accuse and try them by jury, with subsequent establishment of guilt or innocence through the judicial process.

—A person is charged with burglarizing the home of another, forcing entry to steal a television set and jewelry. The burglary may have been accomplished by a drug addict seeking funds to support a habit or by an unemployed husband desperately seeking a way to support his family, but the procedure is the same. Acting in the name of the public, a law enforcement official prosecutes the person involved.

—A state official is charged with absconding with public funds, a crime punishable by up to five years in prison and a fine of up to $10,000.

—A leading industrial firm is charged with polluting the waters of a nearby lake by discharge of an obnoxious and dangerous chemical, a criminal charge punishable by fines and possible prison terms for employees found responsible.

It is important that the reporter distinguish between a civil action and a criminal proceeding, for, while some of the procedures are similar, the philosophies underlying the process and the final actions reached are vastly different.

Civil actions are filed by private individuals or corporations against other private individuals or corporations seeking enforcement or protection of a right or redress or prevention of a wrong. The court acts as arbiter between the parties in litigation, with a judge or a jury deciding in favor of one litigant or the other. Judgment in a civil action can result in award of financial compensation, in some other form of compensation, or in an order directing a defendant to comply with a directive of the court. However, judgment in such a civil action does not impute criminality.

> A woman who claimed that she developed a disabling condition from birth control pills prescribed by a local physician was awarded $180,000 by a Circuit Court jury yesterday.
>
> Mrs. Joyce T. Nether, 1600 Broad St., had sought $1 million from gynecologist Edward L. Humphrey, charging that he was negligent in failing to inform her of "untoward side effects" from use of the contraceptive Ovulen.

However, a crime offends everyone, and officials file *criminal actions* to punish a person or group of persons who commit acts that have been deemed to be injurious to society.

In such cases the defendant is considered innocent until found guilty by a carefully selected jury. Furthermore, that process itself is preceded by another that first determines whether such a trial is warranted. Because the defendant's reputation and possibly even freedom are at stake, the criminal process offers the accused person many safeguards, not the least of which is the potentially lengthy process leading to a finding of guilty or not guilty. Conviction in a criminal trial can result in imprisonment, a fine or both.

Logan County Sheriff-elect Johnson C. Waggoner was indicted Thursday by a special grand jury investigating charges of vote fraud in the county's primary election in May.

Waggoner was charged with "conspiring to defraud the County of Logan of true, honest and uncorrupted services of its election officials." The second of the two-count indictment charged Waggoner with deceiving and intimidating voters.

Conviction on either count carries a prison sentence of up to five years and/or a fine of up to $10,000.

The Complexities of Court Reporting

No area of public affairs reporting is more complex or more far reaching in scope, attracts greater interest or stands in greater need of accuracy to assure total impartiality than is the reporting of the judicial process. Further, the journalist whose major effort is directed toward the court system will find that the process spills over into every other public affairs beat.

—A labor union seeks an injunction in court to prohibit the manager of an industrial plant from locking out workers during a dispute. Coverage may fall to the court reporter, the labor reporter or a person covering the business beat.

—The state government, acting through its attorney general's office, asks a circuit court judge to forbid a county commission from paying additional funds to public defenders.Coverage could fall to the statehouse reporter, the person covering the county beat or to a court reporter. All governments, in fact, are often in the process of suing or being sued, of forcing judicial action or being forced to act through judicial action. States are constantly involved in court litigation—as plaintiff or defendant.

Attorney General S. Baird Singleton is girding for court battle this month in the state's effort to recapture more than $20 million of overpayments to highway contractors during the past 15 months.

Singleton contends that highway contracts did not reflect the federal government's insistence on additional negotiation of penalty clauses for failing to meet agreed-upon deadlines.

—A school district defends itself in court against charges that it has illegally disbursed funds from the federal government for a project not yet officially sanctioned. One of several reporters might be assigned, including the education writer who has followed the dispute.

—A criminal case involving the murder of a prominent member

of the community goes to trial, possibly moving the story from the hands of the police reporter to the reporter covering the county courthouse.

As these examples show, assignment to cover the courts implies much more than a need for knowledge of legal principles and procedures. The court reporter must be an adaptable "generalist," with a grounding in all areas of public affairs and a familiarity with the major personalities who propel movement in each. The court reporter will also find it essential to develop the ability to translate legal terms and actions into terminology understandable to the average reader.

Federal Judge Irving Kaufman has blamed poor communications for causing public discontent with the nation's legal system and says that the news media is largely at fault: "Judges are forced for the most part to reach their audience through the medium of the press, whose reporting of judicial decisions is all too often inaccurate or superficial," Kaufman noted. However, the judge also criticized the legal profession which, Kaufman said, "has failed to appreciate the vital importance of communication between the courts and the public."

While Kaufman suggested that most reporters lack the training necessary to interpret difficult decisions, there is no reason why any competent reporter cannot successfully cover the courts, given proper direction from his or her editors and assistance from the judicial officers themselves. A basic requirement, however, is a knowledge of the system and how it operates. This ingredient, plus care, accuracy and the ability to cut through the legal thickets, can produce an acceptable court report.

Different Methods of Coverage

No consensus exists on how to cover the courts, and every newspaper and broadcast outlet covers them somewhat differently.

The police reporter may take responsibility for covering the municipal court or police court, mainly because he or she is familiar with the cases there. The county beat reporter may cover the circuit or county court, and general assignment reporters are often responsible for regular checks with the clerk of court for possible stories. Courts at the appellate level are often covered by the statehouse correspondent, mainly because many of those courts are located in the state capital.

The full-time court reporter has become scarcer today, but that specific assignment continues to be the one that offers the best way to assure coverage of the judiciary. The various levels of jurisdiction require constant checking and reliable contacts to assure that cases of great public interest and importance do not lie untouched inside the system.

Lack of reportorial persistence will result in an inadequate report that poorly serves the public. Even the most assiduous reporter runs the risk of missing an important judicial development because of the volume of litigation, and a full-time court reporter provides the assurance that it will not remain unnoticed by the public. There is an ever-present need for regular cross-checking among public affairs beats to guarantee a total report. A tip from a state government reporter, for example, often pays dividends with a timely story that might be overlooked at deadline.

> Six nursing homes have filed suit against the State Department of Public Welfare, charging that they were incorrectly reimbursed for services to Medicaid patients for the years 1975 through 1980.
>
> The suit, filed Wednesday in Common Pleas Court in Columbia, charged that the state failed to use the correct inflation factor in reimbursing the nursing homes as required by law.

Outside the court action itself lie other questions germane to the state government beat: What agency will ultimately have to provide the reimbursement? What effect will the action have on the other 500 nursing homes in the state? What will be the final cost? In this and many other instances, more than one reporter may be grappling with details of court actions that have other implications—and other sources of information.

Going About It

Covering the courts is often a laborious process, particularly if the case is a complicated one. The reporter obtains information by examining court records, covering judicial proceedings including trials, and interviewing court officials, attorneys for the various litigants and the litigants themselves. Access to material depends on the willingness of the court officials to make it readily available to the reporter. Few special rights to court records exist, and the reporter relies instead on the general public's basic right of access to records. This right includes attendance at most judicial proceedings and the right to inspect official court records. Depending on whether the right of access is absolute or conditional, the reporter is free to review and take note of pertinent material or decisions. Conditional right of access to some material makes the reporter dependent upon the clerks or judge of the court.

Attendance at judicial proceedings, such as preliminary hearings or trials, is a right granted to the public rather than specifically to the press. A judge may order such proceedings closed to the public to protect the rights of a defendant, to shield a minor or to maintain courtroom order. In practice, reporters are seldom excluded from such proceedings.

Some court records, such as actions of a grand jury, are not public record until they reach the judge of a court or are read in open court. Depending on the jurisdiction, some preliminary records are denied press scrutiny.

Much of the information that is obtained through the courts is conditionally privileged, which means that a reporter can use such material without fear of libel, provided that it is reported accurately and fairly, and without malice. Errors can destroy conditional (sometimes called "qualified") privilege. Careless notetaking by a reporter at a trial or in copying details of a civil complaint is a constant danger. Most states insist that the report must be of a "public and official proceeding," not related material that emerges outside the proceeding. This privilege extends through courts of record.

Some inferior courts, such as the magistrate's court, police court or municipal court, are often regarded as not being courts of record, but the tendency has been to include most of them under record-keeping powers.

Contempt of Court

The court reporter, as well as the general public, operates under a special condition: the judge's power to cite for contempt. Any act which the judge construes as hindering or obstructing the court in its effort to fairly administer justice or to embarrass it subjects a person to contempt of court.

The reporter must always be aware that the judge reigns supreme in his or her court and possesses the arbitrary power to fine and/or imprison anyone determined to be in contempt of court. It is not at all uncommon for a judge to send a reporter to the lockup to cool his or her heels there overnight for what the presiding judge in a case perceives to be an infraction of the rules he or she has set.

Such penalties are enforceable unless they are reversed on appeal to a higher court. Reporters should remember that they are as susceptible to contempt as anyone else, and for the same reasons.

In a pending trial of a public official on sexual misconduct charges, the presiding judge took steps to limit the coverage of the case.

> Although the trial was expected to receive extensive publicity, visiting Judge George J. McGillivery has placed limits on some aspects of that coverage. He has prohibited news interviews with witnesses, or photographing and interviewing of jurors.
>
> McGillivery has also forbidden the photographing of any women called to testify. Some female witnesses previously were reluctant to testify because television cameras are being allowed in the courtroom.

The court reporter or photographer who breaks such rules does so at his or her own peril.

Publication of stories that include criticism of a pending case, which the judge believes has obstructed justice, can create a situation in which the reporter is found in contempt and remanded to jail for a specified length of time or an indefinite period.

Reasons for contempt citations include publication of grand jury testimony which has not yet been made public by the court; serious inaccuracies in reporting a trial, including what the judge perceives as the absence of a complete or balanced report; publication of stories deemed prejudicial to the case; or refusal of a reporter to break a confidence while testifying on the witness stand. Often a reporter will find himself or herself in possession of information that the court sees as important to a case.

The issue of confidentiality between the reporter and his or her sources continues to be debated, and some journalists have spent weeks in jail after refusing to disclose sources of material after being ordered to do so by a judge. Some states have enacted shield laws designed to protect the reporter, but in most jurisdictions the journalist continues to be at the mercy of the presiding judge.

The alert court reporter will find that the contempt process extends to the public, and is often newsworthy, as this Washington Post report shows.

> Each month a diverse collection of divorced fathers who have consistently failed to make regular child-support payments is called to Montgomery Circuit Court to explain why they should not be thrown in jail.
>
> The pageant of wheedling, mumbling, last-minute bargaining and tall-tale telling that ensues during these court sessions is known as Contempt Day.
>
> Yesterday's session offered an education in extenuating circumstances as parents in arrears tried to explain themselves to Judge William Cave.
>
> "I've been trying to get a business started for five years," explained a Silver Spring father who had fallen more than $2,000 behind in child support payments.
>
> But why hadn't he showed up in court last month? "I didn't see my name on the docket," he explained.
>
> The judge was not convinced. He sentenced the man to 90 days in the Montgomery Detention Center for contempt of court. The sheriffs closed in on the father, snapped the handcuffs on and took him away.
>
> It had a chastening effect on the 35 persons waiting yesterday to plead their cases.

Attorneys involved in a court case are also susceptible to citations for contempt. Sometimes the jury's verdict in a case is accompanied by an order from the judge directing that an attorney pay a fine for contempt, on grounds he or she exceeded the bounds of propriety in handling a case.

A Basic Definition

A law is a rule of conduct, action or procedure prescribed or formally recognized as binding or enforced by a controlling authority. These rules are promulgated by the people, legislative bodies, other branches of organized political government, the church and judicial officers themselves.

Custom and conduct dictate adherence to prescribed laws; thus an old and obscure state statute may forbid all smoking on school property, yet custom allows school administrators to smoke in their private offices. An old municipal statute still on the books may prohibit gambling within corporate limits, yet bingo games and frequent raffles may flourish in many churches. "Blue laws" may prohibit the sale of merchandise on Sunday, but officials in a community may look the other way and allow it. The reporter should make it his or her business to know the applicable law and the practical application of it.

All law has its origins in morality, custom, religious decrees, treaties, institutions, legislation and judicial decisions. The law in this country dates to England and can be separated into broad categories—common law and statutory law.

Common Law

This grows out of usage and custom, built up over generations, and is produced by cases decided through the litigation process. It is often referred to as the law of decided cases. Unless specifically changed by statute, common law is generally observed in the United States. One of its significant characteristics is precedent, under which the judiciary makes use of a previous decision to adjudicate the case at issue. Common law has survived because of the willingness of judges to adapt it to changing times.

Although common law is not codified like statutory law, much of it appears in written form through the judgments in cases that are decided and reported. Since most courts maintain records, the ability of the judiciary—and reporters—to research precedent-setting decisions has contributed to the continuing strength of the system.

Equity, an important supplement to common law, also dates to early England, where "law courts" were established to administer the common law. Equity was based on the custom of appealing to the king or chancellor when the common law did not provide relief.

Equity began where the law ended, taking the form of judicial decrees rather than merely a judgment of "yes" or "no." Under equity, judgments take the form of preventive or remedial measures, such as an order calling for specific performance or an injunction or restraining order. Equity is designed to provide remedies not otherwise obtainable.

A glass-making firm may seek an injunction from a judge to restrain employees who are about to strike from leaving their jobs until they bank the furnaces in the plant. A property owner may ask for court relief to restrain a county highway department from cutting down a 100-year-old tree at the edge of his property until a hearing is held on the right-of-way dispute.

There are no separate courts of equity at the federal level, although some states retain separate courts.

Statutory Law

While this country operates today under systems based on the common law which found its way here from England, the framework for both the federal and state judiciary is a mixture of common and statutory law.

Statutory law is created by legislation, and thousands of government bodies, ranging from tiny towns to the Congress, are constantly in the process of enacting them. Being coded, statutory law may replace common law and other judicial precedent. Sections of a code may be revised, updated or replaced outright, calling for care that an untouched section doesn't negate the intent of the legislators.

The influence of statutory law upon the public depends on many factors—enforcement, exemptions, type of statute and jurisdiction. A state legislature may enact a new statute requiring gun registration. Authorities enforce the statute, administering its provisions, but the courts adjudicate the disputes which arise when the law is alleged to have been broken.

Much of this country's statutory law provides for reasonable discretion on the part of the judge, with a jury reaching its decision and a judge pronouncing sentence. A guilty verdict by a jury in a criminal case may give the judge the discretion to set the sentence so long as it does not breach the maximum and minimum penalties provided by the statute.

> Frank J. Hern, a prominent Swiss County coal broker, was sentenced to four years in prison Tuesday after his conviction for interstate transportation of stolen coal.
>
> Hern had been convicted Sept. 1 of fraudulently disposing of more than 2,300 tons of coal taken from Consolidated Coal Co.'s Swiss County mine in 1979.
>
> U.S. District Court Judge Charles M. Francis recommended that Hern serve at least two years of the sentence and also imposed a $5,000 fine. Hern could have received as much as 10 years in prison and been fined as much as $10,000.

Substantive vs. Procedural Law

The home purchaser who files suit in the appropriate court alleging a breach of contract by the firm constructing the house is basing his litigation on substantive law regulating such contracts. *Substantive law* creates, defines and regulates rights.

After the suit is filed, both the plaintiff, the party who alleges injury, and the defendant, the party against whom the suit is filed, follow procedural law, that body of rules through which the substantive law is administered.

Procedural law, with which the court reporter must be thoroughly familiar, dictates the progress of the suit or criminal action and the frequent stories that will be written during the course of important litigation.

A defendant charged with passing a number of fraudulent checks after forging another's name to them is brought to court under substantive law forbidding such action and making it a criminal offense. In appearing at an arraignment before a magistrate who orders a preliminary hearing to determine whether the defendant should be bound over to a grand jury, procedural law is being followed.

The chairman of the Airport Commission who files a civil suit to force the county government to fulfill its financial commitment is relying on the substantive agreements governing the two bodies. But the complaint, the answer and subsequent pleadings flow out of the procedural law which governs the litigation process.

While substantive law and its ramifications constitute the basis for news reporting, the court reporter should not overlook the news inherent in the judicial process itself. Changes in a court system's process of jury selection, for example, are newsworthy because they affect the residents of entire communities.

New legislation, such as the federal statute calling for speedier trials for defendants, often changes the procedures under which courts operate. Movement is under way in some areas to reduce the size of juries in criminal trials from the present 12 members. The U.S. Supreme Court often renders decisions which affect handling of judicial affairs at the local level. The court reporter should remain abreast of such procedural developments through perusal of judicial journals as well as monitoring federal and state actions concerning the court systems.

Jurisdiction

The attorney leaned back in his chair and studied the ceiling, pondering the question by his client. Finally he responded: "Our best bet in winning this case is over in Judge Leander's court. That's where you drew up the contract and filed it, even though you live over in Columbia now."

The attorney subsequently files a complaint in Leander's court and the suit begins its course through the litigation process. The power or right to interpret or apply the law is called jurisdiction. Jurisdiction also sets the limits of that power. The U.S. Constitution or statutes of each state and the federal government determine the jurisdiction of the courts.

In the suit noted, Judge Leander may dismiss it, claiming lack of jurisdiction and recommending that it be refiled with another court.

Original jurisdiction is the power to hear a civil or criminal action and pursue it through the trial process. The district court is the court of original jurisdiction in the federal system; each state has its own court of original jurisdiction.

Appellate jurisdiction is the power to receive a judgment in a civil or criminal action and to uphold or reverse it. Both the state and federal systems embody a system of appellate courts.

Courts of *limited jurisdication* are bound by statute to a specified and limited area, such as magistrate, police or municipal courts. Many states limit these inferior courts to cases involving a maximum of $500, $1,500 or $2,000 in damages. Others limit magistrates to matters involving minor infractions of the law, such as traffic violations. Judgments of these courts are subject to review in courts of original jurisdiction.

The Dual System of Courts

"Don't make a federal case out of it."

How many times have we heard someone use that nearly universal expression in an effort to minimize the importance of an action? While the importance of a state "case" often far outweighs that of a federal "case," the expression helps to explain the dual system of national and state courts in the United States, which exist side by side.

The process of justice proceeds at two distinct levels—a federal system that exists throughout the 50 states and the different state systems themselves, all similar in makeup and function.

Although the judicial systems in the 50 states are similar, wide differences exist in selection of court officers, organization, distribution of functions, jurisdiction and even in terminology. The net result of judicial coverage, however, is the same.

Most of the legal business of the nation is transacted at these state levels, with the federal judiciary empowered to handle only those actions specified by the U.S. Constitution. All powers not specifically delegated to the federal government by the Constitution fall automatically to the states, and so each state's judicial process remains uniquely its own.

The Federal Courts

A simple fork in the judicial highway creates a "federal case" in the process of litigation. It is important that the reporter be able to identify the fork and have a clear understanding of the role and scope of the federal system.

One section of the road leads to litigation in the state courts, the other to the federal courts, with Article 3 of the U.S. Constitution acting as the catalyst:

> The judicial Power shall extend to all cases in Law and Equity, arising under this Constitution, the laws of the United States, the Treaties made, or which shall be made, under their Authority:
>
> —to all cases affecting ambassadors, other public ministers and consuls;
>
> —to all cases of admiralty and maritime jurisdiction;
>
> —to controversies to which the United States shall be a party;
>
> —to controversies between two or more states, between a state and citizens of another state, between citizens of different states, between citizens of the same state claiming lands under grants of different states, and between a state, or the citizens thereof, and foreign states, citizens or subjects.

The Constitution also vests the U.S. Supreme Court with original jurisdiction in all cases affecting ambassadors and other public ministers and cases in which a state is a litigant. With these constitutional limits in mind, the fork in the judicial terrain becomes comparatively easy to identify.

After setting these limits for the federal judiciary, all other judiciary proceedings were left to the state through the 10th Amendment to the Constitution:

All powers not delegated to the United States by the Constitution, nor prohibited by it to the states, are reserved to the States respectively, or to the people.

All judicial power is vested in one Supreme Court and in such inferior courts as the Congress might establish. The U.S. District Court is the federal court of original jurisdiction and serves as a trial court. Most cases deserving public notice originate in the district court, and many conclude at that level, although the appellate process exists.

> A former teller for the Guarantee National Bank pleaded guilty yesterday in U.S. District Court to embezzling $6,700 from the bank last year.
>
> Caesar Willmarco, 25, 1206 Martinez Rd., was employed in Guarantee's main office for three years. He will be sentenced Aug. 23, after probation reports are completed and submitted to the court.

Since federal banking laws cover such criminal activity, these cases are heard in the federal courts. The Congress has enacted thousands of such pieces of legislation, which provide for settlement of disputes in the federal system.

THE DISTRICT COURTS

Every state has at least one district court, with more populous states having as many as four. There are 90 district courts, with each court maintaining from one to 27 judges, depending upon the case load within each jurisdiction.

Until 1891, all cases in the district courts were appealed directly to the Supreme Court. Since that time, appellate courts have taken on the brunt of the appeals process. Federal appeals courts around the country are empowered to review all final decisions of district courts, except where the law provides for a direct review by the Supreme Court.

These are some of the types of cases that would be adjudicated in the federal rather than the state courts:

—A seaman is injured while working on a dredge in the Mississippi River. He files suit, claiming negligence on the part of the firm operating the equipment.

—A New Jersey resident vacationing in Florida is struck by an auto driven by a Florida resident. Claiming that the injuries were substantial and were inflicted through negligence on the part of the Florida driver, the New Jersey resident might sue in federal court. If both were residents of the same state, the suit would be filed in state court.

—A dispute over the right of way for a proposed bridge spanning the Ohio River between West Virginia and Ohio would be litigated in the federal courts.

—Theft of a motor vehicle, with subsequent recovery and arrest in another state, would be prosecuted in federal district court, since federal law prohibits transportation of a stolen vehicle across a state line.

Since the Constitution delegated power over a broad range of activity to the federal government, the federal courts hold jurisdiction in such areas as bankruptcy, regulation of foreign and interstate commerce, patents and copyrights, postal and currency activity, and taxation. Meanwhile, legislation working its way through Congress is annually expanding the jurisdiction enjoyed by the federal courts.

> Charlottesville, Va. (AP)—A federal railway inspector will recommend federal prosecution of two railroads and a chemical company for an Aug. 4 incident in which a railway tank car rolled into Charlottesville leaking the toxic chemical carbon disulfide.
>
> C. K. Kreh, hazardous materials inspector with the Federal Railway Administration, said Thursday that Conrail, the Chessie System and FMC Corp. violated federal regulations by failing to observe proper procedures following an incident involving the same tank car in Illinois, and thus allowed the Charlottesville incident to occur.

A charge of forgery, for example, would be prosecuted in the state courts, but, if use of the mails were involved, the case would be remanded to federal district court for action. A burglary of a post office facility would lead to prosecution in federal court, and possession of a stolen postal money order or social security check would subject a person to federal prosecution.

> Four men who Federal Bureau of Investigation agents say were part of an interstate theft operation were indicted yesterday by a federal grand jury in Cleveland on charges that they stole bulldozers and other construction equipment in Illinois and disposed of them in Ohio.
>
> At least $200,000 in equipment has been identified as part of the ring's thefts, the Justice Department announced.

A huge body of federal laws has grown through legislative action, and a multitude of agencies posesses the power to prosecute those who break the laws. Theft of dynamite in a mining state would be prosecuted by the Bureau of Alcohol, Tobacco and Firearms. Transportation of illegal drugs from the East to the West Coast might be prosecuted by several agencies at the federal level, including the Federal Bureau of Investigation and the Drug Enforcement Administration.

HOW THE DISTRICT COURTS OPERATE

The district court is the workhorse for the federal judiciary. Dockets are separated into criminal cases, civil disputes, admiralty actions and bankruptcy proceedings. Suits are filed with the clerk of district court, whether they are "local" actions or they emanate from an executive agency in Washington, D.C. Federal civil proceedings become public record when the pleadings are filed.

> Washington (AP)—In a major blow to President Carter's anti-inflation program, a federal judge ruled yesterday that Carter had overstepped his constitutional power in trying to enforce his wage-price guidelines.
>
> U.S. District Court Judge Barrington D. Parker said neither the Constitution nor Congress gave Carter authority to threaten to deny federal contracts to companies that violate his "voluntary" guidelines.
>
> The decision does not prevent the president from using his influence—"benign jawboning" in the judge's words—to obtain purely voluntary support for his guidelines from business and labor.
>
> But it disarms the administration of a big club to enforce the guidelines.
>
> The Justice Department said it would seek to have the decision overturned by the U.S. District Court of Appeals. Meanwhile, federal attorneys said, they will ask Parker to delay issuing his order.

The chambers of federal judges often serve as courts of last resort for groups seeking extraordinary legal remedies.

> Plans by the Navy to slaughter more than 3,000 goats living wild on a Navy-owned island off southern California were disrupted Tuesday when a consortium of humane groups obtained a temporary restraining order barring a helicopter hunt that had been scheduled to begin tomorrow.
>
> The order, which expires in 10 days, was issued by Federal Judge Robert Takasugi of Los Angeles a few hours after it was sought by groups asserting that the planned killing on San Clemente Island was unnecessary and inhumane. The Navy said its sole purpose was to comply with the Federal Endangered Species Act.

Such orders often postpone planned action for months while the process sorts itself out in court hearings.

District court judges are provided with an assortment of assistants to help carry on the work of the court, including magistrates, law clerks, bailiffs, court reporters, probation officers and professional administrators to relieve the judges of management duties.

The U.S. magistrate, formerly called a commissioner, is an indispensible aid to the system, with authority to take action on a substantial number of preliminary legal moves in federal cases. As a federal justice of the peace, the magistrate issues arrest warrants, holds preliminary examinations to determine whether to detain an accused person for federal grand jury action, and sets bail for the accused.

Much of the reporter's contact at the federal courthouse will be with the magistrate and his or her assistants, who may assume responsibility in some minor federal cases when the defendant waives his or her right to have the case heard by judge and jury. The magistrate also appoints legal counsel for indigent defendants and is active in pretrial civil proceedings.

Working closely with the magistrate is the marshal, who is empowered to make arrests, guards and transports prisoners, and maintains order in the federal courtrooms. The marshal is also an administrative official, with responsibility for disbursing federal judicial funds, serving court orders and transporting federal documents. The marshal functions under authority of the U.S. attorney general, rather than under that of the district court judge whom he or she nominally serves.

The federal judge, marshal and the U.S. attorney, another important officer of the federal district court, are appointed by the president, with the advice and consent of the United States Senate. Patronage and the wishes of influential members of the president's political party often play a major part in the selection of these federal officials.

THE APPELLATE COURTS

Decisions rendered in the federal district courts can be taken on to the U.S. Court of Appeals and in a few cases directly to the Supreme Court. The 11 appeals courts, often still referred to as "circuit courts," also possess statutory power to review and enforce the actions of many federal agencies, among them some rulings of the National Labor Relations Board, the Department of Labor, the Federal Communications Commission, the Civil Aeronautics Board and the Interstate Commerce Commission.

But most of the work of these courts is of an appellate nature, since it is the first stop from the district courts.

> Richmond, Va. (UPI)—The U.S. Fourth Circuit Court of Appeals has affirmed the 1980 conviction of a West Virginia attorney for mail fraud.
>
> The appellate court ruled that the evidence against Harley C. Majors, a 48-year-old Clarksburg resident, was "overwhelming." He had been convicted by a federal district court in Clarksburg and sentenced to five years in prison.
>
> Major's conviction stemmed from a scheme to obtain money from an insurance company after a suspicious fire destroyed three antique autos.

OTHER FEDERAL COURTS

Several other federal courts which operate with special functions include the U.S. Court of Claims, the U.S. Customs Court, the U.S. Court of Customs and Patent Appeals, the U.S. Court of Military Appeals and the territorial courts.

The U.S. Court of Claims adjudicates suits brought by citizens against the federal government, most of them involving government contracts. Some involve attempts to collect damages for injuries by negligent behavior of federal employees; others are brought in an effort to collect compensation for the taking of private property for public purposes. This court represents an institutional arrangement whereby the federal government can be sued within a fairly narrow range, and eliminates what might become a flood of special legislation in the Congress.

The U.S. Customs Court, which sits at ports of entry throughout the country, reviews rulings and appraisals of imported goods by customs collectors. Its' decisions can be appealed to the Court of Customs and Patent Appeals, which also reviews decisions made by the U.S. Patent Office on patents and trademarks. The appeals court also reviews import practices of the U.S. Tariff Commission.

The U.S. Court of Military Appeals, staffed by civilians, reviews decisions concerning military personnel. While there is no direct appeal from this court, the Supreme Court and federal appeals courts occasionally exercise jurisdiction and become involved in the proceedings.

The territorial courts exercise a function similar to the federal district courts but are tailored somewhat differently depending on specific local needs.

THE SUPREME COURT

At the pinnacle of the federal judiciary, the Supreme Court sits as the final arbiter in the judicial process. Its decisions are final. As a practical matter, however, the court possesses discretionary power to reject an appeal on the ground that the federal issue is inappropriate or insubstantial, leaving the final outcome of the case in the hands of a lower court. This discretionary power has cut down on the appeals from state courts, but the Supreme Court's caseload remains heavy—more than 5,000 cases docketed annually. While full written opinions may number fewer than 200 annually, most of the cases brought before the court are disposed of in some manner—affirmed, reversed, dismissed or remanded to a lower court.

Disputes between or among states are taken directly to the Supreme Court, and the pleadings can take several terms of court.

Cincinnati (AP)—Fish and game officials in Kentucky and Ohio are watching carefully as fishermen slip in and out of what they call the "gray areas" of the Ohio River.

The uncertainty is caused by the boundary dispute currently before the U.S. Supreme Court.

The suit, filed in 1966 by William Saxbe, then Ohio attorney general, seeks to establish how much of the Ohio River is owned by Kentucky.

As it stands now, the boundary is on the north bank of the river. A special master appointed by the Supreme Court has recommended that the low-water mark of the river in 1792 be fixed as the boundary between the states. Dams have raised the river level since that time, causing Ohio to lose land.

Many months later, the court ruled on a case which it had been studying for more than 14 years.

> Washington (AP)—Like the sands of time, the banks of rivers may shift. But the boundary between the states of Ohio and Kentucky remains fixed where it was nearly two centuries ago, the Supreme Court ruled Monday.
>
> In a 6-3 decision, the court said the boundary line between the two states is the low-water mark on the northern shore of the Ohio River as it existed in 1792 when Kentucky was admitted to the union.

The State Courts

The gavel bangs and the municipal court judge pronounces the verdict: guilty, he says of the defendant charged with allowing his dog to run loose on the streets. The dog's owner is fined $25 and charged an additional $15 in court costs as the result of the breaching of the ordinance.

The defendant did not deny the offense, which had led to the dog's biting the daughter of another resident, but pleaded to the judge that it was unintentional. A youngster had left a screen door ajar, and the dog had escaped to begin its foray. After rejecting the defendant's argument and assessing the fine, the judge adds a final statement: "This is the limit of jurisdiction of this court," he admonishes the parties. "For other relief you will have to file action in another court."

Subsequently, the defendant judged guilty decides not to appeal his sentence to a higher court. But the other party files a civil action in circuit court to recover substantial hospital costs and other damages alleged to have been inflicted on the family.

Each state constitution, codification of statutes, or a combination of both specifies the jurisdiction and function of a system of courts. Although many different designations are used, they are generally known as inferior courts, courts of original jurisdiction, intermediate appeals courts and the highest appeals courts. The inferior courts, or courts of limited jurisdiction, such as magistrate, municipal or police courts, are empowered to hear and rule on litigation that is deemed minor, whereas more serious cases are heard in courts of general jurisdiction known as trial courts.

A traffic offense or a dispute over a small claim might be heard in a municipal court, with a judge authorized to hear and weigh the evidence and hand down a ruling that is appealable to a higher court. A more serious charge, such as robbery, burglary or fraud, would be taken to a higher court.

Disposal of a traffic charge may conclude the case in municipal or city court. Suppose, however, that a motorist strikes and injures a pedestrian in a crosswalk while running the red light. The injured pedestrian may seek relief in a trial court, initiating action to recover thousands of dollars in hospital and other medical costs.

The identity of the court of general jurisdiction in which the pedestrian seeks relief depends on the state. In Alabama it is known as Circuit Court; in North Carolina it is Superior Court; in Colorado it is District Court; in Ohio it is the Court of Common Pleas; and in South Carolina it is General Sessions or Common Pleas.

Some court systems lump civil and criminal cases together, often detailing specific judges to hear one or the other; other systems employ separate probate courts; and still others operate separate chancery (equity) courts. In sparsely populated areas, a single judge will serve a judicial district. In metropolitan areas, more than 100 judges are often elected to dispose of thousands of cases annually. Many urban counties provide for trial courts to handle cases that originate in them and intermediate appellate courts to handle the first appeal in the long process toward the state supreme court.

A HIERARCHY OF FUNCTIONS

The lowest court at the state level is that of *Justice of the Peace*, an office that dates to 13th century England. In many cities this inferior court has become *Magistrate's Court*, *Municipal Court* or *Mayor's Court*, administering justice in minor matters. Generally an elective office, the justice of the peace need not even possess a law degree in some areas of the country and is elected for a term of office ranging from two to 10 years. Many JPs, as they are called, continue to perform quasi-judicial duties such as performing civil marriages for a fee, signing county documents and issuing warrants of arrest to law enforcement agents.

Such courts have specific limits, usually set by the state legislature, often hearing civil cases involving no more than $2,000, and criminal cases involving only misdemeanors. Judgments are appealable to the next level of court jurisdiction.

The JP's office is an excellent source of news tips because the justice of the peace maintains a close relationship with police.

Aside from issuing warrants and conducting other business for law enforcement authorities, JP courts are often empowered to hold preliminary hearings for persons charged with a crime, set bail for persons accused of minor crimes, and bind over persons accused of more serious crimes to a higher court or to a grand jury for action.

> A Wellington salesman was charged with armed robbery yesterday after the victim of a knife-point confrontation pointed him out to police.
>
> Arrest records identified the suspect as Paul D. Haynes, 28, 1500 Sussman Ave., who was placed in the county jail in lieu of $15,000 bond set by Magistrate William R. Baker.

Whatever the identity of these inferior courts, their jurisdiction remains limited to misdemeanors and small claims court action.

For a filing fee of as little as $10, a person can seek recompense for any wrong or injury. Usually there is no need to hire an attorney. Buyers of merchandise can sue for damages to the merchandise, people in business may sue to collect unpaid bills, babysitters or day workers may sue for unpaid wages.

The court reporter often finds a wealth of feature material in these inferior courts. A resident filed a 35 cent lawsuit against a soft drink firm, charging that she had purchased a defective can of soda. The firm capitulated out of court, settling for five cases of soda and the 35 cents. Another woman collected $150 in damages after filing suit against a professional laundry and charging that it had shrunk her lingerie to a point where it would not fit.

Usually the claims must be for money only, since some courts are empowered to utilize that specific remedy.

As the courts of general jurisdiction, the county or area trial courts originate the bulk of important cases for the state judiciary. Geographically, the courts generally cover one or more counties. It is these courts that the reporter will monitor most carefully. More serious litigation, both civil and criminal, will work its way through these systems.

More than half the states utilize an intermediate Court of Appeals, which is almost wholly appellate in nature. Some have an elaborate intermediate structure, such as that in New York state, which has more than 150 appellate courts.

Major litigation, both civil and criminal, works its way through the judicial process to a final court of appeals, whose main purpose it is to determine the law rather than the facts. The highest state court may be designated as the Supreme Court, but some states refer to it as the Supreme Judicial Court or the Court of Appeals.

> The state is not liable for the death or injury of persons in state-owned parks if the victims didn't pay to enter the grounds, the state Supreme Court held Wednesday.
>
> It also ruled that a worker who is declared permanently and totally disabled and is being paid benefits for an occupational disease can receive additional disability benefits for a separate injury.
>
> In the park decision, the court considered a case involving a broken ankle a woman suffered when she stepped in a hole and a damage claim by the mother of a girl who drowned in an accident involving a rented canoe.

Staffing the Courts

Judicial officials and the paperwork that flows through their offices are important to the reporter. At an early stage, he or she should make it a point to determine the decision-making process and the flow of documents to assure the quality of the news report.

The functions and responsibilities of each official are fairly clear-cut—from the judge to the probation officer. Other common offices in the system include the clerk of court, bailiff, court reporter, prosecuting attorney, public defender, and other attorneys who have an interest in a particular case.

Depending on the jurisdiction, other officials might include a friend of the court, commissioner, referee, master, receiver and monitor. As already noted, two of the most significant officers at the federal level are the marshal and the U.S. attorney.

The Judge

The chief officer in the judicial process is the judge, and the system revolves around him or her. Judicial records may be maintained in the clerk's office in another part of the building, but the decision-making at nearly every point in the process flows out of the judge's chambers.

The clerk may prepare trial lists called dockets or calendars, with the concurrence of the presiding judge or judges, and final approval rests with that official or officials.

Most of the more than 12,000 judges in state and local courts are elected, but the appointive method is used exclusively at the federal level. Except for inferior court staffing, such as justices of the peace, judges are drawn almost entirely from the legal profession. The 657 federal judges are appointed by the president, subject to confirmation by a simple Senate majority, but other factors intrude to complicate the selection process. Consultation is necessary with the political powers in the home state of the candidate for judicial office, including the senators. This story points up the political problems that often arise.

> Washington—Ohio's two U.S. senators have been unable since January to agree on guidelines for recommending one of five nominees as the new federal judge for Columbus.
>
> John Glenn and Howard Metzenbaum, both Democrats, were called to the attorney general's office Monday to discuss the impasse. A method was suggested for speeding up the process, but Glenn is not entirely satisfied with it, his aides say. Metzenbaum has agreed to the method.
>
> Metzenbaum's press secretary, Roy Meyers, blames Glenn for the delay in making the recommendation. He said Metzenbaum has repeatedly asked Glenn to meet and select nominees, to no effect.
>
> Glenn's administrative assistant, William R. White, blames the delay on published reports that Metzenbaum had tampered with the nominating commission's selections for the two judgeships authorized for the Northern District of Ohio.

Another group which has played an increasingly important role in appointment of federal judges is the American Bar Association's Committee on the Federal Judiciary, which is asked to evaluate potential candidates. The 12-member committee, established in 1946, has become a powerful factor in the nominating process.

Politics plays a part in selection of judges at the state level as well. Proponents of the election method, which is used most often, argue that it is better to select a judge through a partisan ballot method than to engage in what they refer to as the "horse-trading" and the "wheeling-dealing" by political figures. Proponents of the appointive method argue that the judicial candidate who must run on a partisan ballot cannot possibly serve as an impartial judge. Such a political process, they argue, impinges on the basic need for total impartiality on the bench. Furthermore, they argue, the uninformed electorate may not be in a position to evaluate the legal abilities of the candidates.

While some states call for candidacy on bipartisan or nonpartisan tickets, long and loyal service in partisan politics is generally a prerequisite for nomination. Elective terms of office are considerably longer than they are in other public jobs, ranging from four to 12 years, with some terms extending to life.

Some states have undertaken compromises between the elective and appointive method of choosing judges. Under the California plan, the governor nominates a candidate for office, subject to approval by a Commission on Qualifications. The candidate serves for one year, then stands for election to a full 12-year term of office, his or her name being the only one on a nonpartisan ballot.

Under the Missouri plan, nonpartisan nominating boards select three candidates, and the governor is obliged to appoint one of them to a one-year term, subject to confirmation by the voters at the end of the year for a full term on the bench.

The judge rules supreme within the jurisdiction of his or her court, be it inside the courtroom itself during a trial or in administering the far-reaching details surrounding that proceeding. The clerk of court may summon the prospective juror for a term of jury duty, but the judge usually makes the decision to excuse the juror for whatever reason.

As the presiding official, the judge exercises what is known as "inherent power" to assure impartial and efficient administration of justice. Through this means, he or she commands decorum in the courtroom, assures attendance by all of those involved in the disposition of a pending case, and in other ways safeguards the administration of justice. The judge may punish a recalcitrant witness with contempt of court, an attorney who may seek to unduly delay disposition of the case, or a newspaper reporter who the judge believes has interfered with administration of justice.

> Nathan J. Rexrod told Federal District Court Judge Robert Maxwell yesterday that he had more important things to do, such as handle his business affairs, than be sworn in as a juror in Maxwell's court.
>
> Maxwell wasn't sympathetic. He fined Rexrod $150 for failing to show up for jury duty and ordered him to spend 24 hours in the Randolph County jail.

While actions are pending, the judge issues orders (often called rulings or rules) which are directives other than judgments. Orders are issued orally or in writing, often on a motion by one of the attorneys involved in the action. The order may require a witness to appear in court with specific records or may delay proceedings while a defendant obtains information from another jurisdiction.

In jurisdictions in which two or more judges handle actions, a presiding judge is appointed—through seniority, rotation or election. He or she serves as administrative officer, assigning cases to specific judges and ruling on technical matters within that jurisdiction. Occasionally a judge with too many criminal cases being routinely overturned in the appeals process will find himself or herself reassigned to minor civil litigation. The careful reporter will keep track of such reversals, and, while a story of record may be an embarrasssment to the judge in question, it is of interest to the public.

In cases where conflict of interest is possible, the presiding judge may also assign a different judge to hear the case.

Many actions of judges are routine, but others are worthy of coverage, depending upon the importance of the case. The reporter's working relationship with the judge is important, and often a court clerk will send the reporter on to the judge's office for information about a pending case. Most judges will take the time to explain the significance of a ruling to reporters.

The Court Clerk

The clerk and his or her assistants are the officials with whom the reporter will have the most frequent contact. In many areas it is an elective office, although in some places the clerk is appointed by the judge.

The clerk is the custodian of all court records, including the papers and exhibits scheduled to be brought into trial court. All money paid to the court is in the safekeeping of the clerk, who makes regular accountings and keeps records of funds received. All these are public record.

During the course of a day, the reporter will consult with the clerk or assistants to determine suits filed, preliminary motions in pending trials, or papers filed during the course of a trial. Cooperative officials can assist the reporter in assessing the importance of a development in a pending case, although the experienced journalist will generally make his or her own decision on whether or not to cover it.

The clerk or a deputy serves as secretary to the court during trial proceedings, assisting in drawing jury panels, administering oaths to witnesses and jurors, reading verdicts of the jury, polling jurors when necessary, and entering judgments made by the presiding judge.

The clerk is also a source of information for periodic reports on fines collected and forfeitures, comparing them with those of previous years, problems with bonds, and other court-related issues. An attorney for an aggrieved party makes the clerk's office the official point of first contact, filing a civil action there. The clerk assigns a number to it, and it is this number that the reporter uses to call up information on a pending case as it progresses through the judicial process. Through these filings with the clerk, the reporter determines the identity of attorneys retained by the parties in the dispute and frequently contacts them for additional details about a case.

Commissioners, Masters and Referees

Most states appoint special officials to assist the judge in carrying out the work of the court. Some of the duties are partly judicial and partly clerical, such as the taking of affidavits and depositions, approval of bond and examination of sureties in civil cases, and administration of oaths. Court commissioners also handle details of probate and other proceedings.

Masters or referees are appointed at the judicial level to handle special cases, such as those involving technical evaluations. The judge may appoint a master to merely ascertain the facts or to actually try the case, subject to the judge's review.

Receivers are also appointed by the court to serve as temporary custodians of a business while issues in a suit are determined by the court. Each federal court appoints a referee in bankruptcy to determine the facts at issue.

Jury Commission

The task of selecting prospective trial jurors falls to a jury commission, with the clerk of court sometimes acting as a jury commissioner. Under the direction of a commission, clerks comb the register of voters (sometimes utilizing the telephone directory, the city directory or certain tax rolls) for a representative list of veniremen who are summoned by the sheriff or the court to appear as prospective jurors. Hundreds of names are drawn during each term of court. An effort is made to obtain a cross section of representative citizens to serve as jurors.

Prospective grand jurors are selected in a similar manner, in many areas from property tax rolls, since they are being sought as citizens of "high standing" in the community. After the list has been compiled, grand jurors are selected by random drawing.

Although little attention is given by the press to the process of selecting veniremen to serve in the jury system, thousands of citizens are selected each year to participate, drawing many citizens who normally have little or no business with the courts.

Those in some occupations or professions may be exempt by law from the obligation to serve; others successfully petition the court to be dismissed. Attorneys and journalists are often exempt from jury service; so are young housewives with children at home. In many places, a judge may delay jury duty until a more appropriate time of year for an individual. Illness often keeps a potential venireman from duty.

Many human interest stories abound in the laborious selection and rejection process, and the discerning court reporter learns to listen carefully for information that leads to such material. Stories detailing the cost of maintaining jury systems are useful, and the persons who operate them provide human interest material.

Many years ago court officers would fan out around the courthouse, summoning prospective jurors in an effort to fill the jury box in a difficult case. The methods are more sophisticated today, with new systems designed to allow reporting to court by telephone, eliminating the time-consuming process of sitting all day in a room adjacent to the judge's chambers. These modern methods are newsworthy and bear reporting.

> Joseph D. Shank dialed a telephone number he'd been given and listened intently.
>
> He hung up jubilantly, turned to Mrs. Shank and smiled. "I don't have to show up tomorrow. I can take that hunting trip."
>
> Shank, 71 West Ave., is on jury duty with County Court, but a new telephone reporting method has eased the strain of appearing daily in court for three full weeks.
>
> Shank and 200 other veniremen merely dial a special number provided by Court Clerk Jerry Bailey each evening to determine which jurors must report the next day.
>
> Not only is it less disruptive on the lives of those doing jury duty, Bailey says, but it is far less expensive for the county.

Attorneys

Other court officials include both private and public attorneys, who represent litigants before the bench. All are technically officers of the court.

A prosecuting attorney, sometimes called a district attorney or solicitor, is paid with public funds and represents the state in criminal cases. Under a constitutional guarantee of counsel, a public defender is often employed to represent accused persons who cannot afford private counsel.

Private attorneys who represent clients in court are paid by those persons, making special arrangements for remuneration. Often a suit is brought by a private party based on a contingency fee—a portion of the court award being paid to the attorney who takes the case. The reporter should be familiar with lawyers in the community, since many are helpful in explaining technical points in cases such as bankruptcy proceedings, tax litigation and real estate cases. Other lawyers specialize in condemnation proceedings and antitrust litigation.

Other Court Officials

The *court reporter* is important to the journalist covering the judiciary, taking verbatim accounts of all that transpires during a trial. They are appointed to prepare a complete record of the proceedings, known as the transcript, and to make those records available to reporters upon request. The transcripts constitute a public record that is used through the appeals process.

This court record is invaluable to the reporter in assuring a totally accurate account of the proceeding, although deadlines often interfere with acquisition of a total transcript for a day. Nothing breathes confidence into a news reporter covering a complicated trial so much as being able to quickly obtain an exact quotation by a witness or objection by an attorney from a cooperative court reporter at a stenotype machine. Oral instructions rendered by the judge and summations by attorneys are all detailed in the transcript.

Law enforcement agencies generally supply a *bailiff*, who acts as a sergeant at arms for the court, maintaining order, administering oaths to prospective jurors, serving subpoenas for the court and otherwise assisting the judge in the courtroom. The bailiff is often an excellent source of news tips for the reporter who cannot be everywhere at once, identifying persons who may be scheduled to appear and providing information on coming events in the trial process. Bailiffs insure privacy for the jury during deliberations and remain with jurors during periods in which they are sequestered in important cases.

A party who desires to participate in a proceeding but without standing as plaintiff or defendant is given permission by the judge to act as a friend of the court (*amicus curiae*), offering advice or presenting other evidence. Such outsiders in the court process may present briefs or offer testimony because their interests may be directly or indirectly affected by the outcome of the case.

Researching Court Cases

The reporter is interviewing a retired judge on the subject of plea bargaining, after discussing the issue with a number of others.

"It's a questionable practice," the judge says. "The prosecutor wants to dispose of the case. It has no political value so he offers a one-year sentence in exchange for a guilty plea. Heck, the defendant is happy to accept. He saw a 10-year term ahead of him."

The judge adds: "But the Capicello case, where the Supreme Court sent the whole thing back to the lower courts, may change the whole picture." The judge launches into another aspect of plea bargaining, and the subject is changed.

Later, the reporter wonders in checking his notes: What about the Capicello case? Is it really that important? He decides to read it.

Each state has its own record-keeping apparatus, much of it tying with other states' court decisions and the federal court system. The reporter's best source for learning the ropes in looking up the law is the county law library or willing attorneys who can lead the journalist through the procedure.

Whatever the court decision, it will have a title, identity of plaintiff and defendant, docket number, date of the decision and, most important, a summary of the case. The opinion may include a legal analysis of the points of law, and may also include a discussion of other similar cases.

Law libraries, including those in attorneys' offices, contain complicated sets of source materials, but it is not difficult to master the instructions, codes and abbreviations.

With the identification of the defendant, Capicello, the reporter can follow through on his interview and locate the case in question by checking standard court digests. One of the best known, West's Digest, will identify the defendant under the Defendant-Plaintiff Table of Cases, or under another classification, Words and Phrases. The defendant–plaintiff table will direct the reporter to the key number digest classification and case history.

Besides checking the parties involved, the reporter can search under *topic analysis,* words descriptive of *places* where the facts arose, *acts* or *omissions* which gave rise to the legal action or issue, *defense* to the action and *relief* sought.

The digests are quite specific. A case may be listed under Unreasonable Search, for example, but not listed under Search, Unreasonable. It may be listed under Act of Bankruptcy, but not merely under Bankruptcy.

The digest search leads to any number of court reports that cover dozens of volumes of decisions. These include State Reports, Appellate Reports, Miscellanous Reports, and Federal Reporter, Federal Supplement, Federal Rules Decisions, the United States Supreme Court Reporter and United States Reports.

In the case of the defendant, Mario C. Capicello, the reporter locates the information in the defendant-plaintiff table:

Capicello-State of Ohio 2 SC 336

The "2" refers to the volume of the reports that includes the opinion. "SC" indicates that the opinion can be found in the Supreme Court Reporter, and "336" indicates the page on which the opinion begins. Very recent cases won't be found in the bound volumes. Such decisions will be listed in paperbound volumes published several times a month and filed with the bound volumes. The reporter should be aware that a "recent" case can be five or more years old.

Opinions may be only a paragraph in length, or many pages. It is helpful to know their organization so information can be obtained speedily. Most opinions follow a fairly standard form:

1. Title of the case, the names of the defendant and plaintiff;

2. Docket number, the reference number assigned by the court;

3. The date of the decision;

4. A summary of the case prepared by the editor;

5. Headnotes, or short numbered paragraphs prepared by the

editors to indicate points of law and legal issues treated in the case; often, these headnotes are important to the reporter's research;

6. The court opinion, with the name of the justice who wrote it, and generally with a statement that tells what the case is about; the opinion may include a discussion of similar cases, stating the facts in each and how they were decided; the opinion will indicate whether the lower court's decision follows the established law;

7. The court's decision, or ruling.

The reporter will find it important, particularly in criminal cases, to know the kind of proceeding. This information is usually found at the beginning of the opinion.

"This is an appeal from a trial held in Franklin County Common Pleas Court" or "This case reaches us from a writ of certiorari from Orange County Superior Court."

Locating the opinion will not tell the reporter whether the case or statute is still in effect; that is, whether it is still a "good law." It could have been modified or reversed by a higher court. The source to check this is Shepard's Citations, which has been publishing since 1873. Shepard's prepares and continually updates a series of volumes explaining the subsequent history of nearly every case or statute that might be researched. Included are the reported decisions of the federal as well as state courts.

Shepard's provides substantial information about cases, coded in abbreviated form. It provides a list of every other case which has been cited since it was decided, and how these later decisions affected the case. The reporter can also determine whether a case has been criticized, questioned or overruled by a more recent case.

The reporter should take care not to cite a court case which has not been checked. If uncertainty exists, the case should be checked with court authorities. Sources are extensive in the field, and most librarians are familiar with all of them.

Suggested Readings

DENNISTON, LYLE W., *The Reporter and the Law* (New York: Hastings House, 1980). A respected reporter for the Washington Star discusses the techniques for covering the courts.

FRANKLIN, MARC A., *The Dynamics of American Law* (Mineola, NY: Foundation Press, 1968). Through a single action, Franklin provides a detailed introduction to American civil procedure. Also suggested is the discussion of tensions between fair trial and free press from a legal viewpoint.

FRETZ, DONALD R., *Courts and the News Media* (Reno, NV: National College of the State Judiciary, 1977). A California judge offers his perception of the role of the press in the judicial process. Some helpful hints at a practical level for the reporter.

Editors of Congressional Quarterly, *Guide to the U.S. Supreme Court* (Washington: Congressional Quarterly, 1980). Recommended chapters: "The Court and the Press" and "The Court at Work," which offer a study of the court's operations, supporting personnel, and traditions.

CHAPTER 8
Reporting Civil Actions

THE reporter pores over a voluminous sheaf of papers at the front counter of the court clerk's office, reviewing a two-year suit about to go to trial. Several stories have been written during that time, the first detailing a prominent citizen's grievance with the operators of a local cemetery and asking for a substantial money award. Another story has reported the cemetery operators' response to the civil action.

The most recent story several months before has detailed an unsuccessful effort to make the city, nominal owner of the cemetery property, a party to the suit.

A clerk interrupts the reporter. The case will not go to trial after all, he announces. It has been settled out of court that day for an undisclosed sum.

The reporter's final story is brief. Despite his earnest efforts to obtain information from attorneys and from the principals themselves, the specific amount of the settlement remains a secret—at least for the moment. Sometimes the amount of the settlement appears on the record at a later date—through filing of a related court action by one of the parties to the original suit. A good rule for the reporter to follow, particularly in the case of important actions, is "better late than never."

As in this example, most of the civil actions begun in the courts never reach the trial stage, but many of them are worth coverage nonetheless. Natural controversy arising from the legal process is part of what makes civil law news. The identity of the individuals or corporations involved is another ingredient. The effect of the decisions reached by judge or jury is yet another.

Diligence and persistence, coupled with the ability to organize information as actions inch their way through the virtually always laborious legal process, are indispensible elements in covering the courts. A thorough knowledge of the process itself is, of course, basic to success, and the place to begin is with the emergence of the grievance that leads to legal action.

Civil action commences with a dispute between two parties. One contends that he or she has been wronged and seeks redress through the legal process. Advice is usually sought from an attorney, who identifies and researches the relevant law, helping to decide whether or not the issue should be pursued through a court case. The attorney also estimates the chances for recovery.

The proper court system and court is identified, and legal action begins when one of the aggrieved parties, the *plaintiff,* retains an attorney to put the grievance in writing and present it as a formal *complaint.* The complaint details the grievance and asks for specific relief in the form of a monetary award or equitable action.

> A Middletown physician has filed a $2 million suit in U.S. District Court against the Central Hospital, Inc., charging discrimination in the hospital's decision to limit her staff privileges there.
>
> Dr. May Kho Lim, who maintains an office at 300 West St., is seeking an injunction to force the hospital's executive committee to grant her full surgery privileges.
>
> In her suit, Lim alleged that she had been granted surgical privileges from 1977 until this year when the executive committee voted to deny them without giving a reason.

After the complaint is formally brought to the attention of the *defendant* (the other party to the grievance), the defendant's attorney drafts and files an *answer.* These basic actions constitute the beginning of the process called *pleadings,* which may or may not culminate in trial.

Between filing of the complaint and the trial lie months, even years, of pretrial activities which serve to narrow the issues in the dispute and allow both sides to share information about the case.

Failure to settle the dispute during this time leads to the judge's decision that the case is *at issue* and ready to go to trial. A civil suit is decided by judge or jury, with a *judgment order* issued if the judge concludes that the jury's verdict was correct, calling for payment of damages.

Following the trial, an appeal may be made to a higher court, still another time-consuming process.

The scope of the judicial process, together with the complex and heavy burden of total actions begun, functions to create massive roadblocks to comprehensive reporting of the courts by the press. Only a small percentage of actions in the process will be reported to the public, and this is why news judgment plays such an important role in covering the courts.

The type of complaint is important to the reporter. Amount of damage, generally located as the *prayer* at the conclusion of the listing of grievances, the individuals or corporations involved, and unusual circumstances surrounding the dispute are all critical in the decision to report and follow a civil action.

The reporter should observe caution in handling "I am going to file a suit" stories. The best rule is to await official filing of an action before reporting it, but major legal controversies are often an exception. If the mayor threatens to sue the county government to force release of matching federal funds, the public controversy is inescapable. But the attorney for a wronged party who "advises" the press that he is "about" to file suit for his client may be fishing for a way to scare the potential defendant into settling the grievance immediately. The reporter should be forewarned that these things happen.

Following through is important after the initial story is written because the complaint merely outlines the grievance *of one party* and does not necessarily constitute fact. Many newspapers now point this out in stories about originating suits in the system, adding this parenthetical note:

A suit outlines the grievance of one party against another and does not present both sides of the issue in question.

Fairness dictates that a story detailing a complaint by a plaintiff be followed with a story detailing the answer of the defendant.

> The city yesterday defended its action in dismissing four policemen on official charges they were derelict in their patrol duties.
>
> Answering a complaint by Patrolmen Harry S. Reed, Willis J. Sims, Jospeh P. Ridell and James E. High that the city unjustly discriminated against them by its action, City Attorney G. S. Merritt alleged that the four men "illegally conspired to call in for each other during night patrol, allowing each other to remain away from their posts for long periods of time."
>
> "This serious action," the suit's answer stated, "resulted in a dangerous and unwarranted reduction in police patrol."

If news judgment dictates that a story be written on the commencement of a civil suit, care should be taken to follow its progress so that a final disposition of the case can be made public—even years later. Many newspapers utilize clerks to compile and publish lists of suits filed, with final judgments listed as a public service when they occur. Separate ews stories highlight court actions which are deemed of general interest.

The Action Commences

A civil complaint (not to be confused with a complaint filed in the criminal process) officially advises the defendant of the existence and nature of the grievance that the plaintiff presents and puts the defendant on notice that the action is being brought.

Complaints include the following basic information:

—Identity of the plaintiff, the defendant, location and identity of the court, serial number of the case, a factual statement of the plaintiff's claim or claims, and a demand for relief.

The plaintiff may be parent or guardian for a minor child, or for a person who is otherwise incompetent to pursue the case through the courts. Often a substitution is made in identity of a plaintiff or a defendant upon the death of one of the original parties to the suit. Other parties may join the suit as intervenors, and the court retains the discretion to consolidate actions where several relate to the same dispute.

> A judge has ordered six nursing homes to consolidate civil suits they have filed against the state, seeking reimbursement for service to Medicaid patients during the last three years.

In most complaints, the plaintiff details the specific circumstances which led to the action, such as time and place, exactly what is alleged to have occurred, and the parties involved. Following the allegations, the plaintiff lists the specific amount of damages demanded or equitable relief asked, such as money, issuance of an injunction or granting of a divorce.

The amount of money damages is often deliberately exaggerated, and the reporter should take this into account in assessing the value of the news story. The law provides for *general damages*, presumed to have resulted from an injury, and *special damages*, which must be proven. A businessman may allege that his income has been affected by breach of a contract, and the actual amount of damage must be determined by jury or judge. *Punitive damages* are often assessed for malice with the object of punishing the defendant. *Nominal damages* are sometimes awarded merely as vindication of the plaintiff's character. Awards of $1 are not uncommon.

Dealing with the Complaint

This complaint filed in state court provides an example of the type of information available to the reporter, enabling him or her to assess the news value of the suit. A representative news story is culled from the basic information.

Plaintiff ID is frequently inadequate, and the reporter must carefully flesh out a full identification. In this case, a few phone calls were sufficient to establish Ms. Hodges' home address, age and occupation.

IN THE CIRCUIT COURT OF CALE COUNTY, WEST VIRGINIA
MACEL HODGES,
Plaintiff

vs.

doing business as

SISTERS OF THE PALLOTINE MISSIONARY SOCIETY, a corporation d/b/a ST. MARY'S HOSPITAL
Defendant

The reporter will find it easy to return to records years later through this permanent court number.

Civil Action No. 81-2747

COMPLAINT

I.

Suits are frequently filed years later. The reporter should always doublecheck the year in which the grievance was alleged to have occurred.

On November 26, 1980, plaintiff Macel Hodges was a patient in St. Mary's Hospital in the City of Greenville, W. V. and was being treated in said hospital for a nervous condition and was kept on 4 East, a locked ward of said hospital. Said hosital is owned and operated by Sisters of the Pallotine Missionary Society, a corporation doing business as St. Mary's Hospital.

II.

Charges like these are privileged in court actions, but the reporter must always qualify the material that is picked up. It must always be remembered that this represents only one side's version.

It was necessary in order for the patients on 4 East to use the toilet, that they walk through a shower room. Said shower room had developed a leak so that floor from time to time became wet and slippery. The employees of said hospital were aware of this condition and failed to use due care to make the premises reasonably safe and to protect the patients on 4 East from injury.

III.

Like other areas in which direct quotation is used, the reporter must never take liberties. If a suit uses the term "wretching," and the reporter wishes to use it, he or she should pick it up exactly.

Often the reporter must draw a line between "trying the case" in the newspaper and ignoring it completely. So many months or years will elapse before possible trial, there is little likelihood of the former. A suit may appear frivolous, but it is not so to the parties involved.

Plaintiff had an occasion to use the toilet on November 26, and as she stepped from the hall into said shower room she suddenly slipped on the wet floor and was thrown violently to the floor. On her way down she attempted to catch herself on the lavatories and as a result she suffered a severe wretching of her shoulders, back and neck and also took a severe blow on her left hip. When plaintiff recovered her senses, she was able to get to her feet and inform the nurses she had fallen. Plaintiff had planned to go home for a Thanksgiving visit the next morning, but was unable to go by reason of the fall. Plaintiff suffered what is commonly known as a severe whiplash, and for a period of several months suffered great pain in both shoulders and neck. At the present time the pain in plaintiff's left shoulder has been alleviated, but the pain in the right shoulder is so severe that she is unable to perform any task without suffering great pain. Since the fall, plaintiff has on at least a dozen occasions, when the pain radiates from her neck down into her back, fainted and completely lost her senses. Since said fall, she has feared to travel any place without being accompanied by some other member of her family, and when she is forced to travel alone she is continually apprehensive that she might faint and fall upon the street.

IV.

Plaintiff alleges that it was the duty of said hospital to use all due care to keep the premises in a reasonably safe condition in order that patients confined therein would suffer no injury, but that St. Mary's Hospital breached the aforesaid duty and failed to use due care, and that the failure constituted actionable negligence against the defendant; that the negligence of defendant was the sole and approximate cause of plaintiff's injury, and that by reason of the aforesaid negligence plaintiff has been injured and suffered great pain of body and mind and will continue to suffer great pain of both body and mind for the rest of her

The key to most suits lies in amount of damages sought, but that should be only one yardstick used by the reporter in deciding how much of a story to produce.

life. As a direct consequence of the wrong and injury, plaintiff has been damaged to the amount of $120,000.00.
WHEREFORE, plaintiff demands judgment in the amount of $120,000.00 and costs.

MACEL HODGES,
by counsel

Most newspapers consider publication of attorneys' names and their firms a necessary part of the court story. Others look upon it as a form of free advertising for lawyers. The reporter is advised to add the attorney's name unless there is a rule against it.

BARR, NAPIER & COLEMAN
Attorneys for plaintiff
630 Fifth Street
Greenville, West Virginia

BY William K. Napier

The complaint was accompanied by an affidavit signed by Macel Hodges certifying the truth of the allegations. It is often necessary for the reporter to contact the parties involved or their attorneys for ages, addresses, occupations and other explanatory information. With this material in hand and added to the complaint, the reporter is ready to write the preliminary story on the action:

> A 77-year-old retired bookkeeper sued the operators of St. Mary's Hospital for $120,000 yesterday, claiming that she was severely injured in a shower room fall while a patient.
>
> In the suit filed in Cale County Circuit Court, Ms. Macel Hodges, 1920 Earl St., alleged that while being treated for a nervous condition Nov. 26, 1980, she slipped in a shower room, suffering "a severe wretching of her shoulders, back and neck," and whiplash. Since the accident, Ms. Hodges contends, she has fainted on at least a dozen occasions and fears to travel alone.
>
> Hospital personnel, although aware of the leak in the shower room, were negligent in allowing the condition to exist, Ms. Hodges contends. She charged that the Sisters of the Pallotine Missionary Society, who operate the hospital, failed to keep the facility in a "reasonably safe condition."
>
> William K. Napier, associated with the law firm of Barr, Napier & Coleman, is attorney for Ms. Hodges.

Important to this story is the claim of injuries suffered by Ms. Hodges, the total damages sought, and the identity of the defendant, and the religious society which operates the hospital. Ms. Hodges is suing the operators of the hospital rather than the hospital itself.

The Defendant Answers

In the parlance of the prize fight ring, the first blow has been struck. The defendant, in this case the hospital operators, must respond to the complaint with a formal *answer* within a specified time or risk a *default judgment* by failing to submit to the jurisdiction of the court. Answers usually must be filed within 30 days.

In the answer, the defendant may deny some or all of the allegations listed in the complaint, setting the stage for the series of confrontations called pleadings which lead to eventual trial or settlement through other means. The purpose of the pleadings is to identify the issues to be tried.

Here is the answer to Ms. Hodges' complaint, filed several weeks later by the attorney for the operators of the hospital:

IN THE CIRCUIT COURT OF CALE COUNTY, WEST VIRGINIA
MACEL HODGES,
Plaintiff

vs.

SISTERS OF THE PALLOTINE MISSIONARY SOCIETY, a corporation d/b/a ST. MARY's HOSPITAL
Defendant

ANSWER OF DEFENDANT

First Defense: As its first defense to the Complaint of the plaintiff against it, said defendant states as follows:

Like many answers, this is a fairly general defense and there is little the reporter can do about it, unless the party is willing to discuss it further. Most defendants cloak themselves in as much anonymity as possible and hunker down for the long litigation.

1. As its answer to Paragraph I of the Complaint of the plaintiff against it, said defendant admits that St. Mary's Hospital is owned and operated by the Sisters of the Pallotine Missionary Society, a corporation d/b/a St. Mary's Hospital, but specifically denies each and every other allegation contained in Paragraph I of the said complaint.

2. As its answer to Paragraph II of the Complaint of the plaintiff against it, said defendant denies each and every allegation contained therein and demands strict proof thereof.

Second Defense: As its second defense to the Complaint of the plaintiff against it, said defendant states that the plaintiff herself was guilty of acts of negligence which contributed directly and proximately to the incident involved in this civil action, and the alleged injuries and damages suffered by her, therefore was guilty of contributory negligence, and as a result thereof may not recover of this defendant in this action.

The key to this news story probably lies in this third defense—in alleging that Ms. Hodges was herself guilty of negligence which contributed to her fall.

Third Defense: As its third defense to the Complaint of the plaintiff against it, said defendant argues that the plaintiff knew the risks attendant to the circumstances surrounding the incident involved in this civil action, and the alleged injuries and damages suffered by her, knowingly and voluntarily assumed the risks, therefore was guilty of assumption of risk, and as a result thereof may not recover of this defendant in this action.

WHEREFORE, defendant, Sisters of the Pallotine Missionary Society, a corporation d/b/a St. Mary's Hospital, demands that the Complaint of the plaintiff against it be dismissed, and that it be awarded its costs of action.

Peter C. Jenkins

Counsel for Defendant

Be consistent. If you used lawyer for the plaintiff weeks before, you should pick up the counsel for the defendant as well.

PETER C. JENKINS
1190 Wood St.
Greenville, WV

Counsel for Defendant

The answer was accompanied by a Certificate of Service, certifying that the defendant's attorney had provided a copy of the answer to the attorney for the plaintiff.

The operators of the hospital, who have declined until now to respond to any questions concerning the suit, have officially responded to the court. Armed with the court record, the reporter will write a story detailing that response to Ms. Hodges' action.

> The operators of St. Mary's Hospital yesterday denied charges that its employees were negligent in caring for one of its elderly patients, who said she sustained a severe fall during her stay in the hospital last year.
>
> In answering a $120,000 civil suit brought by the patient, Macel Hodges, 1920 Earl St., the hospital operators, Sisters of the Pallotine Missionary Society, alleged that Ms. Hodges herself was guilty of negligence which contributed to her fall in a shower room Nov. 26, 1980.
>
> The answer to Ms. Hodges' charges was filed in Cale County Circuit Court yesterday.
>
> The hospital operators also argued that Ms. Hodges knew the risks involved when she became a patient and voluntarily assumed those risks. They asked for dismissal of the suit.
>
> Peter C. Jenkins is attorney for the hospital operators.

It should be noted that the complaint generally has greater inherent news value than the defendant's answer weeks later. Whatever that newsworthiness, fairness dictates some consideration for a degree of equitable play for both sides of the argument.

While many civil actions are far more complex than this, most of them begin with this basic procedure—a document laying out the complaint of one party and an answer by the other.

Other Responses

A defendant has recourse to responses other than denial of allegations through a formal answer. His or her attorney may file a *demurrer*, stating that the plaintiff's action has no basis in law, or a *plea in abatement*, objecting to the manner in which the plaintiff filed the action. The defendant may cite a lack of jurisdiction over the person or subject matter, object that the venue is improper, or cite lack of a capacity to sue in the first place. The defendant may plead that another action is pending and, thus, that the complaint is invalid or that the action has been brought prematurely. All these tactics require rulings by the presiding judge of the court.

The reporter must be careful to explain the legal terminology, while making an effort to move the story along. Here is how a demurrer action might be handled in a news story:

> The attorney for Langmuir County yesterday asked for dismissal of a Circuit Court suit brought against it by the District Authority, arguing there is no legal basis for the claim.
>
> In a demurrer filed with Judge John T. Scopes, County Attorney Paul L. Craig submitted detailed federal regulations specifying the $3.9 million to which the county claims the authority is entitled.
>
> "None of us has anything to say about how the pie is sliced," Craig argued. "It's all spelled out in these federal regulations."
>
> The authority is suing to increase the amount to $5.6 million.

A defendant may feel that he or she not only owes nothing to the plaintiff but that the plaintiff in fact owes something to the defendant. Then the answer may include a *counterclaim*, which calls for a further reply from the plaintiff. Often an automobile collision is the catalyst in such actions, with each party asserting that the other is responsible and should pay damages.

Judgments Without Trial

In any court on any given day, routine motions are being heard that affect the course of litigation in civil actions. Not all of them are newsworthy. They include efforts to extend the time allowed for filing a pleading, changes in attorneys and other such requests.

In some circumstances, judgment can be made without going through the trial process, and the reporter should be alert to these proceedings which affect the final outcome of an action. Often an abrupt decision to drop an action is as newsworthy or more so than the original filing of the action.

The attorney for one party may move for a *summary judgment* if there is a belief that the defendant's answer is clearly inadequate. Arguments on a motion for summary judgment can be as extensive as a full trial. This motion is used to compel the other party to disclose the kind of proof he or she intends to present at a later date and attacks the facts in the case. Denial of a motion for summary judgment implies that the judge believes that there are genuine issues of fact, and the case proceeds.

Rather than contest the action, a defendant may acknowledge the legitimacy of the plaintiff's claim and consent to a verdict against him or her for a stipulated amount. This motion is known as *judgment by consent* or *judgment by confession*. The advantage to the news reporter is obvious—the specifics of the settlement are easily obtainable, in contrast to the problems of an out-of-court settlement.

In some proceedings, the parties in dispute may jointly produce a consent decree under sanction of the court. While not a judgment, such an action allows both parties to withdraw with an adequate determination of their rights. Antitrust suits are often concluded through consent decrees between private corporations and the government agencies that oversee their operations.

> Washington (AP)—The federal government and 22 manufacturers of folding cartons have agreed to settle a three-year-old civil antitrust suit, the Justice Department announced Thursday.
>
> The consent agreement is subject to approval by a federal district court judge in Chicago.
>
> The government had charged that the firms conspired to fix prices on folding cartons from 1960 to 1976.
>
> A companion criminal case had been resolved earlier this year with the 71 corporate and individual defendants pleading no contest to the charges. Fifteen persons were sentenced to jail.
>
> Under Thursday's proposed settlement, the companies will be barred by court order from conspiring to fix prices, allocating customers, submitting noncompetitive bids or exchanging pricing information.

Discovery

While procedures may vary depending upon the jurisdiction, the law provides assurance that information in the hands of one party in a legal action be made available to the other if it is needed to properly answer the suit.

This disclosure by parties possessing relevant documents or knowledge is called *discovery*. Either the plaintiff or the defendant might be ordered to produce contracts, letters, certificates, photographs, books, bills of lading, promissory notes or other acknowledgements of debt. Discovery helps to narrow the issues in a case by eliminating the necessity of proving the authenticity of documents later in court.

Another method of discovery involves the taking of *depositions*, testimony in writing of a party or witness to the suit taken outside open court. Depositions are ordered by the presiding judge, with notice provided to the adverse party, often specifying the subject matter and whether they are to be oral depositions or written *interrogatories*. Out-of-state witnesses unable to be present to testify in court often respond in this manner. The deposition is similar to the affidavit, except that notice of deposition must be given to the adverse party, whereas an affidavit need not be.

Discovery petitions are routine, but they are sometimes crucial to a civil action in controversial cases. The right of reporters to attend discovery examinations has been affirmed in some jurisdictions and denied in others. They are privileged material when made a part of the court record.

While discovery is basically a provision for the litigants in an action, often the material that emerges is in the public interest. The reporter should be on the alert for important information that surfaces in this manner in court actions.

Remedies

The judicial process itself constitutes the basic remedy for settling grievances among disputants, but special remedies are available to compel enforcement of rights and equitable determination of the issues before the law.

Such remedies are an important source of news, and reporters should be alert to the significance of provisional remedies as a suit commences and extraordinary remedies, legal procedures that are often resorted to when ordinary measures might prove inadequate.

Provisional Remedies

Included among provisional remedies in civil actions are the injunction, attachment, receivership, arrest and bail, garnishment, and claim and delivery.

To restrain performance or require a specific act, the court issues an *injunction*. It is ordered by the judge when no other equitable remedy exists. Following a hearing, a judge may issue a temporary injunction barring striking workers from picketing a plant until their leaders can appear in court to show cause why the order should not be made permanent.

A temporary injunction might delay an official meeting scheduled by the owners of a business firm or protect the holder of a patent by forbidding start of work on a new product. Such an injunction remains in force until it is vacated by an appeal or trial or is otherwise discontinued by the presiding judge. Terms of an injunction may also be modified to allow some action or extended when the order is about to expire without the rights of those involved being determined.

> Washington—U.S. District Court Judge Wilson R. Greene Friday temporarily blocked the Labor Department's efforts to cancel the Armstrong Corp.'s $86 million in government contracts.
>
> Greene said the firm had raised "substantial legal questions" in challenging the department's move, which was based on allegations of sex discrimination.
>
> Greene will hear arguments July 12 on whether he should issue a longer-term preliminary injunction blocking the government's action.

An injunction may be secured for an individual while that person's rights are being determined or for a municipal government which contends that its rights are being violated.

Human Rights Commissioner William Deegan asked for a restraining order against the city today so that he can continue in office until a court hearing is held.

Deegan was dismissed suddenly yesterday by City Manager Alfred Williston on unspecified charges after a series of meetings in Williston's office.

George Lambros, attorney for Deegan, filed suit in Circuit Court for a temporary order blocking the city manager's action.

Following a hearing at which the judge attempts to determine the validity of the request, he or she will issue such an order or deny it. Most injunctions prevent action rather than compel it, and judicial officials usually act quickly so that neither party will be unduly injured by a lengthy impasse. Injunctions are common in disputes between management and labor, with one side seeking to limit the other's actions.

A taxpayer may file suit to restrain a public agency from collecting taxes while the citizen questions the agency's disbursement of funds. An individual or public official may question the manner in which another public official is performing his or her duties, seeking an injunction to restrain that official from exceeding the authority of the office. A person being sued by two or more other persons claiming title to the same property may seek an injunction to protect himself or herself. Federal agencies and private organizations frequently make use of the injunction process to restrain or force action in many kinds of matters.

Pierre, S.D. (AP)—A federal judge ruled yesterday that ranchers must temporarily stop using the chemical toxaphene to combat an infestation of grasshoppers.

District Court Judge Donald Porter granted a temporary injunction sought by the National Audubon Society, which contended that toxaphene was dangerous to wildlife.

The U.S. Environmental Protection Agency had approved the emergency use of the chemical June 22 on 600,000 acres of rangeland after grasshoppers swarmed over the area—as many as several hundred per square yard.

The judge added that he had weighed the Audubon Society's chances of winning a permanent injunction and decided that it had "a strong chance of success." With further court maneuvers by ranchers a strong possibility, this injunction is part of a continuing story dominated by judicial action.

A property owner might seek an order restraining a corporation from making use of some of its property adjacent to his land, seeking a hearing to determine whether his property will be adversely affected.

Malcolm Springs property owners received a reprieve yesterday when Circuit Court Judge Dan Daughtery issued an order prohibiting a public hearing on a proposed county zoning ordinance.

> The residents had petitioned the court to halt the hearing, charging that a nearby landowner was unduly influencing county officials to allow a mobile trailer park on his property adjacent to Malcolm Springs homes.

In this case, the matter was merely a delaying action, since the judge dissolved the injunction within a week and allowed the public hearing to be held at a later date.

Other provisional remedies are available to the plaintiff in a court action. A request may be made for a *writ of attachment* before judgment to assure that the defendant will not dispose of the property in dispute. Such a writ can be requested if there is danger that the defendant might leave the court's jurisdiction with the property. A court official, usually the sheriff or a marshal, is directed to take possession of the property.

If a party in a civil suit has reason to believe that another party might depart a jurisdiction or dispose of property in dispute, he or she can request *arrest and bail*. Following the arrest upon such an order, the party may be required to post suitable bond with the court before release.

The court often appoints a receiver to manage property while the dispute works its way toward trial. The receiver generally possesses some expertise in the management of such property or in knowledge of the property in question. A dispute over ownership of a hotel, for example, might result in temporary appointment of an executive from another hotel chain to operate the disputed property until a settlement can be reached in court.

Wages of a salaried or hourly wage employee can be taken by the court through a *garnishment order* and the money redirected to a plaintiff who has successfully argued that the defendant owes him or her money. This is common practice in the business community.

A remedy similar to attachment is available when a plaintiff seeks property, claiming that it is wrongfully possessed by the defendent. In an action of *claim and delivery*, a court official is directed to take possession of the property and deliver it to the plaintiff, with the plaintiff assuring fairness by posting bond.

Extraordinary Remedies

The reporter should be familiar with a number of extraordinary legal remedies available to litigants in the courts—habeas corpus, mandamus, prohibition, certiorari and the permanent injunction.

The oldest is *habeas corpus* (you have the body), which orders a party to produce a person's appearance in court. The remedy stems from efforts to protect persons against arbitrary arrest and confinement and is often used by prisoners today to obtain further court hearings on their imprisonment. The U.S. Constitution guarantees the remedy in this country.

This writ is often used to force arraignment of a prisoner who has not been officially charged so that charges can be ascertained. Habeas corpus is also used to produce a witness in a legal proceeding or to transfer persons from the custody of one court to another.

After other remedies have been exhausted, the attorney for a convicted person often uses the procedure to challenge the jurisdiction of the court or to question the validity of parts of the legal process used in the conviction.

> The court-appointed attorney for 3-year-old Sheila Bond sought a hearing today on a Welfare Department decision to place the child in a foster home.
>
> Duane L. Selden, representing the daughter of Mrs. Wilson S. Bond, filed a petition of habeas corpus in Domestic Relations Court in an effort to force another hearing in the case, this time in court.
>
> The Welfare Department decision had followed agency hearings in the dispute, in which Mrs. Bond is seeking to retain custody.

When a public official refuses to perform his or her offical, nondiscretionary duty, a citizen may institute a *writ of mandamus* (we command) to force the official to comply with the law. The writ usually commands the performance of and orders the official to appear in court to show cause why the writ should not be made permanent.

Controversies involving quasi-official agencies, such as special district governments and publicly supported hospitals, often surface, with citizen groups active in forcing action on an issue.

> A citizens' organization has filed suit to force the Central Valley Water District to share its new $13.5 million federal grant with the City of Grantsville.
>
> Alleging that federal regulations call for sharing water conservation funds with overlapping governmental units, the Action Council asked Superior Court Thursday to issue a writ of mandamus, directing the district to appropriate $4 million to the city as its share of the grant.

The writ of mandamus does not apply to public officials when another remedy is available, nor is it applicable when discretionary action on the part of the official is at issue. A citizen's group may seek a writ of mandamus directing the police department to enforce anti-fireworks legislation, which the department has chosen to ignore selectively in the past. Or it may command a sheriff to take action on tax collections, but it has no power over setting a specific tax rate.

Individuals frequently make use of the remedy. A stockholder may file suit to compel a corporation to issue new stock or to open its books for inspection. A lawyer may file such a suit against a court, asking that his name be restored to its rolls.

> A Huntsville barber has asked Circuit Court to force the State Barber Board to restore his license.
>
> In a petition for a writ of mandamus filed Friday, William J. Dennison, 67, stated that the board's refusal to reactivate his expired license was "arbitrary and

> capricious, for nowhere in the law is there a mandatory retirement policy for barbers."

Application for a *writ of prohibition* is made to a superior court in an effort to restrain an inferior court from exceeding its jurisdiction. The effect of the order is to halt the proceedings of the inferior court before final judgment in an action. Both public bodies and individuals make use of the remedy.

> Arguing that the Argus Construction Co.'s suit to evade payment of $180,000 for damage to county roads has no standing in Circuit Court, the Doane County Commission asked an appeals court yesterday to halt action and forestall judgment.
>
> In the writ of prohibition filed with the Court of Appeals in the capital, the commission argued that its contract with Argus clearly specified that the firm would be responsible for damage to county roads during construction of three major public facilities.

The writ of prohibition only seeks to prevent an inferior court from exercising jurisdiction; it does not change a final judgment in a case. The *writ of certiorari* is a form of appeal, petitioning another court to direct an inferior court to send the records to determine whether it had exceeded its authority.

> Lt. John Steen, charging that the city's Civil Service Commission had exceeded its authority in upholding his dismissal from the police force, asked Superior Court Wednesday to take jurisdiction in the dispute.
>
> Steen's attorney, Clive Sammons, filed a petition for a writ of certiorari, stating that the commission's action was "capricious, without legal foundation and politically inspired."
>
> Steen, a 14-year veteran of the force, had been dismissed June 14 following testimony in commission hearings that he took unauthorized leave of absence totaling 32 days last year.

Final Pretrial Procedure

Like other pretrial litigation, not all pretrial conference actions are newsworthy. But regular attention to the schedules of judges and clerks will help assure that the newsworthy ones will be reported.

After all the pleadings have been filed and all motions disposed of, the civil action is said to be at issue—that is, ready for trial. Attorneys for the litigants meet with the judge for a *pretrial conference* to finally narrow the issues and to eliminate uncontested questions from the trial proceedings. The conference also serves as a final effort to determine whether the case can be settled without going through the costly trial process.

Following the conference, the judge may issue a pretrial order, setting down the agreements of the parties and the issues in the case. The following is a typical example of a pretrial order following a conference between counsel for a pedestrian injured during a car collision and the defendant who was operating the vehicle:

PARTIES AGREED:

—That plaintiff was struck by defendent's automobile.

—That hospital records may be introduced into evidence without objections.

ISSUES IN THE CASE:

—What degree of care did defendant owe plaintiff at intersection?

—Did defendant commit any act of negligence?

—Did insurance release defendant from any further claims?

—What amount of damages, if any, is plaintiff entitled to recover?

With the issues narrowed to these questions, the case is declared ready for trial by the judge, and it is placed on the trial calendar or docket. Often a pretrial order following the conference is newsworthy because of the time that will elapse between its filing and the trial itself may be months in the future.

Only three questions will be at issue during the trial to determine ownership of the popular White Horse Café in suburban Lucasville:

1. What steps did former owner Jake Carlisle take to validate the contract selling the café to Wendy Lawson for $380,000 in 1979?
2. What is the current marital relationship between the two litigants—Carlisle and Lawson?
3. Who actually owns the White Horse Café now?

These questions were included in a pretrial order by Circuit Court Judge Alvin Spottswood Wednesday directing the long dispute to a jury trial during the next term of court.

The Trial Calendar

Several times a year the clerk's office, which has been mired in routine filings and correspondence, is galvanized into action. The catalyst is the beginning of a new term of court, important to the public because it produces so many decisions. As previously noted, many cases are settled by the litigants before coming to trial, but a new term of court tends to force decisions on the parties.

At the start of each term, the clerk's office makes up and publishes a trial calendar, listing the parties to the action, date of trial and the case number. The calendar, the reporter will soon learn, serves only as a general guide to the activities of the court, since cases are often delayed and sometimes switched for many reasons. Out-of-court settlements immediately preceding the trial date often change the time schedules for the term, with several days originally scheduled for the trial becoming available.

> Amos Johnson's $1 million suit against the Peerless Water Co. was suddenly settled today when attorneys for both parties requested dismissal during opening arguments in the long dispute.
>
> Johnson had charged the firm with illegally tapping an underground water supply, which he claimed had affected the water supply to his 3,000-acre farm near Theopolis.
>
> No settlement figures were supplied by the parties in the dispute, but Johnson's attorney, Stephen L. Womack, commented that his client "is entirely satisfied with the settlement."
>
> Peerless attorney William E. Snider declined to comment, but a source in the clerk's office indicated that the Peerless water tap would remain in place.

A typical circuit court civil jury trial calendar notation provides this basic information:

80-9534 RLG-B&C James Horne vs. Allegheny Railroad Corp. May 3

The first number is the case to which the notation refers. Identifying this number in the clerk's office will bring the file to the reporter for scrutiny. It is the premanent file number, making future access to the material much easier for the reporter.

The initials indicate the attorneys of record for the parties in the dispute—in this case Ralph L. Goodwin for the plaintiff and Bostick & Carruthers for the defendant. The plaintiff is James V. Horne, who has filed the action against the Allegheny Railroad Corp. Tentative date for trial of the suit has been set for May 3. The reporter often will find it helpful to contact the attorneys in a pending trial.

The Trial

Litigation that reaches the trial stage has usually endured protracted pretrial argument, but such jockeying for the best position continues into the trial itself. Actions are often settled while a jury is being chosen and even while the judge is instructing the jury before it retires to deliberate at the conclusion.

Many cases that reach the trial stage are not newsworthy and may usually be disposed of in a few paragraphs or in a daily listing of routine cases. Little or no space is devoted to selection of the jury, arguments or other phases of the trial, unless it is an unusual case.

In newsworthy civil litigation, however, such proceedings are often important to the story, and the news reporter must possess a sound knowledge of the trial process and the issues in the case.

In covering major cases, the reporter may write a daily trial story; in others, he or she may cover a two or three day trial, then wrap it up in a single story. This Washington Post reporter covered a three-day trial, then produced this wrap-up:

> A District of Columbia landlord has been ordered by a Superior Court jury to pay $104,000 to a tenant who was seriously injured when he fell through a stairway that the landlord had been charged with failing to repair.
>
> Robert Walker, a bookkeeper, testified in court that his landlord, William J. Davis Inc., had not properly maintained the fire escape stairway that Walker used to leave his third-story apartment Aug. 20, 1980.
>
> Walker told the jury he climbed down the metal stairs to the first floor in search of his dog. The bottom step had apparently rusted away, he testified, and he fell when he stepped on it.

Impaneling of the Jury

At the beginning of the trial, the clerk calls the case, and attorneys for the disputing parties announce that they are ready. The trial begins with selection of a jury. Both plaintiff and defendant have a right to demand that a jury determine issues of fact in common law disputes. The judge may also insist on a jury trial, although that judicial officer usually determines the resolution of suits in equity.

Juries of six to 12 members are chosen from a venire (a group of prospective jurors summoned to court) and are closely questioned regarding their impartiality through a process called *voir dire* (to speak the truth). The questioning, by attorneys and by the judge, helps to determine jurors' qualifications and possible prejudice in the specific case. Depending upon the court and the jurisdiction, attorneys may challenge one or more of the prospective jurors for cause when an attorney has reason to believe that selection of the juror may adversely affect his or her client's case. Each attorney is also entitled to a specified number of peremptory challenges when no reason need be assigned.

After the stated number of jurors has been chosen, they are sworn in and the trial proceeds.

Presenting the Evidence

Opening statements to the court are made by the attorneys for the plaintiff and defendant. The plaintiff's counsel attempts to explain the suit to the jury and identify the evidence that he or she plans to introduce to prove the plaintiff's case.

The defendant's attorney follows with a statement explaining his or her client's side to the jury. The defendant's attorney may delay the opening statement until the plaintiff's evidence has been presented.

In presenting evidence, the plaintiff's attorney must establish a case, attempting through witnesses and introduction of exhibits to show that there is a cause for the action. Questions are asked in an effort to show that the plaintiff has been wronged, with corroborating testimony from others in succession.

Following direct testimony by witnesses for the plaintiff, the defendant's attorney is entitled to cross-examine them, seeking to discredit their testimony through contradictory statements or through questions about the witness's interest in the case.

Defense Motions

When the plaintiff's attorney has concluded his or her case, the defendant's counsel can preface presentation of his or her defense with a series of motions in an effort to terminate the trial at this point. The attorney may ask for a directed verdict, a demurrer to the evidence (in some jurisdictions) or move for a non-suit.

In asking for a directed verdict, the defense asks the judge to determine whether sufficient evidence has been presented to justify submitting the matter to the jury. Either party may move for a directed verdict, which, if granted, effectively concludes the case.

In making a motion for a non-suit, the defense argues that there is no legal basis for the action, while conceding the truth of the plaintiff's evidence. Such a motion attacks the sufficiency of the evidence rather than the pleading itself. The motion for non-suit has generally replaced the demurrer to the evidence, the defendant's argument that there is insufficient evidence to support the case.

Defendant's Arguments

The attorney for the defendant now presents his or her case, with the defendant often taking the witness stand to testify. Efforts are made to disprove the statements made by witnesses for the plaintiff. Requests are often made for the jury to visit the scene of a dispute, such as land in a condemnation suit for highway construction.

Rebuttal in civil trials allows witnesses to be recalled to clarify important points in testimony.

After both sides have presented their arguments, attorneys summarize their cases with closing statements, attempting to emphasize the points they believe necessary to win their case.

Conclusion of the Trial

Before the jury begins its deliberations, the judge charges the panel, instructing jurors on points of law. The judge identifies the evidence that the jurors are to consider and what verdicts they may return. The jurors then retire to deliberate.

Many states require a unanimous verdict on the part of the jury;

others permit split verdicts in civil suits.

Following the verdict, the attorney for the losing party has a number of options for motions, including a motion to set aside the verdict and grant a new trial. The defendant's attorney may also seek a reduction of damages.

Judgment in the action is satisfied when the clerk issues a writ of execution and the defeated party pays the amount to the clerk.

CHAPTER 9
Law Enforcement

"TEN-FOUR."

The rasping signal ending the exchange crackled over the receiver in the police dispatcher's office. The dispatcher, a young uniformed police officer with a ready smile, flipped a switch, leaned back in his chair and picked up his steaming mug of coffee.

Almost apologetically, he turned to pass the word to the waiting police reporter. "Units all say it's quiet out there." He shrugged. "Two drunks in the can and a minor fender bender out on Eighth Avenue. Pretty dead night, I'd say," he concluded.

With a sigh, the reporter checked his watch, then picked up a telephone to call the newspaper office. It was nearing deadline for the final, 1:04 a.m., and there was nothing to report. The reporter checked out for the night. His total output for the evening's tour of duty:

—Two minor break-ins at local places of business, reported earlier in the evening. An auto-truck collision on the nearby interstate, a spectacular affair resulting in major damage but only minor injuries. Unreported was a family quarrel patched up without incident by a sympathetic police officer. The shift was uneventful.

It was in sharp contrast to the previous day's report. A gun-wielding robber had invaded a local tavern, forced patrons to the floor and took off with $2,200 in bar receipts and a sackful of personal valuables collected from the unhappy patrons. The reporter was fortunate. He was able to reach the scene shortly after conclusion of a high-speed police chase resulting in capture of the gunman. A front-page story.

That breaking story, coupled with an announcement earlier in the day of a detective bureau reorganization and the usual assortment of minor stories, created somewhat of a logjam for the reporter.

Coverage of the police beat is often characterized by these frenetic bursts of activity and frequent lulls.

Complicating Factors for the Journalist

Unlike other areas of public affairs coverage, some special factors complicate the work of the police reporter. The unpredictability of news developments creates more pressure, particularly at deadline time, for the print or broadcast journalist. Consider these factors:

Irregular hours. Police departments operate around the clock, generally on a three-shift basis. Reporters must adjust to and work around these shifts. A "lobster shift" may begin at 11 p.m. and conclude at 7 a.m. or begin at midnight and end at 8 a.m. A normally cooperative police officer can become very uncooperative when roused out of bed by an inquiring reporter at 10 a.m., just after he has drifted off to sleep after a night's work.

Check-in times vary with the police organization, and late-breaking stories often necessitate overtime work. Newspapers handle the shift problem in different ways. Metropolitan dailies may staff police headquarters around the clock, while a morning newspaper in a smaller city may staff the station only during the evening hours, being content with occasional telephone checks during the day and often relying on an office radio monitor to check police frequencies.

The busiest time for the police reporter often occurs at what are usually considered "off hours" for other beats. Inaccessibility of public officials during evening hours sometimes complicates efforts by reporters to get comment on police-related developments.

> A policeman was charged with using excessive force last night in arresting a runaway juvenile. Patrolman Alvin Donovan was suspended from duty by Lt. Allen Bragg, who filed the charge.
>
> Bragg said the youth, a 14-year-old Detroit resident, had been beaten with a nightstick. Police Department officials could not be reached for comment last night.

Associations may be disillusioning. Law enforcement deals at somewhat greater depth with a "criminal element." Whereas the average citizen rarely runs afoul of the law, the lawbreaker is much more apt to occupy the police officer's time. These are also the stories that are more significant and interesting on the police beat. Reporter and officer alike should avoid the tendency to view the underbelly of society through the eyes of a cynic.

Violence is much more common on the police beat, and it appears in the form of homicide, rape, robbery and other major crimes. The perpetrator may be merely a common purse snatcher or the leader of an organized theft ring.

Because the beat lends itself to reporters' disillusionment, newspapers often transfer reporters off the beat after a time, rotating the coverage among several staffers. This too has its disadvantages, as contacts carefully nurtured must be regularly updated by new beat persons.

The duties are often unpleasant. The police reporter should be prepared for obscenities, blood and occasional violence. They are intrinsic to the beat. A reporter's account of a violent death in a Florida field some years ago was all the more vivid because the reporter had personally inspected the site. An escaping prisoner from a county road gang had been struck down by a bolt of lightning in the open field.

After reading a reporter's account of a fatal auto collision, an editor may ask, "Did you check out the intersection yourself?" An occasional visit to the emergency room of a local hospital is rewarding in terms of covering an accident, albeit somewhat unsettling to the stomach. In reconstructing a gruesome, still unsolved murder, the reporter may find it helpful to visit the scene of the crime.

> The trail of blood began behind the old farmhouse, big dark splotches leading grimly across the open ground to the brick well 40 feet distant.
>
> Walsh pointed to the porch, where there were many more splotches. "It looks like she put up a real fight, then she fell and was dragged to the well," he said.

The reporter with "inside connections" who manages to accompany deputies on a drug raid should be prepared to take cover on short notice. Law enforcement officers are paid to accept the danger, police reporters are paid to survive and write the subsequent story.

> Police raided an illegal after-hours club early Tuesday, arresting seven unruly patrons who scuffled with officers and the club's operator.
>
> Joseph Turnbull, operator of the club located at 600 Madison Ave., threatened police with a meat cleaver and had to be subdued by force after emergency backup units arrived.

Reporters at the scene will obtain a much better story, but they sometimes stand in the same danger zone as do the police. It is best to be careful and not take chances.

> Sgt. R. A. Gabbert cut a slightly comical figure as he tiptoed out of the Benson High School science lab, gingerly holding a small brown bottle at arm's length.
>
> But the bottle's contents were no laughing matter. "I

have respect for explosives," said Gabbert, a demolition expert with the state police's hazardous device team.

"If somebody tells me something might blow up, I always take their word for it," he said.

Gabbert was at the school to detonate a bottle of picric acid, a volatile substance that has created a minor sensation in several area schools during the last week.

A constant danger of libel. Danger of defamation is much greater in law enforcement than on other public affairs beats, and the reporter must constantly be on guard. Criminal accusations are particularly sensitive. In addition to knowing the law, the reporter must take painstaking care with names, addresses, exact charges and other vital facts. Minor errors, such as a wrong address, often stir libel suits.

George M. Jones, an unemployed carpenter who listed his address as 124 Elm St., was charged with robbery of Daniels Candy Store last night.

A substance believed to be cocaine was found in his possession, Detective Sgt. Ollie Vance said.

Careful attribution is always necessary. Precision is also required in identifying the charge made against a person. The difference between the charge of sexual abuse and the charge of incest, for example, is sufficient to cause a publication grave problems when the facts are not totally correct. A simple charge of robbery carries a far lesser sentence than does armed robbery, for example. The reporter throws away his or her protection when the published charge is found to be imprecise.

Inaccurate and uncooperative news sources. The pressures of the police beat create a greater likelihood that inaccuracies will creep into news accounts. The lodging of official criminal charges often makes normally open news sources more uncooperative. Police themselves suddenly become unavailable to the press when they believe it is in their best interests to close informational doors.

Lack of cooperation can crop up to bedevil a seemingly open and routine effort on the part of the reporter. Pursuit of a story on an often-robbed fruit stand operator may be frustrated by the reluctant merchant or by police officials who fear that visibility of the issue may hamper investigations.

With so many "official" and "unofficial" sources, the reporter must make special efforts to establish reliable and trustworthy contacts, which are often critical to key information in a story. Human interest stories about members of the force are one way of making it more difficult to close out a reporter at headquarters. The reporter should begin early to develop legitimate and interesting material, not waiting until a sensitive story is sizzling in the frying pan. Feature story possibilities are endless—unusual outside interests, husband-wife teams on the force and sometimes person-related problems, such as having to take second jobs.

One teaches chops.
One cuts them.
Another checks them.
All that chopping is done by city policemen supplementing their incomes by moonlighting on part-time jobs.
The teacher is Detective Danny Lane. He delivers karate chops at a local self-defense school.
Detective Sam Blankenship cuts chops as a meatcutter for a local wholesale food distributor.
Guarding chops, as in pork and lamb, is Detective Arnold Ross, who spots shoplifters at a supermarket.
They are three of more than 100 city policemen, representing half the force, who make ends meet by holding second jobs. Under departmental regulations, officers can work up to 20 extra hours a week at other jobs.

Such stories are relevant, interesting and often sociologically important. As a further benefit, they offer the reporter an opportunity to make friends.

From one end of the city to the other. The police reporter must finally deal with the variety and scope of material on the beat. A major accident on the western edge of the city may be balanced by a simultaneous emergency at the other end. Often hasty decisions have to be made on whether to cover a major church fire or an imminent bridge collapse.

Some police beat stories have little or no connection with crime. Police are generally the first to know about emergencies such as fires, the weather or other natural conditions, power outages and special parade events in communities. It has been estimated that up to 85 percent of a department's time is devoted to responding to service calls, with the other 15 percent devoted to criminal matters. During an eight-hour shift, the police officer becomes a parent, physician, counselor, lawyer and even unpaid insurance company employee.

—A citizen reports a leaking gas main to police or, worse, an explosion caused by gas. The utility handles the details.

—A home emergency necessitates an ambulance trip to the hospital, and police forward the call to the emergency squad.

—Fire calls usually necessitate police department cooperation. Whatever the emergency, the police normally are involved.

The Enforcers of the Law

Although the locale differs, the big-city detective and the rural constable have much in common. The detective is questioning witnesses after a drug raid that resulted in a violent death. The constable is checking into the theft of some cows from Arlie Jacob's farm over on East Ridge.

The men and women who enforce the law in this country work under dissimilar conditions, but the work is the same:

—The small-town constable may be the only law enforcement agent in a Farm Belt community. He may hold another full-time job and act as cop part time, earning as little as $3,000 a year to protect the town's population of 250 persons.

—The 25,000 New York City police officers, traditionally called "New York's finest," enforce the laws of a huge city.

—An agent for the Federal Bureau of Investigation holds a college degree in accounting or law. Hundreds of such agents operate at the federal level, investigating an interstate theft ring, auditing records of a person accused of defrauding the government or cooperating with local authorities in a kidnapping case.

—A sheriff in the South may be charged with keeping the peace over a wide area and may also be responsible for collecting taxes and serving legal papers for the court system.

Reporting in all these jurisdictions falls to the police reporter, who may be a full-time journalist or merely a part-time "stringer" for a publication. Whatever the background, the first step is to sublimate preconceived notions about law enforcement, how it operates and the people who enforce the laws. An open mind, coupled with a dose of healthy skepticism, is essential on the police beat.

To most people, uniformed police officers assume an aura of power unlike other public employees. Some of this stems from early encounters with the law, often unpleasant but rarely more than that. A dressing-down by a police officer for trying to beat a red light can be most uncomfortable, particularly when it is coupled with a summons to appear in court Friday.

The police reporter clears away these biases and adopts the principle that law enforcement officers are like other people—some kind and understanding, a few ill-tempered and intransigent. Considering the pressures of the job, most are well-adjusted, even-tempered personalities. Few persons would fail to succumb to the pressure of easing 20,000 vehicles through a busy intersection each working day without occasionally letting off a little steam. But few citizens are more sensitive than a beat police officer who offers first aid to a stricken pedestrian while awaiting an ambulance.

The typical police officer is a high school graduate; increasing numbers possess college degrees. He or she has completed a basic instruction course in police work with professionals. The beginning salary range for a patrol officer in a medium-sized city is $10,000 to $15,000 annually, with fringe benefits including a clothing allowance for uniforms and equipment, differentials for evening and midnight shifts, substantial sick leave, holiday and vacation time off, and some type of pension plan.

While law enforcement has traditionally been a field dominated by men, women have increasingly become part of the criminal justice system. A dozen years ago, their function was limited to passing out parking tickets and acting as decoys in high crime areas. Today they operate patrol cars, direct traffic and undertake criminal investigations.

Police Department Organization

The office was abustle with controlled activity. At the rear of the room, a secretary guarded the entrance to the police chief's office. A radio receiver crackled in the corner. At the front counter a uniformed sergeant explained to an anxious woman: "We don't take parking tickets here, ma'am. Go down the hall and to your left. Look for a door that says 'Finance Department.'"

In a smaller community, the reporter's regular contact with a police department may be with a desk sergeant who presides over and compiles the daily "blotter," a 24-hour running account of all activity within the department. A fire call, a traffic accident, a police car out of service, a report of a robbery with only bare details—all are described briefly on the blotter.

In the larger cities, that function is being displaced by a service bureau with an office director, secretarial assistance and an official callboard for the press. In the bigger cities, as many as 30 stations or precinct headquarters are required; in a medium-sized city, one central police station is usually sufficient.

No matter what the size of the department, the reporter must first learn the organization, functions and responsibility of the various elements to effectively cover the beat.

The informal structure of the department is as important as the formal structure. Who is actually in charge in the central office? How much day-to-day responsibility does the police chief retain? Who are the department's chief policy-makers? Such organizational questions are important if the reporter is to cut through the frequent red tape and quickly get to the source of news stories.

Setting Basic Policy

While the police chief sets much of the policy for the department, the pragmatic reporter will look beyond that office to the elected officials in the community. It is they who are finally responsible for propounding the laws that assure an orderly community, and they often are more involved in the law enforcement function than they seem to be on the surface.

Be it a city council, a city commission, a municipal board or police commission, the governing body retains ultimate responsibility and control over the police department. Another level of control lies with a city manager or other city administrator, such as a safety director. Involvement of these municipal officials in police department affairs depends on the personalities of the individuals and the tradition of the community.

An ordinance to limit sale of alcoholic beverages after midnight is approved by city council, with a provision in the ordinance for enforcement by the police department. A council member may informally pass on to the department a complaint from a constituent that teen-age gangs are engaging in frequent free-for-alls on neighborhood streets.

> Mayor George Ballinger last night introduced an ordinance designed to regulate the growing number of massage parlors in the city.
>
> The key limitation, which would be enforced by the police department, would prohibit operation of the parlors between midnight and 6 a.m. daily.

In the popular city manager form of government, the police chief is often selected by the city manager, generally with concurrence of city council. Despite the increasingly professional character of law enforcement, the appointment is sometimes political. An unpopular police department possesses the capability of creating major problems for political figures seeking re-election, and police chiefs are occasionally caught in the cross fire between political opponents at election time.

> George P. Slater, heading the slate of independent candidates seeking City Council seats next month, promised to dismiss Police Chief O. T. Wilkins and reorganize the department if he and his group are elected.
>
> The current campaign has been characterized by frequent criticism of Wilkins and the Police Department.

For these reasons, the philosophy of a community's governing body concerning operation of its police department is important to the police reporter, who will follow developments at city hall as closely as the government affairs reporter.

Removal of top police officials is sometimes in the hands of a police governing board or council itself, but more often it is the responsibility of the city manager.

> Clarksburg Police Chief James Shield was relieved of his duties yesterday and returned to the rank of lieutenant, effective immediately.
>
> City Manager Pat Tremont, who ordered the dismissal, said his action had nothing to do with an internal investigation of the department, conducted after two confiscated slot machines disappeared from the collections room.
>
> "It was just time for a change," Tremont said.

The governing body of the municipality usually decides on a basic pay scale, increasingly negotiating with police fraternal organizations or organized labor unions in setting annual increases. It also allots funds for equipment and determines whether increases in staffing are necessary. In this not-too-subtle manner, a council or commission effectively places further controls on the police department.

How the Department is Organized

Day-to-day responsibilities for the department are in the hands of the police chief. In the generally accepted organizational chart, subordinates answer directly to the chief, who appoints division officers, orders promotions and demotions, approves procedures and requests equipment purchases, and often personally checks on important investigations. The chief is also responsible for transfers and suspensions.

In most personnel matters, the reporter will deal directly with the chief, who is often reluctant to delegate authority to release information concerning departmental policy and personnel. The effect of this is to slow down the public's access to important developments, not to cut it off entirely. Personal contact within the department often helps tip the reporter to future developments.

> Foot patrols will return to the city tomorrow when two police officers begin walking the controversial 20th Street bar area from 4 p.m. to midnight in an effort to reduce complaints.
>
> Most of the complaints have been logged after midnight, but Police Chief Louis Sarran explained the 4-12 hours have been ordered "for show."
>
> "This way, the business people will see them for a few hours and the bar customers will know they are there," he said.

Departmental disputes often find their way into print, either from police sources or from officials themselves. Some such disputes become highly politicized, with department personnel taking sides over programs and procedures. A new manual of objectives, for example, may reflect a desire by the police chief to make each officer a generalist rather than a specialist. The detective division may object strenuously but privately to the reporter.

The police chief is usually a key figure in these disputes, occasionally with less control over their outcome than he or she desires.

> Following a 3-hour meeting with the Civil Service Commission, Police Chief William Standiford has postponed an order that eight members of the Police Department undergo retraining.
>
> Standiford confirmed that he had postponed the action, but refused to discuss the matter with a reporter.
>
> He had issued a memorandum last week identifying the police officers as "needing immediate basic retraining" after receiving written reports from their commanders indicating poor performance.

Police department morale is a recurring issue, sometimes creating sufficient friction to involve the reporter on the beat. The astute reporter resists alignment with one faction or another, working to produce impersonal stories about the dispute.

The final word in many department personnel disputes lies with civil service commissions, established to decide merit disputes and other personnel matters, rather than with a city council, police board or mayor.

> A 90-day suspension and reduction in rank for Police Capt. Henry Playford was sustained today by the Civil Service Board.
>
> Playford was reduced in rank to lieutenant and suspended May 10 for failure to take a polygraph test upon order of Police Chief Willis Henson. Playford had appealed the order to the board.

Another area of frequent dispute lies in the police department's relationships with outside organizations and agencies. It may be with the American Civil Liberties Union or with the judiciary; it may be with the county sheriff's department or with a state investigations unit; it may be professionally motivated or purely political.

An active ACLU chapter in a city will often become embroiled in police actions that it believes to be excessive. Acting as an ombudsman for the public, the ACLU may attempt to limit use of deadly force by police officers. It may propose that police training include instruction on alternatives to use of deadly force.

Depending on the area, there are often as many disputes with outside agencies as there are areas of cooperation. The reporter should remember that a police officer may sometimes have a much different perspective than a judge.

> Thirty-four armed robberies have occurred in the city so far this year, and the police chief believes "the entire judicial system is making it tougher for officers to cope with the problem."
>
> The department reported 21 armed robberies in January, 10 last month and three so far this month. That's half the number reported during all of last year.
>
> "I don't want to blame any one person—magistrates, prosecutors or judges," said Chief Earl Durden, "but I am saying the judicial system is just not working right."
>
> Durden said 12 of the 17 persons already charged in connection with 25 of the 34 armed robberies this year "are back on the streets after posting bond."

With the police chief at the apex of the chart, departments are organized in paramilitary fashion, with captains, lieutenants, sergeants and patrol officers. Functions of the various subdepartments have become increasingly specialized, with an administrative unit, a patrol and/or traffic unit, an investigations division containing a detective bureau and a crime prevention unit which deals with the public in education matters and provides information. (See Figure 9–1.)

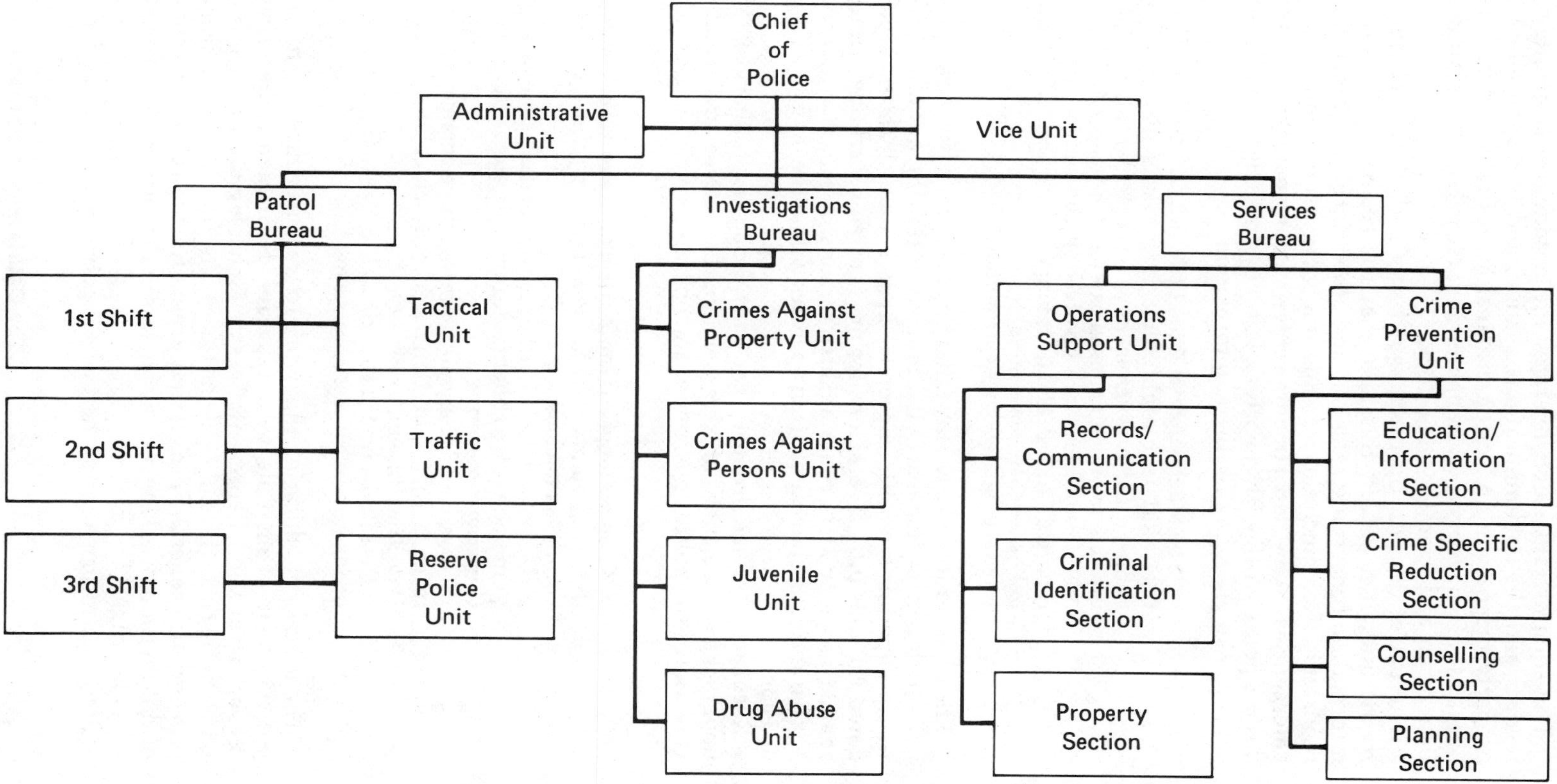

FIGURE 9-1. *An organizational chart for a typical municipal police department.*

The administrative unit operates the headquarters, maintains records and the communications system, and is responsible for property disposition and often criminal identification. A service bureau is often charged with maintaining records and operating a fingerprint and scientific laboratory.

The patrol division operates squad cars and often includes a traffic unit. It is within this unit that the reporter will obtain information concerning collisions and other traffic problems. The reporter is often much closer to this unit because it responds first to emergencies. Some departments refuse to allow patrol officers to discuss police work with reporters, but most investigating officers cooperate in providing firsthand information.

> "Too much snow and too little salt," Patrolman L. D. Otis said last night after traffic was disrupted on slippery Fifth Avenue by a spectacular pileup that injured no one but caused extensive property damage.
>
> Nine vehicles were involved in the snowy jam, Otis reported. Asked about damage, he responded: "I can only guess. It was a mess."
>
> Otis' educated guess: around $15,000.

The reporter looks to the investigations unit for a broad range of information on criminal activity, much of it flowing out of today's vastly superior scientific methods. Larger municipalities break down the unit into several smaller ones, often separating crimes against property and crimes against persons. A separate juvenile section and drug abuse unit often operates within the investigations division.

Recovery of stolen property, car theft, fraud and robbery all fall under the jurisdiction of this section. Detectives are usually veterans of the police department and operate as a non-uniformed unit.

> When a shopper at the Central Mall saw three persons throwing empty coat hangers under a parked car, she became suspicious.
>
> Her suspicions led to the recovery of more than $10,000 in merchandise shoplifted from area stores during the Christmas season.
>
> "It was a mini-shoplifting ring, three outsiders trying to cash in," said Don L. Morris, chief of the city's Detective Bureau, yesterday.
>
> Detectives traced the trio to 115 Burke St., where the goods were recovered, Morris said.

The process of educating the public to ways in which it can best protect itself often falls to a separate department, the crime prevention division. Representatives visit schools and civic organizations to discuss the police department, its functions and crime prevention in general. Special study groups function under direction of this division, working on ways to lessen the incidence of specific types of crime.

Statistical information gathered by the division is shared with the press as well as with other police units. Modern police departments also provide informational services through a counseling section.

> The doors of more than half of the cars stolen in the city were unlocked, a statistical breakdown by the Crime Prevention Bureau shows.
>
> Of 386 motorists whose vehicles were stolen, 202 failed to lock their doors, according to a study of stolen vehicle reports.
>
> "Locking your car may not deter a professional car thief, but it most certainly will cut losses by amateurs," said William Dawson, chief of the unit.

Covering the Police Beat

Although crime reporting has changed, an important basic principle remains. The surveillance function by the press of the law enforcement process continues to be a necessary element in assuring the rights of citizens. The reporting of crime, and its subsequent resolution through the judicial process, is a natural outgrowth of this need.

However, the new emphasis in crime reporting is on the *why* rather than merely on the old *what*—vivid detail of high-speed auto chases and gun-toting badmen cornered in crumbling farmhouses. Some of this stems from scientific crime detection advances, some from a far more sophisticated and better educated audience. However, the human drama continues to play a part in police beat coverage.

In smaller communities, the police beat is not a full-time assignment. A city hall reporter may include it as part of the daily rounds. Some newspapers provide their staffers with radio receivers or "scanners" at home, and it is not uncommon for a reporter to be at the scene of a fatal accident outside his or her regular hours.

Metropolitan newspapers usually detail reporters to the police beat on a full-time basis, some rarely seeing the newsroom. Reporters operate out of a press room at police headquarters, with contact to their office through telephone or teletype. The reporter's auto is usually equipped with a police radio to monitor calls, and a radio telephone may connect the car with the newspaper office or television newsroom.

The police reporter in the smaller city begins the day by studying the running, 24-hour account of all activity. Incoming complaints, vehicles dispatched, traffic accidents, burglary reports and routine messages are all listed, often with scant information. The police blotter serves to alert the reporter to nearly all the activity occurring during a specified period. Not everything is always transmitted to the blotter, however. The alert reporter is aware that references to sensitive stories in smaller communities may be conspicuously absent from the sheet. For this reason, arrest and complaint reports should always be carefully checked as well.

The blotter's brevity is expanded with more detailed information

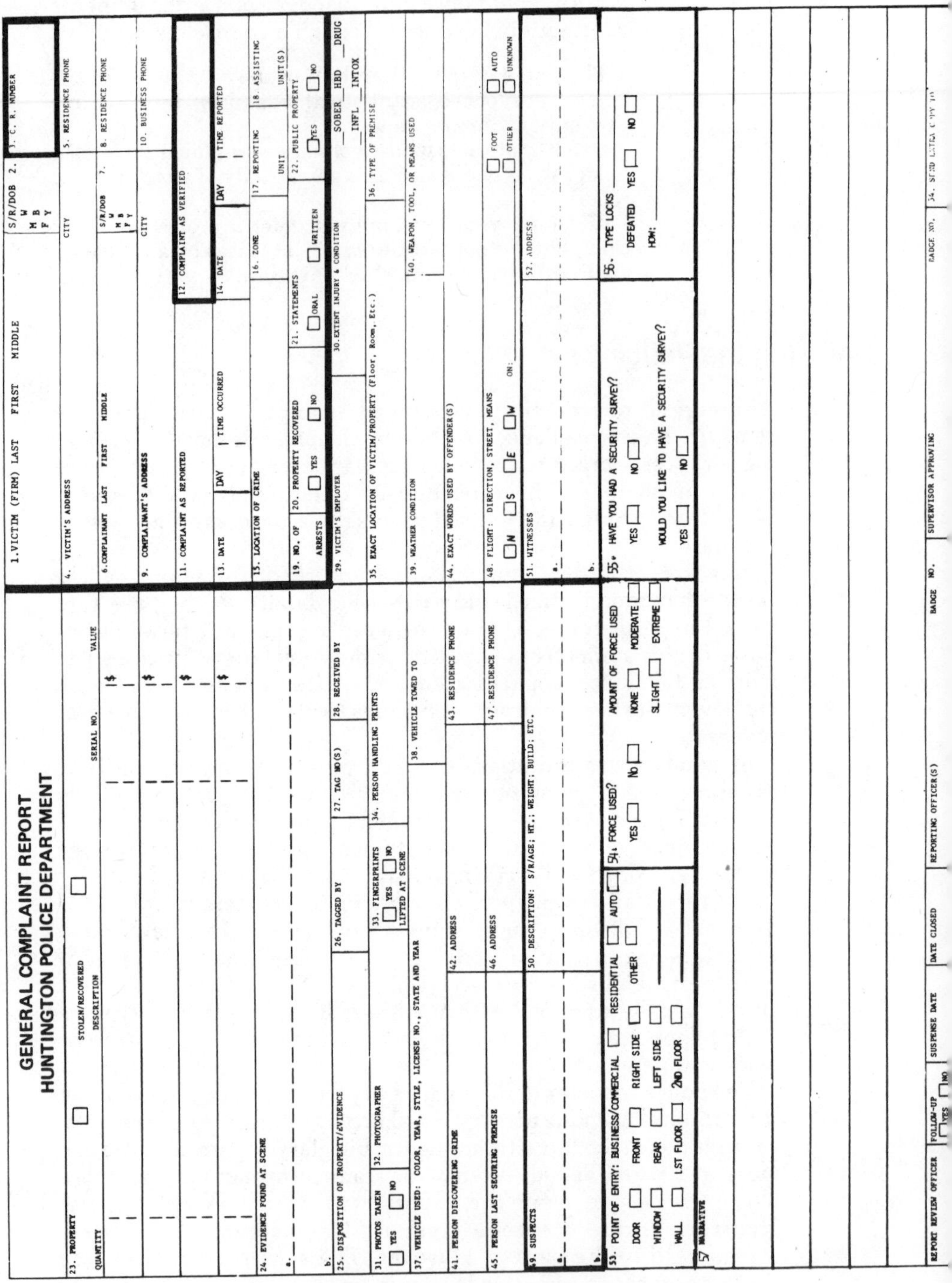
GENERAL COMPLAINT REPORT
HUNTINGTON POLICE DEPARTMENT

1. VICTIM (FIRM) LAST FIRST MIDDLE
S/R/DOB M F W B Y
2.
3. C. R. NUMBER
4. VICTIM'S ADDRESS
CITY
5. RESIDENCE PHONE
6. COMPLAINANT LAST FIRST MIDDLE
S/R/DOB M F W B Y
7.
8. RESIDENCE PHONE
9. COMPLAINANT'S ADDRESS
CITY
10. BUSINESS PHONE
11. COMPLAINT AS REPORTED
12. COMPLAINT AS VERIFIED
13. DATE
DAY
TIME OCCURRED
14. DATE
DAY
TIME REPORTED
15. LOCATION OF CRIME
16. ZONE
17. REPORTING UNIT
18. ASSISTING UNIT(S)
19. NO. OF ARRESTS
20. PROPERTY RECOVERED ☐ YES ☐ NO
21. STATEMENTS ☐ ORAL ☐ WRITTEN
22. PUBLIC PROPERTY ☐ YES ☐ NO
23. PROPERTY ☐ STOLEN/RECOVERED ☐
QUANTITY | DESCRIPTION | SERIAL NO. | VALUE $
24. EVIDENCE FOUND AT SCENE
a.
b.
25. DISPOSITION OF PROPERTY/EVIDENCE
26. TAGGED BY
27. TAG NO(S)
28. RECEIVED BY
29. VICTIM'S EMPLOYER
30. EXTENT INJURY & CONDITION
__SOBER __HBD __DRUG
__INFL __INTOX
31. PHOTOS TAKEN ☐ YES ☐ NO
32. PHOTOGRAPHER
33. FINGERPRINTS ☐ YES ☐ NO LIFTED AT SCENE
34. PERSON HANDLING PRINTS
35. EXACT LOCATION OF VICTIM/PROPERTY (Floor, Room, Etc.)
36. TYPE OF PREMISE
37. VEHICLE USED: COLOR, YEAR, STYLE, LICENSE NO., STATE AND YEAR
38. VEHICLE TOWED TO
39. WEATHER CONDITION
40. WEAPON, TOOL, OR MEANS USED
41. PERSON DISCOVERING CRIME
42. ADDRESS
43. RESIDENCE PHONE
44. EXACT WORDS USED BY OFFENDER(S)
45. PERSON LAST SECURING PREMISE
46. ADDRESS
47. RESIDENCE PHONE
48. FLIGHT: DIRECTION, STREET, MEANS
☐ N ☐ S ☐ E ☐ W ON:
☐ FOOT ☐ AUTO ☐ OTHER ☐ UNKNOWN
49. SUSPECTS
a.
b.
50. DESCRIPTION: S/R/AGE; HT.; WEIGHT; BUILD; ETC.
51. WITNESSES
a.
b.
52. ADDRESS
53. POINT OF ENTRY: BUSINESS/COMMERCIAL ☐ RESIDENTIAL ☐ AUTO ☐
DOOR ☐ FRONT ☐ RIGHT SIDE ☐ OTHER ☐
WINDOW ☐ REAR ☐ LEFT SIDE ☐
WALL ☐ 1ST FLOOR ☐ 2ND FLOOR ☐
54. FORCE USED? YES ☐ NO ☐
AMOUNT OF FORCE USED
NONE ☐ MODERATE ☐
SLIGHT ☐ EXTREME ☐
55. HAVE YOU HAD A SECURITY SURVEY?
YES ☐ NO ☐
WOULD YOU LIKE TO HAVE A SECURITY SURVEY?
YES ☐ NO ☐
56. TYPE LOCKS
DEFEATED YES ☐ NO ☐
HOW:
57 NARRATIVE
REPORT REVIEW OFFICER
FOLLOW-UP ☐ YES ☐ NO
SUSPENSE DATE
DATE CLOSED
REPORTING OFFICER(S)
BADGE NO.
SUPERVISOR APPROVING
BADGE NO.
54. SEND EXTRA COPY TO

FIGURE 9-2. *A general complaint report form.*

from the desk sergeant, investigating officer and the police chief. It should be noted that the police blotter is not a privileged document, so the reporter must obtain specific information from official records. Comments by investigating officers are not privileged either, and the reporter should exercise care that libel is not committed through careless comments by police.

Many departments have abolished the old blotter, using instead a complaint board containing official reports. A service bureau is responsible for collecting and dispensing such information, which remains easily accessible to the press for as long as 48 hours.

The reporter checks a general complaint board for information on all crimes committed within the department's jurisdiction and an accident board, which contains official reports of all traffic accidents. These are privileged documents, along with an arrest record, often called a "rap sheet," that become part of department records. The "rap sheet" is a compilation of information regarding any arrest or temporary detention and includes the identity of the person arrested or detained, the nature of the police contact, the charge (if any) and the disposition or current status of the case.

If the case results in a conviction, police also maintain a conviction record and often compile investigative reports or "statements of fact," which are not generally available to the reporter.

An overnight burglary will be noted on the complaint board identifying the homeowner, valuables taken, method of entry and so forth. The reporter should check with the supervisor on duty in the investigations unit and with the detective who responded to the complaint for any unusual angles. Is the burglary part of a pattern and similar to others? Has there been a rash of them in the area? Was someone at home during the entry?

Oral statements by the detective are not privileged, although his or her comments on the complaint board are privileged.

The reporter will also have access to the lockup to speak with prisoners, although the trend today is to provide jail facilities in a central location, often operated by the county. In such cases, identical arrest records are also maintained at the jail by agencies in charge of the facility.

Identity of victims of criminal acts and witnesses is one of the prime goals of the police reporter, who seeks out eyewitness accounts for more accurate and vivid news stories.

> Two bandits slipped into Willis Drugs this morning, held two employees and three customers at gunpoint and escaped with nearly $2,000 in cash.
>
> "They held us in the corner, grabbed the money and went," said Ted Willis, operator of the store located at 2020 3rd Ave. "It all happened in less than five minutes."
>
> Willis described the men as tall, black-haired with red face masks. "One put the gun (a pistol) to my head and made me face the wall while the other went through the cash register," he said. "I was scared to death."

The reporter should be prepared to make a personal visit if time permits or to use the telephone in search of such material. Effort like this often results in altering a routine story and turning it into a far more readable account.

With the growth of computer use, more detailed statistical information is being compiled by police departments, much of it being made available to the press. A study of the department's statistics bureau often provides interesting and important data.

The data are used in department planning and staffing, but they are also pertinent to the public. Areas with high crime incidence, for example, can quickly be located through use of the computer and detailed incidents in the area compiled for a story.

> The intersection of Central Avenue and Fifth Street, under state study for possible relocation, has averaged five traffic accidents a week for more than two years, a Statistical Bureau analysis shows.
>
> "Collisions at that point and traffic tieups are the reason work needs to be done straightening it out," Supervisor Robert Roane said yesterday.
>
> A computer analysis shows that 517 traffic collisions occurred within one block of the intersection during a two-year period ending yesterday.

Writing the Crime Story

The basic rules for writing the crime story are not complex. There is a need to be straightforward, precise, fair and accurate, which requires both curiosity and care on the part of the reporter. Choice of words is important.

Clichés are to be avoided on every beat, but the field of law enforcement has its own peculiar brand. The reporter should resist the temptation to "launch an investigation," identify an officer as "grim faced," or write that a suspect has "vanished into thin air."

By the end of their first month on the police beat, most reporters have probably covered their first important fire, with not a few succumbing to the temptation to write the most overwritten of all leads:

> Fire of undetermined origin swept through an East Side home about 9 p.m. Wednesday, killing a 72-year invalid.

Most editors have been rejecting this overworked beginning to fire stories for years, and send the reporter back to the video display terminal for something fresher.

> A 72-year-old invalid collapsed and died at her front door as fire swept through her East Side home about 9 p.m. Wednesday.
>
> Police identified her as Florence Louise Wolfe, 806 Kenton Ave. She lived alone, they said.
>
> Assistant Fire Chief Neal Mills said the fire might have been caused by a lighted cigarette that burned a living room chair after Ms. Wolfe fell asleep.

While most fires do bear the label, undetermined origin, during

USE OF FIREARM REPORT

DATE OF INCIDENT TIME

☐ O.R. NUMBER
☐ C.I.

OFFICERS NAME-BADGE RANK SEX AGE | DATE OF APPOINTMENT | ASSIGNMENT

DUTY STATUS ☐ ON DUTY ☐ OFF DUTY ☐ W/PARTNER ☐ ALONE ☐ SPECIAL DUTY ☐ W/AUXILIARY ☐ NON UNIFORM ☐ UNIFORM ☐ OTHER-SPECIFY:

HOW DID OFFICER BECOME INVOLVED IN INCIDENT ☐ OTHER-SPECIFY:
☐ RADIO ☐ ON VIEW ☐ CITIZEN

TYPE OF INCIDENT ☐ DOMESTIC ☐ TRAFFIC RELATED ☐ OTHER-SPECIFY:
☐ ROBBERY ☐ BURGLARY ☐ MAN WITH A GUN

WHY DID OFFICER USE WEAPON ☐ TO PROTECT CITIZEN ☐ TO PROTECT SELF
☐ TO PREVENT DANGEROUS FELONY ☐ TO PREVENT ESCAPE OF A DANGEROUS FELON
☐ OTHER-SPECIFY:

WAS THERE ANY PHYSICAL EXERTION PRIOR TO INCIDENT
☐ PHYSICAL STRUGGLE ☐ RUNNING ☐ OTHER-SPECIFY:

TYPE OF COVER USED BY OFFICER

OFFICERS WEAPON ☐ SHOTGUN ☐ CPD REVOLVER ☐ PERSONAL WEAPON ☐ OTHER-SPECIFY:
MODEL ____ BARREL LENGTH ____ CALIBER ____
TYPE OF AMMUNITION USED

NO. SHOTS FIRED BY OFFICER ____ ☐ SINGLE ACTION ☐ DOUBLE ACTION ☐ TWO HANDED ☐ ONE HANDED ☐ STRONG HAND ☐ WEAK HAND
WAS WEAPON RELOADED DURING INCIDENT ☐ YES ☐ NO

DISTANCE FROM SUSPECT WHEN FIRST SHOT WAS FIRED ____ LAST SHOT WAS FIRED ____
ESTIMATED ELAPSED TIME BETWEEN FIRST AND LAST SHOT: ____
WERE GUN SIGHTS USED? ☐ YES ☐ NO
IMMEDIATELY BEFORE SHOOTING, WAS HANDGUN ☐ HOLSTERED ☐ ALREADY DRAWN

POSITION OF OFFICER ☐ SITTING ☐ KNEELING ☐ SEATED IN VEHICLE ☐ OTHER-SPECIFY:
☐ STANDING ☐ RUNNING ☐ PRONE

INJURIES SUSTAINED BY OFFICER
☐ NOT WOUNDED ☐ SUPERFICIAL ☐ CRITICAL ☐ KILLED
WAS OFFICER HOSPITALIZED? ☐ YES ☐ NO

ADDRESS OF INCIDENT
TYPE OF PREMISES ☐ COMMERCIAL BUILDING ☐ OPEN AREA ☐ STREET ☐ APARTMENT ☐ HOME ☐ OTHER-SPECIFY:

LIGHTING CONDITIONS ☐ INDOORS ☐ OUTDOORS ☐ DAY ☐ NIGHT ☐ GOOD ☐ POOR ☐ DUSK ☐ NATURAL LIGHT ☐ FLASHLIGHT ☐ DAWN ☐ OTHER-SPECIFY:
WEATHER CONDITIONS ☐ CLEAR ☐ CLOUDY ☐ RAIN ☐ SNOW ☐ FOG
WERE GLOVES WORN DURING SHOOTING? ☐ YES ☐ NO

SUSPECT NO. 1 NAME SEX AGE RACE
SUSPECT NO. 2 NAME SEX AGE RACE
MULTIPLE SUSPECTS ☐ YES ☐ NO
NO. MALES ____ NO. FEMALES ____
ANIMAL: ☐ YES ☐ NO
SPECIFY TYPE: ____

SUSPECTS WEAPON ☐ HANDGUN ☐ SHOTGUN ☐ RIFLE ☐ KNIFE
MAKE ____ MODEL ____
CALIBER ____ ☐ OTHER SPECIFY:
TYPE OF COVER USED BY SUSPECT

NO. SHOTS FIRED BY SUSPECT
DISTANCE FROM OFFICER WHEN FIRST SHOT WAS FIRED ____ LAST SHOT WAS FIRED ____
POSITION OF SUSPECT ☐ STANDING ☐ OTHER-SPECIFY: ☐ RUNNING ☐ SEATED IN VEHICLE ☐ SITTING ☐ KNEELING ☐ PRONE

INJURIES SUSTAINED BY SUSPECT
☐ NOT WOUNDED ☐ SUPERFICIAL ☐ CRITICAL ☐ KILLED ☐ UNKNOWN

WAS SUSPECT HOSPITALIZED? ☐ YES ☐ NO
LOCATION OF SUSPECTS INJURY, WHAT BODY PARTS(S) SPECIFY:

REPORTING SUPERVISOR DATE:

S-70.100

FIGURE 9-3. *A "use of firearm report" form.*

preliminary investigation, officials expert in this area often provide information that will take the reader beyond the bare facts.

Exaggerated reports of crime should be avoided at all costs, but literary techniques that will be effective in telling a story should be sought out and utilized.

> John Turner slammed his fist on the table, snatched his woolen cap from his head, jumped from his seat and shouted at the gray-haired man who was examining the parking ticket.
>
> "Give that ticket back to me," he yelled at the hearing examiner, Herman Dorfman. "You're going to find me guilty anyway. You don't give no breaks down here. I'm just wasting my time."
>
> Turner is one of 150,000 motorists who sought hearings last year at the Parking Violations Bureau because they felt themselves unjustly served with parking tickets.
>
> And while in the past, few could expect to win the battles, today the Davids of the driving world are often winning disputes with the Goliath-like bureaucracy responsible for adjudicating parking tickets.
>
> More than 80 percent of the people who show up for hearings have their cases dismissed, or fines and penalties reduced, according to the bureau.

Good writing that focuses on the heart of an issue is important, but so is content.

Carelessness in identification is one of the chief causes of libel suits against publications. That's why the police reporter will exercise such care in obtaining middle initials and correct addresses. When there is doubt, clothing a person's identity with "police listed Jones's address as 124 Cardinal St." will help when exact verification is impossible because of deadlines.

Caution is also necessary in clothing a statement with "alleged" and the "suspect." They are only partial defenses in libel suits and should be avoided. Referring to a person, particularly one who has not been charged, as "the alleged intruder" or "the alleged robber" is not only unfair but unsafe.

The reporter should avoid another danger zone—writing about a specific charge before it is formally placed. A person arrested in connection with a rape or robbery constitutes a legitimate story. But adding to the story, "Brown will likely be charged with rape, according to police," is also unfair and dangerous. Quoting authorities as to their future intention should be avoided.

Caution should also be exercised in incidents involving domestic arguments, a routine complaint in most cities. While poignant stories can be written about wife and child abuse, care should be taken in reporting what a distraught wife says about her recalcitrant husband. She may be willing to "throw the book at him" one night, then deny everything the next day, leaving the reporter high and dry and subject to action in court.

Precision is Important

The reporter must also be precise in routine as well as in major crime stories, avoiding such generalities as "Jones was jailed on an open charge," conveying to the reader that some kind of charge was filed. In fact, no charge may have been filed. Instead, the story will state: "Jones is being detained but has not been charged."

There is a vast difference between the terms "arrest" and "detain." Should a reporter observe a person being taken into custody, then later released, he or she should write that the person was merely "detained and released for lack of evidence" rather than "arrested."

Correct words may be dangerous because of imposition of a preposition. The police reporter should avoid "A Reedsville man has been indicted *for* armed robbery." This oversteps the bounds of fairness and safety because the phrase taken literally means that he has committed the crime. The defendant has merely been held for trial on the charge and is presumed innocent until found guilty. So the reporter will write: "A Reedsville man has been indicted *on a charge of* armed robbery" or "*in connection with* an armed robbery." Precision is essential to total fairness.

Qualifying the Information

The importance of qualifying information cannot be overemphasized. While the word of law enforcement officials is not an absolute defense for a reporter on deadline, it is certainly a mitigating factor.

The temptation would be strong to provide an exciting lead and fast-paced account of the arrest of a husband who shot his wife, then engaged in a shoot-out with police before being shot himself. But because the reporter did not actually witness the affair, the story required substantial qualification. Note the care with which the reporter produced the information.

> A former member of the city School Board was found shot to death in her home yesterday, and police are holding her husband for investigation.
>
> The dead woman is Mrs. Simon Gideon, 54, who served three terms on the board from 1962 to 1974 and did not seek re-election. Her body was found in the bedroom of her home at 3200 High St. by police who were called when neighbors heard shooting.
>
> Police arrested Mrs. Gideon's husband, who is 57, after an exchange of shots.
>
> Det. Sgt. Dan Williams said police found Gideon, an insurance adjustor, in the kitchen armed with a .45-caliber pistol. He fired several shots before surrendering, Williams said, and was wounded in the left arm by shots fired by police. Gideon was taken to Riverside Hospital emergency room, then to the police lockup.
>
> Police had been called to the house once before,

STATE OF OHIO
TRAFFIC CRASH REPORT

OH-4 (Rev. 1/77)

LOCAL REPORT NO. | OH-2 OH-3 OH-5 | CITY CODE | —DEPT. OF HIGHWAY SAFETY ONLY—

ACCIDENT SEVERITY: FATAL · INJURY · PROP. DAMAGE · P.D. UNDER $150

FILE NO. LOCAL USE

REPORTING AGENCY | OH | TIME OF CRASH | DAY | DATE OF CRASH (MO, DAY, YR)

ON PRIV. PROP.

IN COUNTY OF | ON ROUTE, CO. OR TWP. ROAD, STREET ADDRESS | AT JUNCTION OR INTERSECTION WITH

HIT & RUN UNSOLVED · HIT & RUN SOLVED

IN (CITY, VILLAGE, TOWNSHIP) OF | MILES · FEET | N S E W | OF | MILEPOST, JUNCTION, INTERSECTION, BRIDGE, ETC. | PHOTO REFERENCE

FED-AID | LOG-LOC | JUR | TC | FLT | DESCRIPTION | DIR. ALIGN

UNIT NO. 1

TOTAL UNITS INVOLVED

DRIVER — LAST | FIRST | MIDDLE | SEX | DATE OF BIRTH (MO., DAY, YR.) | AGE | SOCIAL SECURITY NUMBER

ADDRESS — NUMBER STREET | CITY | STATE | PHONE | CIRCLE DAMAGED AREAS

STATE | OPERATOR LIC. NO. | RESTR | CLASS | ENDOR | OCCUPATION | DAMAGE SEVERITY: SL · SE · MO · DE

OWNER — LAST | FIRST | MIDDLE | ADDRESS — NUMBER STREET | CITY | STATE | PHONE

VEHICLE YEAR 19 | MAKE | MODEL NAME | COLOR | BODY STYLE | VEHICLE DIR. N S E W | ODOMETER READING | STATE | LICENSE NO. | YEAR

NAME OF INSURANCE COMPANY/AGENT | NAME OF WRECKER | INJURED TAKEN TO | BY WHOM

DAMAGE ESTIMATE: NONE · OVER $150 · UNDER $150 | ALCOHOL TEST GIVEN: NO · YES | TYPE | RESULTS | ORD. OR CODE NUMBER: CITY ORD. · STATE CODE | ORD. DESCRIPTION

UNIT NO. 2

VEH. · PED. · ANIMAL · TRAIN

DRIVER — LAST | FIRST | MIDDLE | SEX | DATE OF BIRTH (MO., DAY, YR.) | AGE | SOCIAL SECURITY NUMBER

ADDRESS — NUMBER STREET | CITY | STATE | PHONE | CIRCLE DAMAGED AREAS

STATE | OPERATOR LIC. NO. | RESTR | CLASS | ENDOR | OCCUPATION | DAMAGE SEVERITY: SL · SE · MO · DE

OWNER — LAST | FIRST | MIDDLE | ADDRESS — NUMBER STREET | CITY | STATE | PHONE

PROPERTY: CITY · COUNTY · STATE · FEDERAL · PRIVATE

VEHICLE YEAR 19 | MAKE | MODEL NAME | COLOR | BODY STYLE | VEHICLE DIR. N S E W | ODOMETER READING | STATE | LICENSE NO. | YEAR

NAME OF INSURANCE COMPANY/AGENT | NAME OF WRECKER | INJURED TAKEN TO | BY WHOM

OWNER NOTIFIED: YES · NO

DAMAGE ESTIMATE: NONE · OVER $150 · UNDER $150 | ALCOHOL TEST GIVEN: NO · YES | TYPE | RESULTS | ORD. OR CODE NUMBER: CITY ORD. · STATE CODE | ORD. DESCRIPTION

OCC. 1 UNIT · WIT.
NAME — LAST | FIRST | MIDDLE | DATE OF BIRTH (MO., DAY, YR.) | AGE
ADDRESS — NUMBER STREET | CITY | STATE | PHONE | SEX

OCC. 2 UNIT · WIT.
NAME — LAST | FIRST | MIDDLE | DATE OF BIRTH (MO, DAY, YR.) | AGE
ADDRESS — NUMBER STREET | CITY | STATE | PHONE | SEX

OCC. 3 UNIT · WIT.
NAME — LAST | FIRST | MIDDLE | DATE OF BIRTH (MO., DAY, YR.) | AGE
ADDRESS — NUMBER STREET | CITY | STATE | PHONE | SEX

OCC. 4 UNIT · WIT.
NAME — LAST | FIRST | MIDDLE | DATE OF BIRTH (MO., DAY, YR.) | AGE
ADDRESS — NUMBER STREET | CITY | STATE | PHONE | SEX

TIME POLICE: RECEIVED CALL | DISPATCHED | ARRIVED SCENE | CLEARED SCENE | OTHER INVESTIGATION | TOTAL TIME

OCC. 1 | INJURED TAKEN TO | BY WHOM | OCC. 3 | INJURED TAKEN TO | BY WHOM | OFFICER'S I.D.

OCC. 2 | | | OCC. 4 | | | CHECKED BY

DR. / PED: DR. 1, 2 · OCCUPANT 1 2 3 4

INJURY SEVERITY
1 Fatal
2 Incapacitating injury
3 Visible signs of injury
4 Claimed injury
5 No claimed injury

RESTRAINTS IN USE
1 Seat belt
2 Harness and seat belt
3 Shoulder harness
4 None in use
5 Other
6 None installed

POSITION
1 Front left
2 Front center
3 Front right
4 Back left
5 Back center
6 Back right
7 Other

CONDITION (PED/DR)
1 Apparently normal
2 Sick
3 Fatigued
4 Apparently sleepy
5 Physical defect
6 Apparently drinking
7 OMVI
8 Apparent drug usage

EJECTION
1 Total
2 Partial
3 Not ejected
4 Trapped

FIGURE 9-4. *A traffic crash report form.*

STATE OF OHIO

REPORT NO. (LOCAL)

TYPE OF CRASH

(Two Moving Motor Vehicles)

1 Head-on
2 Rear-end
3 Sideswipe
4 Angle
5 Turning

(One Moving MV and —)

6 Parked motor vehicle
7 Pedestrian
8 Animal
9 Train
0 Pedalcycles
1 Other non-motor vehicle
2 Fixed object
3 Other object

(One MV Only)

4 Overturning
5 Other non-collision

MOTORCYCLE

UNIT
1 2
Light (up to 100 cc)
Medium (101 to 349 cc)
Heavy (over 350 cc)
Yes / No — Helmet
Yes / No — Extended fork

LOCATION

1 Street or highway intersection
2 Intersection related
3 Driveway access
4 Railroad crossing
5 Bridge (over 20' span)
6 Subway (underpass)
7 Bridge or culvert (spans 20' and under)
8 Interchange
9 Non-intersection

CONTOUR

1 Straight, level
2 Straight, grade
3 Straight, hillcrest
4 Curve, level
5 Curve, grade
6 Curve, hillcrest

OCCURRENCE

1 On roadway
2 Off roadway
3 Off left side
4 Off right side
5 On other roadway (divided highway)

RAMP

Lettercode ________
1 Ramp beginning
2 On the ramp
3 Ramp end
4 At the intersection of two ramps

LIGHT CONDITIONS

1 Daylight
2 Dawn or dusk
3 Dark—no lights
4 Dark but lighted
5 Other ________

CAUSATIVE FACTORS

UNIT
1 2
01 Failure to yield
02 Ran stop signal
03 Driving wrong way
04 Improper passing
05 Improper turning
06 OMVI
07 Driving too slow
08 Traffic signal violation
09 Left of center
10 Stopped or parked illegally
11 Excessive speed
12 Following too close
13 Driver inattention
14 View obstruction
15 None
16 Vehicle defects
17 Road defects
18 Ped. action
19 Other ________

DEFECTS

UNIT
1 2
1 Brakes
2 Lights
3 Steering
4 Tires
5 Other ________
6 None

WEATHER

1 No adverse weather condition
2 Rain
3 Snow
4 Fog
5 Heavy wind
6 Other ________

PEDESTRIAN ACTION

01 In crosswalk
02 Crossing other than crosswalk
03 Walking with traffic
04 Walking against traffic
05 Working or playing in roadway
06 Entering or leaving vehicle
07 On highway but not in roadway
08 Off highway
09 Other ________
10 Working on car

FIXED ROADSIDE OBJECT STRUCK

UNIT
1 2
1 Light or utility pole
2 Bridge or culvert
3 Sign, signal or support
4 Guard rail
5 Fence
6 Tree
7 Ditch or embankment
8 Curb
9 Construct. barricade
10 None
11 Other ________

ROAD CONDITIONS

1 Dry
2 Wet
3 Snow or ice
4 Mud or sand
5 Other ________

NO. LANES

INTENDED DRIVER ACTION

UNIT
1 2
01 Going straight
02 Changing lanes
03 Passing
04 Turning right
05 Turning left
06 Stopped to turn
07 Parking
08 Unparking
09 Parked
10 Backing
11 Stopped in traffic
12 U-turn
13 Merging onto freeway
14 Exiting from freeway
15 Swerving to avoid
16 Other ________

TRAFFIC CONTROL

UNIT
1 2
1 Traffic officer
2 Stop sign
3 Yield sign
4 Railroad signal
5 Traffic signal
6 Official barricade
7 Other ________
8 None

ROAD SURFACE

1 Asphalt
2 Concrete
3 Gravel
4 Other ________

ROAD WIDTH

TYPE OF UNIT

UNIT
1 2
01 Passenger car
02 Single body truck
03 Pickup
04 Van
05 Truck Tractor
06 Tractor/Semi-Trailer
07 Tractor/Double Trailer
08 Fire truck
09 Police vehicle
10 Emergency vehicle
11 Bus public
12 Bus school
13 Bus church
14 Taxi
15 Train
16 Motorcycle
17 Motor scooter
18 Motor home
19 Bicycle
20 Motorized bicycle
21 Animal w/rider
22 Animal w/buggy
23 Farm veh., unlicensed
24 Other ________

TOWING

UNIT
1 2
01 Trailer
02 Camper
03 Other ________

ACCIDENT DESCRIPTION TO INCLUDE POINT OF IMPACT:

—OTHER INVESTIGATION NOTES —

DIAGRAM (Show all lanes, label all units)

INDICATE NORTH BY ARROW

SPEED		
UNIT	STATED	POSTED
1		
2		

SKIDMARK DATA	UNIT 1	UNIT 2
R.F.		
L.F.		
R.R.		
L.R.		
% Gr.		

FIGURE 9-4. (*Continued*).

> Williams said, and added that there was a record of trouble between Mr. and Mrs. Gideon.
>
> Mrs. Gideon was an accountant who worked for several firms in the city. The couple had no children.

Despite the temptation to handle this story somewhat differently, it is always best to use care in qualifying it.

Fairness dictates similar caution in reporting traffic accidents. Claims by persons injured in collisions frequently conclude in court litigation, with judge and jury deciding the outcome. Reporters are often dependent on accident reports turned in hours after the incident occured and upon an investigating officer who arrived at the scene after it happened. The reporter must exercise care in reporting damage estimates as well as other questionable data.

> A car driven at high speed by Howard University student Lorie Wills jumped a curb and crashed into a Central Avenue home near the school last night, sending the occupants of the house dashing to safety. Two rooms sustained major damage, but no one was injured.

The underlined words constitute danger for the reporter, unless he or she personally observed the incident. Such a story requires major attribution before being published, even though it is routine.

> A car that police said was driven by Howard University student Lorie Wills jumped a curb and crashed into a Central Avenue home near the school last night, sending the occupants of the house dashing to safety.
>
> Police said two rooms sustained damage, but no one was injured.

Equal caution should be observed in writing a story concerning a suicide or a homicide. The careful reporter avoids use of the words "suicide" or "murder," just as competent police investigators do. There may be every indication that a person took his or her own life, but until an official ruling is made, the reporter should carefully imply it through the circumstances. The occasion is rare when a reporter can write in a straightforward manner that a person "committed suicide."

Instead, police and press will be circumspect until a coroner or a coroner's jury conducts a hearing and makes a finding of suicide or murder.

> Harlan County Judge William E. Sparkman died this morning of a gunshot wound in the head. Sparkman's body was discovered in the bathroom of his chambers at the county courthouse.
>
> "It appears that the wound was self-inflicted," Coroner Michael L. Smithson said, but added that circumstances surrounding Sparkman's death were being investigated.

Days, even weeks, can pass before an official ruling is returned.

Other Sensitive Areas

Another sensitive area for the reporter is selective law enforcement. It may be the unspoken policy of the police department to minimally enforce some ordinances or laws or to disregard others altogether. Realizing that he or she is neither judge nor jury, the police reporter has a responsibility to so inform the public, sometimes creating friction through publication of the policy.

> Confusion about state-mandated speed limits and differing city ordinances has resulted in an informal Police Department decision to suspend radar surveillance on the west side of the city.
>
> Although police officials declined to confirm the report, patrolmen who asked not to be identified told reporters that the radar units have been taken out of service indefinitely.

Annual crime summaries should be closely scrutinized and every effort made to accurately portray the material. An increase of 7 percent in major crimes, for example, may be accompanied by an increase of 13 percent in arrests for those crimes. So the key might lie in the conviction rate of those arrested and accused of the crimes.

As do other public officials, law enforcement officers sometimes have a vested interest in placing the best light possible on such summaries. Some increases are helpful when budget time comes around, while others fail to win public support during heated election campaigns. Caution should be exercised in treating the material as pure fact. It should be handled as though it were a press release, with the reporter checking it carefully and asking probing questions.

Trends are important to law enforcement and to the public. The reporter should take advantage of advances in the field of crime prevention to keep the public informed. It is becoming common practice for trained dogs to sniff out marijuana and other drugs in school locker searches, but the addition of hypnosis to the crime-fighting arsenal is not nearly so common. New techniques under development may enable medical examiners to tell police exactly when a person died. Medical examiners have had that ability for years on television, but those Hollywood examiners have not yet divulged their secrets to real-life officials.

> Imagine seeing a police officer stabbing the ground with a metal tube able to sense a decomposing body buried 12 feet deep.
>
> That item is not on the market now, but check again in a few years, says John Jupin, county medical examiner.
>
> Such futuristic equipment is an example of the investigative techniques being researched across the country. The advances will enable police and medical examiners to diagnose more accurately what happened when a crime occurred.

Like the police officer, the reporter should remain on top of such developments.

The function of habeas corpus, a remedy to compel police to either lodge a specific charge against a person who has been detained or release the person from custody, also has important implications for the press. The alert police reporter should be familiar with the jail population, learning why prisoners are being detained and the length of their stays in jail. Informative and useful stories often result.

> It's only a few feet from the Dean County jail to the magistrate's court in the basement of the courthouse, but it sometimes takes a long time to cover that distance.
>
> Donald C. Wilson, 27, 60 Burke Ave., was arrested and charged by police with robbery 13 days ago. He was finally given a preliminary hearing yesterday afternoon.
>
> The problem, according to Prosecutor Keith Lyons, was that no one was available to bring Wilson from the jail to the court for a hearing.
>
> As it turned out, Lyons said, Wilson was bound over to the grand jury. "But if the magistrate had decided we didn't have enough to hold him on, that would have been 12 days out of his life."
>
> Public Defender John Simpson, who acted as counsel for Wilson, disagreed.
>
> "That was 12 days out of his life anyway," he argued.

Officials are rarely willing to publicize conditions in jails or other detention areas, and the perceptive reporter must dig beneath officialdom for a more accurate picture of how inmates are being treated. It is often the old story, "out of sight, out of mind" for the public. Within some limitations, reporters usually have access to prisoners, and their views are sometimes newsworthy.

> "There's no stability of mind here," said Charley Gibson, who has been a Rikers Island inmate for three months. "You're better off taking a plea and letting them send you on to prison."
>
> In a series of interviews, Gibson and other inmates at the City House of Detention for Men sketched a picture of life there so bleak, they said, that some inmates plead guilty so they will be moved on to the better conditions of the state prison.

If the police reporter is not careful, he or she can easily become bogged down in day-to-day routine stories, creating an unending series of interesting but quite specific news accounts that ignore the broader brush strokes of law enforcement activity.

Time must be budgeted to seek out and develop stories that cover the entire range of law enforcement. Growth of special police units, and how and why they operate, is important to the public. Many cities have trained officers in handling nuclear material and in responding to nuclear accidents. Others have become skilled in terrorist activity, including handling the sensitive issue of hostages.

The use of deadly force by police officers has stirred emotions in many cities in the United States. The reporter's questions are legitimate:

—When should an officer use deadly force in making an arrest or defending himself or herself? When the officer does so, what agency should decide whether he or she has acted properly or improperly? How do the officers themselves feel?

Police theoreticians are arguing over the issue, and legislators have entered the picture to politicize the debate. It is an area of public interest that should be fully mined by the reporter.

> Police Officer Jeffrey Wingate has faced the wrong end of a revolver before, and it nearly cost him his life.
>
> That's why he is alarmed about his own reaction this week when he and his partner encountered another man wielding a cocked pistol.
>
> "I'd say six months ago I probably would have shot him," Wingate said.
>
> But he says public criticism since then about the use of deadly force has made him—and many fellow police officers—somewhat more hesitant to fire his weapon.
>
> So this time Wingate lunged for the man and subdued him with the help of his partner, Sam Longdon. The gun, it turned out, was not loaded.
>
> But there's always the next time, Wingate said. The officer, who was wounded in the line of duty in 1979, pointed out that just a moment of hesitation could prove fatal.
>
> "I think there is a lot of hesitation. I look for an officer to get killed out of it," Wingate said.

Discrimination in law enforcement hiring has also become an important issue, and the reporter cannot overlook the implications for minority groups in the constant decisions that are being reached by many public bodies on the issue.

Police-Press Relationships

Although most law enforcement officials recognize the function of the press as communicator and interpreter to the public, relationships between police and press sometimes become strained.

Police tend to see themselves as "the good guys in the white hats," fighting crime and keeping the community safe. This image is encouraged because, as former Los Angeles Police Chief Quinn Tamm said, "The police officer, upon whom we depend for the maintenance of peace and order in our society, can function most effectively in a community where he can depend on the support and assistance of the citizens."

The police reporter's goal—to communicate information that may not always please officials—does not necessarily coincide with those articulated by police officials. Unfortunately, stories that are perceived as inimical to a police department's interests cannot be ignored or hidden, making way for only the "good" stories. The police reporter is not a press agent.

Other developments have contributed to the strained relationships which often exist today:

—Police reporters have traditionally taken the word of their police sources with little or no question. But in the upheavals of the 1960s, with demonstrations on the streets and unrest in the ghettos, alert young reporters began asking questions of "the other side," anti-war protesters and blacks in the inner cities. What the press saw as a new fairness was interpreted by police as consorting with the enemy. It created press-police friction which remains in some areas.

—Police resent what they regard as publicity that the press sometimes gives to notorious criminals. By creating a glamorous image, police believe, the press makes it more difficult for them to fulfill their law enforcement responsibilities. What a reporter sees as a fair and reasonable story, police may perceive as detrimental to their interests.

—Despite the reporter's best intentions, information is occasionally published about a sensitive investigation which complicates efforts by police to solve it. A news story may contain sufficient detail about a case to enable a missing suspect to continue to elude the authorities. Police tend to overreact, seeing many stories as jeopardizing their investigations.

—In their zeal to get close to the scene of emergencies, reporters, particularly those lugging heavy camera and broadcast equipment, sometimes get in the way. If other irritating factors are already present, press-police relationships tend to deteriorate further.

To counteract these impediments to good communication, trustworthy contacts should be developed at all levels of law enforcement without compromising the integrity of the reporter or that of the publication he or she represents.

Reporter Bill Hazlett commented on his relationships with police:

> It's a tradeoff. You give them a little, and they give you a little. The key is to make sure you never compromise your primary responsibility—which is to the paper and the public, not the police. A paper's got to have at least one guy who speaks the cops' language these days though, or we'll never get anything from them.

A fine, often shifting, line separates cooperation from cooptation. The astute reporter will learn where it is and how not to cross it. The ranks of law enforcement officials, like other public employees, contain their share of self-serving men and women.

The reporter will identify and work around them, recognizing that the majority of law enforcement people are dedicated to their jobs and are capable of working out a good relationship with the press.

Police-Press Guidelines

Guidelines have become an increasingly useful device in clarifying the relationship between police and the press and in minimizing areas of friction.

With the stipulation that the press play a part in developing them, guidelines—either formal or informal—often provide a means of reducing the traditional areas of conflict to reasonable dimensions. Formulas promulgated by one side and subjected to acceptance by the other have less chance of succeeding.

The objective of the reporter and editor in working out any set of guidelines should be to produce a working document, not one that is cast in stone. The responsibilities of the journalist dictate that a final decision on what to print rests with the editor.

Many police officials, aware of the influence of the press upon public opinion, are increasingly agreeable to consideration of formulas that will facilitate the flow of information when it does not interfere with law enforcement.

In a typical memorandum to members of the force, the chief of a Midwest police department directs them "to engage in a program of complete fairness and frankness with the news media and their representatives."

The memo directs members of the department to facilitate "the maximum flow of information to the public through the media." Such general directives as this can be useful in assuring openness and facilitating the reporter's work. But specifics can be even more helpful.

Desirable goals include rules to obtain information at the lowest possible administrative level within the department, easing the pressures at deadline time. Sometimes designation of specific officers to release information can be helpful.

A typical police memo authorizes bureau, shift and unit commanders or their designated representatives "to release news items regarding the general or overall activities of their respective elements, that is, matters of public record about which they have personal knowledge. This would include information as to violations, crimes reported, arrests made and, where possible, the disposition of the case."

A central file or "booking register" that is easily accessible to the reporter should be a major goal. One typical department memo spells out this responsibility:

> It shall be the responsibility of the commanding officer of the Services Bureau to ensure that a copy of preliminary field case reports is placed on the designated board located at the Information Counter, for use by representatives of the news media. Such reports shall be retained on this

board for a minimum of 48 hours. The central booking register and other "public records" shall also be made available to representatives of the news media upon request.

Press access to scenes of disasters or other emergencies has been complicated by the equipment necessary for quality broadcast coverage in recent years. Press identification cards are as useful as authorities are disposed to make them. The reporter's objective should be to convince authorities that the press has a right to be present, provided there is no interference with personnel at the scene.

There is good leverage in the argument that the press merely represents a multitude of citizens that would otherwise present major logistical problems. A meeting with officials establishing such guidelines for the presence of the press at emergencies is often helpful in clearing the air *before* such a need arises and not during the crisis itself.

No set of police-press guidelines is perfect, however, and gray areas will continue to exist because of the discretionary nature of information in the hands of officials. Good working relationships between reporter and police continue to constitute the major building blocks of effective access.

To Print or Not to Print

A modern approach to protection of individual rights has complicated the traditional ethical considerations of the press in whether to print information or suppress it. Media and law enforcement agencies are approaching the problem more cautiously than in the past. To help assure the right to a fair trial, police, generally with the cooperation of the press, limit some information formerly provided without question. Since at least some of this information can be considered public record, the constitutional issues of freedom of the press (First Amendment) and the right to a fair trial (Sixth Amendment) have come into conflict.

The line separating the legitimacy of both these rights is not always clear, but reporter and editor must undertake to assure that both sets of rights are fulfilled.

Guidelines protecting both these constitutional issues were given strong impetus in 1966 with recommended standards on release of material before criminal trials. The so-called Reardon Rules, formulated by a committee headed by Paul C. Reardon, justice of the Supreme Judicial Court of Massachusetts, were designed to restrict law enforcement officials and attorneys in dissemination of information that could be prejudicial to a defendant's right to a fair trial.

One of the effects of the Reardon Committee report has been the growth of voluntary agreements among the press, law enforcement officials and the judiciary. But despite the proliferation of such agreements, editors usually reserve the right to decide what they will publish or broadcast, while agreeing in principle to adhere to the accepted guidelines.

Law enforcement agencies today make public such factual matters about a criminal case as the following, but they avoid subjective observations:

—Release of the defendant's name, date of birth or age, place of residence; the substance or text of the specific charge against the defendant (such as a complaint, indictment or information); the identity of the investigating or arresting officer and the length of the investigation; and the circumstances surrounding the arrest, including the time and place, resistance, pursuit and possession or use of weapons.

Any details that flesh out such information is considered valid.

However, most police jurisdictions today avoid release of the following details, which might compromise the defendant's right to a fair trial:

—The past criminal record of an arrested person; observations about the person's character; statements, admissions, confessions or alibis attributable to the defendant; and references to investigative procedures, such as fingerprints, lie detector tests or laboratory tests. Any information detailing refusal of the defendant to take various tests would be withheld, as well as discussion of the strength of the evidence, pro or con, and the possibility of a guilty plea by the defendant.

There is some validity to the view that other information tends to create danger of prejudice without serving a significant law enforcement or public information function. These include statements regarding evidence or any other information that might interfere with successful and impartial conclusion to a case in the courts.

Thus, such information may be factual, but the alert reporter who has obtained possession of it faces the issue of whether justice is fully served by using it.

A minister who has visited a prisoner charged with homicide discusses the prisoner's demeanor and reluctantly informs a reporter that the prisoner has expressed remorse. Final judgment on such a sensitive matter lies in the hands of the reporter and the editor, with a healthy dose of advice from legal authorities.

Similar sensitivity applies to coverage of crimes involving juveniles. Newspapers generally avoid identifying juveniles unless they are charged with a capital crime, but this practice appears to be changing. One of the reasons is a Supreme Court ruling in 1979 that a state cannot punish a newspaper for accurately publishing the name of a juvenile charged with a crime.

Fairness also dictates exercise of caution in cases in which publishing the name of one person involved might compromise the identity of a sex victim or a juvenile. A juvenile who accuses her father of incest, for example, is identified for all practical purposes when the father is arrested. At the very least, identification should await formal charges and be handled with care.

The problem is often intensified when juvenile cases involve the children or relatives of prominent individuals. Editors are divided on the issue of using the juvenile's name when that name is news.

As one editor argues, "We're not protecting the public if we don't use names. Names of offenders, particularly in sex crimes, ought to be printed so that people will know who they are and be able to protect themselves." Another editor responds: "The youngster has a right to some protection. The stigma of police involvement can remain with him or her throughout life."

Setting a standard for reporting all juvenile crime news is difficult, but some general guidelines acceptable to press, law enforcement agencies and the courts appears to be a reasonable approach. As Norman Isaacs, former newspaper editor and educator, put it at a seminar on the subject, "The truth is, none of us know what's right or wrong. Many papers will call up the judge when they are confused—but sometimes he's as confused as we are."

The police reporter is occasionally asked by sources to withhold a story from publication on grounds that it might endanger an investigation in process. Each instance should be studied and treated on the basis of that incident alone. The problem has intensified in recent years with increasing danger to hostages taken by militants. Reporters and editors should avoid establishing more than minimal guidelines in this area, even though such standards might ease the strain on the press-police relationship.

The correct position for the reporter is that his or her editors must finally decide the question of whether to publish a story. The key to such a solution lies in a reasonable rapport with police contacts, coupled with an "arms length" attitude. Becoming too friendly can affect the reporter's judgment on the police beat just as it can elsewhere.

Covering Hospitals

Guidelines are similarly effective in dealing with hospitals and other sources of news of an emergency nature. Disputes over access to the news have traditionally surrounded release of information involving emergency treatment.

While the media's responsibility to report the news promptly and accurately is recognized by most hospital officials, hospital administrators retain a moral as well as a legal responsibility for the care and rights of privacy of patients under their care. An effective set of guidelines recognizes both sets of responsibilities.

The reporter's major effort should be directed toward encouraging release of information on *cases of public record that are reportable by law to public authorities*. Examples of these are persons under arrest or held under police surveillance, persons taken to the hospital by police, firefighters or other public officials, or cases involving violence, poisoning or traffic accidents.

Unless hospital officials determine that release of information jeopardizes the health or welfare of the patient, pertinent information will often be released with or without the patient's consent in cases of public record. The reporter should encourage officials to release these basic facts concerning patients brought to the hospital:

—Identification of the person, including name, address, age, sex, marital status and occupation;

—Nature of the accident if such an accident is involved;

—The condition of the patient, including whether he or she is conscious or unconscious, whether there are fractures, head injuries or internal injuries;

—If poisoning is involved, the nature of the substance and the severity of the patient's condition;

—If a shooting or stabbing has occurred, the number of wounds and their location.

The reporter will find officials sensitive to questions regarding child abuse, drug abuse or sexual assault, but often a statement on the medical condition of the patient can be successfully solicited.

Efforts should be made to designate hospital personnel to release information 24 hours a day, where possible. Public information officers are being increasingly designated to facilitate the flow of such information.

The old rules continue to apply, however. Reporters should be sufficiently familiar with the incident to ask *specific* questions. They are much more difficult to turn away. And there is no substitute for personally being on the scene at the hospital rather than relying on the telephone.

State and Federal Agencies

Local police departments frequently turn to federal and state law enforcement agencies for assistance, and a large number of sophisticated organizations operate at these levels.

Their chief advantages in the solution of crime lie in advanced scientific methods and in wide territorial authority, although most of the agencies are limited by statute.

When a person is believed to have fled the state to avoid prosecution, state or county law enforcement officers may ask a federal prosecutor to issue a fugitive warrant, so that a search may be expedited.

An aircraft transporting illegal drugs from another country touches down at an airport, and both federal and state police agencies may be involved in subsequent arrests. In the case of specific law violations, some agencies are in constant communication.

The federal Hobbs Act prohibits public officials from using their offices to extort money. Local police may initiate an investigation and then be joined by agents of the Federal Bureau of Investigation, who make the arrests and prosecute in the federal courts.

Despite statutory limitations, duties and jurisdictions of federal agencies often overlap. One example illustrates this point. The FBI was established in 1908 and was given responsibility for investigating all violations of federal laws except those specifically assigned by legislation to some other agency. In 1973, the Justice Department was authorized to establish the Drug Enforcement Administration, whose mission is to control narcotic and dangerous drug abuse through enforcement and prevention programs. Its primary responsibility is to enforce statutes dealing with narcotic drugs, marijuana, depressants, stimulants and hallucinogenic drugs. However, the Food and Drug Administration, which is engaged in protecting the nation's health against impure and unsafe foods, drugs and cosmetics (1931), also deals in enforcement in that general area.

> Washington (AP)—Federal law enforcement agencies waste untold sums of money because the right hand rarely knows what the left hand is doing, according to a presidential government reorganization team.
>
> More than 100 federal agencies spend $5 billion a year on law enforcement responsibilities, but no one has authority to coordinate their activities, the team says.

The reorganization team concluded that lack of coordination may have resulted from a "meteoric growth in the number of law enforcement agencies." Research disclosed that more than one third of the 113 agencies surveyed did not exist before 1970.

The police reporter may never deal with this multitude of agencies on a daily basis, but he or she should be familiar with them and their method of operation. Regular contacts should be developed with those agencies frequently dealing with enforcement problems at the local level. A current *U.S. Government Manual* provides up-to-date addresses, telephone numbers and often personnel for law enforcement agencies at the federal level.

These are some of the major state and federal agencies with which the reporter will deal from time to time.

State Police Agencies

Paralleling growth of federal law enforcement agencies, state crime fighting units take on this general pattern—a highway patrol, a state militia, a bureau of identification and often a separate division of criminal investigation.

Legislatures set the number of employees and jurisdictions, which often adds a political complexion to the makeup of the forces.

The agency with which the police reporter will most often deal is the highway patrol, which is mainly charged with enforcing the laws along federal and state highways. The reporter should maintain regular contact with district offices and substations of the patrol, but local police departments are usually aware of emergencies involving the patrol through radio monitoring. Some state police forces have taken over law enforcement in rural areas, patrolling highways and investigating crime outside incorporated municipalities.

Police reporters usually do not have the time necessary to cultivate contacts with highway patrol personnel. Often patrol headquarters are far removed from central police facilities and media offices. The key to dealing with the patrol lies in working successfully with dispatchers, particularly on late-breaking stories. If a dispatcher is cooperative, the media connection will result in adequate information.

> A 6-year-old girl was shot and killed and her father arrested after a high-speed chase with a highway patrolman along Interstate 70.
>
> Mary Julia Swift, whom neighbors described as a "quiet, loving and sweet little girl," was shot as her father, Joseph C. Swift, 27, and Trooper W. A. Birke wrestled for a gun after a car chase Thurday night, officials reported.

The flow through the news pipeline tends to become more sluggish when detailed investigations are involved. Many highway patrol systems lack adequate public information officers who can efficiently provide details of important investigations.

The answer for the reporter who insists on thorough coverage is to carefully cultivate sources in the beginning and rely heavily on effective telephone contact.

Most states provide a criminal investigation agency and an identification service, utilized by local officials as well as state agencies. The trend is also toward establishment of state coroner's offices in central locations for autopsies and scientific laboratories.

Although known as the National Guard, the state militia acts as an arm of the state's chief executive in time of peace. Training and regulations are prescribed by federal law, and personnel are paid with federal funds, but the guard actually is a part-time state army. It stands by to maintain order only after it is apparent that local law enforcement agencies cannot cope with an emergency. The guard becomes highly visible after major disasters such as flooding, fires, street riots or other disturbances.

> National Guard units were ordered into the Tug Valley this morning to prevent looting in the wake of widespread destruction from yesterday's flooding by the Needer River.
>
> State Guard Commander Sam Alston said 200 men from the Winston and Chambless areas were en route to the scene.

Miscellaneous law enforcement agencies include one to deal with enforcement of fish and game laws, another which may oversee alcoholic beverage laws, the state fire marshal's office, revenue agents and mine inspectors.

Federal Agencies

The Federal Bureau of Investigation, the federal government's principal law enforcement agency, is the agency to which local police departments turn most often.

Sharp restrictions on release of information characterize the activities of the FBI, which has 60 field division offices scattered about the United States. Agents investigate a wide range of criminal, civil and national security violations, incuding espionage, sabotage, kidnapping, extortion, bank robbery, interstate transportation of stolen property, civil rights violations, fraud against the federal government and interstate gambling violations.

Cooperative services of the FBI utilized by other law enforcement agencies include fingerprint identification, laboratory services and police training.

Agents maintain a low profile in local communities and generally offer little or no information regarding investigations in process, usually resulting in a more formal relationship between reporter and the agency. On occasion, an agent will announce a series of federal arrests and the cracking of an interstate auto theft ring, then quietly resume a low profile again.

> With evidence accumulating that 23-year-old Joanna James has been taken across the state line by her abductor, police called in the FBI for assistance today.
>
> Ms. James was taken from her Mills Lane apartment Thursday night by a masked intruder who police believe was known to her.

The FBI frequently cooperates with state and local law enforcement agencies, sometimes in efforts to extradite suspects from other states and at other times to investigate violations of a person's civil rights. A magistrate may ask the FBI to investigate incidents of alleged police brutality, or to join in a search for a missing state legislator who has been charged with a crime.

Often the FBI works with other federal agencies, such as the Bureau of Alcohol, Tobacco and Firearms, as well as local agencies in seeking solutions to criminal actions.

> A DC-6 cargo plane registered in Nicaragua and crammed with 10 tons of marijuana crashed and burst into flames at a Tristate Airport runway yesterday.
>
> None of the eight persons aboard was injured. All eight face federal charges, and three face additional state charges.
>
> Authorities said the aircraft may have been stolen. Street value of the marijuana was estimated at nearly $10 million by authorities.

Several federal agencies joined the FBI in the case—including the Federal Aviation Administration and the United States attorney's office. Before the investigation is completed, the Drug Enforcement Administration may have a hand in it, creating a logjam for the reporter trying to follow up on an interesting story.

Like the FBI, the Drug Enforcement Administration is an arm of the Justice Department, established in 1973 to control and monitor drug abuse. The DEA conducts investigations of drug traffickers at the national and international levels, but it works closely with local law enforcement agencies, providing specialized training in dangerous drug control to all levels of police agencies.

The DEA carries on its activities through regional field offices and also operates specialized laboratories at key points around the country.

BUREAU OF ALCOHOL, TOBACCO AND FIREARMS

Another federal agency with substantial contact at the local level, the Bureau of Alcohol, Tobacco and Firearms also operates out of regional offices. It is a division of the Treasury Department.

ATF agents are responsible for enforcing firearms, explosives, gambling tax, alcoholic beverage and tobacco products laws. The bureau has two distinct functions: criminal enforcement and regulatory enforcement.

Criminal enforcement activities include elimination of illegal possession and use of firearms and explosives, suppression of traffic in illicit distilled spirits and enforcement of gambling tax legislation.

Its regulatory function assures collection of revenue due from legal alcohol and tobacco industries, and efforts include prevention of commercial bribery, consumer deception and other improper practices in the distilled spirits industry. ATF agents cooperate with state and local agencies in these areas.

> Two miners have been charged with theft of explosives from the Carbondale Mine in Sumter County, an agent of the Alcohol, Tobacco and Firearms Bureau said today.
>
> Agent Harry Purcell identified the men as Wallace Goshen and Will Santana, both of Sumter County. He said the men were in possession of a case of dynamite when they were stopped on U.S. 44 near the mine early in the day.

IMMIGRATION AND NATURALIZATION SERVICE

Administration and enforcement of legislation covering admission, exclusion, deportation and naturalization of aliens lie in the hands of the Immigration and Naturalization Service. Operating through the Border Patrol, the service tries to prevent illegal entry into the United States and investigates and apprehends aliens who enter the country illegally.

Many stories deal with deportation proceedings, naturalization examinations and registration of aliens through the U.S. Postal Service. When prominent persons are involved, the stories take on additional importance.

CUSTOMS SERVICE

In cooperation with the Drug Enforcement Administration, the Customs Service works to suppress illegal drug traffic into the United States, but its functions are much broader. The service enforces regulations on importation of goods into this country and prevents fraud and smuggling through its interdiction program.

The service also enforces some aspects of the environmental programs for other federal agencies, such as prohibition of discharge of refuse and oil into coastal waters, and regulations regarding endangered species and those considered injurious to community health and plant quarantines.

The service, a division of the Treasury Department headquartered in Washington, operates out of 42 district offices with more than 300 ports of entry under surveillance.

POSTAL INSPECTION SERVICE

The U.S. Postal Service provides one of the most important services to the public, with more than 700,000 persons employed by the independent federal agency in 31,000 post offices throughout the country. A special division of the service, the Inspection Service, protects the mails, postal funds and property, apprehends those who are suspected of violating postal laws and investigates internal conditions.

Postal inspectors are called in whenever use of the mails is suspected in illegal activities—fraud or embezzlement through the mails, or mailing of explosives, obscene literature or extortion threats through the mails. Local police are not always privy to these developments, and the reporter should maintain regular contact with the postmaster, superintendent of the mails or inspectors to assure access to frequent stories.

> Two postal employees at the main office have been charged with opening and discarding mail addressed to their relatives.
>
> Harry Hammer, postal inspector in charge of the district, said personal observation led to the charges against John Logan, 1212 Bruce St., and Smith Jordan, 1214 Bruce St.

SECRET SERVICE

One of the best known agencies because of its responsibilities in protecting the president, the Secret Service is under jurisdiction of the Treasury Department. It enforces legislation relating to coins, currency and securities of the Unites States. As the main enforcement arm for the Treasury Department, the service also investigates counterfeiting, forgery, and alteration of U.S. and foreign currencies.

> It was a perfect hiding place—almost.
>
> But because of the persistence of a Secret Service agent, Colbert Hale, 27, 800 20th St., was in the county jail today, charged with counterfeiting.

Agent Sam Winslow, acting on a tip by an informant, found Hale hiding in the chimney just above the fireplace in his apartment.

Winslow had earlier checked the premises without success and had called the informant who insisted Hale was in the apartment. Winslow returned, noticed a wood slat ajar in the fireplace, and located Hale's hiding place.

LAW ENFORCEMENT ASSISTANCE ADMINISTRATION

In an effort to shift more law enforcement authority and power to state and local governments, the U.S. Congress established the Law Enforcement Assistance Administration in 1968, its major purpose being to reduce crime. One of its programs, the National Institute of Law Enforcement and Criminal Justice, provides technical assistance to local authorities, and serves as a national clearinghouse for the exchange of criminal justice information.

Another program, the Criminal Justice Information and Statistics Service, collects, evaluates and disseminates statistics on crime and justice. LEAA activities are coordinated through 10 regional offices.

U.S. MARSHALS SERVICE

The federal marshal is one of the nation's oldest law enforcement jobs, dating from 1789. Traditionally, the marshal's office serves process papers produced by the federal courts, but that responsibility has expanded. Marshals make arrests on the basis of federal warrants and serve as officers of the federal court. The service also acts as jailer, maintaining custody of federal prisoners in transit.

The office is a valuable source for the police reporter, who makes regular checks with it for information regarding cases being brought before a U.S. magistrate for preliminary hearings.

OTHER AGENCIES

More than 100 federal agencies are involved in some manner with law enforcement, many of them as noted with overlapping responsibilities. The *Coast Guard*, a division of the Department of Transportation in time of peace, is responsible for enforcing federal laws on the navigable waters of the United States and on the high seas. The Coast Guard also enforces conservation and marine environmental laws, cooperating with other law enforcement agencies in use of its transportation facilities.

Law enforcement capability is also carried by the *Internal Revenue Service*, which administers all revenue legislation except that relating to alcohol, tobacco, firearms, explosives and gambling.

The *Public Buildings Service*, an arm of the General Services Administration, protects federally owned and leased buildings through sophisticated systems and uniformed personnel. Nearly every community of any size houses the more than 10,000 federal buildings scattered around the United States, and the PBS has a role of management of all of them.

In many states, representatives of the *Mining Enforcement and Safety*

Administration control health hazards and seek to reduce fatalities and injuries in the mineral extraction industries. Facilities are inspected and assessment of penalties is made for violating the law. Enforcement of laws in its area is also the responsibility of the *Fish and Wildlife Service*, which manages and protects wildlife resources throughout the United States. Representatives often engage in cooperative ventures with state wildlife officers.

Other federal agencies that hold law enforcement power include the *Environmental Protection Agency*, the *Federal Trade Commission*, the *Equal Employment Opportunity Commission*, the *Securities and Exchange Commission* and others.

Suggested Readings

SHAW, DAVID, *Journalism Today* (New York: Harper's, 1977). In Chapter 4, "The Press and the Police," this newspaper ombudsman suggests reportorial methods for dealing with law enforcement officials.

ROYKO, MIKE, *Boss: Richard J. Daley of Chicago* (New York; Dutton, 1971). Chapter VI is a study of police relationships in an urban community.

Police and Society (Beverly Hills, CA: Sage Publications, 1977). Chapter 10, "The Limits of Police Reform," David Bayley; Chapter 11, "A Regulatory Theory of Policing," R. Sykes.

FRIENDLY, ALFRED, and RONALD L. GOLDFARB, *Crime and Publicity* (New York: 20th Century Fund, 1967). Chapter 1, "The Complaint" and, Chapter 2, "Is Crime News Fit to Print?"

SNORTUM, JOHN R., and ILANA HADER, editors, *Criminal Justice: Allies and Adversaries* (Pacific Palisades, CA: Palisades Publishers, 1978). This discussion of the "managers" of the criminal justice system helps the reporter understand the relationships among them and the accused, including the plea bargaining process.

CHAPTER 10
Reporting Criminal Actions

THE police reporter is pleased with himself.

So is his editor.

With precious little time remaining before deadline, the reporter has produced a highly readable account of a criminal investigation involving two men suspected of committing a series of armed robberies in search of drugs. An exciting midnight auto chase has resulted in the arrest of the pair.

The police reporter has had to bring into play all the skills he possesses to tie up the story in time for the newspaper's final edition: a personal capacity for being in the right place at the right time, good communications with the police, reliable sources, and the ability to quickly organize and dictate a complicated story. It has been a good news day.

However, as the heavy metal door of the lockup bangs shut against the jailed suspects, a different kind of drama emerges.

The setting changes. Noisy street scenes and police station confrontations give way to quiet courtrooms as the case begins its circuitous route through the judicial process. And while its interest and importance to the public may not appreciably diminish, entirely different kinds of stories emerge from the courts.

An Important Judicial Mechanism

As noted, the judicial forum exists to allow private disputants to argue their cases before an impartial tribunal. But the courts serve another equally important function, providing a mechanism by which a person charged with a public offense is accused and brought to trial, with subsequent punishment or acquittal.

It is through this process that the state, acting in the name of the public, endeavors to punish a person who commits an action that is deemed to be injurious to society.

A criminal action in the courts is prosecuted by a district attorney, a prosecuting attorney or a state's attorney, following a nearly universal process of arrest, accusation, pleadings and trial, with a lengthy appeals process culminating the procedure.

The proceedings in a criminal action are designed to safeguard the rights of the accused person, by far the most important truth in the criminal process for the reporter.

Every accused person is guaranteed the rights to notice of charges against him or her, to bail, to be represented by counsel, to a speedy and public trial by an impartial jury, to refuse to testify against himself or herself, to confront and examine accusers, and to be tried only once for the same crime.

The state goes to court in an effort to prove that criminal guilt has been established beyond a reasonable doubt. Anything less than that demands acquittal of the person charged.

From the very beginning of the process, the reporter must exercise the utmost care that news accounts assure the presumed innocence of the accused. At most, the accused is charged only with a specific crime, even when details seemingly point to guilt.

In the case of a suspect who is arrested and charged with assault and robbery, for example, it is not only unfair but dangerous for the reporter to predict on the basis of conversations with law enforcement authorities that further charges will be made.

> A police department spokesman said two counts of rape, two counts of aggravated robbery and one count of kidnapping will probably be filed against Smith this week.

Reporting in this manner is totally inappropriate. Only *after* a suspect is officially charged with such crimes should they be reported.

Nowhere in public affairs reporting do the rights of the people to know and concomitant rights of the individual stand in constant danger of collision along the thin line separating them.

How much detail does the reporter have the obligation to provide in preliminary stories involving criminal action prior to a trial? Who should be quoted and at what length? How should incriminating evidence be handled in news stories? How much and what kind of detail should be provided on the suspect's background?

The handling of crime news has been under constant and often critical scrutiny for many years, with the press attempting to balance conscientious reporting of crime in an effort to inform and protect the public, while minimizing the sensational aspects and protecting the rights of the accused.

Policies differ from newspaper to newspaper and in broadcast newsrooms as well. Metropolitan newspapers have been accused of sensationalism in reporting crime news, while publications in smaller communities are often accused of suppressing similar information that is deemed to be important to the public interest.

The answer lies in a thoughtful commitment on the part of the press to objective coverage which balances the public's right to pertinent details in criminal actions with an insistence on the accused person's right to fair treatment in the courts.

The Nature of Crime

Two members of a political party argue in a public hallway over a long-standing personal difference. Suddenly one of them strikes the other, sending him to the hospital with a fractured jaw and other injuries. The injured man swears out a complaint that a statute prohibiting such assaults was breached, and the attacker is formally charged with simple assault. A city court judge, after hearing the evidence, pronounces the defendant guilty of violating the law, suspends a 30-day sentence and fines him $200.

Unless the defendant seeks an appeal to a higher court, this concludes the "criminal" aspects of the case.

However, the injured party has further recourse to the courts if he wishes to file a civil action to recover medical costs and other damages he feels he has sustained. Civil action often follows criminal cases in court.

Depending upon the nature of the crime, criminal actions can be pursued in federal as well as in state courts. The celebrated break-in at the headquarters of the Democratic National Committee in Washington's Watergate Complex in 1972 offers an excellent example of federal-state and criminal-civil overlapping cases:

—Five men were arrested at gunpoint by District of Columbia police June 17, 1972 and charged with burglary. At this point it was a local case, but two days later the Justice Department announced that it would conduct a full-scale criminal investigation by the Federal Bureau of Investigation.

—On June 20, Chairman Lawrence O'Brien announced that the Democratic Party was filing a $1 million civil suit in federal court against the Committee to Re-Elect the President, a Republican organization.

—On July 31, *The Washington Post* reported that a $25,000 check intended for President Richard M. Nixon's re-election campaign had been deposited in a bank account of Bernard Barker, one of the defendants in the still-local burglary case. Federal investigators had traced money found in the burglary suspects' possession to Barker's bank account.

—The FBI and the Office of Federal Elections, a new congressional watchdog agency, joined District of Columbia police in the case the next day, as the affair began emerging as a federal criminal action.

—Meanwhile, civil litigation continued in the federal court as the Republican Party Sept. 13 filed a countersuit against O'Brien and the Democratic Party, accusing them of using the court "as a forum in which to publicize actions against innocent persons which would be libelous if published elsewhere."

—The Watergate affair officially became a federal criminal action on Sept. 15 when a grand jury indicted seven persons (including two former White House aides) on charges of conspiring to break into the Democratic headquarters. The indictments included charges of illegal wiretapping, a federal offense.

An out-of-court settlement later concluded the civil action, while most of those involved in the criminal proceedings were convicted and imprisoned for varying terms. The case illustrates how criminal action frequently shifts from one court to another, depending upon the nature of the crime and the jurisdiction of the court.

Rights of the Accused

The court serves as a referee in determining whether one individual has wronged another. It also referees the criminal action.

A prosecuting attorney or district attorney prosecutes the case as a representative of the public, but it is important at the outset that the reporter always remember that the accused person has his or her rights safeguarded by the U.S. Constitution. In all the proceedings that will be covered and reported by the press, the accused is presumed innocent until proved guilty. Thus, the court reporter will avoid writing that a jury "has found the defendant innocent." The defendant cannot be *found* innocent, because he or she *is* innocent until found guilty. Properly, the defendant is acquitted of the charges against him or her. While this may be considered a technical point, it is important to remember the rights of every accused person, which are assured by the Fifth Amendment to the Constitution. Its terms are unequivocal: No person shall be deprived of life, liberty or property without due process of law.

These are the other basic rights that are important to the reporter in the criminal process:

—The accused person is guaranteed the right to notice of the nature and cause of the accusation.

—To have the assistance of counsel, even if the public must provide it.

—To reasonable bail, as determined by law.

—To a speedy and public trial by an impartial jury.

—To refuse to testify against himself or herself.

—To be able to confront and examine his or her accusers.

—To be tried only once for the same crime.

Recognizing each of these basic guarantees, the reporter will cover the court developments that reflect each step through the often lengthy process. Although the process may take different paths, the guarantees remain the same.

Following arrest, an accused person might be taken directly through arraignment, where notice of charges is given; then bail might be set. Depending upon the nature of the charge, the accused might be incarcerated until he or she is notified of the charges against him or her. In some cases, the accused is released on his or her own recognizance or a small amount of bail; in serious offenses where there is danger that the accused person may flee the jurisdiction, a judge may refuse to set bail at all.

> An oil worker at the Marine Terminal was arrested this morning and charged with the murders of a Toneyville woman and her three children whose battered bodies were discovered Monday in her stucco house on Broad Street.
>
> Wesley Starke David, 28, who gave his address as 1905 Oak St., was charged with four counts of murder and placed in the Dale County jail shortly after 10 a.m. without bail.
>
> Magistrate Gerard Osburne issued the state warrants for David's arrest. Under state law, a magistrate cannot set bail in a capital offense.

Every story should reflect a responsibility to safeguard the rights of an accused person. No one should be incriminated or his or her motive imputed for a crime. Speculation regarding guilt or innocence should always be avoided, with all pretrial publicity being combed to assure that the judicial process is being fairly reported.

The reporter should beware such off-hand comments from arresting officers as "we caught them red-handed," or "I had a hunch that he was the one who did it." Most law enforcement officers are far more cautious today, but such incidents do persist and the reporter should be cognizant of the dangers they pose to fairness.

Public Involvement in Crime

crime: the commission of an act that is forbidden.

Stripped to its simplest definition, crime is an offensive act that is committed against all the people in a community rather than merely a wrong that one individual perceives another as committing against him or her.

But the nature of crime itself and the multitude of offenses create a much more complex relationship between those who commit crime and those who accept responsibility for punishing the criminal. Some crimes are inherently wrong (*mala in se*, or wrongs in themselves), such as robbery or assault. Others are merely prohibited by law, such as failure to register as an alien in this country.

Newsworthiness sometimes depends upon the degree of seriousness of a criminal act. A misdemeanor implies a minor offense, such as a traffic violation or a gambling charge. More serious crimes, such as burglary, extortion, kidnapping and murder, are identified as felonies, with conviction calling for longer prison terms or fines. Some jurisdictions distinguish between misdemeanors and felonies with a maximum sentence of a year in jail for the former.

Since punishment varies so greatly, it is important that the reporter learn to distinguish the specific classes of criminal acts. Conviction on a simple robbery charge might be punishable by two years in prison, while a more serious charge of armed robbery could result in up to 10 years in prison. Still another charge, robbery with a deadly weapon, might be punishable with a sentence of up to life imprisonment.

Kinds of Crime

Common law differentiates among the kinds of crime:

—Crimes against the person, crimes against property, crimes against the habitation, crimes against the public peace and crimes against authority.

CRIMES AGAINST THE PERSON

Crimes against the person range from simple assault, merely threatening someone without actual physical violence, through homicide, the gravest of all crimes against the person. Simple assault may be punishable by up to 30 days in jail, whereas assault with intent to maim could draw up to 10 to 20 years in prison.

The reporter must always take care to identify the exact charge in a crime. When a person forcibly takes a person away against his or her will, the charge may be kidnapping; when a person is taken away by persuasion but without violence, the charge might be abduction. Unlawful carnal knowledge of a person without his or her consent constitutes the crime of rape, but less serious charges might be lodged against a person in this category—molestation or even sexual harassment. Most newspapers carefully mask the identity of victims of sexually inspired crimes, and some now explain in a footnote to the story their reason for doing so:

(*The Morning News* does not normally use the names of persons reporting incidents of sexual abuse to law enforcement agencies.)

The most serious crime against the person is homicide, and, as with other crimes, knowledge of the various degrees is important to the reporter. The killing of another human being, either intentionally or by accident, is always among the most newsworthy of criminal actions. And since punishment is generally most severe, its news coverage is the one that calls for the most care.

The law recognizes two types of homicide: justifiable and felonious. A police officer who must shoot and kill someone in the line of duty may be charged with justifiable homicide and in fact may be forced to traverse the entire judicial process through the trial. A charge of justifiable homicide may be placed against a homeowner protecting his or her family against an intruder.

Different degrees of felonious homicide exist, ranging from first-degree murder, a premeditated act with intent to do harm, through second-degree murder, which is an intentional act but committed as the result of extreme provocation or in the heat of passion, to murder in the third degree—known as manslaughter.

A willful, deliberate and successful attempt to murder, or when such action is accompanied by commission of a felony such as robbery or burglary, is punishable by a sentence of life in prison or death. A husband who finds his wife with an adulterer and commits murder may be charged with murder in the second degree. Often this is classed as justifiable homicide, and the defendant is freed.

The less serious charge of homicide is manslaughter, which is often placed following a fatal automobile accident. The charge becomes more serious when the defendant has broken a traffic law or is deemed to have acted in an irresponsible manner. The charge may be dropped in its entirety if the defendant has been found to be acting within the law.

Juvenile defendants, who are not normally identified in news accounts, are often identified in capital cases such as homicide.

CRIMES AGAINST THE HABITATION

The original concept of "habitation" as a dwelling place has been expanded to include almost any building in which people live, work, engage in recreation or otherwise inhabit. Arson, the act of burning such a building, and burglary, the act of entering a building for a felonious purpose, are recognized as crimes against the habitation.

These felony charges are often coupled with others, such as burglary with intent to commit bodily harm or burglary with intent to sexually assault. Possession of a dangerous weapon while burglarizing a home carries a more serious sentence than does simple burglary. Willfully setting fire to another's property, including setting fire to one's own property for fraudulent insurance purposes, is known as arson. This charge becomes murder when a person is killed as a result of a deliberately set fire.

> A murder charge will be placed against the arsonist who touched off a fire that gutted the vacant Marshall Building on State Street yesterday, police said.
>
> Fireman Wilson Jent, 28, was killed instantly when a falling timber struck him as he and 32 other firemen fought to contain the blaze that State Fire Marshal Soward Fell said was deliberately set.

CRIMES AGAINST PROPERTY

The right of a person to be secure against theft is indisputed in common law, but statutory legislation has also been enacted to meet changing conditions and further protect the individual. There are various degrees of crimes against property, ranging from simple theft of a purse to robbery with a dangerous weapon and extortion or embezzlement of funds from a company for which a person is employed. Sentences upon conviction vary from state to state.

Larceny or theft. Taking property that belongs to someone else is known as larceny, although some jurisdictions have abandoned that term in favor of theft, including embezzlement and obtaining money under false pretenses. Lack of violence generally characterizes this charge, and the sentence varies with its degree of seriousness.

Robbery. Robbery constitutes a crime against the person as well as a crime against property. It is basically larceny or theft through intimidation or force, inferring violence or potential violence. The victim need only be placed in a state of fear for the robbery charge to hold. The instrument used is often the determining factor in degree of seriousness. Robbery with a dangerous weapon such as a knife or gun compounds the felony and carries a far more serious charge. Some state codes call for a mandatory sentence ranging from 10 years to life in prison upon conviction.

Clichés abound in describing details of robberies, and the reporter should be alert to the danger inherent in a news story with frequent references to the "stickup men," the "bandits" and the "thugs."

Embezzlement. Appropriation of a person's property through any fraudulent means constitutes embezzlement. Often the charge is brought against persons handling money or property of others, such as bank or other business establishment employees, servants and public officials.

A person is deprived of property which is rightfully his or hers through breach of confidence. This charge is often combined with others which constitute a crime, such as obtaining funds under false pretenses.

False pretenses. Deliberately misrepresenting facts with intent to deceive or defraud has been established as a statutory crime. The swindler represents himself as a successful businessman in an effort to persuade his elderly fiancé to assign property to him before the marriage. Other common offenses against property include extortion or blackmail, an effort to obtain money or property through the use of threats or intimidation, and forgery, the signing or creating of a written instrument with intent to deceive or defraud. Altering a check is considered to be a forgery. The crime becomes more serious when the forgery is sent through the U.S. mails and is often prosecuted in the federal courts rather than in the state judiciary.

Receiving property stolen by another is punishable by a prison term. Concealment of such goods or reselling them leads to this charge. Professional receivers of stolen goods are known as "fences" in the underworld.

Malicious mischief. Deliberately destroying property belonging to another is classified as a misdemeanor or a felony, depending upon the extent or seriousness of the harm done. Tampering with another's automobile, damaging trees and shrubs on another's property, or harming pets or animals belonging to another are all classified as malicious mischief.

CRIMES AGAINST THE PUBLIC PEACE

The statutes of most states are weighty with laws governing public morality and decency. The apartment dweller who offends the neighborhood with frequent and raucous parties or the homeowner who has turned his front lawn into a graveyard for junked automobiles can be prosecuted for disturbing the peace. Depending on the community, accepted standards of social conduct govern these incidences. Some areas continue to enforce "blue laws" that forbid various activities such as operating a place of business on Sunday.

Although statutes are gradually changing, accepted standards of morality are still embodied there and class as crimes such acts as fornication, adultery, bigamy, incest, seduction, prostitution, sodomy, gambling obscenity, indecency, and contributing to the delinquency of a minor. Civil rights legislation has led to the demise of a number of statutes, such as vagrancy or loitering, which formerly was the vehicle for simple arrest of persons on the streets.

Obscenity laws are also in a state of uncertainty, with definitions of what is obscene dependent upon the jurisdiction and the accepted social values of the people who live there. The same applies to riot actions, disturbance of public assembly. When statutes designed to curb individual actions have resulted in a weakening of the rights of the individual, conflict has arisen over them and many have been overturned in recent years.

CRIMES AGAINST AUTHORITY AND JUSTICE

A body of legislation has been established to deal with willful interference into recognized functions of government. They include statutes forbidding any obstruction of justice, such as interference with a police officer in the performance of his or her duty; resisting arrest or hindering the arrest of another; breaking out of prison or aiding another in avoiding custody; concealing a felony or withholding evidence leading to disposition of a crime; perjury, which is the giving of false testimony under oath in a judicial proceeding; or bribery, the offering or giving of a reward to a public official who is performing his or her duty, with intent to corrupt the official.

Tax evasion, postal violations such as theft of mail, and contempt, which is a willful violation or disregard for judicial proceedings, are also classified as crimes against justice or authority.

MISCELLANEOUS CRIMES

State and federal codes include a wide variety of other statutes prohibiting specific offenses. These include traffic safety laws that have been enacted to protect the safety of the public, food and drug laws, and fish and game statutes. Many are punishable by fines; others carry jail or prison sentences upon conviction.

Arrest, Accusation and Pleading

The cutting edge of the law enforcement process, and the point at which the reporter will most often enter the picture is the arrest. Commission of a crime does not have to be directly observed for an arrest to take place, but there must be reasonable suspicion that a person has been involved in some manner.

The arrest can be simple and often observed by the reporter at the scene, or it can be verified through police or court records. Because of its serious nature, however, the reporter should *always* verify that the action occurred.

> A man who police said used a dozen aliases was charged yesterday with passing $20 counterfeit bills in the Front Street district.
>
> He was arrested after a suspicious jewelry store clerk quietly called police while ostensibly making change for a purchase.

Following the arrest, the police official swears out a formal complaint with a court official, usually a magistrate, who issues a warrant of arrest for the specific person or persons. The process is often reversed, however, as when the officer first files the complaint and the court official issues the warrant, after which the arrest is made. A complaining witness can also swear out a complaint against a person if he or she is convinced that a crime has been committed.

Following the arrest, the suspect is "booked," with the arrest being formally recorded, at a jail, in a police station or in a magistrate's office. The defendant may be incarcerated pending arraignment or released on bail or on personal recognizance if the charge is not serious or if the individual is well known, or the case may be dismissed.

The accused has a right to a speedy arraignment. Its purpose is to identify the defendant, to advise him or her of the charges filed, and to inform the defendant of his or her constitutional rights. The reporter covers an arraignment to determine the specific charges that the defendant faces and the defendant's plea.

> Arrington physician Louis C. Milton pleaded not guilty this morning to three separate indictments charging trafficking in drugs.
>
> The 55-year-old Milton, who has been practicing medicine at 710 S. 11th St. for more than 27 years, sat pensively throughout the 10-minute arraignment in

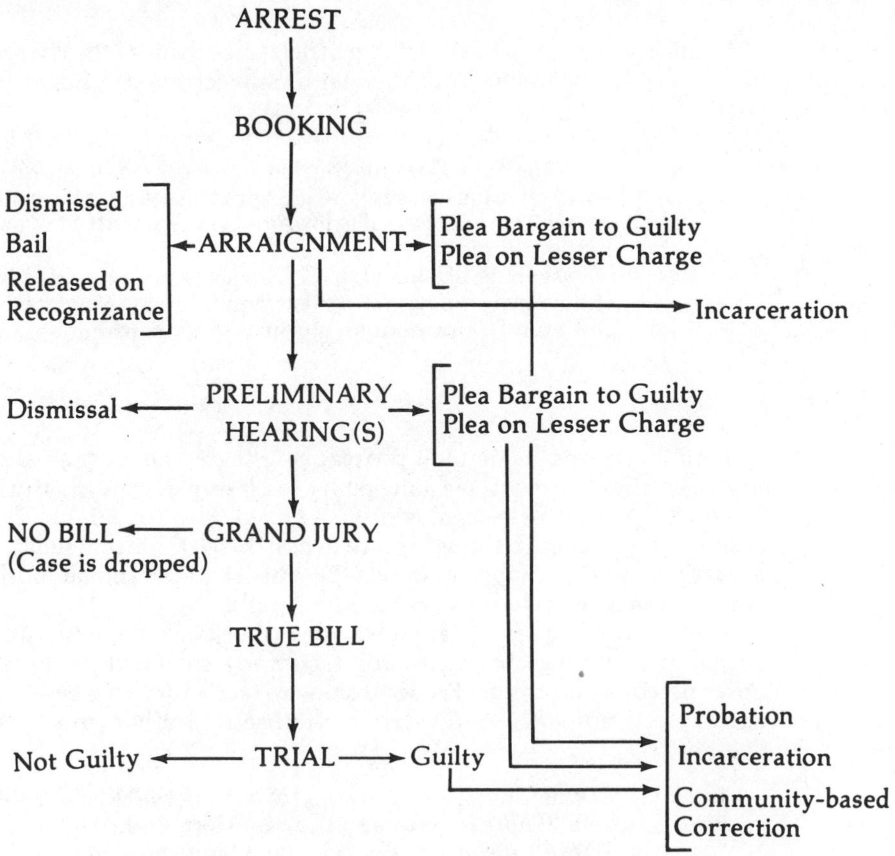

FIGURE 10-1. *A flowchart showing the sequence of events which lead a criminal suspect from arrest to trial.*

> Lawrence County Common Pleas Court, only answering a few personal questions from Judge Forrest McClanahan. Milton's bail was continued at $50,000.
>
> The indictments, returned July 31 by a county grand jury, accused the physician of "aiding and abetting and trafficking in drugs" during a 13-month period concluding with the indictments.

The process advances with one of these pleas:

—Guilty.

—Not guilty.

—*Nolo contendere* (I will not contest it), which is equivalent to a plea of guilty and which throws the defendant on the mercy of the court.

—Not guilty by reason of insanity (a defense that may admit the crime, but argues that the defendant was not in control of his or her faculties when the crime was committed).

At the arraignment, the presiding official may dismiss the charge or set specific bail which must be met or subject the defendant to jail.

> A 300-pound Danville construction worker was charged with felonious assault after witnesses told police he attacked the patrons of a downtown tavern with a broken bottle last night.
>
> Joseph T. Skeen, 30, 2577 Terrace Ave., remained in the county jail under $5,000 bond set by Magistrate Silliman Edens at an arraignment this morning.

Plea Bargaining

In an increasingly common procedure, the defendant may also use a bargaining process, pleading guilty to a lesser charge. In return for such a plea, a costly trial is often avoided. Plea bargaining has become a popular, although controversial, part of the judicial process, and the reporter should be sufficiently familiar with pending cases to accurately project the details.

A defendant frequently bargains with authorities for a reduced or suspended sentence in return for testimony that will implicate other persons in the case. Prosecutors who fear a jury trial because their case is not sufficiently strong often seek plea bargains with defendants.

> Washington (AP)—Daniel Minchew, the chief accuser in a Senate investigation of Sen. Herman E. Talmadge (D-Ga.), pleaded guilty today to submitting a false $2,289 expense account to the Senate.
>
> The one-count plea resulted from negotiations between Minchew's attorney and government attorneys, who said that Minchew had admitted additional financial wrongdoing.
>
> No sentencing date was set. The charge carries a maximum five-year prison term and $10,000 fine. Justice Department attorneys said that, as a result of the plea bargaining agreement, they are dropping plans to seek other indictments on charges of embezzlement, fund conversion and fraud.

Plea bargaining takes place throughout the judicial process—even after a trial is concluded. Sometimes the court adjourns for hours or days to allow the defendant time to consult with his or her attorney on the plea.

Plea bargaining tends to complicate the reporting process, since much of it remains closeted in private negotiations among attorneys in the case. The reporter is generally forced to rely on vague reports of a "deal" being struck, speculation by other officials and other inappropriate sources. It constitutes a dangerous reporting area.

Further complicating the reporter's job, plea bargaining is criticized as promoting a double standard of justice. Increasing examples in recent years point directly to the problem.

> Washington (AP)—When former Vice President Spiro T. Agnew pleaded no contest to income tax evasion and quit, the Justice Department agreed not to prosecute for conspiracy, extortion or bribery.
>
> Agnew got probation and a $10,000 fine.
>
> When former Atty. Gen. Richard G. Kleindienst pleaded guilty to a misdemeanor, failure to testify fully to a Senate subcommittee, the Justice Department agreed not to prosecute for perjury, a felony.
>
> Kleindienst drew a suspended sentence.
>
> Had they been anyone else, would Agnew and Kleindienst have fared as well? Is there a double standard at the bar of justice? Can the powerful and the wealthy use their stature and money to extract a better deal?

A Maryland panel of judges gave prison sentences to two former associates of Agnew who had furnished key testimony against the former vice president. The action, according to press reports, stunned the prosecutor's staff, which had recommended and expected leniency for the men. In some states, efforts are under way to outlaw plea bargaining through changes in legislation.

Preliminary Hearings

Unless an indictment has already been returned by a grand jury, the defendant is entitled to a preliminary hearing (sometimes called a preliminary examination). Its purpose is to determine

1. whether or not a crime has been committed, and
2. whether or not there are reasonable grounds to believe the defendant was involved.

At this hearing, the defendant is confronted with the evidence to support the charges against him or her. The hearing is essentially one-sided because the defendant presents no witnesses, and the reporter must take special care to avoid a prejudiced news report. In some jurisdictions, the defendant can request a closed preliminary hearing, asserting that it helps preserve the right to an impartial jury by preventing dissemination of only prosecution testimony through the media.

Closed pretrial hearings were given new and broader impetus July 2, 1979 when the U.S. Supreme Court gave trial judges wide latitude in barring reporters and the public from pretrial hearings if the judge believes publicity might be a threat to a fair trial.

In a 5–4 opinion, Justice Potter Stewart wrote "To safeguard the due process rights of the accused, a trial judge has an affirmative constitutional duty to minimize the effects of prejudicial pretrial publicity." Following the ruling, many judges closed preliminary hearings as well as pretrial hearings to the press.

After the prosecuting attorney has presented the state's case in a preliminary hearing, the presiding judge may hold the defendant to answer and order the case to trial or dismiss the case and release the defendant if he or she feels that the evidence is insufficient.

Other Routes to Trial

Felony cases reach trial court by two routes other than the sworn complaint:

1. Through an *information*, which is an accusation by a prosecutor of a criminal offense. If the district attorney or prosecuting attorney has knowledge that a crime has been committed and has evidence to suggest that an individual is involved, the official may swear out an information and submit it to the court for action. The defendant is again entitled to a preliminary hearing, and the process of determining whether a trial is warranted is repeated. The filing of an information has the advantage of speed, with the district attorney sidestepping the often time-consuming grand jury process.

2. Through the *grand jury*. A specially impaneled group of men and women meets to consider whether or not persons accused of crimes should go to trial. After hearing testimony, the grand jury votes a *true bill* if it believes that there is reason and evidence to support a trial. It votes a *no bill* if it believes that such evidence is insufficient. The prosecuting attorney presents the evidence and requests that an indictment be returned in cases before the jury.

> The grand jury may well be cumbersome, amateurish, time-consuming, annoying, emotional and the fifth wheel in the legal process, but on balance—as was well demonstrated by the persistent 1973–74 "Watergate" grand jury—it does appear to serve as a potentially powerful arm of direct democracy—*if* one is willing to accept the philosophy of the institution in the first place and if one has faith in the competence and intelligence of one's fellow citizens.

Henry J. Abraham's pithy assessment of the grand jury system, which continues to serve as a body of inquiry in many states, may find disagreement among the public, but it remains as a major means of determining whether or not there is sufficient evidence to warrant a trial on criminal charges.

A grand jury can open an investigation on its own, or it can rely on the prosecuting attorney to prepare cases for consideration. It considers evidence in cases of persons arrested and being held in jail or who have been released on bond. During the course of an investigation, the jury can subpoena witnesses, call the accused as a witness, and seek any information that might lead to a decision on its part.

> A special grand jury will examine the records of the Oxford Urban Renewal Authority to determine whether relocated families have been cheated out of thousands of dollars.
>
> A subpoena issued yesterday by Circuit Court Judge Henry L. Mannington directed URA Director Thomas R. Wilson to bring records on relocation before the grand jury tomorrow. Requested records span the period from Jan. 1, 1980 to July 12 of this year.
>
> Prosecutor Earl Ross, who accompanied deputies when the subpoena was served, said there is reason to believe that unnamed officials may have pocketed money earmarked for families forced to leave their homes and move elsewhere in the Elm District Project.

Grand jury sessions are traditionally secret, mainly to protect innocent persons. Many indictments are studied, but never returned. The jury generally considers only the prosecuting attorney's evidence in a case, and the accused may have little or no opportunity to present his or her own case or cross-examine witnesses. As a practical matter, the reporter should be aware that the prosecutor may not always be completely objective in treatment of a pending case. Human frailty or overriding ambition on the part of an official sometimes acts to unfairly obstruct justice. A reporter with good investigative instincts can minimize the incidences of such actions with close scrutiny, a healthy skepticism and probing questions.

The grand jury has another important function—acting as an investigative body to public agencies. Operations of county facilities, such as nursing homes, hospitals and jail facilities, are often investigated. Questionable bail practices by bondsmen in a city may be investigated by a grand jury, leading to changes in the system and even to indictments on conspiracy and extortion charges. When a grand jury conducts its own investigation and returns accusations, it is called a presentment.

While the access of the press to the grand jury is limited, the alert reporter can find ways to carefully collect and publish information coming out of the privacy of the grand jury room, often by observing who enters and departs from the proceedings, thereby obtaining a picture of who and what are being investigated.

Grand jurors are sworn to secrecy, but witnesses are free to discuss their own testimony. Extreme care should be exercised, however, to assure that the witness has not been specifically admonished to secrecy by the presiding judge. General information is often available from a prosecuting attorney and the presiding judge, if they choose to divulge it.

Access to grand jury transcripts is generally regulated by the judge, and transcripts are not available until after the indictments have been returned and the grand jury dismissed. A portion of a transcript may be sealed by the judge until the trial has been begun.

The federal government also impanels grand juries for purposes similar to the county bodies, with the federal bodies binding over defendants for trial and investigating possible abuses by officeholders and government employees.

Grand juries consist of from six to 30 members, chosen at random from among the public. In the past, they were chosen from property tax rolls and thus did not ideally represent a cross section of the community as do trial jurors. Increasingly, however, nominations are being made on a more equitable basis.

Terms of grand juries are limited, ranging from a month to a year before jurors are discharged, but a presiding judge may occasionally extend a jury's term if its business has not been completed. The presiding judge instructs the jury, which appoints its own foreperson and secretary before getting down to business. Length of sessions vary, with some juries meeting every day for a week before recessing, while others meet one day each week for extended periods.

The reporter should watch for new procedural developments in the juries as well as in the courts. Sometimes they are more newsworthy than the lists of indictments returned.

> A new procedure for grand jury deliberations promises "far more efficiency," County Prosecutor John J. Cummings announced yesterday.
>
> Cummings said he would break with tradition by calling the grand jury into session every two weeks throughout the course of the three-month term. In the past, juries have convened only once each three months.
>
> "Things will come up as they occur, instead of waiting and waiting and waiting," Cummings said. "Cases essentially will be fresh when they go before the grand jury," he added, giving the members "a far more accurate" account of each case.

Pretrial Pleading

Prior to trial, many courses of action are open to the defendant through his or her attorney, mainly through motions attacking the accusation. The defendant may file a demurrer, challenging the accusation on the grounds that the facts stated in it do not constitute a crime or that a crime is charged for which the defendant does not have to respond. If the judge sustains a demurrer, the case is dropped unless there are circumstances in which the complaint, information or indictment can be amended and resubmitted. The defendant can deny that the court has jurisdiction to try him or her for the offense charged (plea to the jurisdiction) or can request a change of venue when there is a question as to whether or not the defendant can obtain a fair trial in that area.

> Ronald Wilmer's request to change the site of his trial on charges of murder was denied today, but Circuit Court Judge David Haswell left the door ajar to reconsideration later.
>
> Wilmer, 24, is scheduled to begin trial Monday on charges that he killed three persons during a March 12 crime spree along the coast.

> Haswell said he denied the request "based on the showing here today." Defense attorney Cleveland Eames based his motion on pretrial publicity and a fund-raising effort for one of the victims.
>
> "Monday morning when we start to impanel a jury, if I get the idea this is not the place for the trial, I'll change the venue," Haswell said.

A motion may be made to set aside the charge for factual or procedural deficiencies. The defense attorney argues that the prosecuting attorney's complaint, based on evidence presented at a preliminary hearing, is not sufficient to prove what it charges.

The defendant's attorney may offer a motion to suppress evidence that has been obtained illegally and is not admissable in court, such as illegal police search and seizure or illegal arrest. It is from pretrial hearings such as these that the press is being barred more frequently.

The defense attorney may also ask the judge to dismiss the charge because the defendant has been denied due process, as when notice of his or her constitutional rights is not given when an arrest is made.

Lengthy legal maneuvering often takes place during efforts to extradite a person accused or convicted of an offense to a court which demands his or her surrender. Proof from a state or nation is demanded that the person is indeed a fugitive from the jurisdiction. Uniform extradition legislation has standardized the procedure in recent years, but frequently such efforts are newsworthy.

> Michele Sindona, an Italian financier who once controlled the Franklin National Bank, won a court decision yesterday that bars his extradition to his native Italy.
>
> The decision by Federal District Court Judge Herman L. Werkman represents a significant victory for Sindona, who has conducted a two-year struggle to avoid extradition on fraud charges involving the collapse of Italian banks he had controlled.

Criminal Trial

As a bailiff intones, "All rise," the black-robed judge strides into the courtroom, and the crowded chamber suddenly quiets. The judge takes a seat on the raised bench and the crowd settles back expectantly. A trial is about to begin.

Across the land, the cast of characters in this drama of an American institution is similar: In front of the judge and closest to the action sits a court reporter, expert fingers ready to negotiate the keyboard of the stenotype equipment. Every question asked, every answer given will be recorded with monumental efficiency in a complete transcript of the proceedings.

At a table facing the bench sits a defendant formally accused of committing a crime, flanked by one or more attorneys acting in the defendant's behalf.

At an adjacent table, public officials charged with prosecuting the indictment or indictments against the accused whisper last-minute instructions to one another. The prosecuting attorney, often with several assistants, orchestrates the effort.

The poker-faced bailiff, present to maintain the decorum of the court, stands unobtrusively near the door to the judge's chambers.

Lined up at a nearby table are reporters awaiting opening arguments in what promises to be a newsworthy case. The jury of 12 persons has been chosen and sworn, and the trial is about to begin.

Although the scenario itself is unchanging, the participants themselves are as dissimilar as are the elements of the population. The defendant may be indigent, with public defenders, or a wealthy industrialist, with a dozen attorneys. There may be two witnesses scheduled, or 25. Testimony may be dramatic, or it may be cut and dried, as the trial works its way toward a conclusion.

To reach this trial stage, the participants have traversed the entire pretrial process, including a series of official hearings and unofficial meetings to determine whether the case can be settled before trial and to assure the rights of the defendant.

Most trials lack the newsworthiness that compels a news reporter to cover them daily, listening to all of the evidence and carefully sorting it out for the reader. Instead, the major interest is in the final result, and the reporter checks regularly for the judgment or judgments—guilty, not guilty or dismissal.

Regular daily checks with court clerks will assure that the less important cases are covered in the press. If preliminary stories have been written concerning a case, the matter should always be disposed of by a story; that is, the material should not be left hanging. The reporter can guarantee a final public accounting of such a case with his or her own personal file of information on the case which the reporter originally covered.

Officers of the Court

The chief officer of the court is the judge, who presides over the trial and issues rulings on all points of law dealing with procedure, submission of evidence and witnesses, and determination of the substantive law in each case. Except when the case is tried without a jury, the judge leaves the determination of facts to that body.

The reporter should remember that the judge is also supreme in the criminal courtroom, with nearly unlimited power to find anyone within its jurisdiction in contempt of court. If the judge decides that the press or one of the attorneys in the case is obstructing justice, he or she may find them in contempt, punishing the offender by setting a jail term or a substantial fine.

A court clerk serves as the judge's right arm during the trial and is an important source of information to the reporter. Records of all the judicial proceedings maintained in the clerk's office are indispensable to accuracy of stories concerning the trials.

All proceedings of the trial are recorded by the court reporter, also an indispensable court officer to the press. Exact testimony of witnesses, details of evidence, objections made by attorneys for both sides, and court rulings are all taken verbatim by the court reporter through shorthand, stenotype or tape recorder. In important trials, newspapers often arrange to obtain a daily transcript of the proceedings for accuracy and thoroughness. Nevertheless, most of the material depends on the reporter's notetaking ability, with frequent spot checks of confusing testimony with the court reporter.

Other officers of the court include the bailiff, whose duty it is to maintain order in the courtroom, and attorneys for both sides.

Setting the Stage

While care should be taken to avoid interpreting actions, events and testimony, important trials often merit a description of the setting, the principals and drama of the event. The reporter should avoid use of overly descriptive "labels" for those involved, concentrating instead on helping the reader to gain an understanding of the issues involved and the stakes.

A folksy, red-suspendered defense attorney, in contrast to the decorous gray-suited prosecutor, offers the reader a picture of the trial scene which can otherwise be obtained only by sitting in on the trial itself, something that few people do.

> Conover—As though he were only a passerby, former state liquor commissioner Brian L. Jeffries has listened quietly to the shrill arguments that have resounded for 10 days through the courtroom where he is on trial.
>
> Jeffries, now a practicing lawyer in Conover, is charged with defrauding the state of thousands of dollars while he served as commissioner from 1975 to 1979. Prosecutors are attempting to prove that he accepted cash payments from liquor companies and appropriated hundreds of cases of alcoholic beverages to his own use during those years.
>
> Despite his bright plaid jackets—which appear out of place among the somber blue and gray suits of most of the attorneys, Jeffries has remained a passive figure on the fringes of the proceedings.
>
> Defense attorneys Rudolph Bulgarelli and Timothy Barber offer a vivid contrast to their client and to one another. Bulgarelli's red suspenders and folksy manner disarm witnesses, who are startled when the fatherly, friendly voice switches suddenly to a booming, accusing baritone.
>
> Barber, polished and sophisticated, hammers at witnesses from the outset of his questioning. Some of his remarks have provoked the ire of presiding Judge John Willingham, who keeps a tight rein on courtroom procedure.

Important Elements in the Trial

While specifics vary from state to state, these are the basic steps through which the process evolves in a criminal trial on a felony charge:

—The jury is selected and sworn.

—The accusation is read in open court, and the defendant's plea is recorded.

—The prosecution makes an opening statement, explaining to the jury how it intends to prove its case. Stories are frequently written based on the opening remarks of both prosecution and defense.

—The prosecution presents its case, calling witnesses and presenting evidence that it believes will be a factor in convicting the defendant.

—The defense makes its opening statement, carefully explaining why and how it will show the defendant to be innocent of the charge. This opening statement is sometimes made immediately after the prosecution offers its opening statement.

—The defense presents its evidence, with the burden of proof on the prosecution. The defense merely has to prove reasonable doubt that the defendant committed the crime.

—Both sides present rebuttal evidence in an effort to weaken the other side's case.

—Both parties sum up their case to the jury, seeking to strengthen their cause.

—The judge instructs the jury on the law, explaining what possible verdicts can be returned and the jury's limitations.

—The jury retires to deliberate and return a verdict. If it cannot reach a verdict in a reasonable time, the judge can rule a mistrial, and the case may be retried or simply dropped.

—If the defendant has been convicted, sentence is passed, sometimes following extensive presentencing investigation by court officials. Judgment is then executed, with the convicted defendant remanded to custody or to probation proceedings. Often the sentence is suspended in light of probation officers' reports.

Course of the Trial

Selection of the jurors who will render final judgment is important to both sides as well as to the public. Traditionally 12 jurors are chosen, with alternates occasionally selected in potentially lengthy and complex cases so that sudden illness of a juror would not affect a final verdict and abort the proceedings. Alternates do not vote unless they must substitute for one of the 12 jurors in the case. Some states have adopted legislation permitting fewer than that number, except in capital cases.

The story covering the final verdict in a criminal case should be written in a straightforward manner, with prompt efforts made to determine from the principals whether appeals would be made.

> A federal court jury convicted John and Edward Schneider today of plotting to blow up the Olde Mill Elementary School in October, a plot the brothers claimed was promoted by undercover police.
>
> The jury returned its verdict against the Schneiders—John W., 28, and Edward S., 26—less than two hours after it received the case from District Court Judge Joseph Kinnear.
>
> Each brother was convicted of conspiring to violate the rights of schoolchildren, of attempting to damage an institution receiving federal aid, and attempting to interfere with a court order—Federal Judge Richard Donlevy's decision to desegregate the city's public school system.
>
> Attorneys for both defendants said they will appeal the verdict.

As the trial proceeds, there are special points at which the reporter must take particular care, such as admissibility of a defendant's confession or an admission or acknowledgement of a fact tending to prove guilt. Admittance of a confession must be preceded by proof that it was given voluntarily, without extortion or threats by authorities.

The reporter should also exercise care to properly use the appropriate words in writing about testimony. There is a vast difference between "testified" and "admitted" and between "acknowledged" and "described."

During cross-examination, the reporter should be aware of the significance of what the previous testimony has been. A witness who earlier may have stated flatly that a marriage was legal may admit under cross-examination that he is not fully certain. Such nuances can dramatically change the course of a trial.

To cover a trial effectively, the reporter should anticipate developments, frequently checking with attorneys for both sides during court recesses. Some information is worth advance notice in news stories; other material is obtained when disclosures are made during the trial itself. Whether or not the defendant will testify in his or her own behalf, "surprise" witnesses who may be called to testify, shifts in the order of key witnesses—all provide clues to the course of the trial. Conversations with the attorneys and the court clerk help keep the reporter closer to the day-to-day proceedings.

While the ubiquitous telephone is a necessity for the reporter, it cannot replace actual presence at the courthouse. Personal legwork often provides the kind of additional information that humanizes court coverage.

> A mistrial was declared in a Superior Court case yesterday after two women members of a deadlocked jury became locked in combat.
> Judge Wilson C. Rivers stopped the jury's deliberations, declared the mistrial and sent the bristling jurors home after squeals and sounds of a scuffle filtered into his courtroom from the small adjacent jury room.
> The jury had been deliberating for two days in the trial of three men charged with armed robbery when an argument broke out between the two women over the evidence in the case, according to witnesses.

Being personally present at trials often adds important ingredients to the stories that are finally written. The official court record is, of course, available to the reporter, but timeliness dictates on-the-spot coverage in important trials. Only a day's personal coverage could produce material such as this:

> A key witness in the murder trial of James H. Allen testified Monday that the killer of 19-year-old Mark Patterson "appeared to be laughing" when he pulled the trigger of a gun as Patterson ran from him.
> But the Common Pleas Court jury sitting in the case won't be allowed to consider that testimony.
> The witness, Carol Jean Hale, testified she saw Patterson shot to death Jan. 9 after a scuffle with two men behind his father's business, Auto Parts Inc., 1400 Cleveland Ave.
> Of four witnesses to the scuffle, only Ms. Hale has identified Allen, 20, as the killer. She said he pointed the gun at Patterson and fired three times, hitting Patterson from about 20 feet away.
> Judge Harley Meyer told the jury to disregard Ms. Hale's conclusion that Allen was laughing. But he did allow her to testify, "I could see his teeth. His lips were turned up. His eyes were bright."
> Ms. Hale, a psychiatric nurse, said she watched the shooting from her second-floor office just north of the Auto Parts parking lot.

The reporter must have the patience to wait through lengthy deliberations by a jury in important cases, often piecing together details that will convey much more than a cut and dried acquittal in a murder case.

> A few scraps of paper from the wastebasket in the now-empty juryroom gave evidence of the lack of accord that plagued jurors through several ballots until unanimous agreement was reached.
> On discarded pieces of paper five persons had voted "not sure," "undecided" and "not committed." Two "guilty" votes were found along with one "not guilty." The basket was littered with other discarded ballots shredded beyond recognition.

Even though the understanding of the reader may be advanced, care should be taken in interpreting testimony. Editorializing, of course, should always be avoided.

Free Press vs. Fair Trial

After a suspect had been apprehended and charged with murder in Chicago in 1967, a local minister visited the suspect in jail. As the minister emerged from the conference, he reluctantly informed reporters that the supect seemed remorseful. The comment was duly reported, but for years the propriety of publishing such a damaging comment prior to trial has been debated.

At the heart of the debate lie two basic rights as expressed in the U.S. Constitution:

1. Congress shall make no law . . . abridging the freedom of speech, or of the press (First Amendment)
2. In all criminal prosecutions, the accused shall enjoy the right to a speedy and public trial, by an impartial jury of the state and district wherein the crime shall have been committed. (Sixth Amendment)

Any actions abridging these basic rights are forbidden, yet each has traditionally encroached upon the domain of the other.

Today the journalist faces an even more complex responsibility in determining whether publication of such a statement as that issued by the minister is in the interest of a totally fair trial. The merits of publishing certain information concerning criminal cases must be weighed as must the shifting, often contradictory, series of judicial opinions that have tended to further confuse the issue.

While the U.S. Supreme Court ruled in 1976 that judges may not generally impose orders on the press forbidding publication of information about criminal cases, the same court three years later made an about-face and granted judges broad discretionary power to order courtrooms closed to the press and the public during pretrial hearings.

In the celebrated "Nebraska case" in 1976 (*Nebraska Press Assn v. Stuart*), the court ruled that judges could not gag the press in criminal cases, even if the judge believes that such an order will help to assure the defendant a fair trial by preventing prejudicial publicity.

But in 1979, in *Gannett* v. *DePasquale*, the court ruled that a trial judge has an "affirmative constitutional duty to minimize the effects of prejudicial pretrial publicity" and has the right to bar the press from pretrial hearings.

The effect of the court's rulings was to create confusion among the nation's judiciary as well as the press over its interpretation.

Unofficial efforts were made by individual justices to explain the thrust of the rulings. Justice John Paul Stevens said that the effects of the ruling have been exaggerated and warned that the country's trial judges should not use the latest ruling "to unnecessarily exclude the public from judicial proceedings."

Federal Judge Irving R. Kaufman suggested that the question cannot be answered in absolute terms. "There is a vital affinity between an independent press and an independent judiciary," Kaufman noted. "Yet, recently and with greater frequency, it appears that the courts are wielding the cutting edge against the press."

"At what point," Kaufman asked, "does a criminal defendant's right to a trial free from the taint of prejudicial publicity override our devotion of the concept of a public trial?"

Supreme Court justices were not unanimous in their opinions limiting press access to court proceedings. Justice Harry Blackmun, a dissenter in the 5-4 ruling in 1979 on pretrial limitations, said the result of the Supreme Court action "is that the important interests of the public and the press in open judicial proceedings are rejected and cast aside as of little value or significance."

Chief Justice Warren Burger, who concurred with the majority, pointed out that "by definition, a hearing on a motion before trial to suppress evidence is not a trial; it is a pretrial hearing." Another justice who voted with the majority, William Rehnquist, argued that the Sixth Amendment gives the public no definitive right to attend criminal trials.

Major elements of the press opposed the 1979 ruling, arguing that 90 percent of criminal cases are disposed of before coming to trial and viewing the pretrial limitations as a basic limitation on the right of a defendant to a public trial.

However, the court clarified its position somewhat in a significant 1980 decision, holding for the first time that the First Amendment to the Constitution gives the public and the press an all but absolute right to attend criminal trials.

Ruling in the case of a Virginia judge who had closed a 1978 murder trial to reporters and spectators (*Richmond Newspapers Inc. v. the Commonwealth of Virginia*), the court held that "absent an overriding interest" to the contrary, the trial in a criminal case must be open to the public.

While the ruling did not clear up all of the problems associated with the Gannett-DePasquale opinion on pretrial procedures, it had the effect of repudiating much of the reasoning in that case. Spokesmen for the press applauded the Supreme Court ruling, pointing out that it was the first time the court had recognized there was a constitutional right of access to information.

A Reporter's Guide to Legal Terms

Knowledge of these basic legal terms will help the student to avoid the temptation to impart information to the reader only in "legalese." Legal terminology generally must be explained.

Action in personam: An action against the person, based on a personal liability.

Action in rem: An action to recover a specific object, usually an item of personal property, such as jewelry or a car.

Adversary system: The system in

use in this country in which each of the opposing, or adversary, parties is given the opportunity to present and establish opposing contentions in court.

Affidavit: A written statement subscribed to before a notary public or other official who has the authority to administer an oath.

Alias: A fictitious name assumed by a person.

Allegation: The assertion or statement to a party in an action, submitted in a pleading, setting out what the party expects to prove.

Amicus curiae: A friend of the court; one who joins an action, with permission of the court, and volunteers information.

Answer: A pleading by which a defendant seeks to resist a plaintiff's allegation or allegations against him or her.

Appellate court: A court that has jurisdiction of appeal and review as opposed to a trial court.

Arraignment: The process of bringing a prisoner to court to respond to a criminal charge and to officially hear the charge(s) against him or her.

Assignment: An act by which a person assigns his or her rights to property to another.

At issue: When the parties to a suit reach a point in the pleadings that is affirmed by one side and denied by the other, the case is said to be "at issue" and ready for trial.

Attachment: A remedy that enables a plaintiff to acquire a lien upon property for satisfaction of judgment.

Attorney of record: The attorney whose name appears in the permanent files or record of a case.

Bail: Security obtained by the court which allows a person to go free pending appearance in court on a specified day.

Bench warrant: A demand issued by the court itself for the arrest of a person or attachment of property.

Binding instruction: The jury is told that, if it finds certain facts to be true, it must find for the plaintiff or the defendant.

Bind over: To hold on bail or trial.

Brief: A document filed by counsel in court, usually setting forth facts and law in support of his or her case.

Burden of proof: In the law of evidence, the necessity of indisputably proving a fact or facts.

Certiorari: A writ directing judges or officers of inferior courts to certify or to return the records of proceedings to the higher court for judicial review.

Change of venue: The removal of a suit from one geograpical or judicial area to another.

Chattel: Tangible property, such as personal possessions, machinery, stocks and bonds, as distinguished from real property.

Circumstantial evidence: Evidence of an indirect nature.

Collusion: A secret, deceitful arrangement between two or more persons.

Complaint (civil): The initial pleading on the part of plaintiff in a civil action.

Complaint (criminal): A sworn application for a warrant of arrest, alleging that a law has been broken.

Contempt of court: Any act that a judge considers has embarrassed or hindered the court in its effort to administer justice.

Contract: A written or oral agreement between two parties which is considered enforceable by law.

Declaratory judgment: Court decree that declares the rights of a party to an action or expresses the opinion of the court on a question of law.

Decree: An order or a decision by the court. Decrees can be final or interlocutory, provisional or preliminary.

Demur (demurrer): A pleading admitting the truth of the facts in a civil complaint, or answer, but contending the legal insufficiency of the complaint.

Deposition: Testimony of a witness taken outside of court.

Discovery: A proceeding that enables one party to become informed of the facts known by other parties in the action.

Double jeopardy: The constitutional prohibition against more than one prosecution for the same crime.

Easement: A privilege or right acquired to use the land of another. A public easement is acquired by condemnation, such as a public utility's right to place power or telephone lines across property.

Embezzlement: Fraudulent appropriation of money or property entrusted to one person by another.

Eminent domain: The right of a government to take private property for public use.

Enjoin: To require a person through court action to perform some act or abstain from one.

Escrow: A party to a pending agreement deposits something of value, often a deed, with a third party, usually a bank or other such institution, to be surrendered to a second party when final action is taken in a proceeding.

Extradition: The surrender by one state or jurisdiction to another of an individual accused or convicted of an offense outside its own territory and within the territorial jurisdiction of another.

Felony: A serious crime, generally punishable by imprisonment in a penitentiary.

Forgery: Altering or falsely copying, with intent to defraud, any material which, if genuine, might be the foundation of a legal liability, such as a check or deed.

Fraud: Intentionally perverting the truth; resorting to a deceitful practice with intent to deprive another of his of her rights.

Garnishment (garnishee): A court decree applying money or property of one person toward the debts owed by that person to a creditor.

Grand jury: A body whose duty it is to study complaints and accusations in criminal cases and to indict or dismiss persons accused. (As distinguished from a petit jury, the ordinary jury of 12 or fewer persons who sit at the trial in civil or criminal actions.)

Habeas corpus: A writ directing a person to appear before a court or judge. Most commonly, it is directed to an official detaining another, commanding him or her to produce that person, so that the court can determine whether due process of law has been observed.

Indictment: A written accusation by a grand jury, charging that a person has committed a crime.

Injunction: A mandatory or prohibitive order issued by a court.

Instruction: Directions given by a judge to a jury concerning the law in an action.

Interrogatories: Written questions by a party to an action served on the other party who must provide written responses under oath.

Libel: Defamation of a person or group by print, pictures or signs. Generally any publication that injures the reputation of another.

Lien: A charge imposed on specific property, which is security for a debt.

Mandamus: A court order that compels action.

Manslaughter: The unlawful killing of another without malice. It may be voluntary, upon sudden impulse, or involuntary in the commission of an unlawful act.

Master: A court officer, usually an attorney, who takes testimony and reports to the court, such as divorce hearings.

Misdemeanor: Minor offenses, sometimes punishable by less than a year in jail.

Mistrial: An invalid trial, usually

aborted because of lack of jurisdiction, irregular procedure or disregard of some other fundamental requisite.

No bill: A grand jury returns a "no bill" when it finds that evidence is insufficient to warrant the return of a formal charge.

Nolle prosequi (nolle pros): The prosecuting officer in a criminal case declares that he or she will no longer prosecute the case, with the effect of dropping the charges.

Nolo contendere: A pleading by defendants in criminal cases, which literally means "I will not contest it." The effect is to throw the defendant on the mercy of the court. Corporations often agree to plead to this, agreeing to pay damages but without admitting guilt.

Plaintiff: A person who brings an action in court.

Pleading: The process in which parties to an action alternately present written contentions, with each serving to narrow the field of controversy until only a few points remain. At that time the action is said to be "at issue" and ready for trial.

Preliminary hearing: A hearing to determine whether a person charged with a crime by a magistrate or judge should be held for trial.

Presentment: A statement in writing by a grand jury to the court that a public offense has been committed without a bill of indictment being first submitted to the jury.

Probate: The process of proving that a will is valid.

Probation: The process of allowing a person convicted of a crime to remain free under suspension of sentence and generally under supervision of an officer of the court, such as a probation officer.

Prosecutor: An official who initiates the prosecution of a person accused of a crime and who performs the function of trial lawyer in behalf of the public.

Quash: To overturn, annul or void a summons or indictment.

Remand: To send a prisoner back to custody after a hearing that has not resulted in final judgment; also, the action of an appellate court in returning a case to the court of original jurisdiction for final disposal.

Search warrant: An order directing an officer to search a specified property to determine whether a crime has been committed.

Slander: Defamatory words spoken that tend to prejudice another in reputation or livelihood.

Specific performance: A mandatory order in equity to perform a specific action.

Subpoena: An order for a witness to appear and give testimony before a court.

Substantive law: That law dealing with rights, duties and liabilities, as distinguished from adjective law, the law regulating procedure.

Summons: An order directing the sheriff or another officer to notify a person that an action has commenced against him or her in court and requiring appearance to answer the complaint.

Tort: An injury or wrong committed against the person or property of another.

Transcript: The official record of a proceeding.

Trespass: Any action in which entry is made or unlawful injury is done to another's property.

True bill: A grand jury's endorsement of a bill of indictment when the jury feels that there is sufficient evidence to support a criminal charge.

Venire: A writ summoning persons to court to act as jurors but used popularily to identify the group of names summoned.

Venue: The place in which the alleged events from which a legal action arises take place.

Voir dire (to speak the truth): The preliminary examination conducted by the court of prospective jurors or witnesses regarding qualifications.

Warrant of arrest: An order or writ issued by a magistrate or other authority to a sheriff or other officer directing the arrest of a person to be brought to court.

Warranty deed: A document giving title to land or other property, including a covenant guaranteeing the validity of the title.

Writ: A court order requiring the performance of a specified act or providing the authority to have it done.

PART THREE

THE PRIVATE SECTOR:
People Make It "Public"

CHAPTER 11
Covering Politics

All of the Great Patriots now engaged in edging and squirming their way toward the Presidency of the Republic run true to form. This is to say, they are all extremely wary, and all more or less palpable frauds. What they want primarily is the job; the necessary equipment of unescapable issues, immutable principles and soaring ideals can wait until it becomes more certain which way the mob will be whooping.

With these pithy generalities, the late H. L. Mencken marched into the battleground of the 1920 presidential political campaign. But he also possessed the capability of being far more specific about his subjects—the political figures of that day—as his further comments indicate:

Of the whole crowd at present in the ring, it is probable that only Hoover would make a respectable president. General Wood is a simple-minded old dodo with a delusion of persecution; Palmer is a political mountebank of the first water; Harding is a second-rate provincial; Borah is steadily diminishing in size as he gets closer to the fight; Gerard and the rest are simply bad jokes.

Political coverage today is more restrained, but the reality of 1920 remains—almost anything goes in politics. The political reporter of the 1980s will still have to negotiate a course through land mines that dot the landscape—politicians who attempt to use the press, sources that mysteriously dry up at inopportune times, and outright lies and deception, all perpetrated in the name of "good government."

politics: the science and art of political government; the conducting of or participation in political affairs, often as a profession; political methods, tactics, etc.

Webster's definition does not nearly encompass the complexities of the process by which this country is governed. Companion definitions are necessary to clarify the journalist's role: "political" is defined as "being concerned with government, the state or politics; engaged in taking sides in politics."

This act of taking sides is one of the most important elements in the political process, and the reporter who does not immediately recognize its implications will encounter far more formidable land mines in the political battle zone. For political office—the legal position from which individuals or groups design and implement public policy—and politics itself are inevitably intermingled.

The effective politician is usually an officeholder—but not always. Whatever the role of a politician, be it U.S. senator, precinct committee member, unpaid adviser to a governor or the secretary of a political organization, the individual wields some measure of power. And all or part of that power lies in effective organization.

Edmund Burke's 18th century description of a political party is not realistic today. He suggested it was "a body of men united, for promoting by their joint endeavors the national interest, upon some particular principle on which they are all agreed." Since organized political parties in the United States tend to sidestep many major issues and to avoid views that might alienate important segments of the party, the practical political structure today does not embrace that ideal. The strength of the political party lies in its ability to compromise differing viewpoints.

A more practical approach today would be to categorize political parties as organizations of diverse groups that seek to acquire office and direct policies, often for mutual gain. Be it a farm organization, a labor union or an association of business executives, the group often promotes its own interest in advance of others.

> The State Council of Retail Merchants put public pressure today on Democratic members of the state legislature to resist a sales tax increase and turn instead to some other method of balancing next year's state budget.

In this instance, a pressure group is clearly setting its interests—aimed at avoiding placing other problems on business establishments—ahead of other interests. Many organizations, such as chambers of commerce, industrial development groups, labor unions, businesses and churches, see themselves as part of the political process. The reporter's job is to be sufficiently familiar with the groups to identify their role in the process.

Rhetoric vs. Reality

rhetoric: insincere or grandiloquent language.
reality: the quality or state of being real.

The political reporter requires more than a sharp pencil to deal with the realities of his or her job; an instinct for what is real and unreal is necessary, so that the public can be assured the reality it requires to make some measure of informed decisions.

Political officeholders and would-be officeholders lean toward ornate oration, declamation and occasionally verbal tub-thumping. One of the basic and most important jobs of the political reporter is to cut through the excess shrubbery and reach the roots of the verbiage, eliminating the protective coloration employed by most politicians. Thus, the reporter will correctly translate to the reader or viewer this exchange with Vice President Nelson Rockefeller in 1976:

Reporter: Mr. Vice President, do you see the possibility that you will be nominated at this year's Republican National Convention?

Rockefeller: I cannot conceive of any scenario in which that could eventuate.

Translation: The vice president sees no possibility that he will be nominated.

Many such responses by politicians are far more detailed than this comparatively simple exchange, and they are not limited to the elder statesmen of the parties. A much younger candidate is often as obscure, as reporters covering California Gov. Edmund Brown, Jr. discovered during the 1976 primaries:

Reporter: Gov. Brown, isn't your 1976 candidacy really aimed at a 1980 candidacy?

Brown: My equation is sufficiently complex to admit of various outcomes.

Translation: It certainly is possible.

Aside from such translation ability, the reporter's other tools include insistence on total fairness and balance in coverage, the ability to work with widely disparate interest groups, an intimate knowledge of those involved in politics and the organizations within which they function, and the realization that objectivity must be closely monitored when close professional relationships are involved.

Writing About Politics

Whether print or broadcast oriented, the political reporter must first be cognizant of the dissimilarity between his or her role and that of the political figure:

Politician: actively engaged in conducting the business of government or party politics, or trying to reach that level.

Political reporter: actively engaged in reporting the affairs of the politician and the party, whatever those affairs may be and wherever they may lead, as they affect the public interest.

As a practical matter, of course, the goals of the politician and the journalist do not often coincide. The politician is seeking power and attempting to secure it, often through popular election. The journalist is engaged in seeking out and publishing the truth. Politicians, even those most nearly at the level of angels, do not always care to find the truth emblazoned across the front page of a newspaper or coldly broadcast to constituents across the region.

A certain amount of calculated mystery is desirable for the political figure, particularly when the facts may not enhance his or her image or advance a specific political cause. On the other hand, the reporter is concerned with sweeping away such cobwebs for the public.

One of the problems in covering politicians lies in cutting through the veneer that often obscures the real people and the real philosophies. The reporter should watch what they do, rather than merely listening to what they say. What's their record? How successful have they been? What does the campaign platform say, and how does it square with the record? How successful has their approach been? What are their *real* philosophies? Such questions are not easily answered, but they are at the heart of the political reporting process.

To begin, the reporter must have a working knowledge of the people in a political organization, how and where they function as a hierarchy, and what they see as their goals. Next, a knowledge of the legislation which has developed to govern the political process and judicial action which has affected it is necessary.

But the reporter must be able to do more than merely understand the process: he or she must establish working relationships with political figures that will withstand the reporter's ethical tests. The successful reporter operates closely with politicians, often obtaining important stories through personal approaches.

> State Senator James B. Taylor, whose stand on abortion on demand has made him a controversial political figure, has decided to seek a second term in the legislature, a source close to Taylor indicated yesterday.

In this case, the "source" was the senator himself, acting to foreclose other candidacies within his own party without publicly committing himself. The reporter's interest lay in alerting readers to the candidacy. So while the goals of reporter and politician differed sharply, the instrument used to achieve the goals was the same.

However, carefully constructed ground rules are necessary to protect the reporter and the public from being compromised by the relationship that brought the news break in the first place and to assure that the story was not merely a trial balloon floated by a cautious politician to test the waters. The reporter's instinct plays a big part in determining whether the political figure is using the press only as a sounding board.

Good ground rules would specify that any trial balloon carry the danger of including a public warning that might prove embarrassing to the politician who floated it. The reporter's best rule is to avoid anything beyond a purely professional relationship with any political figure.

It is difficult to root out all bias in human relationships, and there is a natural tendency to view matching political philosophies in a more favorable light. The solution to minimizing this natural bias is for the reporter to maintain a healthy skepticism, whoever the party and whatever the issue.

The reporter must forever ask why, and for what purpose, adopting a cooperative attitude but maintaining a certain aloofness.

Author William L. Rivers, a former reporter, is led inescapably to the conclusion that the proper role of the political reporter is that of adversary:

> However friendly an official and a reporter may seem to be, however often they may drink together or have lunch together, however happily they may remember their college years together, there should be a degree of tension between them when they serve their professional roles.

Rivers concludes that a proper adversary relationship is a delicate balance of tact and antagonism, of cooperation and conflict. How effectively political reporters maintain that balance determines the measure of how they do their job.

Political Party Structure

Political parties serve as the principal medium through which the electorate attempts to influence public policy in this country. While many independent voters and candidates have emerged to play a part in the system, most of the electorate depends upon organized parties to determine officials and direction of policy in government. The reason is not complex: there is somewhat greater assurance that influence will be felt through concerted action.

The vast bulk of those who nominally categorize themselves as members of the major parties—Democratic and Republican—are members through voter registration only. Except at election time they do not normally participate in day-to-day functioning of party affairs.

That is left to a far smaller group of interested persons who wield the power and influence to affect decisions at the topmost echelons of government—local, state and national. These are the party members with whom reporters must successfully deal if politics is to be fully and accurately portrayed to the public.

Successful officeholders are often important members of this party machinery, and thus public office and organized politics become part and parcel of each other.

> Republicans unanimously elected Sheriff Ted C. Farr chairman of the County Republican Executive Committee last night.
>
> After the meeting, Farr, 51, who is serving his second term as sheriff, said party harmony would be his major objective.
>
> "We are a minority party," he pointed out, "and it is essential that this committee work together if all our goals are to be met."

From Precinct to National Committee

Political parties are structured in the shape of a pyramid, with a multitude of local organizations operating the bottom levels and the national committee functioning at the top, with headquarters in the nation's capital.

The party's strength lies in the organization and effectiveness of the precinct, the smallest political unit. Voters are registered in specific precincts, which range in size from a few dozen persons in rural areas to more than a thousand in metropolitan communities. Precinct workers, under the direction of the precinct committee head, function as doorbell ringers during political campaigns and poll watchers on election day, and handle many other volunteer jobs. The key to elections, particularly in the big cities, often lies with the precinct chief, who knows his or her district thoroughly and can effectively get out the vote on election day.

The next level in the party's structure may be the ward, city or township committee, depending upon the size of the community. The ward committee usually consists of precinct committee members who elect a chairperson. These are the groups that select candidates for local tickets and wield influence on officeholders.

Although the bottom of the pyramid, with its proximity to the "grass roots," wields substantial influence on the success of the party, it is much less visible than the national offices. Party power gravitates to the candidates who win office; after an election their influence is far more pervasive, for they control the purse strings and patronage.

Between the top and bottom of the party pyramid lie the county and state committees, all functioning to tie local and national organization together. These interrelated organizations are essential to success.

An active party leader, for example, might serve as a local official and also be elected to state party office. Thus, Sheriff Farr, while chairing the county executive committee, has also been elected a member of the State Republican Executive Committee. Furthermore, he was a delegate to the Republican National Convention, completing the chain of office as a successful wielder of power in the typical political party.

While the parties enjoy legal status, government regulates many of their activities through the legislative process, setting dates for primary elections and determining deadlines for candidates. The parties themselves have adopted rules that bind members to conduct party business under their aegis and determine their candidates through primary elections or conventions. Successful primary candidates represent the party in general elections.

Legislatures also affect party affairs through enactment of laws governing campaign contributions and the method in which they are reported to the public. Elected state officials, as members of organized parties, play a part in legislation dictating dates for pimary elections, looking to the party's interest.

> Gov. Randall Dole today asked the state legislature to enact a law setting the first Tuesday in June as primary election day. The first Tuesday in May is presently primary day.
>
> Shortening the time between primary and general elections will enable candidates with fewer resources to better compete with wealthy candidates, Dole explained.

The reporter can be sure that the shift in primary dates is in the interest of the governor's party as well as in the interest of the candidates he espouses.

A party is only as effective as its committees at the local level, and efforts are made to develop strong organizations locally. However, factionalism exists in some form in many of them. When this disrupts the organization, officials at the next level attempt to contain it as much as possible, while preserving an outward show of equanimity.

> Depending on which faction is correct, the chairman of the County Democratic Executive Committee is either State Sen. Robert Morris or Sheriff Herbert Gartin.
>
> The executive committee was evenly split last night, with 16 members voting to re-elect Morris and 14 members supporting Gartin. Two proxies from absent committeemen were cast for Gartin, but Morris ruled them invalid. The Gartin faction walked out, met in an adjacent courthouse room and elected Gartin chairman.

Power in political parties is not always where it appears to be, and the effective reporter will know its specific location and use.

Is the party chairman the real boss or merely a figurehead? Who is actually determining party policy at this level? What's the background and interests of the dissident factions and how much strength do they possess? Who owes what to whom—and why?

Armed with the answers to these and similar questions, the reporter can more accurately cover the party processes. Party organizations operate in comparative secrecy, but their substance as well as their style should be an open book to the reporter.

The chairperson calls meetings of the local committee, presides at such meetings and serves as the visible head of the party at the local level. Because much of the effort at the precinct level is voluntary, the successful party leader must be capable of effectively motivating people. Many factors motivate party workers—philosophical, social and acquisitive—and the reporter should be aware of these factors. Two examples illustrate the point:

1. Peg Aldridge chaired the Union County Republican Council and was a visible figure in the community. Her photograph appeared regularly in the newspapers as an active social worker, hospital auxiliary organizer and school carnival sponsor. In the wake of the Watergate scandal, voters dislodged her party from county office for the first time in 30 years. Aldridge and other members of the party leadership disappeared from public view, major internal shakeups occurred and the party reorganized. However, Aldridge remained as chairman and resumed her rounds of social activities. The reason was obvious to reporters: the real power in the party rested elsewhere, among far less visible personalities. Aldridge was merely a figurehead.

2. Clyde C. Stephens, a wealthy local businessman who backed an unsuccessful candidate for governor, was succeeded as chairman of the Caine County Democratic Committee by Homer L. Harris, a retired railroad employee. Reporters were aware that Stephens lost the chairmanship and most of his political power because he could not overcome the handicap of backing a losing candidate. On the other hand, Harris remained neutral in the governor's race and his neutrality paid off in the race for chairman.

The political reporter develops a finely tuned antenna that points unerringly to areas of greatest influence and to those who are actually making party decisions. Many factors produce this influence—wealth, prestige, old family ties, length of service to the party, organizational ability and personal or professional friendships.

Elections: The Moment of Truth

Intraparty disputes and decisions aside, the highlight of the political process is Election Day, when arguments over public policy and political figures are settled in polling places by the voters. That process begins with registration of eligible citizens by a duly appointed or elected registrar, continues through an often frenetic campaign to the voting and final tabulation, and finally to an official canvass by an elections committee which certifies the winners.

The process does not always end there, however, because legislation provides for legal challenges, which are often taken to state election officials or the judiciary.

> Jody Snedden, unsuccessful candidate for the House, complained that her Democratic opponent, Rep. Albert Ensign, the winning candidate, had committed election irregularities.

> Her complaints were detailed yesterday in a letter to Secretary of State James A. Munck, whose office said it is investigating the matter.
>
> Munck's office has the authority to appeal to Circuit Court for relief for Ms. Snedden.

Unless they are formally registered, citizens are not permitted to vote. Registration, therefore, is an important instrument in party effectiveness. The precinct captain realizes that all the effort in the world to get voters to the polls won't bear fruit unless they are duly qualified.

So political parties act as a catalyst in registering potential voters, but newspapers and broadcast outlets encourage registration too through public service campaigns. Sometimes the interests of a minority party are better served by a low voter turnout than by a high one.

> Based on registration figures, heavy rain forecast for tomorrow may keep voter turnout low and enhance Democratic State Senator William Woodbury's chances for re-election. Registered Republican voters outnumber their Democratic counterparts in Wayne County, 36,416 to 29,677.

Some states continue to permit nomination of candidates by caucus or convention, but most have shifted to the method of nominating by direct primary election. Local conventions are generally cut-and-dried affairs, with delegates being routinely elected to the state conventions which nominate the candidates. Aside from nominating candidates, the state convention delegates adopt a party platform and select members of the state executive committee. It is particularly important at the caucus level for the reporter to gauge sentiment for the candidates, as delegates are often taking party instructions to the state level.

Caucuses, once the mainstay of the systems for choosing party candidates, have fallen by the wayside, but they continue to serve a somewhat different function. Caucuses are called by political leaders at all levels of government to determine many party matters. Some are tightly controlled, others are freewheeling affairs, but the press is usually barred from the sessions, being informed of the results following the meetings.

A persistent political reporter with a good range of sources inside the party can usually locate people who will enlarge upon the bare details provided by the leadership.

> A majority of the Randolph County Executive Committee voted Friday to oust Chairman Howard (Red) Simons, the *News-Herald* has learned.
>
> Officers, including Simons, refused to discuss the meeting, but reliable sources said 19 of the 31 members attended the meeting at the American Legion Hall and voted 18-1 to remove Simons as chairman. The sources said Simons was not present at the meeting.
>
> Simons' position as chairman has been in dispute since he was elected two years ago by a vote of 16 to 15.

Political reporters should avoid the temptation to ignore local party matters unless they deal with intraparty squabbles or other visible issues. By following affairs closely, the reporter can accurately point to political developments long before they become campaign fodder at election time.

Polishing the Ability to Solve Problems

Sooner or later, the political reporter, no matter how experienced he or she may be, will be confronted with a version of each of these problems. No assaults on the integrity of the press or on reportorial quality are necessary if care is taken to address the problem directly and forcefully.

Depending on the specifics and personalities involved, each reporter will find slightly different solutions without compromising basic journalistic virtue.

Keeping Confidences

The soundness of maintaining the confidence of sources applies to any beat, but in the world of politics, where not a few confidences are sacred, failure of a reporter to maintain one could result in the loss of many others.

While others in the political battle zone take sides, the competent reporter should operate in such a manner as to earn respect, if not always the confidence, of both the "ins" and the "outs." They may not hasten to clasp him or her to bosom, but political figures will deal with the independent reporter on the assumption that they will obtain at least an "even break." Most ask no more than that.

In *Public Officials and the Press,* Richard Lee suggests some of the qualities that engender respect for political reporters, including enterprise and correct interpretation of events.

"They can spot a phony a mile away," one politician said. "There is enough sophistication in the press that you can't put something over on them." Lee suggested that those evaluations derived from genuine admiration for the ability and skill of political reporters.

A final note of caution:

—The reporter who values his or her reputation will avoid making promises. The world of politics is a giant arena liberally laced with doses of behavioral sensitivity; the philosophy of "You do this for me and I'll do that for you" prevails. The political reporter will leave the business of making promises to the people whom he or she is covering.

Selective Perception

Psychologists define perception as the process through which we become aware of our environment by organizing and interpreting the evidence of our senses. Yet from childhood on, people subconsciously tend to see what they want to see—and with which they tend to agree.

The problem of selective perception confronts reporters as well as other mortals, but journalism is a particularly harmful area for it to surface.

The nature of their beat places reporters in closer juxtaposition to current events and issues than many others. It is just as natural for them to harbor legitimate private opinions in seeing these events develop as other people. The problem becomes even more complicated with the kaleidoscope of activity that springs up during a political campaign, and the danger is always present that the busy reporter will tend to remember facts as they unconsciously enhance his or her own views of events or issues.

The reporter must constantly be on guard against the danger of selective perception. For example, a political candidate has finally endorsed a project with which the reporter privately agrees, but which the reporter did not expect the candidate to endorse.

> County Commissioner Jules Simon has reluctantly endorsed the proposal to create a $3 million watershed in the south of Lake County. Simon's opponent, John Jennings, had endorsed the project last week.

Nowhere in the remainder of the account is Simon's "reluctance" reflected; the insertion of the word merely emerged out of the reporter's subconscious feelings about the candidate's timing of the announcement. Selective perception often involves only the use of a word or phrase, but it can affect the meaning of an entire story.

Another example suggests that the problem of selective perception can worsen under deadline pressure. Coverage of two recent presidential inaugurations by the same newspaper contained a certain amount of "color" in the accounts. It is much too simplistic to point to the newspaper's endorsement of one successful candidate and lack of endorsement of the other.

Although the integrity of the reporters was unquestioned, a charge of selective perception could have been lodged through a careful study of these leads in retrospect.

> WASHINGTON—Richard Milhous Nixon was inaugurated for a second term as president today and appealed to the nation and its allies to show greater self-reliance "as we stand on the threshold of a new era of peace." In a ceremony that mingled the martial spirit of brass bands and cannon, the peace prayers of clergymen and the distant shouts of protesters, the 60-year-old president took the oath of office. . . . Inauguration day broke cold, and a sharp wind sliced across the dirty Potomac, snapping the half-staff flags as it swept up Pennsylvania Avenue past the $235,000 presidential reviewing stand and on up to the Capitol.
>
> —Jan. 20, 1973

In contrast to this lead was another four years later in the same newspaper but by a different reporter:

> WASHINGTON—Jimmy Carter today became the 39th president of the United States and spoke softly but passionately of a new beginning for the country. In the gentle cadence of his native Georgia, the 52-year-old Democrat took the oath of office. . . . "I have no new dream to set forth today, but rather urge a fresh faith in the old dream," he said in a brief inaugural address that, in homiletic style and moralistic tone, reiterated many of the populist themes of his long campaign . . . a 12-minute address that reflected the strong religious tone of the ceremonies and focused on the nation's spiritual lineage, stressing human rights, human dignity and a new role for the country as an international symbol of decency, compassion and strength.
>
> —Jan. 20, 1977

Coping with selective perception calls for special perception on the part of political reporters that the potential is always present for misrepresentation of important points or issues.

Carefully Setting the Scene

Properly backgrounding political stories is important to a better understanding of them, and the amount of detail will depend upon the story and the setting of an event. Whether a long-ago litany of basic information or merely a brief paragraph to bring the reader or viewer up to date, the reporter should be always prepared to provide the necessary detail.

The 1976 announcement by a candidate for governor of West Virginia that he favored liberalizing strip mining laws in the coal fields could not have been placed in proper perspective by the reader unless his opposition to that issue as a 1972 candidate was pointed out. A long memory is as important to the reporter as it is to the politician.

Equally important is the necessity for setting the tone of a political event. The demeanor of a candidate is important; the dignitaries who have joined him or her on the platform and the mood of the crowd all play a part. Public officials and candidates do not function in a vacuum. They are affected by people and events, and the political reporter should seek to carefully and fairly reflect this in coverage.

This 1962 Associated Press story provides an example of the importance of setting the tone for a political event:

> Beverly Hills, Calif.—An embittered Richard M. Nixon, his hopes for a political comeback in ruins, congratulated Gov. Edmund G. Brown Wednesday, bade farewell to public life and, in an angry denunciation of the press, told newsmen:
>
> "You won't have Nixon to kick around any longer. Because this, gentlemen, is my last press conference."
>
> The 49-year-old Republican former vice president, eyes swollen from lack of sleep and flashing anger, accused the press of distorting his statements. In one

breath he said he had no complaints. Then he aired a few.

"Thank God for radio and TV," Nixon said through tightly compressed lips, "for keeping the newspapers a little more honest."

Nixon, who lost the 1960 presidential election by the narrowest of margins, lost his usual polished composure before newsmen and television cameras in the ballroom of the Beverly Hilton.

In this story, the emotional element needed to be stressed to accurately put the scene in perspective. However, caution should be exercised in setting the tone without unnecessary adjectives which might subtly alter the focus of the story.

In analyzing political developments, care should be used. Different interpretations can be placed on events, creating the impression of partiality. Ron Nessen, former journalist and press secretary to President Gerald Ford, made this point during the 1976 presidential campaign. In discussing press "mistakes," Nessen wrote,

> On the day after a handful of Democrats voted in Florida in October for half the delegates to the Nov. 17-19 nonbinding state presidential-preference convention, *The Washington Post* told its readers:
>
> "The first thing to remember about yesterday is that nothing really happened."
>
> The second thing to remember is that the *Post* made that "nothing" its lead story, devoting 41 column inches to it that day and 101 column inches the next day under the bylines of such world-class writers as David S. Broder, Martin Schramm and Myra MacPherson.
>
> Some "nothing."

Deadline pressure makes such entrapment more susceptible, and the job of avoiding these problems should begin with the reporter on the scene.

The Importance of Following Through

What'd he say?

When'd he say it?

There is a tendency to separate the political campaign and assumption of office into two distinct worlds—one of promises, the other of performance. In fact, the two are inseparable, with one closely following on the heels of the other and accountings to be ultimately made. What more capable person to assist with these accountings than the reporter who originally transcribed the promises as they were being made?

In theory, the office-seeker becomes the policy-maker, with a higher duty to perform. In practice, the politician remains the politician, keeping his or her candidate's hat close by for frequent forays back into that world. The officeholder must be carefully monitored as he or she replaces promises with reality.

The politician-officeholder may in fact become the property of another reporter covering a different beat, but the need to compare past promises with present practices is inescapable.

What *were* those promises? How will they be implemented? Who's going to be involved, and how do they feel about them? Where's the money coming from? How will they affect present policies? To ignore promises is to allow the public officeholder an unwarranted luxury, one that the reporter and the public can ill afford.

"Following through" encompasses many levels of reporting. Thus, the reporter will take care that developing stories are not left unattended for any length of time. A county executive committee's inability to select a chairperson may result in adjournment of the meeting without making a choice, but the reporter can be sure that efforts continue vigorously behind the scenes. So he or she will follow the story there. Other assignments should not be allowed to get in the way of uncompleted stories.

Persistence is one of the great virtues in the field of political reporting. Success demands that politicians not be allowed to "get off the hook," and the tenacious reporter will insist on responses to pertinent questions.

One of the values of television is its visual insistence on honest answers. The political figure who offers to appear to enhance his or her visibility takes on the responsibility of responding in a straightforward manner. In this case, however, the broadcaster was not sufficiently persistent:

Q. Mr. Mayor, is the special Council meeting to choose a replacement for Councilman Bailey still scheduled for tomorrow at 2 o'clock?
A. Yes it is.
Q. Have you and Council decided on a replacement?
A. I'm sorry, Don. I just can't go into that now.
Q. I can understand that (and the subject is dropped, leaving another reporter to bulldog the story).

In this instance, the reporter allowed the official to effectively close the subject and in fact sympathetically aided the official in closing it. Insistent questioning is often necessary to shed light on an important subject. It is common for politicians to want to refuse to discuss issues, and the role of the reporter is to gently but firmly force them to allow the public some insight into their thinking.

Reluctance to respond to questions should be met by equal persistence, a reminder by the reporter that the public is asking for the answers, not merely the journalist. A common reportorial maneuver is to point out to the reluctant politician that rumors or reports have surfaced and that it is in her or his interest to dispell them.

Every effort should be made to obtain responses on the reporter's terms, rather than on the politician's conditions.

Setting Ground Rules

The adversary conditions of the relationship between the press and politicians dictates that a set of ground rules be established to ensure that each side understands the roles and goals of the other.

The candidate needs political office to acquire the power to direct public policy. To win that office, the candidate must carefully plan and execute a campaign. The goal of course is to present the candidate in such a way that the electorate will respond favorably.

The reporter has a different goal—to present the candidate, the candidate's views of the issues and his or her philosophy as accurately as possible. Since these aims do not always coincide, ground rules are necessary. They may be quite specific or merely implied, but they should be capable of covering all of the exigencies that might arise in the relationship.

The following are some of the "gray" areas that ground rules would cover:

1. Accepting remarks "off the record." With shirt unbuttoned, tie tossed carelessly on a nearby chair and cocktail in hand, the candidate stretches out on the divan and expansively says, "Now, gentlemen, this is off the record but . . .".

Long before this scene unfolds, the rules should have been spelled out between the reporter and the now tieless candidate. Nothing is ever "off the record." The reporter will get far more stories than he or she will lose with such a rule. At the very least, the question should be addressed before the comments are made, not after.

2. "Exclusive" stories. Rules should be clear about accepting exclusive stories on the condition that they are tailored to suit the desires of the politician. If it boils down to the question of how much the reporter will "give" in return for special treatment, clearly set ground rules should apply, with limits established and agreed upon. The final decision always rests with the journalist on how a story is to be handled, and his or her judgment should be the bottom line.

3. Acceptance of gratuities. Is lunch or dinner going to be "on the candidate"? Will accepting an open seat on the candidate's aircraft en route to the next campaign stop affect the reporter's coverage? Will the mere fact of such an acceptance destroy the reporter's credibility? Is attendance at the candidate's posh party going to create such a credibility problem? The political reporter, with financial assistance from his or her employer, should always lean toward plebian ground transportation, the lonely motel room and dinner for one when there is such a problem. It is much safer.

4. Prepared texts and departures from them. Texts are often prepared for the press, but the candidate frequently departs from them in the course of changing audiences and conditions. Material is added or deleted. A good set of ground rules, specifying that the importance of the material dropped or deleted is the key, is helpful to the reporter. Why was the

material dropped or added? This question will help to determine whether the omission should be noted.

Other problems will arise, necessitating similar decisions. A campaigning candidate, for example, has given an informal and negative response to a campaign issue. In the activity of the campaign, the informal, almost off-hand comment is temporarily forgotten. Later the candidate offers a different, positive response to the issue, duly included in the news reports. The reporter' s dilemma: What should be done about backgrounding the candidate's earlier moment of candor? A sound set of ground rules specifying that the importance of the issue will determine whether it is used by the reporter will protect the journalist.

Listening to Dissidents

That ancient slogan, "Never put all your eggs in one basket," is never so pertinent as it is on the political beat. The friendly source of yesterday may be the hostile source of tomorrow. By cultivating honestly all shades of the political spectrum, the reporter will add immensely to his or her news report.

Another slogan is equally apt: Always cultivate the dissidents. They are present in all political hierarchies and are often ready to clarify murky actions of those in power. They will be present at the secret caucuses in which major political decisions are thrashed out—often with bitter exchanges.

> The Clay County Republican Council has decided to drop its opposition to changes in state laws governing campaign contributions, it was learned last night.
>
> The council met informally last week at the home of Chairman Douglas Monroe to resolve the controversial issue, according to reliable sources who attended the meeting. None of the council's officers would discuss the report of the action.

In such cases, it is always best to obtain two separate sources for confirmation, to corroborate the events as fully as possible. No source should be underestimated in keeping track of the inner workings of the political parties, but the reporter should take care to assure that information supplied by dissidents is not unduly colored by natural bias.

A Common Interest

The political reporter's relationships with his or her sources constitute a curious mixture of friendship and ill-feeling. It is natural for the politician to attempt to place the emphasis on the positive and just as natural for the reporter to probe for the negative.

But being close to the mainstream of current events, and following them in depth, reporter and politician also find much in common. There is always a current subject that interests everyone. Furthermore, the long campaigns, with many hours on the road and away from home, create a certain camaraderie among reporter, candidate and candidate's staff. With so much background in political affairs, the reporter is often regarded as an "insider" and is frequently called upon for advice by politicians. With this, it is naturally difficult to avoid becoming "one of the crowd."

But, by the same token, the reporter who faithfully reports the foibles of a political figure, occasionally details his or her eccentricities and generally does a competent job will engender a certain animosity, whatever the personalities involved.

A reasonable "arms length" position is necessary to assure reportorial fairness and balance. It is somewhat like walking a tightrope, but the sound political reporter can successfully negotiate the course by following a good set of ground rules.

Monitoring Public Opinion

It had been a long and tiresome day, but a fruitful one. The reporter's notebook was crammed with quotes from dozens of men and women, and the tally of yesses and noes marched across the white pages like stiff little soldiers.

The reporter had been measuring public opinion at a busy suburban mall, an assignment that had grown out of a newsroom decision to poll citizens on an important upcoming election.

In studying his notes later, however, the reporter was disturbed. Did the line of marching yesses and noes, and the accompanying quotes designed to humanize and focus the cold statistics truly reflect the issues of the political race? He wasn't at all certain.

In his uncertainty, the reporter was pointing to a series of unanswered questions important to the validity of his assignment:

—Had the right questions really been asked, and in the right way?

—Did the sample of persons he had interviewed truly represent the voting population?

—How would the resulting news story or stories affect the race?

Suddenly the long hours out in the parking lot closed in on the reporter, and some even more specific questions arose:

—How about the young mother carrying a tired child past the reporter who refused to answer any questions? Would she and many others like her affect the results? Would their refusals to participate be prejudicial to the survey?

The reporter was asking legitimate questions about an assignment that has become increasingly commonplace in the past few years.

The importance of measuring public opinion in this country is undisputed. It constitutes a vital segment of modern mass communications, and it is conducted carefully or sloppily depending upon the methods used and the researchers doing it. The job of the reporter is to measure and report public opinion without misinforming himself or herself and thousands of readers or viewers on the receiving end of the reports.

Opinion surveys implicate every public affairs beat, but usually are most visible on the political scene. The political reporter, therefore, must not only know how to accurately conduct and report a survey, but must be capable of verifying the validity of those conducted by others.

Who's Doing It and Why?

Before the advent of professional polling organizations, and even now among uninformed and usually unreconstructed journalists, reporters engaged in their own unofficial and amiable brand of polling. They talked to precinct captains in the big cities, counted crowds at staged political events, sampled the private views of hangers-on traveling with candidates and surveyed the opinions of other reporters on the campaign trail.

The rise of "precision journalism" has tended to improve on that old informal pattern. Reporters and editors now require a minimum knowledge of modern research methods and competent analysis to successfully complete a polling assignment.

They obtain their expertise from a wide range of sources—the pollsters who have become increasingly professional as social science research has offered more sophisticated tools, researchers themselves who are steadily developing better methods of acquiring and translating such material accurately and understandably, new generations of sophisticated computer equipment, and the reporter's own instinct for greater accuracy in an important and relatively unmined field.

Polling has become the legitimate business of reporters and news organizations who continue to react to the public's constant questions, "Who's ahead and WHY?"

The shortcomings of the old and imperfect technique at the suburban mall can be analyzed by the reporter, and adjustments effected that will assure a far more accurate reading of the issue. These are some of the areas that require such analysis:

The Questions. Before ever asking the first question, the reporter carefully analyzes the type and wording of those to be asked for clarity, bias and imprecision. Are they loaded in favor of one answer? Do they assume too much knowledge on the part of the interviewees? Do they make poor comparisons? Are they too simplistic or too complex?

Questions should be checked to assure that they do not ask more than one question, yet allow for only one answer. People tend to favor the positive and prestigious rather than the negative, dangerous or unknown, and this should be taken into account in formulating questions. Questions should be carefully scrutinized to eliminate those that might be loaded, or weighted in favor of a particular answer.

Questions can be tested in a number of ways, pretesting them in a systematic manner or trying them out on colleagues. If the reporter stumbles over questions while reading them aloud, chances are the people he or she is polling will stumble too. Filter questions designed to determine whether some or all of the questions are really pertinent to the issue can also be helpful prior to a survey. Special care should be taken in presenting a sensitive or emotional topic whose results might be completely misinterpreted.

Even the order of the questions often plays a part in the overall results. Timing of the questions is important too. The reporter's results can be affected by dramatic breaking news on a certain day, affecting the way that interviewees perceive the questions.

Sampling. The key to successful sampling is the basic requirement that every person in a community or group, whatever its size, has a known (ideally it would be equal) opportunity to be interviewed. The reporter must be able to assure readers or viewers that the sample surveyed is representative of the larger population or group from which it is drawn.

Stopping people on a street corner does not assure that the sample will be representative. Neither does drawing names out of a hat, although ideally if all members of a group or community were represented in the hat, this could be a legitimate selection mechanism.

The manner in which the sampling is planned and conducted is vital. For example, a telephone survey can be effective if a truly random sample can be systematically produced. Every 50th name in the directory might be contacted, but must be reconciled with the possibility that many unlisted numbers not taken into consideration will affect the final results. The 15 or 20 percent of subscribers who refuse to be listed can dramatically affect the results if they are not taken into account. In the same way, using only half the directory names might improperly weight the sample in a community by dropping out a specific segment of the population.

The reporter should be able to determine the range within which the survey has a good probability of representing the larger population or group of people. This sampling error depends on the size of the sample, the probability level and determination of the diversity or dissimilarity of the group being studied. These factors can be broken down into arithmetic terms and evaluated.

Size of the sample can play a part in its accuracy. Up to a point, the larger the size, the more accurately the reporter can generalize to the larger population.

But size alone does not insure accuracy. Even the largest sample of the population may not be accurate if it is not representative, that is, if everyone in the sample did not have the same probability of being chosen.

The probability level—the odds that results of a survey lie within an acceptable error range—is important to the credibility of the survey. Because of these variables, the reporter must carefully study the type of sampling and survey methods used in his or her poll, or in the polls of others.

Interviewing. The basic interview techniques studied in advanced reporting courses are quite valid in conducting surveys, although studies indicate that journalistic interviews are often flimsy instruments for accuracy. If the reporter is not careful, answers tend to change in accordance with who's asking the questions. The presence and/or personality of the interviewer can affect results dramatically.

Some studies suggest that "verbal conditioning" can have an effect on the responses of an interviewee. Through subtle leadership, people can be encouraged to use or avoid certain words and phrases.

An open-minded, nonjudgmental, low-profile approach to surveying is essential, all of these suggested by a common sense approach and sensitivity to the task.

Similar care should be exercised in making use of information supplied by polling organizations. Hiring and training practices can affect the data compiled, and the reporter should attempt to determine the extent to which the organization supplying the material has attempted to train competent interviewers.

A familiarity with the advantages of face-to-face, mail and telephone interviewing is also desirable.

Evaluating and Reporting the Results. In evaluating the material collected during a survey, the reporter asks the most important question of all:

—What do the figures say?

The planning that goes into preparation of a survey helps provide the answer, but other important questions lead to the answer:

—What actual percentage of the planned sample was interviewed?

—How valid is the sample?

—Are missing answers a factor in the final results?

—Did filter questions, designed to determine whether some or all of the questionnaire is really pertinent to the interviewee, actually do their job in the sample of persons surveyed?

For the reporter, analyzing and communicating the results is the bottom line. Research has provided some other effective guidelines in making this job easier.

Care should be taken in generalizing beyond the specific sample surveyed, and in reflecting a "horse race" mentality. The question of who's ahead is relatively meaningless unless issues and the *why* are included. The reporter should be careful in drawing conclusions from only a few response categories or questions, since it might create an unfair news report. Often the results of a single survey can be compared with some other survey to improve the accuracy of any conclusions.

Such guidelines would have alerted the reporter surveying at the suburban mall that the effort he was undertaking carried the risk of many deficiencies. Quality of the questions was suspect. Interviewing techniques were questionable. The survey failed the sampling test, since merely stopping individuals at a shopping center does not provide a representative sample.

To call his effort a survey and generalize to a larger group would be misleading. The reporter's solution in this case is to make it very clear that only a group of people were questioned at a shopping center, without generalizing to a larger group.

Without this kind of care and questioning, most newspaper and broadcast surveys will fail the sampling test.

News accounts should include some of the basic information about how the survey was handled. It helps to include in sidebar stories the actual key questions asked.

Care in conducting the reporter's own survey is only part of the obstacle in accurate polling reports. In *Newsroom Guide to Polls & Surveys*, G. Cleveland Wilhoit and David H. Weaver suggest important questions to be asked about other surveys, with some of the answers necessary to accurate news stories:

—Who sponsored (or paid for) the poll and who conducted it?

—What was the population (or universe) sampled?

—What was the completion rate?

—How and when were the interviews done?

—What is the purpose of the survey or poll, and who is going to use the results for what purpose?

—Was anything found that is not being disclosed to the reporter?

—Is data being released selectively, raising the question that less flattering results are being avoided?

In insisting on answers to such questions, the reporter can contribute to public knowledge about a candidate or issue. Surveys should not be treated as fixed or immutable facts, but as shifting and changing sets of statistics. They are only as effective as reportorial care and treatment allow them to be.

Suggested Readings

Kaufman, Herbert, *Politics and Policies in State and Local Government* (Englewood Cliffs, NJ: Prentice-Hall, 1963). Chapter 3, "Everyone's in Politics" and Chapter 5, "State and Local Government in Perspective."

Lee, Richard, editor, *Politics and the Press* (Washington, D.C.: Acropolis, 1970) Two chapters recommended: "Appraising Press Coverage of Politics" by William Rivers and, "Politicians and Biased Political Information" by David S. Broder.

Bendiner, Robert, *White House Fever* (New York: Harcourt, 1960).

Sorauf, Frank, J., *Party Politics in America*, 4th ed. (Boston: Little, Brown, 1980).

Crouse, Timothy, *The Boys on the Bus* (New York: Random House, 1973). Chapter IV, "The Heavies" and Chapter V, "More Heavies."

Wilhoit, G. Cleveland, and David H. Weaver, *Newsroom Guide to Polls & Surveys* (Washington, D.C.: American Newspaper Publishers Association, 1980).

Meyer, Philip, *Precision Journalism* (Bloomington, IN: Indiana University Press, 1979). A reporter's introduction to social science methods.

CHAPTER 12
Covering Labor

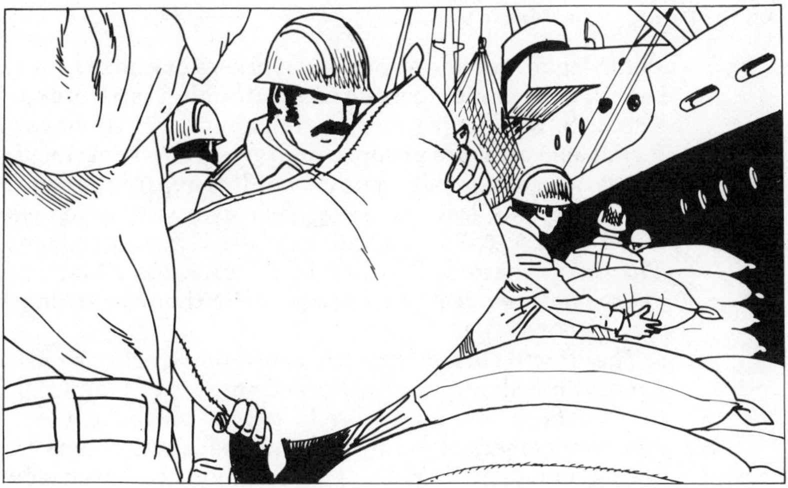

IN an East Coast city, a ragged line of men carrying signs breaks. Several scream obscenities at a television crew atop a truck as it slowly cruises past the entrance to the food warehouse. The work stoppage has not been authorized by the union representing the workers, and nerves have been rubbed raw on the disorganized picket line set up overnight.

The communications breakdown between the workers and the company that employs them is total. The TV reporter later tells his news director, "The feeling out there at the warehouse is just plain *mean*."

In a Midwest city, 14 men, distinguished only by the color and cut of their tailored business suits, file quietly into a paneled conference room at a downtown hotel and take seats on either side of a long mahogany table. Along one side are executives representing major trucking firms. On the other are representatives of unionized drivers seeking a new contract that will replace the one about to expire.

The talks are in their final stages, and journalists wait patiently in an anteroom as the negotiators hammer out an agreement that will satisfy all the men in the business suits.

Between these two dissimilar scenarios lies the bulk of employer-employee activity which constitutes the "labor beat" for the mass media today. However, much more than merely "labor" is involved. The entire range of business and industrial affairs is at its base. Extending outward are the complex relationships between the millions of men and women in the work force and the corporations that employ those countless organized and unorganized workers.

The economic and social implications of these relationships for the general public are only one of the reasons for the need to completely and accurately cover them.

Minor Proportion, Major Voice

While labor unions—groups of workers organized for the general benefit of their members—constitute only a small proportion of the total U.S. work force, their activity and visibility have produced a formidable pressure group. Union growth was spectacular through the early years of this century, but it is apparently leveling off.

In 1978, the last reporting year available, union membership stood at 22,798,000, according to the U.S. Department of Labor. The union share of the total labor force was 22.2 percent in that year. Those modest percentages belie the true strength of organized labor.

The effectiveness of union organization is epitomized by the giant American Federation of Labor—Congress of Industrial Organizations (AFL-CIO), an umbrella group which includes nearly 17 million members of many craft and industrial unions.

Paralleling the growth of labor unions has been emergence of substantial protective and restrictive legislation at the federal and local levels, affecting virtually the entire U.S. work force and complicating the task of the labor reporter. For, despite the vast body of laws which interlace labor-management relations, unions enjoy legal status as a component of the "private" sector, similar to the corporations with which they deal.

As with decisions made by private industry, those of organized labor are also fundamental to the well-being of the general public. The need for the press to accurately portray these decisions and activities is unquestioned for the following reasons:

AN AUTHORITATIVE VOICE OF MILLIONS

The economic impact of unions on society as the recognized voice of millions of salaried and hourly wage earners is undisputed. At nearly every political level, the action committees of labor unions, serving as influential pressure groups, carry enormous weight.

> Joseph L. Powell, state president of the AFL-CIO, appeared before the Senate Finance Committee yesterday to support removal of food from the current 5 percent sales tax.
>
> "It's a dollars and cents proposition with the workers," Powell warned. "Legislators are going to have to give them relief in this election year."

As a pressure group seeking decision-making access to government, the effectiveness of organized labor is unquestioned. Such groups usually win more battles than they lose.

The frequent threat of nationwide work stoppages is very real to the consuming public, which depends on labor-management peace for smoothly functioning economic lifelines as well as earning power. A strike in western truck gardening centers hits as close to the average family as does a lockout of workers by management of a trucking industry. Issues in contract disputes are recurring items in the news until their eventual resolution.

> Government mediators were asked yesterday to join the negotiations between the major auto manufacturers and the United Auto Workers Union as the deadline for reaching the contract settlement neared.
> Meanwhile, both sides prepared for the eventuality of a work stoppage that will affect the entire industry as well as the rest of the country.

GROWTH OF REGULATORY AGENCIES

In the wake of complex labor legislation, a multitude of regulatory agencies has sprung up to deal with labor-management affairs. While this proliferation has been greatest at the federal level, state and local agencies have contributed to the weight of government involvement.

> The president of the State Labor Council asked the Labor Department yesterday to clarify new legislation mandating stronger safety measures in the construction industry.

If the new law has been reported superficially before, it cannot be now. The labor reporter must ask these questions: What's in the legislation? Who is affected and how? How will current standards be changed? What's the reaction of the construction industry as well as officials charged with enforcing the legislation? Will the legislation change the timetables for completing current projects?

The role of the courts in labor-management relations is also important. While legislation may allow an industrial firm to seek a restraining order against a union, the judicial process is generally entrusted with the responsibility for granting or refusing an order.

> Circuit Court Judge Will Robinson yesterday issued a back-to-work order to striking employees of Vesco Engineering Co., directing them to resume bargaining in an effort to end the 26-day strike.
> The court order was issued on the basis of a contract provision calling for a seven-day "cooling off" period between the parties, which Robinson ruled Engineering Local #627 did not observe.

A basic knowledge of the courts and how disputants work their way through the process is one of the requirements to competently cover the labor beat. The reporter must also be familiar with the relief afforded to the arguing parties through the agencies themselves.

> Attorneys for Teamsters Union Local 71 filed objections with the National Labor Relations Board Wednesday, complaining of company tactics the union says cost it last week's election at the Fiber Industries plant.

These were the major objections filed by the union, which lost the representation vote, 883 to 1,272:

—Several days before the election, plant workers received a phonograph record dramatizing a Teamster strike riot.

—Just before the vote, all plant workers were required to attend a company meeting at which armed county deputies were present.

UNIONIZATION OF PUBLIC EMPLOYEES

In recent years, another factor—unionization of public employees—has added a new dimension to the labor beat, complicating the traditional employer-employee relationship. Policemen, firemen, postal workers, deputy sheriffs and refuse removal workers have joined other wage earners in the private sector in establishing bargaining units and frequently engaging in work stoppages against the public that employs them.

Terminology differs. Some of these public employee units refer to themselves as "associations," others as "action committees," and many prefer the traditional designation of "union." Whatever the terminology, growing numbers of public employee units, many of them militant, are engaging in the collective bargaining process over wages, working conditions and other issues.

Teachers have left the classrooms for the picket line; firefighters have struck in major cities, standing by while houses and business establishments have burned to the ground; hospital workers have walked out. For those accustomed to traditional public employee loyalty, the effect has been traumatic, sometimes leaving a residual bitterness that has influenced the life of a community.

Teacher organizations have been in the forefront of unionization, although many prefer to reach agreement with employers through "associations." Such groups resist recruitment by AFL-CIO teacher unions, preferring to handle collective bargaining through their own, often informal, organizations.

The American Federation of Teachers will conduct a major recruiting drive in the state during the next 30 days, using as its rallying point the need for more discipline in schools.

The AFT, backed by the AFL-CIO, will conduct workshops in nine cities to prepare for the drive, a spokesman for the organization said yesterday.

Balancing "Pluses" and "Minuses"

The union organizer shook his head vigorously. "Look," he told his listeners at the entrance to the plant, "you're either with us or against us. There's no halfway."

Support and nonsupport of the labor movement are much more complicated than this, but the fact remains that there is little unanimity on the virtues of organized labor or its faults. In covering labor, the reporter should have a good understanding of its role and be aware of the advantages and disadvantages that are ascribed to it.

Media coverage of labor affairs elicits a broad range of human response from the public: bitterness over the issues dividing disputants, a deep pride by some in fellow workers' efforts to better themselves, chagrin over mounting labor costs and the need to provide a margin of profit, and the effects of those costs on prices paid by the consuming public. Arguments over the benefits and drawbacks of the organized labor movement have been more than a century in the making, and they constitute the cutting edge of the labor-management relationship.

No consensus exists at any level, and even the experts disagree on the merits of the movement. Supporters, however, cite the following "pluses" for it:

1. Unions help people to earn more money through the collective bargaining process. Monetary implications are always present in nearly every story the reporter covers.

2. Unions help to assure better working conditions, something brought about only through pressure of organized labor. The labor reporter is constantly scrutinizing the humanizing elements of the workplace.

3. Unions offer workers greater job security and assure equal opportunity to workers. Thus, the wave of antiquated plant closings in some sections of the United States takes on particular significance to the reporter of labor affairs.

4. Labor offers incentives to work toward the status of "journeyman" and thus earn more money. A basic question for the reporter here is the efficacy of such incentives in today's society.

5. Unions provide a steady, reliable work force, stabilizing employment.

6. Through unionization and its organization, working people are assured a greater voice in their own affairs. Part of the reporter's task in covering union activities is to reflect this, either in its success or failure.

No unanimity exists on these traditional credits. Balancing them, detractors of the organized labor movement offer another list, detailing what they believe to be the disadvantages or "minuses" of labor unions:

1. Unions cause workers to be too regimented, and because everyone earns very nearly the same salary, union workers tend to lose the incentive to "get ahead," cutting productivity and costing employers money.

2. Unions create an "us versus them" climate at work, tending to lower morale and again diminish productivity. Such a climate can complicate the reporter's job of monitoring the relationships between labor and management.

3. Unions diminish the flexibility of a business or industry, and union militancy keeps management from realizing the most profit for its owners or stockholders.

4. Organized labor has become too big, like big business, and wields far too much power in this country. The reporter's job is to identify the figures who wield this power, their interests and philosophy.

5. Through their excessive power, unions can injure the economy when strikes occur in strategic industries. The reporter addresses this argument by assiduously providing facts and figures that shed the most light on an always arguable dispute.

There is small hope of reconciling these conflicting viewpoints. The reporter can only accept them as a totally impartial observer, even though he or she may be a member of a union personally, and go about the business of communicating the labor beat to the public.

The Labor Beat's Special Set of Problems

The public affairs reporter must accept from the very beginning the proposition that in almost every labor dispute the parties will dig in at opposite ends of the spectrum. They will do so for a variety of reasons:

1. The parties gain bargaining advantage and appear to give up substantial ground during negotiations while actually retreating only to their true position. Thus, the reporter's efforts in such disputes should be directed toward determining and reporting that "true" position.

2. Negotiators for both sides are always under pressure to produce agreements most beneficial to their clients—the union members or the company's stockholders. So the reporter gets threats like these from both sides: A prolonged strike at the White Consolidated plant "would jeopardize the future of the plant." The general manager of another firm says he and the company's owner have discussed the possibility of closing the plant because of the prolonged strike. The union negotiator threatens to break off talks per-

manently if management does not recognize "the reality of the situation."

3. Wounds created by antagonists in previous bargaining encounters may heal slowly, and feelings of personal injustice may persist. Moreover, such feelings often extend to journalists who may have been perceived as not presenting one side's story fully or fairly.

Whatever the battleground, the reporter had better be prepared to take a middle course. Management may refer to a "strike" by its employees; the union leadership may respond to the "lockout" of workers by management. Where the issue is unclear, the reporter wisely refers to the dispute as a "work stoppage." The use of terms when covering emotional disputes requires care.

Unions organize to obtain better contracts for workers in the job market. But unless there is an increase in efficiency, the costs of higher wages and improved fringe benefits are nearly always borne by the public that purchases the goods and services produced. Thus, the economic give and take between organized labor and management holds enormous implications for the millions who are not directly touched by a specific negotiating issue.

Often the problem in reporting on labor is not whether there is anything to write about but, rather, how to sort out the most important issues for the public.

Consider the following special problems that the reporter must face to cover the labor beat competently:

An Unpredictable Beat

One need only reread the "pluses" and "minuses" to recognize that there are always two widely divergent views to every labor dispute. And as with the business of covering politics, neither side—labor nor management—will ever be completely satisfied with the newspaper accounts or the broadcasts produced by the press. Negotiators on both sides will constantly nitpick at minor points, often complaining of reportorial "bias," in an effort to get their story across.

Further, nothing is cut and dried or predictable about most labor-management disputes. What an "expert" sees as early resolution of a difficult sticking point in a bargaining session may be non-negotiable a day later. Reporting in such shifting sand calls for careful attribution of comments on "how it looks" to observers of the dispute.

In attempts to influence public opinion and otherwise gain a bargaining advantage, parties on both sides often float "trial balloons" through the media. Sometimes they are an effort to gauge public opinion; other times they are designed to assess the reaction of the union membership. Like his or her counterpart in politics, the labor reporter must carefully appraise the validity of such material and the effect it may produce, weighing it against the needs of the reader.

A "Private" Organization

The nature of organized labor as a "private" rather than a "public" enterprise poses a further special problem for the reporter, who has no more warrant to freely enter a union hall when a meeting is in progress than to enter a corporate boardroom when the directors are in session.

No legislation or freedom of the press decree opens labor meetings to scrutiny by the press.

> In what was described as a "raucous meeting" last night, Carpenters Local #1376 voted to break off bargaining with three local prefabricated housing firms and strike at midnight Oct. 15.
>
> Although reporters were barred from the union session and officials declined to comment, it was learned that the vote was very close.

The reporter is dependent upon his or her skill in gaining personal access to such meetings or at least obtaining reasonably accurate information on a secondhand basis. It is never easy.

Problems are compounded during contract negotiations when cadres of government mediators are invited to join the disputants, while reporters nearly always cool their heels in anterooms, awaiting word of progress or stalemate. Each side appears to provide its version of developments, while the mediators remain silent. Such secondhand and often biased information makes the reporter's task doubly difficult.

Personal Conflicts

Relatives, friends, and even the journalist are often members of labor unions or associations, creating a great potential for conflict of interest. While few professional journalists will consciously allow this to interfere with their news judgment in a labor dispute, the elements may be present at a subconscious level. The solution lies in the ability of the reporter to sort out his or her natural biases and thus consciously control them.

Relationships with sources are often complicated by their transfer from one side to the other. Excellent contact with a union attorney may carry over when the attorney shifts allegiance to management, or the change might make communication more difficult.

> Enoch Marsden, president of the 3,200-member United Mine Workers local at Bluefield, has resigned to become personnel coordinator for Eastern Coke Co.
>
> "I'd say the main reason is a guy has to make a living for his family," said Marsden, a graduate of Potomac State College, whose father was also a miner.

Emotions Run High

Work stoppages, particularly those that are unauthorized by the union leadership, tend to become highly emotional. The livelihoods of many are at stake, and strong feelings exist on both sides. The reporter is going to find it difficult to argue with a burly union official who clearly sees his job—organize the plant—and whose inclination is to act first, then think, at moments of crisis. There may be more punches thrown than merely fun and games out on the picket line.

> Salinas, Calif. (UPI)—Striking lettuce workers attacked harvesting crews in the Salinas Valley today and two persons were stabbed, authorities said.
>
> It was the first serious outbreak of violence in the two-month strike by the United Farm Workers union against six large lettuce growers.
>
> A spokesman for the Monterey County sheriff's office said several hundred strikers attacked crews in a number of fields. The two persons stabbed were not seriously injured.

In this case, the reporter was not present, but often he or she will find the story at the center of the action, with its inherent dangers.

Emotional complications extend beyond the strike experiences and are basic to the labor-management adversary relationship. On the one hand, workers trying to cope with rising prices and erosion of their earning power are negotiating to protect their interests and those of their families. On the other, management seeks to protect itself by keeping its overhead to a minimum and not dropping profits to a point considered untenable.

The labor reporter, caught in the middle, must take care that already passionate sentiments are not inflamed, further escalating the problem of settling the differences in a dispute.

Perceptions Complicate Relationships

The wide range of lifestyles, social and economic traditions, and personalities in organized labor presents another special problem for reporters. Working groups possess widely differing and sometimes quite negative perceptions of the role of journalists. The pipeline to the leadership often depends on how individuals perceive the press: friend or enemy?

How well a spokesperson is able to articulate his or her side's viewpoint also plays a part, with some leaders capable of presenting their case to the public more effectively than others. The reporter will have to balance the highly paid public information officer's presentation of his firm's stand with the part-time union secretary's response. One may be much better thought out than the other.

The reporter's job will also be made more difficult because one side may *want* the exposure, whereas the other refuses to "go public" with the labor disagreement.

> A member of the committee negotiating settlement of the 11-day dock strike blamed the press for yesterday's breakdown in negotiations.
>
> Grant Savage, president of the striking Longshoreman's Union, complained that the list of grievances submitted by the union should not have been publicized by the press.

In this case, the ability of the reporter to obtain information of legitimate interest to the public was seen by one side as inimical to its bargaining interests. The ethical considerations that frequently arise will have to be settled in the interest of the public.

The Reporter as Economist

While the reporter does not have to be a graduate of the Wharton School of Business to cover labor, he or she should be familiar with the economic system and standard accounting procedures common in the United States today. Ability to understand and accurately translate pay rates and scales, complicated fringe benefits and Bureau of Statistics data is necessary if the reporter is to fully portray the issues in disputes.

Frequently the pay scale itself is not the major issue in a labor dispute; protection of job places, retirement benefits, working conditions and safety factors may underlie the inability of disputants to reach agreement.

> With a strike deadline looming, spokesmen for the Pressman's Union said today that only insistence on elimination of 11 jobs by Mortello Publishing Co. separated the two sides from agreement.
>
> "Mortello wants a crew of 37 men to do the work that 48 have kept busy on in the past," William Priest, business manager for the union, said.
>
> Company officials had said last week that the 11 jobs in question would be eliminated through retirements and other attrition.

The key question for the reporter: What are the similar manning requirements elsewhere? One possible answer would be for the reporter to go to outside experts or seek information from comparable nondisputing firms in other areas. Government statistics might supply a definitive answer, something the parties in the dispute will not.

An area's economy is an important element in covering labor news. The decision of a major foundry to close its plant permanently may be traced to government studies that show lower auto industry demand will result in elimination of more than 17,000 jobs during the next several years.

No Longer a Full-Time Job

A final complication in reporting labor news lies in the tendency of most newspapers and broadcast outlets today to lump the labor beat with the business and financial beat or to treat it as a part-time effort for general assignment reporters. The effect is to devote more time and space to labor news during periods of final negotiations or work stoppages. Considering the impact of organized labor on society, this trend ignores much of the bulk that underlies the tip of the iceberg.

The unionization process itself at the frontiers of the movement, new approaches to benefits, health and safety measures, automation in industry, and the nature and ethic of the work force itself are issues that offer far-reaching implications to the public. Entrusting these kinds of issues on a part-time assignment basis overlooks the importance of the labor beat.

From Agriculture to Industry . . . and Beyond

Union-busters, using tactics that would make a gangster blush, and their counterparts, the strong-armed labor organizers, exist today but in a somewhat different form. The tactics of 100 years ago in the labor movement have almost—but not quite—disappeared, to be replaced by somewhat less physical confrontation. Scars remain from those long-ago organizing wars, however.

Although labor unions had appeared in the United States by 1800, fewer than a million workers held union membership in 1900. Spurred by labor legislation, the growth of unions was spectacular during the 1930s and received impetus from wartime economic conditions.

Three million workers were enrolled in 1933 alone, and the number had swelled to 12 million by 1944. Growth was steady to more than 18 million in 1956. The union movement parallels the growth of a goods-oriented society in this country.

Corporations began employing large numbers of people to handle tools and machinery under conditions and on terms over which the workers themselves had little or no control. Recurring abuses led to large-scale organization of workers with similar skills and occupations. The early craft unions prospered during economic expansions and faded during periods of recession. Bargaining as it is known today was virtually non-existent.

By the mid-1800s the labor movement was developing into a more cohesive structure, and in 1866 a federation called the National Labor Union was organized. It survived for six years before becoming a political party which subsequently collapsed. However, the organization was the forerunner of growing pressures for a nationwide organization that would serve as an umbrella for the various occupations and trades.

The Noble Order of the Knights of Labor, organized in 1871, was briefly successful before a spectacular failure within a decade. Its goal was to unite all wage earners into one organization, a plan that was distasteful to skilled artisans. The Knights climbed to a spectacular 600,000 enrollment before fading around 1890.

A key element in the disintegration of the Knights was the organization of the American Federation of Labor, founded in 1886 as an answer to the desires of skilled artisans for their own union. Led by Samuel Gompers, a young leader from the Cigar Makers Union, the AFL marked the beginning of organized labor movement as it is known today.

The AFL was the first union to successfully survive the rigors of expansion and recession of the U.S. economy and to achieve a permanent status, whatever the economic conditions. Its growth was based on two basic policies:

1. The AFL guaranteed "trade autonomy" to national unions which belonged to it. Thus, those unions retained the authority to make final decisions for themselves.

2. AFL membership assured "exclusive jurisdiction" to those member unions, giving a union the authority to organize a particular occupation and to protect itself from possible competition from other unions.

This craft union approach by the AFL was virtually unchallenged until the 1930s, when the Committee for Industrial Organization emerged within the AFL to provide workers in one industry with a single organization. Such industrial unionism is characterized by membership based on employment in one industry, regardless of skill or occupation.

The group broke away from the AFL in 1935 to form the Congress of Industrial Organizations (CIO). The breach persisted until 1955, when the two organizations merged to form the American Federation of Labor-Congress of Industrial Organizations (AFL-CIO).

Divergent economic trends have created an ebb and flow in union fortunes, with some experiencing spectacular growth and others a gradually eroding membership. The Teamsters Union claimed 100,000 members in 1933, but that figure had climbed to a million by 1951 and to 1.9 million by 1978.

Meanwhile, the United Mine Workers, with the biggest membership in the country from 1898 to 1940, lost members to drastic shifts in energy production. UMW membership was 600,000 in 1951 but had dropped to only 245,000, including 80,000 pensioners in 1980.

As the older unions experienced such shifts, others succeeded because of the changing society. While some of their numbers may be numerically small, they are important to the public affairs reporter because they constitute the "frontier" of organized labor. Thus, a new labor organization, the United Farm Workers Organizing Committee, formed in 1962 to represent grape pickers in California vineyards, had by 1966 won the right to represent its workers, long regarded as unorganizable because of their migratory patterns. Teachers represent another frontier of union activity, with dramatic organizational growth in recent years. Membership in teachers' unions stood at 165,000 in 1968, but had climbed to more than half a million 10 years later.

One of the important roles of the labor reporter is to reflect these far-reaching changes as well as the day-to-day functioning of the labor movement. A spurt of activity in one area may affect an entirely different spectrum of the public.

Traditionally unorganized public employees such as the police, firefighters, public sanitation employees and others have created powerful pressure groups through organization. Even those without the right to strike have won substantial gains in wage and benefit provisions and in the structure of the work force itself.

In 1978, the latest year for which figures are available, nearly 1.4 million federal employees were members of labor unions. Unionized workers at the state and local levels that year totaled 2.242 million. The growth of some unions has been dramatic. In the past decade, the State, County and Municipal Employees Union recruited 655,514 new members to total more than 1 million members.

What is different for the reporter, however, at this level is that workers are not bargaining with private corporations but, rather, with representatives of the public—mayors, county commissioners, city managers, fire and police chiefs, governors and state agencies.

The new development serves to complicate the bargaining process as well as compound the problems of reporting on the issues involved. Does the public official, who represents the public, have a different frame of reference than the negotiator for the city's biggest private industry? Or are the goals similar—getting the best "bargain" that the mayor or governor can get in labor negotiations?

> More than a year after city officials paved the way for contract negotiations, the Police Benevolent Association will present wage and benefits demands to the city tomorrow.
>
> "We aim to get a binding contract down on paper," said Lt. Vincent Catola, PBA vice president.
>
> The City Commission formally recognized the PBA as bargaining agent for the police 13 months ago, and Catola blamed inertia on the part of the city as the reason for the lengthy delay.

Political bodies have been affected by new organization too. Candidates for public office must look over their shoulders on the issue of public unions, and they are being pressed to declare themselves.

> Democratic candidates for the House of Delegates from Harrison County favor some kind of collective bargaining for public employees short of the right to strike.
>
> Their Republican opponents, however, are divided on the issue, with two strongly opposing any such rights and one agreeing with the Democrats.

In fact, public employee unions are already in the process of arguing with one another over jurisdiction and effectiveness and jockeying for power among local and state agencies. It is fertile ground for the labor reporter.

Labor Organization

The heart of union organization beats strongly at the local level, whether in the garment district of a metropolitan city, an industrial suburban community, or in a semirural area with merely a few industrial plants spread over miles of countryside.

Popularly elected members administer the affairs of the locals, often with a business agent employed to direct the day-to-day financial affairs. Frequently a part-time salaried member will assume responsibility for maintaining an office and calling meetings.

Meetings are held regularly, with dues-paying members participating in the decision-making process at this level. Much akin to a fraternal organization, the local provides an opportunity for a social outlet as well as the more serious business of protecting the rights of union members by dealing with employers at the bargaining table. Often the president, vice president and/or secretary assume the bargaining function instead of the paid business agent.

Duties include pressing grievances of workers with management as disputes arise, although a shop steward chosen by fellow workers in a plant often assumes that responsibility.

The membership of a local may be spread through a community in various plants or businesses, or it may be concentrated in a single location.

The Art of Politics

Personalities and politics play an important part in union activity, with officeholders and would-be successors jockeying for positions of power within the organization. Old friendships and alliances are often important in success of union leaders, although empathy with the needs of rank-and-file members is a key element in acquisition of power. Effectiveness in negotiating contracts with management sometimes provides the springboard to more important positions.

> Hiram Wilson, a 28-year-old lathe operator at Kelso Industries who chaired Local 694's negotiating committee with the firm last year, announced yesterday he will be a candidate for president of the union in May.

The reporter looks for success stories such as these, as well as for the failures, in signaling future power changes within a union.

The candidate will find that support of the rank and file is necessary to maintain a power base within the union, but the leader who also has the confidence of the industrial community is generally more effective in leading the organization.

However, such confidence occasionally backfires in heated union election campaigns with opponents hurling charges that a candidate is "in the pocket of management and cannot be trusted." Sometimes, the successful labor leader will combine a public demeanor of truculence with private expressions of willingness to cooperate with management and be successful.

While these inside maneuvers are not always exposed publicly, the reporter who is close to the scene has a fuller picture of the workings of the system and can communicate the overall impact upon the public much more effectively.

Confidence: A Key Element

Confidence of the union's leadership is essential if the labor reporter is to function effectively at the local level. It is certainly more difficult to operate without that confidence. Even with such rapport, however, the reporter can expect to be frequently barred from union meetings, ejected from headquarters and forced to accept press handouts in lieu of firsthand coverage.

The labor reporter treats this as a fact of life and works hard to secure alternate news sources to whom he or she can turn for reasonably accurate information. The sources may be dissidents who want to keep affairs of the union public for a variety of reasons or merely union members who have no axe to grind and no compunction about "telling it like it is." Comparing information provided by the union leadership with such alternate sources helps to assure a complete and balanced story.

Such problems of access become more pronounced during periods of negotiation with management over new contracts or during heated election campaigns.

> Bakers Local #1600 voted 56-51 last night to demand a recount in the recent elections that brought a new slate of officers to power.
>
> Reporters were barred from the union hall on Jefferson Street, and union officials provided only the results of the vote.
>
> However, other sources said the dispute will be taken to circuit court this week. They added that last night's session was tumultuous, with constant banging of the gavel by new President Will Gammick.

Other benefits accrue from a good relationship with union leaders. A war of words may be part of the dispute, but tips leading to hard facts may put the issue in better focus. Or permission may be obtained to study disputed company documents possessed by the union.

> The president of the union representing 2,200 striking employees of the White-Westinghouse plant said the firm's chief officer was talking nonsense when he said a prolonged strike will jeopardize the future of the plant.
>
> The strike at the plant on Phillipi Road is in its second week.
>
> William Farley, president of Local 745 of the International Union of Electrical, Radio and Machine Workers, waved an advertisement clipped from Friday's *Wall Street Journal.*
>
> The ad announced the seventh consecutive year of record sales and earnings for the company.

Being in the right place at the right time often helps the reporter. And persistence and good humor, coupled with the appearance of never giving up in pursuit of a story, are sometimes perceived by union members as a worthwhile quality. The reporter is seen then as a "good guy" who is only doing his or her job.

Links with Other Unions

Although local autonomy is traditional in the union movement, strength in numbers is essential for maximum influence in dealing with management and participating in the outside political process.

To assure coordination of widely divergent and individualistic locals, intermediate labor councils and federations help tie national union organization to the local level. Relationships among these groups often provide material for the reporter, and power struggles are sometimes made more visible through negotiations among them.

Local memberships choose representatives who form coordinating councils and boards at the county, district and state levels, their major purpose being to create unified activity in contract and other demands. Another important function, particularly at the state level, is the unification of lobbying efforts to influence legislation. While state federations have little power in the internal operation of locals, they are effective as organized pressure groups.

> The State Federation of Unions yesterday called on legislators to ignore the right-to-work proposal introduced in the Senate Monday.
>
> The proposal, backed by a group of seven senators from the southern end of the state, would drop the present requirement that an employee be a union member in good standing in order to be employed.

State Government's Involvement

Labor was not specifically mentioned in the federal Constitution, and the earliest legislation emerged at the state level. Under the 10th Amendment, all powers not reserved to the national government were delegated to the states, and the states began early to enact legislation to assure the well-being, safety and health of workers.

At a much later date—near the end of the 19th century—the present body of federal labor legislation began to develop, under the power of the federal government to regulate commerce and prescribe regulations for industry doing business with the federal government under contract.*

The labor reporter should be familiar with legislation affecting

* One of the Labor Department's important agencies is the Office of Federal Contract Compliance, which establishes policies and coordinates the federal program to achieve non-discrimination in employment by government contractors.

safety and health standards, especially since their enforcement frequently becomes a major issue between unions and management. Regulations at the state level cover such disparate areas as guards on dangerous machinery, adequate ventilation, rest room facilities, washrooms and fire safety rules.

Extensive safety codes have become common in all the states, but changes in legislation are often introduced in the interests of one group or another. Since so many workers are affected by statutory changes, the legislative process itself becomes part of the labor reporter's beat.

> A legislative committee has decided to study safety codes relating to the construction industry in the wake of the deaths of three workers who were killed in a machinery accident in Youngstown last month.

Officials at the municipal level often promulgate regulations affecting the safety and health of workers.

Protection of children in the labor force followed the early emphasis on safety, and legislation prohibiting employment of children before certain ages appeared. Legislation was subsequently broadened to include protection for adult women and, for certain hazardous occupations, adult men.

As the growth of social legislation increased, states began adopting laws compensating workers for injuries sustained in employment. *Workmen's compensation* legislation to insure individual workers became common. In most states, the employer supports the program by funding the insurance; the cost is ultimately passed on to the consumer.

A body of legislation has also grown up around *fair employment practices*, to prevent discrimination toward blacks, Spanish-Americans and other minorities. All the states have also enacted legislation to protect workers who find themselves unemployed. A typical *unemployment compensation* system provides for a fund composed of contributions from employer and employee. Weekly benefits depend on the length of time the worker has been employed and compensation during that time.

States have also established procedures for *settlement of wage disputes*, although the federal government has tended to preempt this function in instances where the national interest can be said to be affected. The two major approaches to such settlements, both at the state and federal levels, are through mediation and arbitration. The labor reporter should be familiar with both.

In *mediation*, designated private individuals or public officials attempt to bring the disputing parties together, seeking to reach a voluntary settlement. The parties are encouraged to make mutual concessions, but the mediator or mediation panel has no power to make binding decisions, merely using "their good offices" to help settle the dispute. Powers of mediators vary from state to state, with some having power of subpoena and other means to bring the parties together.

In *arbitration*, the parties to the labor dispute agree in advance to accept the arbitrator's decision. The arbitrator or a panel of arbitrators hears and considers all sides of a labor question and then returns a binding decision. Since it is a much stronger form of settlement procedure, arbitration is used much less frequently than is mediation.

Other labor involvement by the state includes operation of *employment agencies*, which are an excellent source of statistics on job markets and unemployment data for the reporter. The federal government has operated a grant-in-aid program to states for many years, assisting in the funding of these agencies. States also regulate private employment agencies, including limiting fees and discouraging disreputable practices.

Federal Government Involvement

The federal government asserts itself in labor activities through the legislative process and through administrative rulings and interpretations by agencies and boards.

The objective of these government units is to properly balance the rights of organized workers, of non-union employees and of the public itself. This process implies a certain degree of sensitivity to various segments of the public not always evident in other boards or agencies. The reporter's access to information is affected by the pressures on federal officials to avoid any show of partiality toward one group in dealing with labor matters.

While the labor spotlight generally falls on the legislative process and the agencies that administer the rules, the courts constitute an important source of decision-making. Elected officials tend to be more sensitive to public opinion than is the judicial branch of government, and the courts are less innovative than are the other branches in the area of labor.

> Circuit Court Judge Robert Timmons yesterday refused to grant an injunction to halt a work stoppage at the Stone & Webster cement plant because of repeated acts of violence on the picket line.
>
> Instead, Timmons urged authorities to police the Wilson Road area 24 hours a day to assure protection to workers who want to cross the picket line.

Judicial interpretations of legislative action have always been vital to the extent and importance of labor legislation. Effectiveness of the provisions of the Railway Labor Act of 1926, which dealt with the rights of workers to join unions, was contingent on the Supreme Court's action. The act was the first of its kind to pass the scrutiny of the court.

Federal involvement in labor affairs is a fairly recent development, but it has enlarged in massive detail since the 1930s. A Bureau of Labor was created by the Congress in 1884 and placed under the Interior Department. After a period under the aegis of the Commerce Department, the agency became a separate Department of Labor in 1913, charged with "administering and enforcing statutes designed to advance the public interest by promoting the welfare of the wage earners of the United States, improving their working conditions and advancing their opportunities for profitable employment." Since then, the department's scope has broadened to administer legislation and executive orders relating to labor union activities. Also included are such areas as manpower training (Comprehensive Employment and Training Act of 1973), standards of employment, safety and health activities (Occupational Safety and Health Administration), and labor statistics (Bureau of Labor Statistics).

Key Legislative Actions

Among the legislative actions which have changed the course of labor-managment relations in the United States, the National Labor Relations Act of 1935 (known as the Wagner Act) is considered by organized labor to be the most decisive. Quality coverage of union-management disputes is contingent upon a basic knowledge of its far-reaching provisions. While the Wagner Act did not legalize unions or the bargaining process, it was designed to protect the rights of workers in practice as well as in theory.

Its three main provisions included prohibition of employer conduct designed to interfere with a worker's right to join a union, a new method of organizing (by use of the secret ballot election) and the establishment of a federal agency, the National Labor Relations Board, whose function it is to administer and enforce the law.

The NLRB is an independent, quasi-judicial agency of the federal government, but it must seek enforcement of its decisions through the courts. Since board members are presidential appointees, NLRB actions have often been the center of political controversy.

A second milestone in federal labor legislation was the Fair Labor Standards Act in 1938, which established a minimum wage pattern, a basic workweek with provisions for overtime, and prohibition of child labor.

And a third piece of legislation, the Labor Management Relations Act in 1947 (also known as the Taft-Hartley Act) modified and broadened the scope of the Wagner Act and outlawed the "closed shop."*

The Taft-Hartley Act, an amendment to the Wagner Act, was designed to balance regulations placed upon employer conduct in labor relations in 1935 with new provisions regulating union conduct and setting up categories of unfair union practices. To facilitate the collective bargaining process, the Taft-Hartley Act created a new independent agency, the Federal Mediation and

* Under the "closed shop" contract, the employer agrees to hire only union members. After this legislation was enacted in 1947, many states enacted "right to work" laws that prohibited the closed shop at the state level. However, many states permit the closed shop, and the issue has become a highly political one.

Conciliation Service, whose duty is to prevent or minimize interruption of commerce growing out of labor-management disputes. The service possesses no law enforcement authority, relying on persuasive techniques to help bring about agreement between employer and employee.

The most dramatic provision in the legislation was a process for settling disputes that might "imperil the national health or safety" of the country. The provision allows the president to appoint a board to determine the issues in such a dispute and then ask for an 80-day "cooling-off" period through the courts in an effort to resolve the issues.

Another important piece of legislation in 1959 provided for fuller access to the union democratic process by members by giving them mechanisms through which they are assured of greater participation in regular union elections. These rights were provided by the Labor-Management Reporting Act (the Landrum-Griffin Act), which includes a "bill of rights" for union members and provisions for regular union elections.

Also important to the labor reporter is a provision requiring each labor organization to file annual financial reports (detailed income and expenditures statements) with the Labor Department. These documents, which also include any "conflict of interest" transactions by union officials, are subject to public inspection.

In 1970, Congress established an agency to develop and promulgate occupational safety and health standards, the Occupational Safety and Health Administration. This Labor Department agency offers an example of federal jurisdiction and its implications for the labor reporter at the local level.

A scaffold being used in construction of a cooling tower for an Ohio River power plant collapsed in 1978, resulting in the death of 51 workers. In the aftermath, the prime federal agency with jurisdiction was OSHA, whose interest lay in development of occupational and health standards, enforcement of those standards and investigation to determine compliance with regulations.

Since OSHA staffs 10 regional offices around the United States, the reporter covering the aftermath of such a disaster would deal with the regional office in Philadelphia. However, at some point the main Washington office itself would become involved, leading to a final story in the investigation that concluded with other government agency involvement.

> Washington—The Occupational Safety and Health Administration charged yesterday that a construction firm committed "willful" safety rule violations that contributed to the deaths of 51 men in a West Virginia scaffolding collapse earlier this year.
>
> The agency cited Wilson Industrial Contractors for 16 violations of federal safety rules, 10 of them "willful" and six "serious." The finding of "willful" violations means the agency can turn the matter over to the Justice Department for possible criminal prosecution.

In such cases, source points are important to the labor reporter, who must be familiar with the functions of such agencies as well as with their powers and limitations.

However, all labor news is not concentrated in legislative action and subsequent agency activity, often spilling over into the political arena as well.

> Charleston, W. Va.—President Carter, fulfilling a promise he made three months ago at the height of the nation's longest coal strike, appointed a 13-member Commission on the Coal Industry today to conduct a year-long study of the bitter relations between management and labor in the mine fields.
>
> The president chose a political fund-raising stop in this state capital to announce his decision.

Labor Disputes: Strike or Lockout?

No area of labor-management relations is more visible or newsworthy than the sound and fury of a work stoppage. Machinery grinds to a halt or is often operated by shirt-sleeved management executives in an effort to forestall a total shutdown of operations. The union operators of the machinery leave the plant and set up picket lines in an effort to bring the operation to a total halt. There is pushing, shoving and shouting at the entrances to the plant, with occasional violence inflicted on machines as well as on angry workers. Here is where labor reporting becomes most sensitive.

There is a middle ground in such disputes, precarious though it may be. Occupying it are the mediators themselves and the labor reporter. Even the terms used in describing a work stoppage (see the glossary at end of this chapter) must be chosen with care. Union spokespersons may object vigorously to use of the word "strike" by the press, arguing instead that workers have been "locked out" of their jobs by management. In turn, management may complain that the walkout is a "wildcat strike," unauthorized by the leadership of the union and thus in violation of written agreements between the two parties. Care must always be taken to differentiate between a work stoppage and an official strike called by the union.

Collective bargaining has brought about a more structured approach in reporting labor disputes, often making them more difficult to cover because of the sensitive role played by the mediator or arbitrator. At one time, the reporter could successfully deal only with the union and management of the company, each seeking to publicize its case through the press. Insertion of government restrictions into the bargaining process has caused both sides to become more cautious in disputes, particularly in complicated negotiations. Spokespersons tend to weigh their words more carefully, often providing less information to the press. Instead, they lay it on the bargaining table in private grievance sessions.

This approach, while still breached regularly by both sides as they continue to try to bring public sentiment to their point of view during negotiations, places greater responsibility upon the reporter to conduct preliminary spade work on the issues involved. Long before expiration of contracts, the reporter should be identifying and writing about the key issues that could create a final breakdown in communications between the disputants and force a work stoppage.

Is the percentage of wage increase the major point? Are fringe benefits an issue? What about manning of the assembly lines? Is a potential cut in standby staff the problem? Is the bargaining agent the real issue?

The emotional upheaval of a contract expiration without renewal is no time to try to identify the factors that created the crisis in the first place. If the issues have been competently reported upon before workers begin walking a picket line, the public will have been provided with a better perspective and will have been better served.

After a work stoppage occurs, the labor reporter will have to be in two places at once—near the picket line and close to the negotiating sessions. After each session, the reporter will have to ascertain whether or not any of the issues have been resolved and whether or not the parties are any closer to final agreement. The process can be laborious.

> Negotiators for the Food Processors Association and the union which represents workers in six plants emerged from their 11th bargaining session yesterday with agreement on an 8 percent across-the-board wage increase but with the other major issues unresolved.

Meanwhile, the parties in the dispute are also far apart in assessing effectiveness of a work stoppage. One side minimizes the effect of the strike, pointing out that "we're still operating at nearly full strength," with the other side insisting that the strike is "100 percent effective." The truth may be somewhere in between.

Whether authorized or unauthorized, work stoppages are generally intense experiences, with the reporter responsible for faithfully communicating the mood of the picket lines. Such a charged atmosphere calls for low-pressure approaches, and the reporter should attempt to become as much a part of the scene as possible. Without assured police protection, it may be a time to discard television equipment, note pads and even coats and ties. The alternative may be an unwanted jostling by picket line participants.

The reporter with excellent union contacts may be able to breathe a bit easier during touchy picket line confrontations, but there is never a guarantee that his or her "friends" will be on hand at the time they are needed most.

At the point of a work stoppage, the reporter's relationships with union leaders and ability to deal evenly with them is vital. If earlier stories have been reasoned and fair to all parties, there is less risk that a break in communications will occur.

Nothing is more difficult to overcome than the charge by angry strikers that "the press is out to get us." Amid such a din, the disclaimer by the reporter that he or she is "only doing my job" goes totally unheeded.

Work stoppages are often complicated by insertion of more than one union spokesperson in a labor dispute. Thus, a strike by the Fraternal Assn. of Steel Haulers incurred the wrath of the International Brotherhood of Teamsters, which refused to sanction the strike. In this case, the reporter had to deal with the Teamsters, a 2-million-member organization which included 10,000 truckers who haul steel products; FASH, an association of 20,000 truckers who are merely members of an association; and trucking companies which maintain close ties with both labor groups.

The reporting is complicated by the fact that one party may not have the right to bargain for its members as an "official" union recognized by management. Conflict often occurs when an official labor organization attempts to become bargaining agent for law enforcement groups which have been traditionally represented by fraternal police organizations.

> A union seeking to represent the city's 98 patrolmen is seeking a temporary injunction to block contract discussions between city officials and the Fraternal Order of Police.
>
> Food Store Employees Union, Local 325, filed the request in Circuit Court yesterday, claiming that the constitutional rights of the policemen were violated by not allowing them to vote to decide whether the FOP or the union should represent police in bargaining talks.

The potential for violence is also enhanced by involvement of additional elements into an already complicated equation. The belief by substantial numbers of non-striking workers in their right to work often leads to conflict.

> Scattered acts of violence in the area followed the midnight walkout of gasoline truckers yesterday, including the shooting of a non-striking trucker near the Ohio state line.
>
> Rock-throwing incidents were common as negotiators continued to try to hammer out an agreement.

Staffing of strike-bound areas is complicated by the round-the-clock nature of the dispute, and reporters must often accept sensitive information about violence secondhand. Care must be used to corroborate such information and to attribute it properly.

Because they are by definition unauthorized, wildcat strikes are particularly sensitive. Grievances will be more difficult to ascertain, and accurate information will be lacking. "Official" spokespersons won't be as readily available, and the reporter may have to follow them into the field.

> A three-day wildcat strike that has idled more than 7,000 coal miners in western Pennsylvania erupted into violence yesterday as state police scuffled with a group of 300 picketers near Blairsville.

Not all such labor disputes reach this stage, however. While the uncertainty of a strike deadline approaches, many are settled at the bargaining table at the last minute.

> After a tense morning session, Milton city employees approved a 9 percent wage and benefit package yesterday in a three-hour afternoon meeting with City Manager Richard Burt.
>
> At the midday break, negotiators for both sides had grimly refused comment, but by the end of the day left the Council chambers with smiles all around.
>
> "We're satisfied with the contract," said a beaming Gerry Spalding, president of the 285-member American Federation of State, County and Municipal Employees Local 597.

Union organizing efforts in non-union industries must be reported, along with the occasional violence they incur. The frequent jurisdictional disputes among various groups of workers also make news.

> The question of who should be first on the scene of a medical emergency has become the subject of a tense jurisdictional dispute between police and firemen in Cincinnati.
>
> At the center of the controversy is determination of who will assist residents who suffer heart attacks, near-drownings or other emergencies.

While most such disputes may not be as dramatic, they form a regular pattern in many industries that depend upon workers who are members of several different unions.

Such labor coverage is earthy and of particular interest to readers because their basic economic interests are at stake. The ability of the labor reporter to successfully bridge the gap between corporate boardroom and union hall is essential when contract time nears. So is a knowledge of courtroom procedure and the ability to negotiate a picket line. But the true test of the reporter's ability will occur when a labor issue has come full cycle. Having covered contract negotiations, the tense strike watch, picket line encounters, a settlement by harried bargaining officials and complex details of the final document, the reporter shakes hands with both sides and finds, not necessarily affection or friendship, but respect for a job competently handled.

A Labor Glossary

This minimum vocabulary of basic labor terms is essential to the beginning reporter:

Arbitration: A method of deciding a dispute in which the involved parties have agreed in advance to accept the decision of a third party.

Check-off: An employer agrees to deduct union dues from workers' paychecks and turn them over to the union.

Closed shop: A place of employment

which requires labor union membership as a condition for the employment. See open shop.

Company union: An organization of employees at a single corporate enterprise or plant, as distinguished from a labor union, which covers a wider area.

Jurisdictional dispute: An argument between two (or more) unions over the right to perform certain work. Such disputes often lead to work stoppages.

Mediation: Private individuals or public officials, acting as third party, offer assistance in bringing the disputants together to settle differences.

Open shop: A place of employment which does not require labor union membership as a condition for employment. See closed shop.

Preferential bargaining: Preferential status is given by an employer to a single bargaining agent. In a preferential shop, an employer agrees to give preference to members of a particular union when hiring new employees.

Right-to-work law: A law which permits an employee of a firm to work without being forced to join a union.

Scab: A derogatory term for an employee who continues to work during a strike in his or her place of employment.

Secondary boycott: A party in a labor dispute that refuses to deal with a customer or supplier of an employer with whom the boycotters have a dispute.

Shop steward: An employee designated by the union to discuss grievances of fellow union employees with management.

Wildcat strike: A walkout by some or all of the employees of an industry or single plant that is not authorized by the union.

CHAPTER 13
The Economics of the Private Sector

THE date: any time during the 1940s, 1950s or 1960s.

The place: the business desk of almost any newspaper in the United States. The editors are busy putting the finishing touches on these offerings to their readership:

> An open house is planned Saturday at the new distribution facility of the Buckeye Biscuit Co., 925 Greencrest Drive.
>
> David J. Cooper has been named national sales manager for Nulook Fashions, Inc., importer and wholesaler of wigs and hairpieces. Nulook maintains its national headquarters at 700 Long St.
>
> Central Bag & Burlap, in its 24th year of distributing textile bags and specialties, is growing into a full-service packaging supplier with emphasis on supplying the bag needs of industry and agriculture in the state.

This represents the "older" tradition of reporting business that was common in past years.

The time shifts to the present. A new dimension has been added to the old "business beat," and editors are working toward deadline with a different kind of copy:

> Almost everything about American land is known except who owns it.
>
> The vast mineral resources of the United States are assessed and quantified, mountains are measured, and ground cover and soil are analyzed. Uranium deposits

are pinpointed and vast areas of coal reserves surveyed.

The concept of land ownership is quite another story, despite its position as one of the most valuable of capital assets in a nation where capital is pre-eminent.

A secret document indicates that Jimmy Hoffa, the businessman, was deeply involved in the operation of the now bankrupt Great American Coal Co. and its subsidiaries until the day of his disappearance, July 30, 1975.

The document shows that labor leader Hoffa had a keen business eye and an interest in shaping the policy of the firm in which he had apparently invested.

These examples of the traditional business page content and a more contemporary questioning and even investigative approach illustrate the dramatic changes that have taken place in reporting economics during the last 20 years. The task of reporting the economics of the private sector is far more complex than this, however. In this vast country, with its far-flung local, state and federal government agencies looking on as regulators, the private sector continues to operate in a free-enterprise existence all its own, creating new and different informational needs.

The old "business beat" included announcements of personnel changes, openings of new stores, occasional news of record quarterly earnings by a local industry, and regular roundups assessing the economic vitality of the community. The page was fleshed out with a look at the real estate market, a national business column and a local feature story detailing an elderly downtown merchant's success for over a generation.

These traditional staples continue to serve as the backbone of many a newspaper's business page, but the emphasis is shifting to include a new generation of subjects and issues much closer to the reader.

—The issue of offering tax abatements to new industry as an inducement to locate in area industrial parks. Officials of financially strapped school districts are criticizing the eroding tax base.

—An in-depth report on the lagging home computer industry, once thought to be heading toward status as a billion-dollar mass market.

—Executive changes in a troubled industrial firm which signal major shifts in the company's objectives and possible economic consequences for the community in which it is located.

The approach is both broader and deeper today, with an emphasis on "what it means" and "what's ahead" for readers and viewers. The burdens on a press already saddled with an information explosion are considerable.

Reasons for a New Range

The old "business beat" actually encompasses a whole stable of beats—from extraction of raw materials from the earth through production and on to distributors and finally to sellers and buyers. Strictly speaking, the term "business" can no longer serve as an umbrella. Industrial production, distribution through the transportation process and the role of the financial community are equally important. The reporter's job is to address the entire range of the economics of the private sector.

These are some of the reasons for this growth:

1. New relationships between private enterprise and government at all levels, characterized mainly by more involved regulatory practices, has created an even greater need for news coverage.

2. A heightened awareness on the part of the public to economic affairs beyond its immediate concerns has created a new and dynamic "news" market. Realization that economic events occurring in far-away places affect everyone has further whetted the public's appetite for information. The old question, "How does it affect me and my pocketbook?" continues to be answered, but in far more sophisticated ways.

3. The age of technology has created a new market for economics reporting. New products and systems for modern living are being produced, advertised and marketed. It is natural that news reports accompany these developments, assessing the products in some way.

4. Joining this new technology is a new consumerism, with its probing questions, and new marketing strategies on the part of private enterprise to cope with them.

5. There is a new awareness on the part of the public of the influence of the "business world" on where it works, where it lives, what it earns and what it consumes in necessities and luxuries.

The old "business beat" is not dead. It has merely become more sophisticated in its expansion to become the "economics of the private sector" and one of the most important assignments in any newsroom—print or broadcast.

The Range of Story Material

The range of story possibilities which affects and interests the reader or viewer is endless, covering Main Street USA, the huge financial centers, the trading markets of the world and the vast breadbasket of this continent.

The reader now can understand how the daily "fixing" of gold prices in a distant London office affects the dollar in his or her wallet, the interest earned on the dollar in the bank and the future price of a set of gold inlays for his or her teeth.

Other types of economic developments are also important:

—The elderly owner of a neighbor drugstore finally capitulates to a huge new "superpharmacy" that offers thousands more items at far cheaper prices. The proprietor retires, discharges his four employees, and negotiates sale of his corner property as a beauty shop. It is a poignant story that affects more than a neighborhood; it is a sign of the times.

—An out-of-town development firm announces acquisition of a substantial tract of vacant land that it plans to develop as a shopping mall. The development threatens the resurgence of the city's old downtown area, which is being renewed and holds promise as a major community center.

Competition for the public's business carries different implications for different segments of the community: For the consumer, the new mall will mean a greater variety of shopping sources; for the downtown business owner struggling to renew the blighted area, the new mall is a threat to survival. The new mall will bring mixed blessings to the financial community—new ways to lend money, but a threat to mortgages held on downtown property. For the city official trying to remain within a tight budget, the mall means that some taxpaying businesses may be forced to close because of the competition at a time when every dollar counts.

The implications at this local level are enormous, and the economics reporter will have his or her hands full trying to develop them all.

—An industrial firm announces that it will close its local plant, a common rumor for months, putting 1,000 persons out of work. The effect on the community will be devastating, and the reporter begins work to assess the damage to the area's economy.

None of these matters is complex, but all of them will require considerable legwork on the part of an astute reporter to fully develop. Other examples of the private sector's economic life are more complicated:

—The electric utility, a privately owned enterprise, files a petition to raise rates, citing increased costs and a resultant drop in return to its financial investors.

To effectively cover the story, the reporter must understand the complex rate structures that have been developed and be able to digest the firm's balance sheet in fairly presenting the important points to a concerned public. As the case moves ponderously through the state utilities commission hearings, the reporter will have to follow and understand in some measure the technical arguments that will lead to a final decision.

—A local industry beset by financial problems wants to restructure its payments on old bond issues floated years before. It seeks to maintain its solvency in a time of crisis. Since it is a publicly owned corporation, the details are easily obtainable, but not so simple to report.

The reporter's job is to make them easily understandable to the public, which could be affected if the project fails and the firm closes its doors.

Reporting the economics of the private sector is a mixture of minor items and major developments, all in some way affecting the readership or viewership. To do his or her job well, the economics reporter cannot become bogged down in routine; rather, the reporter must be well organized to handle the wide range of material the beat offers.

Subject to limitations of space, time, staffing problems and, not least, pressures from the private sector itself, the community's total economic system is the beat. It is all fair game for the reporter.

The Private Sector: Profit and Risk

While it is basic to the U.S. system, it should be remembered that there is a formidable difference between the so-called "private" and "public" sectors in this country. The goal of any business system, which includes its industrial capacity and its financial manipulations, is to produce goods and services that satisfy the wishes and needs of the consumer public, and with maximum efficiency.

"At the same time, all businesses operate on a profit or loss system—and this involves risk-taking," says Harold S. Mohler, chairman of the board of the Hershey Foods Corp. "Profit is essential for business to develop, providing a return on the owner's investment in the business, whether it is a one-person operation, or a multinational corporation employing thousands of people around the world."

As a business executive, Mohler makes the point clearly: "As a member of a business management team, if you forecast correctly about your customers' needs, and meet these needs efficiently, you are rewarded with good earnings. If your forecast is inaccurate, you are punished with a loss."

To put it another way, the main interest of business, perhaps the overriding one, is survival and ultimately success. The profit motive must be uppermost through the various stages—from planning to production to distribution and finally selling.

On the other hand, the journalist's interest often lies in how that business, its operations and the products it produces affects the public. These subtle sets of priorities sometimes are in conflict. Each party should endeavor to understand the priorities of the other, while not always agreeing with them.

A simple story makes the point effectively:

—An employee at a major grocery store accidently cuts off his finger while working at a meat-cutting machine. An ambulance is dispatched, rushing the employee to a nearby hospital where expert surgeons reattach the finger. A reporter describes the incident in a news story, but the store manager, believing that the incident will injure his store's reputation and business, is incensed over the story and is harassing the injured employee, warning him to say nothing further to the press.

There should be no argument that the incident is newsworthy or that a subsequent follow-up be made to determine whether the reattachment of the finger was successful. However, pressure from management is so great that there is understandable reluctance on the part of the employee to discuss the incident, lest he be summarily dismissed. It will be difficult to communicate the importance of such a follow-up to someone who so firmly believes that his or her success as a manager is in jeopardy.

While this incident may not totally qualify as a "business" story, it illustrates the problem the reporter faces in dealing with individuals in the private sector.

Part of the problem lies in lack of understanding, part in ignorance of the other party's function in society. The proper function of the press is to serve as information conduit, which often encroaches on the profit-making factors of the business community.

Arthur R. Taylor, a broadcast executive, put it this way:

> The crux of the problem lies in the sad fact that business and the press have too little mutual respect and too little understanding for each other's vital role within the American system. It is the role of the press to report fairly and objectively on the events around it. It is the role of business to produce and sell goods and services of quality—hopefully for a legitimate profit. And it is the role and duty of both to serve the public to the best of their abilities.

Such conflict is inevitable. The business executive sees a news story one way, the reporter sees it another.

Two Perceptions of News

A seemingly routine request to City Council by an industrial firm to rezone a parcel of land or to close a little-used street in an industrial area may be the first tip to a reporter of a major expansion. The reporter will naturally be on the lookout for such routine items, remembering that the industrialist will think of it as a news story only after complicated preliminaries are complete. Responding poorly to questions, he may consider the reporter "nosy" and snappishly suggest that plans have not yet been "finalized."

Such an industrial expansion is often news long before the firm's public relations department is ready to provide the announcement in the form of a packaged news release, a press conference and artists' renderings of the new plant. Businesses are also fond of tying such major announcements to paid advertising.

While the planned announcement may be newsworthy, the reporter's function is to communicate such information at the earliest stage, not merely when it is convenient for the company.

The firm looks for the most advantage to itself in its community role in releasing the information; the reporter is merely exercising his or her function of providing the news rapidly and accurately.

Some Complaints About the News Media

"Can't the press ever get anything right?"

That complaint, often unjustified but often containing elements of truth, complicates the journalist's job of reporting the news of the private sector. Antagonism does exist between the press and those it covers.

In criticizing what he calls the "armed camp mentality" that exists between business and the media, writer Carl Tucker points out that "both a free press and profits are essential to the workings of our system of governance." He urged that "newsmen and businessmen/women recognize each other as legitimate partners in our national enterprise." Another economics writer, Louis Banks, cites the conviction of business "that the great power of the media is used selectively to sour the body politic on corporate product, profit and practice."

Specific complaints against the media include publication of careless news stories, quoting business executives as saying things they never said, comparing "apples with oranges" in producing controversial business stories and committing error of fact.

A favorite story still making the rounds of the business community years later indicates the depth of feeling in some quarters:

> A New York reporter covered the opening of the new Pan Am Building in mid-Manhattan, explaining how the modern structure located directly over Grand Central Station was so accessible to the public. Railroads chugged into the basement, helicopters landed on the roof, and buses were right at the doors.
>
> The reporter also noted the easy access by auto, pointing out that Juan Trippe, then president of Pan American Airways, could descend on express elevators to Park Avenue and slip into a waiting chauffeured Cadillac a few steps away.
>
> The story showed imagination, but a minor problem arose. Readers called the business journal to point out that Trippe, being a director of the Chrysler Corp., would not be likely to use a General Motors Corp. product.
>
> At the behest of his editor, the reporter visited the Park Avenue ramp and identified Trippe's Chrysler Imperial parked at the door.

Thus, the credibility of an otherwise good story was tarnished by a single error of fact. But such minor errors are the ones that the business community and the public often remember, negating the results of a good effort on the part of a reporter.

Banks cites other complaints against the press:

—Ignorant reporting, tangling complex business or financial facts into erroneous conclusions. A power company spokesman says, "Newspapers should send out reporters to cover energy who are willing to learn enough about the business they cover to write about it intelligently."

—Oversimplification.

—Sensationalism. Business sees the media as ignoring "constructive" progress and believes that the press gives headline attention to the "bizarre, odd, inconsequential or exceptional."

—Business complains that "good news" is seldom printed or broadcast, whereas the "accident in the plant, the problem in environmental control or the slur of the competitor becomes surefire copy for news stories."

There is often truth in these complaints.

Some Complaints About Business

Countering these complaints, the press argues that business and financial leaders are secretive and inaccessible and provide the wrong kinds of mechanisms to respond to media inquiries. They also charge frequent and deliberate distortion.

Dan Cordtz, economics editor for the American Broadcasting Co., agrees that there is tension and animosity between the press and business, but argues that the press is not "anti-business." Instead he sees as the problem the public's perception of what is news.

> More often than not, what gets a company into the news is something bad, or at least something unflattering. The average person isn't really interested in business per se, and even less interested in most individual companies. So the kind of news that grabs people tends to be things like price increases, or product recalls, or a strike or some such thing. And that's just the kind of thing most executives would just as soon not see on the front page or any other page.

As a consequence, the reporter's relationships with a company suffer under these conditions, with his or her sources either unwilling to communicate at all or becoming very defensive and belligerent and uncooperative.

Washington reporter John M. Berry says that business creates problems for itself by refusing to meet with reporters and adds that business people often do not realize that they are communicating even when they issue a "no comment."

> I fully realize that a private enterprise is a private enterprise, and there's no law that says any businessman has to talk to me. But when they choose not to, they lose an opportunity to have their view expressed—and they have to be prepared for the consequences.

The wish of many business, industrial and financial executives to construct and maintain a favorable public image tends to create barriers to better press-business relations. Thus, a public information office will distribute vast amounts of routine statistics and other information in press releases that must be carefully combed for newsworthy information. Much of the information is designed to enhance the corporate image, while the important information is hidden far inside the material.

Layoffs of hundreds of workers at a major plant become "production adjustments"; the loss of an important production contract becomes a "contractual renegotiation."

Journalists argue that this tendency to minimize adverse developments fosters mistrust of the business community, with conviction by the press that facts are being withheld or twisted. One reporter says,

> You call a company president, get referred to a public relations man who gives you a prepared handout telling you about the excellent state of that business, and adds a few well-chosen "no comments" and you are supposed to write a story.

A corporation may be receiving exhaustive media coverage, yet none that it approves. Executives often fail to understand that the press cannot operate merely as a public relations tool, a business blotter or a booster of the corporation.

SOME RESPONSES BY BUSINESS

The business community has responded in numerous ways to what it perceives as deficiencies of the press. Corporations sponsor "news media seminars" to openly discuss their credibility; television broadcasts such as the U.S. Chamber of Commerce-sponsored show are produced. The organization bills its telecasts as a way to spread its "pro-business, pro-free-enterprise philosophy."

Business also offers substantial annual prizes for excellence in writing, the objective being to influence reporters to write about a particular subject. Some business journalism prizes, sponsored by news organizations and universities, have lofty and serious purposes. Others, as Chris Welles of Columbia University, suggests, are bestowed for a different purpose:

> Next November, three fortunate journalists will receive the Recreation Vehicle Industry Award, which carries with it a $1,000 prize and an all-expenses-paid trip to the National Recreation Vehicle Show in Louisville, Ky. It is unlikely that anyone involved with the event, including the

journalists, will look on it as anything more than what it really is: a promotion.

"We wouldn't want anyone to lose their objectivity," says RVIA public relations director Gary LaBelle. "But we hope, when people are writing a story about RVs and know about our award, that they will go out of their way to do an especially nice story."

Nearly 300 such contests award various prizes annually, mostly by such business-related groups as the National Association of Realtors, the National Bowling Council and the Helicopter Association of America, whose principal and undisguised aim, says Welles, "is a public relations boost for themselves and their members."

Other sponsors, however, take elaborate steps to insulate themselves from the selection process by turning over the selection of winners to disinterested groups such as universities.

This competition may sometimes help to bridge the communications gap between the press and business community. Better insurance, however, lies in insistence on the part of all parties of a scrupulously fair, totally accurate and constantly balanced economic report for every community.

Monitoring the Community

At its most elementary level, each segment of the private sector affects the public in many different ways:

—A merchant opens for business. What he produces or sells is news. How he does so may be news. The merchant's relationships with the people he asks to do business with may also be news. Where the merchant locates and how he affects those around him may be news. People are employed by him, deal with him as brokers, buy from him, sell to him and earn money by investing in his firm as stockholders.

So, many readers may have a vested interest in the activity of the firm—whether it is a retail business, an industry or a public utility that happens to be privately owned and operated. From this level, it is only a step to the larger community, with its broader implications for greater numbers of people.

One of the most important functions of the press is to regularly monitor the economic well-being of the community, through careful observation of the private as well as the public sector. The traditional approach at the "local level" is to periodically present a business and industrial review, carefully packaged in a special section containing advertising from those being reviewed, and offering merely a superficial and generally "upbeat" report to the public.

A more honest and thoughtful monitoring does not await the onslaught of the annual packaged review but deals instead on a daily basis with the frequent economic successes and reverses encountered by any community.

The reporter is always searching for specifics in these assessments, rather than the generalities which are often offered in hopes that the problem, if there is one, will go away. What retail merchant will willingly agree to discuss with an economics reporter his grim six-month sales figures—"it's all downturn, plus as much as 10 percent"?

What real estate broker is going to admit to the press that his staff is selling "far fewer properties" and admit further that "the immediate future is not at all bright"? And what president of an industrial firm wouldn't be reluctant to admit that a major work force layoff is imminent?

It is much easier of course to monitor the economic well-being of the city when all indicators are positive rather than negative. Fairness to readers and viewers demands reporting of the entire spectrum. The key to successfully handling these "negative" swings is to monitor on a regular basis rather than to wait until a definite swing has occurred. Day in, day out reports achieve a quicker and more objective news report.

The reporter cannot assess most communities' well-being by means of press releases extolling the virtues of sale-priced merchandise during "Spring Sales Days." He or she should be searching out more important and more accurate indicators:

—An honest gauge of real estate activity. How do current property listings compare with the totals of six months or 12 months before? The Multiple Listing Service can provide the figures.

—New building permits, comparing them with previous reports. Permits for improvement and alteration are often a gauge of the activity in a community. So are changes in interest rates for mortgages taken out at savings and loan institutions.

—Changes in the city's bond ratings. Such changes often indicate localized economic problems.

—A survey of new orders being placed with local industrial firms. Monitoring such information will often reveal slowdowns or speedups in the local economy. Also important are delays or speedups in planned expansion by business and industrial firms. Such information, coupled with unemployment figures at the local level, often offer a much more accurate picture of economic activity than will the traditional roundup of comments by well-known civic figures.

—Changes in activity in banks and savings and loan institutions. Declines and increases in loans to corporations and individuals are watched closely as indicators of economic activity.

—Close monitoring of government's access to funds to provide continuing services to the public. Problems with the tax base and the city's spending plans also serve as local economic indicators.

Other indicators are also important. Production of public utilities, postal receipts obtainable from the federal agency, vehicular sales in the area, the average workweek and plans for purchasing new equipment offer the reporter the opportunity to build strong economic monitors.

Agencies such as the local Chamber of Commerce, development boards and university departments with an interest in economics often serve as good sources for specialized economic indicators. Even the courts are a source of such indicators. Increases in filings for bankruptcy are often one measure of the community' s vitality.

Localizing Economic Stories

New information-gathering techniques, coupled with the ability to quickly and efficiently process material through computers, has resulted in a massive outpouring of economic data from government agencies. The reporter will find access to such publicly produced data easier than to the material produced by private organizations. However, not all private data are carefully guarded for competitive as well as personal reasons, and the reporter will find some of it accessible and useful.

With access to federal economic data, the reporter can effectively localize much material, making it more meaningful to the reader. A city's unemployment rate, with attendant breakdowns of various industries, is just as important to readers as the periodic issuance of the national unemployment rate.

A wire service story containing specific figures on spending for private and public construction around the nation offers the opportunity for local surveys of the construction industry to determine how closely the national pattern conforms to that of the area.

> A surge in apartment construction fueled by major developers is helping the city avoid the downward national trend in new construction, the city's Development Board said yesterday.
>
> "We're optimistic this difference will continue into next year," Daniel C. Fogerty, executive director of the board, said, but added, "a long-term national slowdown will inevitably affect us."
>
> A U.S. Commerce Department report this week placed the nation's spending for new construction at 11.8 percent below the same period last year.

Regular monitoring of the Consumer Price Index at the national level brings regional and local figures as well. The Bureau of Labor Statistics breaks down figures for various areas and often offers detailed reasons for upward or downward changes in the indexes.

> Consumer prices continued to rise in the Tristate area last month, reflecting higher costs for housing, trans-

> portation and medical care, the Bureau of Labor Statistics reported Thursday.
>
> However, the national Consumer Price Index continued to outpace the regional figure, rising at an annual rate of 11.6 percent. The comparable area figure was at an annual rate of 10.7 percent, Warren Norwood, regional commissioner for the agency, said.

Other statistics covering an indicator's various components, such as fuels, utilities, food and clothing, offer further opportunities to develop local stories on how various industries are affected. Often, the effect of national trends on local communities can be translated into very specific and personal stories.

High interest rates for mortgages may create a softening of a city's real estate market, visible through sharp drops in classified advertising in local newspapers and in real estate closings. Because of the inability of potential home buyers to raise necessary down payments, the rental market booms and merits reporting. The reasons for the high interest rates also merit coverage.

Lost in the barrage of economic stories might be the plight of the professional real estate broker and hundreds of other persons whose livelihoods depend on sales in the housing market. However, some digging on the part of the reporter might uncover the reasons why sales representatives do not suffer as much as they might seem to during such periods of real estate inactivity: many salespersons may be part-time employees who merely return to being full-time housewives until business improves, leaving the field to the full timers.

> Lois Jackson didn't show up for the weekly meeting at Specialty Realty Co. yesterday.
>
> Instead, she watched the morning talk shows, then planted tulip bulbs in the afternoon. Mrs. Jackson is one of the victims of the dramatic drop in the real estate market that has sent her and hundreds of other part-time real estate sales people to the sidelines.
>
> "It's just a temporary thing," she theorized over coffee in the pleasant Oak Ridge home she occupies with engineer husband Herbert and two teen-age children. "When the market improves, I'll plunge back in. Meanwhile, there's lots of reading to catch up on."

Similar possibilities exist in the retail sales market, with students returning to or dropping out of college until employment conditions improve. Research into the socio-economic lifestyles of other families might also uncover related stories—two-job families that become one-job families during periods of recession or high unemployment.

> Families that relied on two or more paychecks to qualify for a Columbia home are finding the going increasingly tough as unemployment takes a bigger bite.
>
> "We are getting some families with problems," Ralph

> L. Staper, vice president of Downtown Savings and Loan Association, said this week. "We're trying to work with them until they get on their feet again."
>
> Staper estimated that up to 15 percent of the association's customers are in danger of losing one of the family paychecks.

Private organizations often collect data that has application at the local level. The National Association of Purchasing Management, an organization of purchasing agents, regularly surveys its membership to determine trends in purchase of industrial building blocks such as fuel, steel and plastic. Purchasing agents among local industry help to flesh out an economic picture that starts at a national level but is finally localized.

Trade associations regularly monitor their specific businesses, providing forecasts and other information that can be checked locally.

> Delays in pickups and deliveries, caused by shortages of diesel fuel, will frustrate the estimated 4.3 million people moving to distant cities this summer.
>
> "Loaded vans are already running into the problem," said Cliff C. Knowles, director of the Household Goods Carriers Bureau, a trade organization representing 80 percent of the nation's moving firms. "We expect it to be much worse when business peaks this summer."
>
> While families planning interstate moves can expect problems, Knowles said, the 17.4 million people planning local or intrastate moves will have far fewer problems.

In many such cases, other groups and agencies can provide further information. The reporter has access to the American Movers Conference, another major trade association representing the industry, and the Interstate Commerce Commission, the federal agency which regulates the industry.

The frequent home and trade shows that attract huge crowds to auditoriums around the country are also a source of information to economics reporters. New products that appear headed for broad public acceptance receive their first viewing in these arenas. Reporters alert to new developments frequently develop stories on problems faced by old products challenged by new ones. Manufacturers, sellers and experts in the field gather at such shows in the big cities to discuss trends in their business.

> Manufacturers and sellers of home video recording equipment fear the advent of new technologies will hopelessly fragment consumer demand.
>
> "We're already afflicted with two cassette formats and tough price competition," moaned Raymond C. Scites, vice president of Panatonic Corp., at the 16th annual Consumer Electronics Show in Chicago. "There could be some big problems ahead."
>
> A new video disk system, a $700 machine utilizing a

laser pickup and phonograph-like record to display movies on a television screen, is being demonstrated at the show.

The Reporter at Work

Competent monitoring of the community's economic life requires the journalist to have some knowledge of how business and industry operate and a willingness to break down the technicalities and explain them in understandable terms to the reader.

This implies a reasonable understanding of the terminology common to the economic sector. The reporter worth his or her salt won't have to resort to a glossary to reconcile a proposed new excise tax with a firm's future growth. Nor will it be necessary to consult a dictionary for a definition when a firm announces an internal audit to check its own control procedures in assessing a government charge of questionable practices.

It will be necessary to learn how to read a financial report before the necessity of studying one on deadline for a news story arises. Any business officer of the firm for which the reporter works will be willing to lead him or her through the intricacies of the double-entry process, the basic accounting system that records most transactions of corporations, public and private. Furthermore, many sources routinely supply booklets explaining how the system operates.

As already noted, the tendency on the economics beat is to operate informationally through "spokesmen," trained to carefully provide data on the terms of and in the interest of "business." The reporter's constant companion is an inner compulsion to obtain answers to questions that will enlighten issues beyond the barriers sources erect.

Information from spokespersons often begins the news story process, but direct access to the decision-makers concludes it. The reporter should make every effort to obtain firsthand information from "the horse's mouth," as it were. This is not always as simple as it sounds; yet persistence will often pay off in the form of such access to those who actually make the decisions.

Delay or postponement of an important project may be newsworthy, but in a negative way. Officials find no reason to emphasize such negative aspects of the development. Unless they are specifically asked about it, they will allow time to take care of events to their satisfaction.

The Diamond department store, key anchor in the new Suburban Mall being constructed on the West Side, has postponed indefinitely its plans to open a store in the mall, the president of the company said yesterday.

However, developers of the mall say the decision has had no effect on progress of the project.

Anthony Cafano, president of Youngstown Developers, said construction on much of the 150-store project is on schedule for an opening next year.

E. K. Braun, president of the Diamond Group, ad-

> mitted that the decision to postpone construction in the mall was made in New York corporate headquarters several months ago. "The general economy and high cost of borrowing money has forced us to rethink our expansion plans," he said.

Another important part of the reporter's job is to monitor continuing stories common to the economics beat and not allow them to become lost in the welter of new stories that are constantly breaking. A "tickler file" is helpful in assuring that such stories are not buried in the press of other responsibilities.

> With the long lines at gas stations now only a memory, dealers and motorists appear to be growing less diligent in observing the odd-even gasoline sales restrictions imposed during the summer crisis.
>
> Informal checks of stations show that motorists with odd-numbered license plates are pulling up to pumps on even days, and vice versa, to make illegal purchases.
>
> "With nobody in line, I'm not going to turn them away," said Jerry Lavecca, manager of a Shell station on Locust Avenue.

Catching up with "old" stories or keeping up with developing ones are an important part of the economics beat.

The careful economics reporter also watches the legal advertisements closely, because overlooked business developments often crop up there. Such monitoring serves as insurance that a major development is not overlooked.

> A new downtown bank designed to provide services especially to the elderly has been proposed by a group of nine local businessmen, physicians and lawyers.
>
> The application to organize the new firm has been filed with the Comptroller of the Currency in Washington, according to legal notices in today's *Journal-Herald*.
>
> Attorney Leon S. Oxnard, a spokesman for the proposed bank, said efforts are being made to lease the vacant facility formerly occupied by the now defunct Downtown Athletic Club at 410 Front St.
>
> "The organizers see a need to offer special banking services to the elderly," Oxnard said. "That's our wave of the future."

Regular checks of new corporations chartered by the state should also be conducted. Many newspapers routinely publish the names of new firms, but merely listing them offers few clues as to their makeup. Identity of the incorporators often provides information of greater interest. A state charter can be obtained for as little as $100, but capitalization is usually far in excess of that figure, and the impact on the community may be much greater. Close study of the types of firms being chartered often reflects the growth of specific types of business activity.

Monitoring the manner in which firms do business is also a source of newsworthy material. Changes in credit card procedures or utility bill payments often make news, and these in-house or industrywide developments affect thousands of persons doing business with the firms.

> Area banks have been raising the cost of low-balance checking, partly to discourage people who like to bounce checks, a survey of the institutions indicates.
>
> Banks are doing this by offering only accounts that charge a flat monthly fee that decreases as the account's balance rises.
>
> "The old 'thrift' accounts are going out of style," William J. Searles, vice president of Bank One, said. Those accounts merely charged customers on the basis of number of checks written.
>
> "People would come in, put in $25 and start bouncing checks all over town," Searles said. "We're trying to chase off the ones that give us a bad name."

Government Involvement

Through regulation, direct and indirect assistance, and credit agencies, government involvement in the economics of the private sector has become increasingly complex in recent years. Some of these relationships concern significant aspects of doing business, whereas others are merely bookkeeping measures designed to routinely secure data for census or survey purposes. At both levels, the relationships may have importance to the reporter.

Nearly 90 federal agencies regulate private enterprises in the United States, creating massive paperwork that flows into and out of federal offices. Business complains that many of the rules are unnecessary and that the cost of complying with regulations has forced firms to pass on the costs to the consuming public.

Time magazine has commented that the systems intended to protect the public sometimes abuse it with the proliferation of rules: "Big Brother, in the garb of the government regulator, has infiltrated virtually every corner of private enterprise, imposing standards on everything from smokestack effluents to the shape of toilet seats."

"Alphabetical watchdogs proliferate," *Time* reported, "the likes of EPA, OSHA, NHTSA and CPSC, mostly accepted by business as well-meaning but roundly condemned for pickiness, overzealousness and bureaucratic tunnel vision."

Whatever his or her reaction to these charges, the economics reporter will have to face a fact of life: the work of many government agencies affects the firms and individuals on this beat, and a knowledge of it is essential. Few reporters have the time to remain abreast of the 70,000 pages produced annually in the *Federal Register*, the publication produced daily by the government that announces most of the rules and regulations proposed for business, industry and finance. Instead, most reporters at the local level rely on well-placed sources to keep them informed of developments that affect the economics of the community.

Frequent wire service stories and reports in business journals signal decisions that can lead to localized coverage.

> Washington—The agency that regulates federally chartered savings and loan associations, the nation's principal mortgage lenders, has proposed a major change in regulations intended to strengthen the financial structures of the lenders.
>
> The Federal Home Loan Bank Board proposes to give lenders more latitude in offering "variable rate" mortgages, those with interest rates that rise and fall according to credit market conditions.
>
> Another important effect, the board says, will be to protect home buyers from being locked into high 30-year mortage rates.

Many questions can and should be answered locally. What will be the effect on area lending insitutions? Will it help to cushion a forecasted drop in mortgage lending and homebuilding activity? How might borrowers react to the new variable rate plans? Good legwork will answer these questions for the readers.

The source of a significant development is never certain. It may emanate from the nation's capital or from one of the many business and financial centers around the country.

> Cleveland (AP)—Banking officials say they're worried that Ohio banks will join a growing movement to abandon the Federal Reserve System and switch to state charters.
>
> "The trickle of members leaving the system has turned into a flow, and it might grow into a flood," said Martin Abrams, a spokesman for Cleveland's Federal Reserve Bank.
>
> Only about one-third of the banks throughout the country are members of the federal system, but those banks have 70 percent of total bank deposits.
>
> Cleveland officials said they are concerned about 37 Ohio banks which hold about $2 billion in assets and which eventually might leave the system.

The implications of developments such as these are important for many communities. What banks are involved in the federal abandonment? Is it a concerted effort? What are the provisions associated with the state banking charters the firms would have to obtain? How will such action affect individuals with accounts in the banks? What effect might such action have on the state agency involved?

Federal Boards and Agencies

Many independent federal boards and agencies provide documentation on the industries and individual companies that they regulate, including annual reports, financial statements, economic impact statements, and records of complaints and investigations. It is not difficult for a reporter to thoroughly research the inner workings of firms involving the public interest through documents and other information.

For this reason, it is important for the economics reporter to be familiar with the various boards and agencies and their basic functions and operational formats.

An airline decides to drastically adjust its service to a Midwest community and creates the possibility of disruption in the transportation sector. If statements from airline officials prove unsatisfactory to cover the story, the reporter can obtain traffic records and denied boarding reports from the Financial and Traffic Data Section of the Civil Aeronautics Board, which regulates the air carrier. Information is also available on finances and statistics on performance from the CAB, should the reporter desire it. There is every reason to document the story through these sources, should it warrant the time.

A community's problems with charter flights can be thoroughly documented in another office of the CAB. The Bureau of Pricing and Domestic Aviation collects information about charter tours, contracts, prices and insurance data.

A wealth of similar material is available from other federal regulators acting independently of the executive departments—the Interstate Commerce Commission, the Occupational Safety and Health Review Commission, the National Transportation Safety Board, the Commodity Futures Trading Commission, the Securities and Exchange Commission, the Federal Communications Commission, the Nuclear Regulatory Commission and the Federal Reserve System.

The ICC was created by Congress to regulate carriers engaged in interstate transportation and that includes trucking companies, railroads, bus lines, freight forwarders, water carriers, transportation brokers and express agencies. The reporter will find that any companies subject to ICC regulation must do business within scrutiny of that agency, which settles controversies over rates and charges among competing modes of carrier; rules on applications for mergers, acquisitions and consolidations; prescribes rules for operation; and investigates complaints against the firms. Records of protests, complaints and investigation are available to the press.

Other agencies also provide this kind of information. The Occupational Safety and Health Review Commission makes available transcripts and decisions concerning the safety and health of any firm that is involved in interstate commerce. The National Transportation Safety Board provides safety reports on aircraft, railroads and pipelines, and a reporter can obtain accident reports and hearing transcripts on agency investigations.

The economics reporter's access to agency information is often restricted only by time and effort. Activities in commodities trading, which affect the consuming public as well as the firms doing business on the various trading exchanges, are regulated by the Commodity Futures Trading Commission. Registration is required for brokerage firms, including financial statements, principals in the firms and their addresses. While the agency has a reputation as one of the federal government's weakest regulatory bodies, its procedures for settling customers' claims and grievances are available to public scrutiny.

> Since last spring, the CFTC has shut down about 75 sellers of off-exchange commodity options and similarly illegal investments. It won a dispute in September with the giant Chicago Board of Trade, the nation's biggest futures exchange, when a federal court upheld its authority to order emergency halts in trading. The CFTC is also concluding several long-standing and major investigations, including its inquiry into the New York Merchantile Exchange's handling of an alleged crisis in potato futures trading last year.

One of the most important independent agencies is the Securities and Exchange Commission. A knowledge of its role and responsibilities is indispensible to the economics reporter. Enabling legislation creating the SEC in 1934 provided for full disclosure to protect the public against malpractices in the securities and financial markets. A wealth of information is available to the reporter concerning many major corporations that may operate in his or her community, with the information often more accessible from the agency than from the firm itself.

More than 11,000 companies selling shares of stock to the public come under the scrutiny of the SEC, and many basic documents that must be filed by the firms to do business are part of the SEC's public files. It is easy to obtain a description of the company and its subsidiaries, location and description of all properties owned, major lawsuits in progress, and identification, relationships and remuneration of all the officers of the firm.

Also readily available are changes and developments in such areas as competitive conditions, possible bankruptcy proceedings, any major disposition of assets, changes in methods of doing business and changes in indebtedness. Local firms that have a substantial impact on the community can often be monitored through these public records. Without even resorting to access to the firm itself, the reporter can determine sales, revenues, sources and application of funds, gross profits and net revenue, any defaults or nonpayment of dividends, and lists of principal security holders.

A firm's parent company may take actions that affect a local subsidiary. The journalist can stay abreast of current developments, such as changes in control of the firm, who obtained control, the nature of the transaction, loans and contracts that could result in future changes, and major acquisitions and their effect on the local plant. Even the sources used to purchase such acquisitions are available. Armed with such information, the reporter is much better equipped to produce accurate stories on local developments that affect the community.

The agency itself should be closely watched because of its impact on the investing public and the corporations it monitors.

> Washington—In its efforts to reduce regulation and make it easier to raise capital in public markets, the Securities and Exchange Commission has been increasingly disregarding the warnings of its enforcement division that investor safeguards are being eroded.
>
> The growing isolation of the enforcement division is reflected in a recent series of actions taken by the commission despite the vigorous dissent of division officials. These included measures concerning earnings forecasts, advertising by mutual funds and stock sales by smaller firms.

Another important source of financial information is the Federal Home Loan Bank Board, which supervises and regulates savings and loan associations, the private firms that lend money on homes and businesses in virtually every community in the United States. The board collects and files basic data on the makeup of the institutions, investments by individual members and profit pictures of the organizations. The board also operates the Federal Savings and Loan Insurance Corporation, which insures the savings deposited in the banks.

The banks of the United States are regulated by the Federal Reserve System, the central point for administering and making policy for the nation's credit and monetary affairs. Banks must file annual reports with the Federal Reserve, showing financial condition and shareholder information.

The Federal Reserve influences the lending and investing activities in most communities through its regulation of commercial banks, including tightening and loosening the cost and availability of money and credit. Its influence over credit conditions affects public borrowing and lending, and the reporter should be familiar with the Federal Reserve's reporting procedures.

> It's a buyers' market, but who's buying?
>
> House prices and mortgage rates, which surged upward following the Federal Reserve's credit-tightening measures Oct. 15, now have begun to drop perceptibly because of customer resistance.
>
> The average price of a new home in the metropolitan area dipped from $102,600 in September to $96,400 in December. Resale houses, which sold for an average of $105,600 in September, sold for an average of $86,700 in December, according to the Federal Home Loan Bank Board.
>
> "The market has indisputably gone into a deep freeze," said William D. O'Connell, vice president of the U.S. League of Savings Associations. "A lot of people don't think that a warm spring will help," he added.

Other agencies also maintain a close scrutiny of firms doing business in specialized areas. The Federal Communications Commission requires annual reports and other documents from companies it regulates—radio and television broadcasting; telephone, telegraph and cable television operation; two-way radio and radio operators; and satellite communication.

Such companies do business via the public airwaves, and they are more closely monitored than are many other private corporations.

> Investigations had dragged on for years—and the final decision came only after intense debate. But last week, by the narrowest of votes, the Federal Communications Commission stripped RKO General, Inc. of licenses for three major television stations in Boston, New York and Los Angeles.
>
> The reason: the FCC said RKO and its parent company, General Tire & Rubber Co., had engaged in misconduct "so extensive and serious" that they could not be trusted as broadcasters. It was the commission's most sweeping disciplinary action ever—and if it sticks, the action could cost RKO and General Tire broadcasting assets worth well over $100 million.
>
> —*Newsweek*

Another independent agency becoming increasingly important is the Nuclear Regulatory Commission, which licenses and regulates the uses of nuclear energy to protect the public health and safety and the environment. Companies that operate nuclear reactors do so under the watchful eye of the NRC, which sets standards for operation. Safety rule violations can be documented through the agency.

The Executive Agencies

The executive agencies parallel the independent agencies of the federal government in imparting important economic information to the media. One of the most important is the Department of Commerce, which encourages and promotes the nation's economic development and technological advancement. Its many divisions offer sound and factual data on development that affect local communities, such as information on finances, growth and production in industries.

The department's *World Traders Data Reports* provide background on companies that may be considering locating in a community, including size and organization, sales area, products, financial references and general reputation. (Banks often offer credit information on foreign firms that are proposing a U.S. location.)

The Department of the Treasury is also a good source of economic information, through the Comptroller of the Currency, which regulates currency and banks; the Customs Service, which administers the tariff laws; and the Internal Revenue Service, which administers most of the tax laws in this country.

The Department of Energy, established in 1977, has become a consolidation point for all the major energy regulation in the United States, including the Federal Energy Administration, the Federal Power Commission and the Energy Research and Development Administration. Firms dealing with power production and supply are regulated by the new department, which documents to the public such material as ownership, organization and financial structure of the privately owned firms. It also serves as regulator for all forms of energy in the nation, including the vast oil and natural gas industries, coal production and research into new forms of energy. Its policing powers should not be overlooked.

> Washington (AP)—Texaco, Inc. and the Atlantic Richfield Co. overcharged customers by almost $200 million after the Arab oil boycott of 1973-74 sent fuel prices soaring, the government charged today.
>
> The accusations by the Energy Department brought to $5.2 billion the amount of pricing irregularities charged against the nation's 15 largest oil firms. That sum is equivalent to a 5-cent-a-gallon increase in the price of all gasoline sold in the U.S. in a year.

The Legislative Process

Economic news is not restricted to the executive branch. By "scratching" a legislator, the reporter could well uncover an economic issue that affects the reader. Congressional hearings should be monitored closely, for it is there that the rules and regulations ultimately promulgated by agencies are argued and hashed out.

> Washington—Pan American-National will drop all of its charter flights and some scheduled flights in an effort to cut fuel costs and reduce expenses, the company's president said today.
>
> Other steps to be taken, Daniel Colussy said in testimony before the House Aviation subcommittee, include scrapping previous plans to expand worldwide services 10 percent next year.
>
> Colussy testified in favor of pending legislation that would permit international carriers to pass through increased fuel costs in much the same way that domestic carriers now do under terms of the deregulation act.

Congress frequently calls on various departments and agencies to undertake specific investigations involving economic issues, such as an effort to update bankruptcy statutes. The results are often newsworthy and offer the opportunity to localize a story.

> Less than half of 1 percent of American farmland was owned by foreigners or American corporations with 5 percent foreign ownership Oct. 31, the Agriculture Department reported yesterday.
>
> In its first analysis of congressionally mandated reports on foreign ownership of farmland, the department said such ownership is so small that it probably would cause few problems overall but might affect local areas where such ownership is high.

Close scrutiny of the total report will determine those areas in which such foreign ownership is heavier, such as Oregon, South Carolina, Nevada and New Mexico.

Economic activity in the federal bureaucracy is so widespread that it is impossible for a single reporter to keep track of it. The key is to adapt the needs of a story to what is available among the agencies. To do this successfully, the reporter must have a "handle" on those agencies which affect his or her area or specific economic activity. It is complex, but capable of being sorted out.

State and Local Government

While federal involvement in business activities is substantial, state and local government relationships should not be overlooked. At the state level, insurance companies, utilities, retail outlets and many other private businesses are regulated to some degree. Some state offices regulate pharmaceuticals and cosmetics; others control water and air pollution.

Economic development agencies work actively to acquire industry for depressed areas of the state.

> A band of Maryland state officials, led by Gov. Harry Hughes, will swoop down on the Silicon Valley of California in a carefully planned April raid on the electronic industry.
>
> The effort is calculated to lure some of the fastest-growing businesses in the nation from their western stronghold.
>
> The Silicon Valley north of San Francisco is the home of the semiconductor industry—the people who put little green digits on watches, calculators and computers on desks. It's the place where Maryland's economic planners have stuck their red pins hoping to lure a major addition to the state's manufacturing base.
>
> While state employees are at work on a four-color brochure extolling Maryland's allure, a California consultant is at work looking for leads.

Local government should not be overlooked. Many cities have established development offices to assure even economic growth, gathering local statistics and serving as a clearinghouse for information that focuses on economic issues.

Private developers often cooperate with local government in projects that enhance economic growth.

> A zoning change that paves the way for a $13 million housing development on the West Side was approved yesterday by the Municipal Planning Commission.
>
> The development, which will include 206 rental townhouses and 100 apartment units, has been proposed by

Rush Industries, a firm which has built extensively in the midstate.

Harold M. Denning, president of the firm, said the project is being financed with loans from the state's Housing Development Fund.

The Public Information Officer

Whatever these men and women may choose to call themselves—public relations counsel, publicity advisers, special assistants to the president, goodwill ambassadors, molders of the mass mind, shepherds of herd reactions, mouthpieces, advocates at the court of public opinion, front men or spacegrabbers—they seek approximately the same thing. They are paid for using their ability and ingenuity to the end that the interests they represent, whether it be a transit corporation or a visiting magician, appear before the public in a light which is favorable and pleasant, or at least in a guise as friendly as the circumstances will permit.

The editors of Stanley Walker's day saw the press agent as a counsel for a special interest. Walker, a New York editor when he penned those words in 1934, represented one side of the equation. The press agents of the early 20th century represented the other—often richly deserving the epithets hurled at them by men like Walker.

Press agentry has evolved into public relations and public information, far more sophisticated vehicles which cover both internal and external communications efforts in corporations and government offices.

Today's corporate public relations office deals with employees of the firm, stockholders, customers, government officials, community neighbors and journalists. The range of communications is wide, covering advertising, speech writing, editing of house organs, legislative lobbying and extensive distribution of press releases explaining the corporation to these various publics.

But while the role is far more sophisticated than in Walker's day, the function remains basically the same: public relations constitutes a planned effort to influence opinion through acceptable performance based on two-way communication.

(*Webster's* defines public relations as "promotion of rapport and goodwill between a person, firm or institution or other persons, special publics, or the community at large through the distribution of interpretive material, the development of neighborly interchange, and the assessment of public reaction.")

Corporation efforts in public relations range from one-person offices to giant nationwide organizations, but whatever the size the relationships with the media are a curious mixture of friendships and animosities. There are several reasons for this.

1. Many public relations practicioners are former journalists, and fully one third held their first jobs in the news-gathering business. Many organizations today continue to require that

applicants for public relations jobs have several years experience as reporters.

2. Astute public relations people follow the news as closely as do most reporters and are familiar with current events. They travel in the same world as journalists, often attending the same professional meetings. News gatherers are comfortable with those who have these common threads of interest and awareness, and besides, they are generally interesting to talk to. Journalists at the management level often mingle with public relations counterparts at civic functions.

3. The journalist's world, like that of the public relations person, includes relationships requiring organizational reality. This give-and-take behavior, "You do this for me and I'll do that for you," is dangerous, but it often exists in the practical world of communications.

With these friendships, however, a concurrent animosity exists. Author Scott Cutlip suggests that the basic conflict between journalist and public relations person lies "in the never-ending quest by the media for exciting news, in their efforts to keep the news stream uncontaminated, and the need for money coming into their cash registers." Cutlip adds that the media's definition of news is at the heart of the problem.

More to the point is the dissimilarity in roles. While both are communicators, one represents a client or employer, the other sees his or her representation as a broader one—that of representing the public. So the reporter's perception of what is printable as news and in what form is often at variance with that of the public relations person.

Like a government official, the public relations person may not lie in response to a reporter's question, but may not always volunteer the truth. "You didn't ask me" may be the response, one that the reporter may find difficult to accept.

Recognizing these problems, the journalist should set clear ground rules in an honest effort to maintain lines of communication. Public information officers can often be helpful, if care is taken to avoid cluttering the business pages with unnecessary trivia that is crowding out important stories and ensuring that proferred material is straightforward and useful to the reader.

Care should also be taken to avoid distortion, through unchecked use of professionally prepared materials such as news stories, tape recordings and quality photographs. Most press releases are written from the client's point of view rather than from the viewpoint of the reporter or editor.

The reporter will be wise to remember that public relations people serve two functions: to create and cultivate a positive image for their organization and to serve as an information outlet or information center.

Within limits, this second function can be important to the

journalist, with pertinent questions answered, interviews set up with executives and much time saved in the process. But that first function is never far from sight. If the reporter understands and accepts this, the two adversaries can find common ground.

The following are suggestions for dealing with a public relations practitioner:

1. Set the ground rules for the relationship early, recognizing that misunderstandings can lead to animosity. Always use an even-handed approach, avoiding threats or intimidation to obtain information.

2. Determine how much authority your public relations source possesses to provide important information; then make efforts to develop sources beyond that point if necessary.

3. Do not promise a public relations person something you are not certain you can deliver, such as an agreement to place the emphasis in a sensitive story on a certain point. The best approach is never to promise anything.

4. Do not accept gratuities in any form from public relations people, including such items as lunch or dinner. Pay your own way, or encourage your editor or publisher to pay it for you.

5. Remember that public relations people can be helpful in cutting through red tape and supplying important information at deadline time. A "thank you" never hurts.

6. You don't want your source to lie to you, so don't lie to him or her. Be cautious and wary, using a healthy skepticism rather than a cynical approach.

7. Always try to explain why you did not use information provided to you that created special problems for your source. Acknowledge receipt of special material, even though you may not be able to use it.

8. Avoid violating confidences with public relations people, and try to observe release dates, although you may be the final judge.

Generating Ideas

Enterprising economics reporters generate ideas for important stories in unlikely places. The University of Missouri School of Journalism's annual business journalism awards, presented for excellence in reporting the American economy, offer examples of the variety.

—William P. Dougherty, a reporter covering Alaska, documented for the first time the extent of foreign ownership of Alaskan fisheries and outlined the complex interrelationships of the multinational corporations involved. Dougherty traced the corporate histories of every fish-processing firm in the state, following the firms as they merged, gave birth to subsidiaries and died, only to rise again under new names. He drew a detailed portrait of what happens when foreign ownership becomes dominant in an industry.

—Two reporters for the *Pottsville* (Pa.) *Republican* found apparent irregularities in the enforcement of environmental laws and workmen's compensation claims while pursuing an investigation of a bankrupt Pennsylvania coal company. Evidence showed that the firm, with assets of more than $260 million, had been deliberately liquidated and that state government had ignored warnings, and determined that, in the end, businesses and the Commonwealth of Pennsylvania were left with millions of dollars in bills.

—Peter Meyer produced for *Harper's* magazine a survey of land ownership in the United States, who owns it and who controls it, filling a vital need for information about land use for economic development, the energy shortages and the great westward movement of the population to regions where vast quantities of land are owned by the federal government.

—Virtually all published material concerning the cotton dust dilemma in the textile industry has focused on the direct effects of the dust on textile workers, the government's efforts to set standards limiting exposure and the cost of those standards to the industry. Reporter John A. Byrne investigated another major problem—compensation claims by workers who were alleged to have byssinosis, known as "brown lung." His reports offered a view of the trade-offs and the conflicts of interest that the occupational disease has created in the American textile industry.

The need for this research and balanced reporting of the economics of the private sector is unquestioned. Ralph Otwell, editor of the *Chicago Sun-Times*, put it this way:

> It is the destiny of a free-enterprise press to be a freewheeling press, spurning the complacency that business leaders would enjoy and rejecting the lethargy that public officials would encourage. As long as the business community exercises the power and control it does over the lives and lifestyles of 210 million Americans, there will be that constitutional mandate for the press to stop, look and listen at everything that business does.

A Reporter's Guide to Business-Financial Terms

This brief listing of terms common to the economic community provides the reporter with a base upon which to build. Areas such as accounting, the stock exchanges and commodity markets require further refinement of the journalist's vocabulary.

Amortization: Gradually paying off a long-term debt, by several different methods.

Articles of incorporation: The charter granted by a state authorizing a corporation to conduct business. It provides information on the incorporators, purpose, place of business and sometimes capitalization of the firm.

Assets: The published value of a company's resources, usually in terms of dollars.

Balance sheet: A formal statement detailing the financial status of a company at a given time.

Bank reserve: The cash that a bank is required by law to maintain in proportion to its total deposits.

Bankruptcy: Abandonment of a business and assignment of its assets to its creditors, thereby discharging the operator from future liability. A *petition in bankruptcy* filed in the courts is *voluntary* when filed by the debtor and *involuntary* when filed by the creditors of the firm.

Bear: One who sells securities or commodities with the expectation of buying later at a lower price; the securities or commodity market is said to be a *bear market* when there is a downward trend in prices and influence of bears predominates. See bull.

Bid and asked prices: Prices offered by prospective buyers and prices asked by prospective sellers, the difference representing the *spread* in which sales are usually consummated.

Blue sky laws: Legislation which regulates the sale of securities to protect the investing public.

Bond: A formal certificate of debt, usually long term, with the borrower promising to pay the lender of funds a specified amount at a fixed rate of interest at specified times; governments as well as private enterprises *float bond issues* to raise capital for many different reasons; the *bond markets* are the source of interaction for these negotiations, usually in the form of bids for the bonds; bonds are *rated* by experts on the basis of their soundness, with interest rates varying on the basis of "prime," "high grade," "sound," "medium grade," etc.

Book value: The probable value of a stock at liquidation; *market value* represents the selling value of a stock at any given time, taking into consideration present and prospective income and dividend payments; *par value* is the monetary value assigned to each share of stock in the charter of a corporation.

Broker: A person dealing in purchase and sale of securities or commodities, with activities regulated by the Securities and Exchange Commission.

Bull: One who purchases securities or commodities in anticipation of a rise in their prices; a rising market is a *bull market.* See bear.

Capitalization: The capital structure of a company; the sum of all of the securities it has issued, including the book value of its stocks and bonds and its surplus. Some firms have a complex *capital account;* others are much simpler.

Cash flow: The aggregate of the depreciation taken by a firm (or the depletion in the extracting industries) and the retained earnings in a specified period. Cash flow is often significant because it enhances a firm's ability to expand operations or modernize without the necessity of having to borrow money or increase its long-term debt.

Charter: Authorization through a written document to create and organize a corporation.

Clearinghouse: A central agency, usually voluntary, for collection, classification and distribution of information; banks maintain a local clearinghouse to facilitate daily exchange of checks, drafts and notes.

Commercial bank: A bank accepts deposits that are payable on demand and makes short-term loans to depositors and others; such a bank makes a *commercial loan*, usually repayable in less than a year. See savings bank.

Commercial paper: Short-term negotiable instruments, such as notes and bills, handled by banks.

Commodity market: Organized trading in specific commodities, such as agricultural products, precious metals and other articles of commerce; *commodity exchanges* and *boards of trade*, located in major cities around the world, deal in *futures*—products that will be deliverable at later dates.

Common stock: See stock.

Consolidated statement: A financial statement itemizing the operations of a parent company and its subsidiaries.

Consolidation: The merger of two or more corporations.

Corporation: A body formed and authorized by law to act as a single entity, although composed of one or more persons; it can engage only in activities specified by its *charter* or *certificate of incorporation* and is a legal entity, separate from the owners; a corporation makes possible accumulation of large amounts of capital, is highly permanent since its stock can be transferred and offers its owners limited liability for corporate debts. See partnership.

Debenture: A long-term bond secured only by the assets and general credit of a corporation rather than by a mortgage; repayment is sometimes contingent upon the profits of the firm.

Debits and credits: See double-entry accounting.

Deflation: A period of generally declining prices; *inflation* is a period of rising prices.

Depletion: Exhaustion of a *wasting asset*, or natural resource, such as oil; the government offers *depletion allowances* to encourage research for new sources and methods of extraction.

Depreciation: Gradual reduction in the value of an asset due to physical wear, obsolescence or decline in the market value; the cost of an asset is *amortized* over the period of its benefit.

Discount rate: The interest rate used by banks to convert future payments to present values, with the rate varying with conditions in the money market.

Dividend: Distribution of the earnings of a corporation to its owners; earnings may be paid in the form of a *cash dividend*, a *stock dividend*, or with other securities, known as *dividend in kind.*

Double-entry accounting: The system of recording the transactions of a corporation that maintains the equality of the accounting equation; the *debit,* or expense of doing business, is listed on the left-hand side of the *account*; the *credit*, in the form of revenue or net worth, is listed on the right-hand side of the account, with the resulting totals equaling each other.

Dumping: The sale of goods abroad at prices lower than those charged in the country in which they were produced.

Exchange: A transaction between one entity and another, technically a *reciprocal transfer*; the term also refers to a market where transactions occur, such as the New York Stock Exchange.

Exchange rate: The price of one country's currency in relation to another country's currency.

Excise tax: A tax on the manufacture, sale or consumption of goods produced.

Fair market price or value: The price or value determined by a willing buyer and a willing seller, each acting in his or her own interest.

Fair trade price: A minimum sale price for a product, determined by agreement between manufacturer and seller or distributor; illegal in some states.

Fixed assets: Assets of a relatively permanent nature, such as real estate or production machinery.

Fixed liabilities: Long-term loans, such as bonds and debentures.

Float *v*: To sell on the market a new issue of securities.

Float, *n*: The checks that are in transit between deposit in one bank and collection in a second.

Futures trading: Trading of various commodities, such as wheat, corn, beef and other products, and providing for delivery at some future date, usually one to eight months; also known as *contract trading.*

Hedge: The purchase or sale of one security or commodity in an effort to protect against possible loss in another transaction.

Holding company: A company that confines its activities to owning stock in other companies and supervising management of those firms; a *conglomerate* operates dissimilar lines of business.

Income: The excess of revenues (and other gains) over expenses (and losses) for a specified period; the *earnings per share* is usually shown on an *income statement.*

Industrials: The market term used to designate securities of industrial corporations; the Dow Jones Industrial Average is the best known market indicator.

Insolvency: Inability to pay debts when they come due; a company may be insolvent even though assets exceed liabilities.

Installment: Partial payment of a debt or the collection of a receivable, usually in fulfillment of a contract.

Intangible asset: A nonphysical asset such as a copyright, a patent, a trademark, goodwill, a lease or franchise, exploration permit, an import or export permit, or any other right that gives a company a preferred position in the marketplace; *tangible assets* have a physical form.

Interest: The charge for using money, usually expressed in an annual *rate.*

Interlocking directorate: Individuals serving on the boards of directors of two or more corporations doing business with one another.

Internal audit: An audit conducted by employees to determine whether internal control procedures are working; *external audits* are conducted by outside accountants and government auditors.

Inventory: Raw materials, supplies, work in progress and finished goods on hand which serve as a balance in an asset account.

Investment: An expenditure to acquire assets in order to produce revenue; when acquired, the investment becomes an asset.

Investment trust: A company whose income is derived solely from the holding of securities of other corporations.

Investment banker: Assists in financing long-term capital improvements for business.

Investment tax credit: A reduction in tax liability granted by the federal government to firms that purchase new equipment.

Invoice: A document detailing a sale or purchase transaction.

Kiting: The illegal practice of taking

advantage of the *float*, the time that elapses between the deposit of a *check* in one bank and its collection in another.

Lease: A contract calling for the user to pay the owner for use of an asset; a *cancelable lease* allows the lessee to cancel at any time.

Liability: A legal obligation to pay a definite amount in return for a current benefit.

Lien: The right of one person to satisfy a claim against another by holding the other's property as security.

Liquid: A business with a substantial but unspecified amount of *working capital*, which may be cash, current marketable securities or current receivables; a company closes its business by selling its assets and *liquidating*.

Merger: Two or more corporations join to form a single economic entity.

Mortgage: Conveyance of property as security for payment of a debt or a loan and becoming void upon payment or performance.

Municipal bond: A bond issued by a city, county, state or other public body to raise money; interest on such bonds is usually exempt from federal income taxes and some state taxes; often referred to as "tax exempts."

Mutual fund: An investment company, regulated by the federal government, that issues its own stock to the public and uses the proceeds to invest in securities of other companies.

Negotiable: Checks, notes and stocks which are legally capable of being transferred by endorsement.

Net income: The excess of all revenues and gains over all expenses and losses for a given period; *net assets* are the owners' equity.

Offering: Putting a security or commodity up for sale.

Operating expenses: Expenses incurred in the ordinary activities of a corporation, including selling, general and administrative expenses and excluding costs of goods sold, interest and income tax expenses.

Option: A legal right to purchase something within a specified time at a specified price.

Outstanding: Something that is unpaid or uncollected.

Overhead: Any cost not specifically associated with the production, distribution or sale of goods or services.

Over-the-counter: Negotiated transactions of securities as opposed to the auction procedure used in organized exchanges.

Partnership: A contractual agreement between two or more persons to do business as a legal entity, with each assuming responsibility for the liabilities and conduct of the business; in a *proprietorship*, an individual takes responsibility for the business. See corporation.

Patent: An exclusive right granted by the federal government which excludes others from manufacturing, using or selling a claimed design, product or plan.

Point: With reference to a stock, a point is $1; to a bond, a point is $10.

Prime rate: The rate for loans charged by commercial banks to their preferred customers, their best risks.

Profit and loss statement: See income.

Proxy: Written authorization given by one person to another so that the second can act for the first.

Purchase order: Written authorization to a seller to deliver goods, with payment to be made later.

Quotation: The bid and asked prices of a stock at a given time; the *closing quotation* is the final price for the trading period.

Receivable: In accounting, any *collectible*, whether or not it is currently due.

Receivership: Operation of a business by a court-appointed officer pending disposition of litigation affecting the firm.

Registration statement: A statement required by the Securities Act of 1933 of most corporations wishing to issue securities to the public; the Securities and Exchange Act of 1934 requires statements from companies desiring to trade their securities in public markets; the statement discloses financial data and other items of interest.

Reorganization or recapitalization: A major change in the structure of a corporation that leads to changes in the rights, interests and implied ownership of the security holders; often approved by a court to forestall bankruptcy.

Research and development: Part of the cost of doing business; *research* seeks new knowledge that will be useful in creating or improving a product, process or service; *development* translates the research findings into a new or improved product, process or service.

Royalty: Compensation for use of property, often copyrighted material, natural resources or a specially produced product.

Savings bank: A financial institution whose basic function is to gather savings and invest them in sound, long-range investments; *savings and loan associations* are nonprofit mortgage banking institutions designed to promote home ownership. See commercial bank.

Severance pay: A monetary payment, usually based on years of service, to a worker whose employment is terminated through no fault of his or her own.

Sinking fund: Earnings earmarked for reduction of long-term debt.

Speculator: An investor who seeks early and substantial returns, usually with an element of risk.

Spot trading: Trading in the commodity market calling for immediate delivery; also called *cash trading*.

Stock: A holding in a corporation, attested to by issued certificates of ownership; *preferred stock* is a claim on income or assets of a firm after bondholders have been satisfied but before *common stock* claims are satisfied; a *stock dividend* is paid or distributed to existing *shareholders;* the right to purchase a specified number of shares of stock at a specified time is called a *stock option*; a *stock split* occurs when the number of common shares is increased without additional capital contributions by shareholders; the places in which organized security trading is conducted are called *stock exchanges.*

Subsidiary: A company owned by another which owns at least 50 percent of the voting stock.

Trademark: Distinctive words or symbols which uniquely identify a corporation's product or service; the *trademark right* excludes others from making use of them.

Treasury bond: A bond issued by a corporation and then reacquired; *treasury stock* is capital stock issued and then reacquired by the corporation, resulting in a reduction of stockholders' equity.

Treasury certificates, notes and bills: The federal government borrows money for specified periods of time through issuance of these documents.

Voting trust: Stockholders agree to deposit their shares with a trustee, giving him or her voting rights on the stock for a specific period of time, but retaining other rights.

Working capital: The excess of a corporation's current assets over its total current liabilities.

Suggested Readings

KIRSCH, DONALD, *Financial and Economic Journalism* (New York: New York University Press, 1978). This former financial writer has collected an impressive amount of helpful information, including several chapters that are a must for the young financial reporter. They include: Chapter 2, "Creation and Growth of a Corporation," Chapter 3, "The Ten Key Stories," Chapter 4, "The Interpretation and Meaning of Economic Indicators," Chapter 5, "The Interpretation and Meaning of Financial Statements," which takes the reporter beyond the top stories that routinely cross his or her desk to more subtle and often far more important stories.

ARONOFF, CRAIG E., *Business and the Media* (Santa Monica, CA: Goodyear, 1979). A collection of essays discussing the economics of the private sector from a number of different perspectives.

SILK, LEONARD, *Economics in Plain English* (New York: Simon & Schuster, 1978).

SIMONS, HOWARD, editor, *The Media and Business* (New York: Vintage, 1979). These case studies are useful in putting the relationship between the media and business in perspective.

JABLONSKI, DONNA, editor, *How To Find Information About Companies* (Washington: Washington Researchers, 1979).

CHAPTER 14
Consumer Affairs

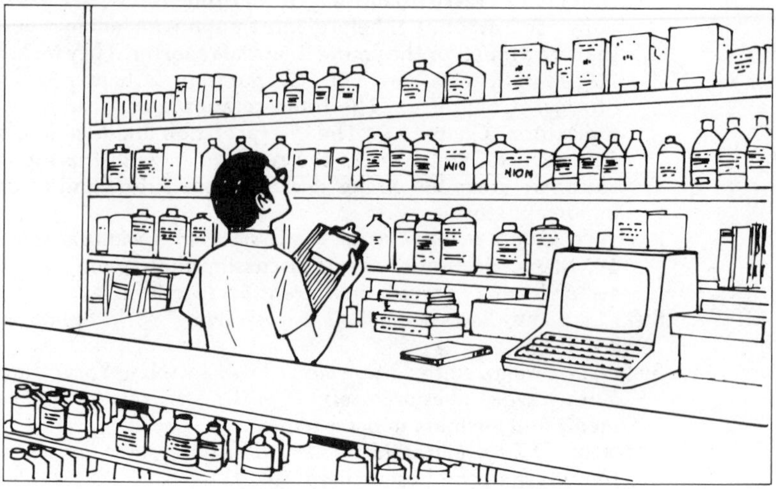

—The reader complaining to the local newspaper editor is irate. He and his family had become ill after consuming hamburgers at a nearby fast-food restaurant and felt strongly that it had been caused by the food. "Somebody ought to close that place down," he grumbles. The complaint is the newspaper's fourth during a two-day period.

—The airline had canceled its nightly feeder flight from the Pittsburgh airport, leaving 11 passengers stranded until the next day. "Service problems" with the aircraft were listed as the reason, but an unhappy passenger later complains to the newspaper editor after a civic club meeting. "The problem is that this happens all the time," he growls.

—A homeowner receives a letter from her insurance company announcing an increase in rates, citing the cost of covering "appurtenant private structures" as the reason. The homeowner objects, pointing out that no such structures exist on her property. The firm responds that it is an "automatic increase."

Are there stories here?

In each case, other questions will have to be asked to legitimately respond. But depending on the resources of the publication or broadcast outlet, the strength of its commitment to fully and fairly report general-interest news to readers or viewers, and the judgment of editors and reporters involved, these could indeed constitute stories of interest and importance to consumers.

In the case of the fast-food operation, the reporter checks the local health department, local hospitals, the local operator of the franchise, and the national office and then goes back to the complainants. The answer might lie in a roundup of these kinds of problems in the industry rather than a focusing on a specific incident.

In the airline cancellation, the reporter contacts airline officials for information, federal agencies for official records of flight cancellations and possible patterns, local airport officials, ticket offices, other airlines for patterns and other complainants.

The homeowner's insurance complaint leads to the insurance agency, consumer protection agencies for other complaints, the state insurance board for records of complaints and authorized rate increases.

There is much legwork involved, but all are worth pursuing.

Coverage of consumer affairs, for all its treacherous shoals and reefs, is often the most rewarding of all public affairs reporting. It is here that a reporter may feel most sensitively that a wrong has been righted, that fairness has been fully served and that the reader or viewer has been given "an even shake."

But it is also a high-risk beat, with greater danger that a story will be unfair or contain unwanted inaccuracies because of the new ground that is being constantly tested.

The Reporter and the Modern Consumer Movement

The relationship of distribution of goods and services to individuals who ultimately purchase those goods and services constitutes the modern consumer movement. Midway between producer and consumer, the journalist functions as an honest information broker, providing perspective on what has become an infinitely complex marketplace.

The reporter's objective is making certain that everyone receives a fair hearing—producer, distributor, sales representative, deliverer and consumer.

One of the chief components of the consumer movement is the demand for information, a demand that can be at least partially satisfied by the mass media but further fulfilled by books and periodicals directed to special consumer audiences.

Yesteryear's questions were simple:

—Where can I buy it and how much does it cost?

Today's questions, from more sophisticated consumers, are far more complex and demand greater depth of information on the part of the press:

—How dependable is the product? What is its quality and how does it compare with others of its kind? How safe is the product? What are the production conditions, and how do they affect me, the consumer? What are the social costs involved in producing the product?

The issue is made more complicated because of the media's own involvement in a part of the process—as an advertising and marketing vehicle for many of the products themselves. Despite this complication, the press today is attempting to respond to this surge in information demand, within the limitations of space, time and resources.

One reporter's in-depth account of an aborted fraud scheme, months in the making, may be epic; another's account of a manufacturer's warning about a deficient electrical device may be merely a routine paragraph or two.

No matter what the length of the story or difficulty of assignment, the breadth of consumer affairs reporting reaches every desk in today's modern newspaper office:

—The financial writer for a newspaper reports the closing of two outlets for a major national hardware store chain and then discusses the problem of their customers' service warranties on recent purchases.

—The editor of the "Family Living" section ponders publication of a story warning of cancer-causing agents in various hormonal treatments, looking ahead to local angles and sources—physicians, pharmacists, health care agencies and the university's research center.

—A sports writer, noting a certain deficiency in quality and quantity of parking around a popular city stadium, identifies what he considers the safest, most efficient and most cost-reasonable sites. Meanwhile he studies the next move—discussing the issue with city officials.

—Following complaints, the travel editor investigates the travel agencies operating in the community, explaining discrepancies in fees and in guarantees of resort bookings. The editor has already checked the state attorney general's office for possible violations of law.

—The court reporter covers a series of consumer complaints originating in small claims court, resulting in editorials on the newspaper's page of opinion that the municipal court system be updated. Many consumer stories conclude in the judicial process and wind up in the hands of the court reporter.

In this sense, consumer affairs reporting transcends a single beat, spreading instead to every journalist on the staff and constituting basic "pocketbook" stories that affect every reader or viewer in some way.

Some Historical Dimensions

It was only when the whole ham was spoiled that it came into the department of Elzbieta. Cut up by the two-thousand-revolutions-a-minute

> flyers, and mixed with half a ton of other meat, no odor that ever was in a ham could make any difference. There was never the least attention paid to what was cut up for sausage; there would come all the way back from Europe old sausage that had been rejected, and that was moldy and white—it would be dosed with borax and glycerine, and dumped into the hoppers, and made over again for home consumption.

Most consumer historians date the consumer protection movement from these and like passages written by Upton Sinclair in *The Jungle,* published in 1906 and possessing a fiery strength that lit up the country. Sinclair's novel about the Chicago stockyards was an immediate and smashing success. For all its melodrama, the book carried with it the conviction that all the injustices actually occurred, if not to the immigrant hero, then to other mistreated workers of that period.

The Jungle was not designed for reading at the breakfast table. Sinclair, who as a young writer spent weeks observing life in the stockyards by wearing old clothes and carrying a workman's dinner pail, designed his novel as a weapon, a potent propaganda tool. As it turned out, few politicians could withstand such angry and naked words on paper. Their constituents were reading this stomach-turning account of the way their main courses were being prepared for the tables of America:

> There would be meat tumbled out on the floor, in the dirt and sawdust, where the workers had tramped and spit uncounted billions of consumption germs. There would be meat stored in great piles in rooms; and the water from leaky roofs would drip over it, and thousands of rats would race about on it. . . . These rats were nuisances, and the packers would put poisoned bread out for them; they would die, and then rats, bread and meat would go into the hoppers together. . . there were things that went into the sausage in comparison with which a poisoned rat was a tidbit.

Such graphic passages by Sinclair galvanized Congress into action by the middle of 1906 and led to enactment of the first Pure Food and Drug Act, which provided the public with at least limited protection from impure foods and drugs.

Sinclair's exposé of the meat packing industry and the subsequent uproar was the opening chapter in the battle for consumer protection.

The traditional Latin phrase, *caveat emptor*—let the buyer beware, had more meaning prior to passage of that legislation, but it remains the practical watchword in today's marketplace. However, its impact has been diminished through development of further protective legislation and greater consumer awareness.

The first consumer protection law was enacted in 1872, making it a crime to defraud through use of the mails. Until the uproar over *The Jungle*, legislation was laboriously enacted piecemeal, with limited and superficial protection aimed at impurities in foods rather than the broader issue of government regulation to assure quality.

Early consumer groups were also limited, and a New York organization, the Consumer's League, was the first, in 1891, to press for social reform. The movement began to spread, and the National Consumers League grew into 20 states. The 1906 legislation stimulated growth of these consumer groups, called leagues, committees and clubs, and encouraged further reform. Weaknesses in legislation gradually brought on a lethargy that lasted into the 1920s. It fell to two other writers, Stuart Chase and F. J. Schlink, in 1927 to again galvanize the public and politicians into action.

In the book, *Your Money's Worth*, they pictured the consumer scene as a "Wonderland of conflicting claims, bright promises, fancy packages, soaring words and almost impenetrable ignorance." Chase and Schlink attacked high-pressure salesmanship and called for scientific testing and establishment of product standards to protect consumers.

In contrast to Sinclair's novel, *Your Money's Worth* was highly readable non-fiction produced by a certified public accountant and an engineer-physicist. Their approach was factual rather than propagandistic, and their material read much like a reporter's investigative story today:

> The firm (Mack, Miller Candle Co.) sold as "beeswax altar candles" a candle containing less than 50 percent of beeswax, although the practice of the Catholic Church required more than a 50 percent beeswax content. Analysis by the Bureau of Standards showed that the company's candles contained only 11.5 percent of beeswax.

In their chapter on adulteration and misrepresentation, the authors clinically covered dozens of such examples, ranging from solid cotton blankets labeled as "woolnap" and containing no wool, to firms selling pure food gelatin in which glue had been substituted for gelatin.

Much of their information came from findings by federal agencies in existence at the time and from congressional hearings:

> An amusing note appears in the Congressional hearings on the "truth in fabrics" bill: white salmon, it is noted, has been dyed pink and sold as pink salmon.

Chase and Schlink researched congressional testimony by a laryngologist from Philadelphia, Dr. Chevalier Jackson, who told a committee that a number of dangerous lye products, such as drain pipe cleaner, bore either no poison label at all or only a very inconspicuous one.

> One product cited contained 75 percent of the violently corrosive poison, sodium hydroxide. Far from bearing the poison label, the printed matter read: "does not injure the finest fabric or the most delicate skin."

Chase and Schlink checked the findings of the National Fire Protection Association and reported that

> Four worthless and unsafe electric irons selling for $1.00 each were found to burn out in from 3 to 35 minutes. 15,000 dozen of these were imported by one New York dealer.

Far from merely mining public records, Chase and Schlink constituted themselves as a committee of two to survey and investigate consumer affairs for themselves. As they duly noted in *Your Money's Worth*, the authors "found 18 out of 22 gasoline pumps giving short measure" in a single Illinois community.

In their summary, Chase and Schlink declared, "It is the consumer's move. If he wants to leave Wonderland, there is a way out, and the clear possibility of drastically reducing the cost of living. He can get his money's worth if he is willing to organize to get it. The market responds to organized pressure."

They recommended that the consumer adopt these and other stances:

—Ask advertisers to produce the scientific facts upon which their claims are based.

—Refuse to deal with firms making fantastic or misleading claims or who are guilty of unfair competition.

—Call the attention of editors to misrepresentations either known or apparent in advertising.

—Look for weights on package goods; figure out how much you are paying per pound. Then look at your bank balance.

—Ask why baking powder or bread comes in 14½ ounce packages instead of pound packages and why soap and a host of other things have no quantity marking at all.

A half century later, they are still valid.

A Continuing Upsurge in Interest

Your Money's Worth focused a vague discontent among consumers into new product-testing laboratories and by the early 1930s led to updating of the Food and Drug Act. Cosmetics were included in food and drug protection, and new labeling standards were added.

Following World War II, there was a new upsurge in consumer protection interest, and in 1962 President John F. Kennedy articulated the points that were to become a powerful grass roots movement. In his Consumer Message to Congress, Kennedy laid out a "Consumer's Bill of Rights":

—The right to safety, to be protected against the marketing of goods which are hazardous to health or life.

—The right to be informed, to be protected against fraudulent, deceitful or grossly misleading information, advertising, labeling or other practices and to be given the facts needed to make an informed choice.

—The right to choose, to be assured access to a variety of products and services at competitive prices; in those industries in which government regulations are substituted, an assurance of satisfactory quality and service at fair prices.

—The right to be heard, to be assured that consumer interests will receive full and sympathetic consideration in the formulation of government policy and fair and expeditious treatment in its administrative tribunals.

Subsequent development of consumer programs reflected a growing awareness of those principles, spurred along by pressure from organized consumer groups.

Legislation was enacted that year requiring that drugs be proven effective and approved by the federal government before they could be marketed. Subsequent administrations continued to reflect the new consumer awareness, and "truth-in-packaging" legislation (the Fair Labeling and Packaging Act) was passed by Congress in 1966, requiring that household products be labeled clearly and accurately as to contents, net quantity and manufacturer. It barred use of qualifying words such as "jumbo ounces" or "giant half quart."

By 1967, a National Commission on Product Safety was established to identify categories of potentially harmful household products and report back to Congress. That commission was followed in 1971 by a Consumer Product Safety Act which established an independent commission with power to set and enforce safety standards for thousands of household, school and recreation products.

Meanwhile, the consumer movement picked up new impetus in 1965 with publication of Ralph Nader's book *Unsafe at Any Speed*, which quickly became a best seller. Nader charged that the high incidence of death and injury on U.S. highways was largely the fault of auto manufacturers who sacrificed safety for styling in the interest of higher profits.

Consumer advocate groups sprang up in the wake of Nader's attack on the auto industry and included the Center for the Study of Responsive Law, Public Citizen, Inc., the Center for Auto Safety and the Public Interest Research Group. By 1970, Congress had enacted a national traffic and motor vehicle safety act, a wholesome meat act, a natural gas pipeline safety act, an occupational safety and health act and truth-in-lending legislation.

The nation's capital was awash in outspoken consumer advocacy groups, and the Federal Trade Commission, the Food and Drug Administration and other federal agencies were charged with failing to defend the interest of consumers. A major reorganization of the FTC was instituted in 1970, taking the form of expanded field offices to speed up complaints. The FTC's power was further broadened in 1970 when the Supreme Court ruled that its authority to protect consumers went beyond antitrust laws.

Today an Office of Consumer Affairs, operating within the Department of Health and Human Services, analyzes and coordinates federal activities in the field of consumer protection.

By the mid-1970s, agencies and consumer advocate organizations had placed large segments of the nation's business community on the defensive with charges, citations, cease and desist orders, and new regulations:

—The Interstate Commerce Commission in 1975 issued new rules governing interstate shipment of household goods.

—The Federal Trade Commission the same year accused the nation's major car rental firms of conspiring to monopolize automobile rentals and keep prices artificially high at U.S. airports.

—As part of an investigation of air safety, a group headed by Ralph Nader charged in 1970 that small plane manufacturers were producing "the most lethal of the major forms of transportation in the U.S." The report charged the Federal Aviation Administration with inadequate supervision of the industry.

—The Supreme Court ruled in 1975 that setting of uniform minimum fee schedules by lawyers constituted price fixing and was a violation of antitrust laws.

Six Different Views

Nowhere will the reporter deal with sources offering a greater divergence in their perception of the marketplace and how it should operate than on the consumer affairs beat. The point of view shifts with the individual and his or her sponsors.

—The housewife may want only assurance that the purchase she has just brought home from the store has been carefully pretested.

—The store owner is cognizant of this, but has a different problem: how to dispose of many of these items to cover the cost of doing business and make a reasonable profit.

—The advertising sales representative may be sympathetic to the housewife's demands but has another problem: how to help the store owner create a strong demand for the product.

—The manufacturer has still another problem: producing the product cheaply enough and in sufficient quantity to assure a profit.

—The consumer advocate, persistent and sometimes strident, wants only assurance of the product's quality and safety and a fair sales approach.

—The government agency official, armed with a directive to assure quality, safety and/or performance, cannot promise it absolutely without an army of inspectors.

In a sense, the consumer affairs reporter must see the marketplace through the eyes of *all* these participants and add an additional ingredient—that of filling a totally impartial communications gap.

For all practical purposes, does the reporter become a consumer advocate when he or she decides to pursue a story?

There may be some validity to such a claim by some of these participants in the marketplace, particularly those with axes to grind. The reporter will simply have to do his or her job and stay in the middle of the road.

As the labor reporter finds that the objectives of management and unions often sharply differ, the consumer affairs reporter will learn that the interests of the business community and the buying public do not always coincide.

A news story may have the effect of alerting the public to a problem, but it also poses the danger of injuring someone's business, sometimes quite unfairly, or of impugning the motives of a professional group without cause.

The reporter who digs up unsavory but factually accurate accounts of a fraudulent roofing contractor must exercise care that an entire roofing industry is not tarnished with publication of the story. Another reporter uncovers details of a highly questionable real estate transaction by a broker and follows it through its final resolution before the State Real Estate Board. Suspension or revocation of the broker's license should mirror the fact that this could happen to anyone in the marketplace but also reflect the fact that it constitutes a specific incident, not necessarily an industry-wide approach.

Accuracy is equally important. Jack Foster put it this way to his Gannett Group co-editors:

> It's impossible to lay too much stress on accuracy. Not only is the newspaper's credibility at stake, but businesses could be driven to the wall, families broken, bread taken from the mouths of children by inaccurate consumer reporting. Stories that nail a business should be checked, double-checked and triple-checked. Every effort must be made to get response from the target, and the response should be in the same story. Response in a follow-up story may get lost.

The Demands of the Beat

With so many voices clamoring to be heard, and such a wealth of information that strikes directly at a newspaper's readers, the consumer affairs reporter is pressed to make rapid and correct decisions in a demanding field.

Aside from the danger of becoming a consumer advocate and the risks of inaccuracy or unfairness, there are many other impediments:

—Sources of information are not always readily available. The target of an investigation is often uncooperative and even threatening, drying up information pipelines and tying up a reporter's time in trying to pursue a legitimate story. Often the reporter will hear, "I'll sue you. You'll hear from my lawyer" or "I'll have your job for this, if you print that story."

Maintaining a cool head, the reporter will go about the business of contacting people around the subject, agencies that may have information relating to the story and other sources. Every effort should be made to convince the subject, angry though he or she may be, that it is in the best interests of everyone to clear the air with a legitimate news account.

While government agencies are increasingly helpful, offices are often located in other cities, with telephone contact not always the most effective method of obtaining detailed information. Some agency officials may be difficult to reach and apathetic to requests for information. Refusal to give up and knowing where to go are among the reporter's best tools. Frequent changes in regulations also complicate the reporter's work.

Often private sources offer information to the consumer affairs reporter that is not easily obtained elsewhere. For example, the Association of Home Appliance Manufacturers compiles product performance reports that show how products of various manufacturers measure up to uniform standards.

—Traditional beats at least offer the reporter some patterns, but consumer affairs reporting often tests new ground. The question, "Is there a story here?" must be answered more carefully.

The old adage, "Money makes the world go 'round," is familiar to all, and the reporter will learn that the business and financial communities do not always appreciate the efforts of a journalist whose material has the potential for casting an unfavorable light on their activities.

Business enjoys and encourages "upbeat" news stories, but the consumer affairs reporter is often cast in the role of a "heavy" because of material that carries negative connotations. A series detailing the incidence of warranty complaints to the Better Business Bureau may not make business happy. Neither may a story that examines in detail the desperate shortage of downtown parking, for it could send many potential customers out to the suburban shopping malls. What the consumer sees as a "positive" and productive story may exist as a threat to the business community.

Advertising departments of newspapers and broadcast outlets have been known to come under intense pressure from local retail outlets, lending institutions and public utilities. Because of this, the reporter is well advised to solicit the advice of his or her editor on potentially controversial consumer stories. A publisher may feel discomfort from the legitimate exposé of a specific advertiser, but he or she may find it difficult to disapprove if the story is fair and accurate. It is best to be practical—the publisher may kill the story anyway.

The most important rule here is that the reporter has the backing of his or her employer. Consumer affairs will be difficult if not impossible to cover without implicit support. Otherwise, there is danger of merely going through the motions.

—The consumer affairs reporter, more than most, must wrestle with the problem of translating highly technical material into the language of laypersons. Coping with information on musical "woofers and tweeters" can be as complicated as a pharmaceutical development requiring the posting of names of specific generic drugs.

A report by an agency that monitors air pollution and deals with specific particulate matter in the atmosphere may involve research in charts and statistics that will frighten all but the most persistent reporter. Similar problems exist in the technical "legalese" contained in the small print of a product warranty.

The reporter should never hesitate to ask questions. If one source cannot help translate material, there are others. It will not pay for the reporter to be shy about seeking advice. It's far better to display one's ignorance before one expert than in a story beamed to thousands of readers.

—Reporters and editors are constantly bedeviled by their own self-censoring concerns. Are they being fair in pursuing the story? Have they become, in effect, consumer advocates in the manner in which they have covered it? Is a sensitive story going to help many readers but affect the community adversely?

Constant questioning of motives is necessary to allay such doubts and ensure objectivity and balanced reports. Gannett editor Barney Waters cited problems that occur when the consumer reporter strays from these guidelines. His newspaper had published a series based on information gathered from a former used car salesman:

> We called it, simply enough, "Confessions of a Used Car Salesman." In the series, the fellow told the consumer reporter little "tricks of the trade," such as stuffing banana peels into axles to disguise rear end noises; a guy who visited used car lots regularly to set back mileage figures on the speedometers at $10 a job; warming up engines each morning so that they would start right up; etc. The series, we thought, was a sincere attempt to alert potential car buyers to possible pitfalls in dealing with unscrupulous vendors.
>
> We told the army of auto dealers who descended on us, "We didn't mean you guys. We mean unscrupulous used car dealers."
>
> "Who are they?" they asked.
>
> "Well, uh, whoever does those things."
>
> And while we are all well aware that these things happen all over, our

unnamed source—who certainly didn't want to change his status of anonymity—was the only proof we could offer that such things indeed did occur in Brevard County, Florida.

Reviewing the problem later, Waters listed what he believed were the basic errors in reporting the story:

1. We placed too much faith in the word of one person, however expert he may have sounded.
2. We were lulled to sleep by a näive belief that if it's good for the consumer, how much can it hurt?
3. We didn't give the used car dealers a chance to respond to charges from one of their former salesmen.
4. Our timing was terrible. It was an exposé of used car sales methods at a time when the auto industry was reaching up for rock bottom.

Such broad-brush consumer reporting is unfair and should be avoided. The reporter and editor should always ask themselves whether their approach is totally professional, a question that should answer itself.

—The potential for defamation, resulting in expensive libel action, is present to a greater degree in consumer affairs reporting than in many other public affairs beats. A government agency's report on defective equipment in the auto industry may constitute a legitimate story, but use of potentially defamatory words could bring on a libel suit.

An expert's opinion that training procedures at a local school of cosmetology appear to be "incompetent" should be edited as closely as another's comment that a recent business transaction seemed "unprofessional."

The following is a list of some other "red flag" words and phrases that could endanger an otherwise impartial consumer affairs story—and the interests of the public—unless thoroughly and carefully documented:

altered records
adulteration of products
cheats or cheating
collusion
corruption
credit risk
defaults
false weights
fraud or fraudulent
illegitimate
sharp dealing or wheeler-dealer
short in accounts
shyster
smooth and tricky
sold out to a rival
swindle
unethical
unworthy of credit

Sources, Contacts and "Expert" Advice

Consumer reporting helps people to cope with changes in buying practices, business practices and legislation affecting those practices. Under this broad umbrella lies nearly every aspect of modern living:

money, people and their relationships with one another, finished goods, services provided, recreation, insurance, property, foodstuffs and transportation, to identify a few. The range of reporting is nearly endless, bounded only by the energy, time and resources of the journalist.

Out of this variety flows contact with many levels of citizens and corporate enterprises, government officials and private organizations. The ability to relate to sources at all these levels is essential to success on the consumer affairs beat.

THE CONSUMER

Citizen-consumers constitute an important level. As material is published which relates to them, readers will identify with the issues and often contact reporters to discuss their concerns.

A contact with the reporter may be made merely to air a personal complaint; often a telephone call, letter or personal visit will open the door to a more general problem that leads to a major story. A consumer with a questionable consumer warranty may in fact reveal hundreds of others with similar problems. A complaint about the practices of one small loan firm may lead to the exposure of a communitywide problem and subsequent legislative action.

Frequent visits from average citizens are time consuming, but they often yield important story leads. The reporter should develop the capability for patiently hearing complaints but without spending a full day on them. Personal complaints must be separated from those that suggest general-interest story material. The reporter's own nose for news, matched with opinions from his or her editors, will most often decide the newsworthiness of material.

MEDIA OMBUDSMEN

It should be remembered that the average reader or viewer may subscribe to a broader definition of "consumer affairs reporting" than the journalist. While some information may not be so labeled, it represents important information to thousands of persons. A review of a local visit to a restaurant, concert or movie provides consumers with information enabling them to make intelligent choices in spending money. It is not considered "hard news," but the consumer sees it as useful information.

The same can be said of the numerous ombudsman services that have been adopted by newspapers and broadcast outlets around the United States, often cast as "action lines" or "consumer hotline" columns. To many consumers, these question and answer columns are as much consumer affairs as are major news developments and often hit much closer to home.

The format is fairly standard: Readers write or call and detail their complaint, and a reporter or staff researches it. The complaint and its resolution are later published.

Consumers are drawn to these ombudsman services, because many find themselves in a situation that can only be resolved through the threat of adverse publicity to a business establishment. At the same time, businesses often feel threatened by them.

Care must be taken that a business is not unfairly attacked by a dissatisfied customer.

A furniture company and an irate customer may be unable to settle their differences without seeking redress in small claims court. The customer turns to the newspaper's action line to solve the problem. The onus is always on the reporter or action line staff to ascertain the *absolute facts* in the dispute, time consuming and not always easy to do. In the interests of fairness, it should be done and the results published. Demands of a fair and equitable ombudsman service dictate substantial resources on the part of the newspaper or broadcast outlet to allow this research to be carried out. Unfortunately, this is not always the case. A publication that commits itself to such an ombudsman service should also commit its resources to a fair and accurate report.

General interest stories often emerge from modest questions to an action line column. One reader's complaint that she was charged sales tax on wall-to-wall carpeting installed in her home as a permanent fixture led to the discovery of violations of the state's consumer sales practices act by carpeting firms. Consumers became eligible for sales tax refunds, but new issues were raised: Did the act also mean to include other permanent fixtures for homes purchased in stores, such as door knobs, built-in cabinets and appliances?

> Merchants should not charge their customers sales tax on household appliances and other items they sell and permanently install in the home, State Department of Taxation officials say.
>
> But fixtures and home appliances the buyer purchases and later installs himself are subject to the standard 5 percent sales tax.

GOVERNMENT OFFICIALS AND LEGISLATORS

A pending consumer bill may be locked up in a legislative committee, requiring knowledge of the legislative process, the issue and the personalities involved. Elected officials have become increasingly sensitive to consumer issues.

> Washington—U.S. Sen. Howard Metzenbaum swung a roundhouse punch yesterday at what he called a lack of consumer protection policies in the current administration.
>
> The Ohio Democrat specifically targeted for criticism the administration's backing of petroleum deregulation, calling the policy "a disaster and an abomination." Metzenbaum said the American consumer "has not been winning here in Washington. He has lost and lost, again and again."

Many stories can be "localized" as they appear, but basic information from federal and other agencies is often equally effective "as is," as this Associated Press story shows:

What are you really getting when you buy a product "as is"?

The Federal Trade Commission says many people are confused by the term, particularly when it comes to used cars.

In most states, the FTC says, if you buy a car marked "as is," the dealer is not legally responsible for any repairs needed later on. And "later on" can come as quickly as five minutes after you drive away.

An FTC survey showed one out of three consumers believed that even if a car were purchased "as is," the dealer would still have to pay for some of the repairs if the car broke down within 30 days.

CONSUMER ADVOCATES

Advocates see their function as specifically and fully protecting the consumer. They are vigorously committed to their cause. And while their information may be regarded as "expert," the reporter must remember that they are advocates and, as such, provide only one side of the story. They can be tremendously helpful in broadening the reporter's knowledge of an issue, so long as the advocacy function is recognized.

PROFESSIONAL AND BUSINESS PEOPLE

Dealing with people whose occupation is their livelihood or whose funds are tied up in a business requires a somewhat different approach. A store manager who perceives a consumer problem as threatening to his or her interests will refuse to cooperate with a reporter who can promise nothing but what the manager sees as "bad publicity." It is going to take every persuasive power possessed by the reporter to convince a reluctant businessperson that his or her best interest is at stake in openly discussing the problem and that the press is not out to "get" him or her.

Unsubstantiated rumors are always worse than the real thing, it should be pointed out, and the opportunity to provide his or her side of the story will be helpful to the businessperson. The implicit threat that the story is going to be published anyway because of its newsworthiness may also have to be used.

With all his or her persuasive techniques, the reporter may still come up empty-handed. Trying to change the businessperson's mind through someone else is often helpful. A business associate, relative or even another newspaper staffer may succeed where the reporter has failed.

Corporate executives deal with the press through public relations offices, necessitating another different approach. They must be convinced through an intermediary that their best interests are at stake in providing information to the press. The reporter should not give up after a "no comment" but apply persistent pressure until the end.

AGENCIES THAT SERVE A VARIETY OF PUBLICS

At every level, the reporter is going to be dealing with public agencies whose employees and clients do not always see an issue the same way.

A health department may be under public criticism because of its intention to change regulations providing for free immunization shots for pre-school children. Caught between a board of directors concerned with tightening a budget and angry parents, employees of the department will be understandably reluctant to comment. The reporter will have to work his or her way through the agency hierarchy to find someone willing to enlighten the public on the issue.

TALKING TO THE "EXPERTS"

Out in the world where nearly everyone has an opinion, it is easy to find instant "experts" who are willing to discuss a controversial consumer issue. It is not so easy to locate one who is really qualified to do so, however. Experts can generally be found at institutions of higher learning or government agencies that constitute impartial and unaligned publics in a controversy.

An argument over feasibility of developing borderline land by property developers may call for the opinion of a geologist in the state department of natural resources or a professor in the city's university system. Members of the school of business in a local college can often be persuaded to discuss and even research a controversial study affecting business or industrial property and effects of zoning changes.

Physical education experts might help settle an argument over the usefulness of a new exercise product on the market that "guarantees" weight loss. A nutritionist or home economist will often provide sound information on the efficacy of a new foodstuff ingredient.

The consumer reporter should take the time to research education facilities in the community and agencies to determine what contacts could be fruitful, should the occasion arise to make use of them. Analysis of economic trends usually falls to an expert in a university's business or economics department. Other areas in which expertise can be counted on include a school of pharmacology, accounting, health services, nursing, marketing or management departments, a college of science and even a music department. Qualified experts are available, and their comments often add an extra dimension to consumer affairs reporting.

Consumer Coverage: Reporter at Work

The consumer affairs reporter need not be a supersleuth, lurking in back alleys for scandalous "scoops" that will shake the business community to the core. Controversial material has a place, but so does any routine story that promises to interest or inform readers. By the simple expedient of contacting local experts, the reporter can produce "how to" stories that will generally touch a responsive chord in most readers. The examples are endless:

1. How to cope with door-to-door sales representatives.
2. How to get the most out of your medical dollar.
3. How to complain effectively.
4. How to cope with postal service problems.
5. How to go to small claims court for relief.
6. How to reduce your grocery bill while continuing to eat well.
7. How to buy a used car with some assurance of safety.
8. How to handle auto repair.
9. How to obtain income tax refund forms.

These examples are basic "pocketbook" stories, but each offers the reporter an opportunity to explore a specific area which often yields clues to other information the reader should possess.

While researching the small claims court story, for example, interviews with attorneys, court officials and litigants themselves may uncover reasons *why* people go to court, as well as *how*.

In researching methods for getting the most out of the medical dollar, the reporter may also quickly determine *why* costs of medical care are so expensive and *who* actually determines how much people pay.

In this way, one consumer affairs story often leads to others containing related material, some of it not strictly on the consumer affairs beat. The reporter should not hesitate to tackle unglamorous stories; they often lead to what turns out to be the best of the week.

An endless variety of material also exists in "what it means" stories. Changes in quality standards for consumer goods often necessitate unraveling complicated information.

> Dating of a wide range of new products in the grocery stores will provide consumers with protection from outdated products, but it's going to cost them more.
>
> That's the consensus of merchants and distributors who responded to the new regulations putting a "Last Date to Be Sold" line on breads, cakes and other bakery goods in the stores Monday.
>
> "I expect prices to go up 10 percent or 11 percent because of returned items," Fred C. Brown, distributor for Betsy Brown Breads, said yesterday.

New regulations and new products, and how they affect readers or viewers, provide a constant source of material. Other consumer stories stem from frequent price changes, and the alert reporter explores the *why* as well as the *what*.

Surveys should be carefully constructed to answer questions in widespread price-changing situations, including different levels of reportage. The attendant at the gasoline pump often reveals more about a developing trend than will the distributor or manufacturer, although they too should be contacted.

> The attendant named Rob shook his head as he filled the gas tank at the 7th Avenue station.
> No, he told his customer, he didn't really know why the price of gasoline continued to rise.
> "Mister," Rob said, "I don't think it's ever going to stop." Then he added, in a confidential tone:
> "I'll tell you what, though. They're about to put new faces on these pumps, and you'll be buying by the liter next week."

News developments emerge in many shapes from many sources, and new consumer protection codes provide a wealth of information. A city's plan to begin a program of inspection of food service establishments generates comment from local health department sanitarians who will administer the program, a cross section of the establishments that will be affected, and from officials on how the program will work and what it means to the consumer. Many newspapers routinely publish violations of health codes, listing establishments in violation and the reason. An afternoon tour with an inspector gives the reporter an opportunity for a close-up view of the program and its effectiveness.

Routine coverage of health inspection is occasionally broken by more dramatic developments, and the reporter's contacts will be helpful when serious charges are leveled.

> A pattern of widespread routine payoffs by city restaurateurs to health inspectors has been found by undercover investigators, Police Commissioner John Swardson disclosed today.
> Because of the findings, Swardson said, the Health Department will move to revoke or suspend the license of any restaurant found to have offered or paid a bribe to an inspector.
> Seven restaurateurs accused by investigators of offering them unsolicited bribes, ranging from a free meal to \$50, face administrative hearings, the commissioner said. The two-year inquiry has been conducted jointly by police and the Health Department.

Most communities have some form of local consumer protection agency in operation, but officials in some of them continue to oppose such agencies for a number of reasons—cost of the service, pressure from local merchants and others. The reporter will find that these agencies and their officials are key consumer contacts.

The agencies must overcome the natural reservations of business, which often sees the agency as an "enforcer" and publicist for consumer advocates. "I'm sure they (local businesses) breathed a collective sigh of relief when they found we weren't going to be some kind of gestapo," said the director of a city's new consumer agency. The agencies work closely with the business community in educating and informing the public of its rights, using their law enforcement powers with care.

"An 18-year-old will go all over the state just to find the right car," one agency director notes, "but he'll go down to Joe's Money Mart and end up paying 40 percent interest. They simply don't know how to get credit. Nobody, not even their parents, ever told them."

Such agencies can be tremendously helpful to a reporter in pointing to such consumer-oriented stories that otherwise might never see the light of day.

> If someone offers you a "free vacation" in Las Vegas, the best thing to do is call his bluff.
>
> Bogus certificates for three-day/two-night vacations in the gambling city are apparently being sold throughout the area, says Jon Reed, director of the Consumer Protection Office.

While law enforcement aspects of such consumer protection agencies provide the most dramatic stories, their education function acts as the trigger for many other routine accounts. Federal funding usually can be found behind most local agencies, generally in matching amounts. A consumer credit counseling service may offer assistance to anyone who asks for it, helping those with massive credit problems. New community service councils are being established to look after the interests of consumers.

> The Community Service Council has proposed a new system to provide the public with a faster and easier way to settle grievances against merchants and manufacturers.
>
> The system would provide for establishment of consumer-claim centers around the city, with officers empowered to award quick judgments and pay settlements to persons with legitimate complaints.
>
> Since the money would come from a government-organized fund, the problem of collecting Small Claims Court judgments from recalcitrants would be overcome, says a CSC official.

At the state level, the focus of consumer protection agencies is on protection rather than on education. The state attorney general is often entrusted with this task, and new legislation puts enforcement teeth into regulations.

> Thirty Instant Muffler shops in the area have been taken to court by Attorney General William C. Brown on charges they violated state consumer laws while doing repair work on cars.
>
> Brown filed a $400,000 suit in Common Pleas Court yesterday, charging that the shops charged customers for unnecessary repairs or services.

Common problems handled by the attorney general's office include disputes involving credit agencies, most business establishments, lending institutions and mail-order companies. The office should be checked regularly for new rules affecting consumers.

> New rules governing automobile rustproofing go into effect today.
>
> The rules, promulgated by the consumer protection division of the attorney general's office, set specific requirements for firms to detail work that will be done on rust-damaged areas.

Other state agencies often have a hand in consumer protection. State property commissions investigate land-grabbing schemes, legal services offer assistance, police agencies often function in the consumer affairs field and the agriculture department is active.

> Meat quality in the state has improved in recent years, and artificial preservatives have largely been eliminated from meat, an Agriculture Department official says.
>
> Of 885 meat samples taken by employees of the department's consumer protection division last year, only 37 violations were found, G. Harold Arms, director of the division, noted yesterday.
>
> "None of the violations involved preservatives," Arms said. "We used to find preservatives all the time, but we broke that up."

Federal, state and local agencies are the reporter's major weapon in producing accurate and balanced consumer news accounts. Whether the information is obtained from the federal government's Consumer Product Safety Commission or from the local Better Business Bureau, the "official" imprimateur of the agency offers a safe umbrella for the reporter.

Ideas for consumer-related stories come from many sources, and organization of an effective file can assure quick reference when a subject seems ripe for localization. Not all wire service stories reach publication, and a telegraph editor should be encouraged to pass on discarded consumer affairs material. Many newspapers are publishing in-depth stories on specific issues, and exchange papers should be checked regularly for material that may also be relevant to readers in the community.

A Consumer Checklist

The consumer affairs reporter should regularly monitor such special publications as *Home Furnishings Daily, The Wall Street Journal, Changing Times, Consumer Reports, Money* and others. The *Federal Register* points to new regulations about to go into effect, and many federal agencies publish newsletters on consumer affairs.

The American Council on Consumer Interests produces a newsletter, and the federal Agriculture Department publishes *Farm Economics Review*, often helpful in consumer affairs. Many attorney general offices issue bulletins warning of shady practices, and other agencies offer guides to use of public services.

The Federal Trade Commission publishes *FTC News*, the Office of

Consumer Affairs distributes *Consumer News*, the Department of Energy offers *Energy Reporter*, and the Department of Transportation publishes *Transportation Topics*.

The reporter will find a wealth of information at his or her fingertips through federal agencies. Questions involving business practices can be addressed to the Office of Ombudsman for Business at the Commerce Department; consumer education information is available at the Office of Education; housing questions can be answered through the Department of Housing and Urban Development; and many sources of information are available on product safety. Sources include the Consumer Services Office of the National Highway Traffic Safety Administration, the Bureau of Drugs at the Food and Drug Administration, and the Agriculture Department.

A number of helpful books should also be useful, including John Dorfman's *Consumer's Arsenal*. This book includes a tactical manual designed for consumers but offers the reporter a helpful state-by-state listing of consumer protection agencies as well as a "complaint encyclopedia" telling where to go with what complaint.

Consumer Sourcebook, by Paul Wasserman, lists government organizations, private associations and trade names.

Mission of the Reporter

In 1926, a New York advertising agency proclaimed, "We who have to bring in the business must get out before the beloved customer and shout, search, halloo, promise, concede, coax, be funny, coo, thump, seek, knock, punch and *get* the order."

That was the salesman's mission in the 1920s. More than half a century later, the consumer affairs reporter's mission is the same: to place the "business" in perspective so that the shouts, halloos, knocks and promises can be more easily analyzed by the public.

PART FOUR

PUBLIC AFFAIRS:
An Overview

CHAPTER 15
Government and Media in Conflict

THE mayor was red-faced and incensed.

"You were unfair," he hissed to the reporter as he entered the council chamber. "Don't you know how you put me out on a limb and sawed it off? You emphasized all the wrong points in that HRC (Human Rights Commission) story."

As the mayor stalked away, forestalling a response by the reporter, a pleased bystander leaned over and nudged her.

"Good story. You finally got our side of the story. Don't listen to old Foxy," said the bystander, a council member who had witnessed the exchange.

Nowhere is the public affairs reporter's role more complex than in relationships with public officials, all of whom have what they firmly believe to be the most efficacious programs and priorities, not the least of which is survival in public service. A seemingly straightforward reportorial account of the issues surrounding a controversy will be construed as total hostility by one party and as blatant cronyism by another, depending upon the circumstances.

Deeply etched in the psyche of many journalists is an image of St. George (themselves), armed only with a slender lance (typewriter, video display terminal or minicamera), sallying forth as the "good guy" to do battle with the Dragon (all self-serving politicians and administrators in government), who if not held in check will devour all in its path. Their unassailable assumption is that anyone on the public payroll is guilty of engaging in activities inimical to the public interest and that the journalist's life-and-death task is to discover and expose these malfeasances.

Reality, however, dictates a far different image and spans a much broader spectrum. At one end stands the militant and hostile St. George. At the other stands the fawning sycophant, intent on merely serving as a public relations mouthpiece for the public official.

Occupying the shifting center are the journalists and officials who perceive a healthy adversary relationship as a service to the public. However, establishing a legitimate operating range is difficult if not impossible, and these questions remain:

1. Of what exactly should the adversary relationship between press and government consist, if indeed there is to be such a relationship at all?
2. How far is too far in such a relationship?
3. To what extent should the press cooperate or collaborate with government without compromising its principles?

One reporter suggests that the adversary relationship is simple: it is responsibility for achieving different goals. A working press seeks to know; a bureaucrat seeks to preserve the status quo and is reluctant to tell.

Another sees the adversary relationship as skepticism of public policy, with the press firmly holding the institution of government to account for all its actions.

Still another sees the relationship as not unfriendly but, rather, as a continuing effort to exert constant pressure to obtain information in the public interest. Respect for each other's position serves as the benchmark in the relationship between reporter and official.

Compounding such an effort to quantify the relationship, however, the official definition of adversary tends to place it at the more hostile end of the spectrum. Says *Webster's*,

adversary (adjective): having or involving antagonistic parties or interests.
adversary (noun): one that contends with, opposes or resists; antagonist, enemy or foe; an opponent in a game.

Press-government relationships should not be characterized as a game, but their frequently antagonistic nature often places the relationship at one end of the spectrum. These enemy-focused definitions must be tempered by the reportorial necessity for objectivity and balance. As examples, try to place the following overt acts along the spectrum between total hostility and outright cronyism:

—An officeholder takes the reporter to lunch and refuses to allow him or her to pick up a share of the modest check.

—At a later date, the officeholder calls the reporter to provide what he describes as an "inside story" on how the decision was made to permit construction of the new power plant and asks the reporter to print it.

—The reporter later contacts known antagonists of the officeholder and seeks what the reporter believes to be "the goods" on him.

—The reporter checks with another officeholder before writing the story on an issue in which the second official has only a peripheral interest.

—The reporter rides with the officeholder to a meeting of the legislature in a distant city, talking politics and listening to the officeholder's reminiscences about his days as a struggling young attorney trying to support a family.

—The reporter waits until the officeholder leaves the city, then visits his secretary in an effort to pry out information on support for a federal judgeship nominee.

—The reporter knows the officeholder is holding informal meetings with associates to settle sticky issues before they are aired in public, but does not report such sessions.

—The reporter knows about such meetings and arranges to be outside the door when the group breaks up, asking individuals what they discussed and their stands on the issues.

Many variables will, of course, influence the response of the reporter on each of these examples, perhaps even the size of the lunch check or the reason for the visit to the legislature. The size of the publication and city in which the reporter is operating will also influence the response. Is the lunch meeting for routine material or for information that holds more important implications? Has the reporter sufficient experience to recognize that he or she may be compromised in a subtle manner by the lunch meeting?

The relationship between reporter and public official is also shaped by the length of time they have dealt with one another and by the possible friendships produced. Superiors also play a part, either by exerting pressure on the reporter to resist all blandishments or to succumb to those that promise newsworthy results.

Location plays a part. The reporter may be operating in a small city or in Washington, D.C. The public official involved may possess sufficient prestige that this question becomes irrelevant. A powerful U.S. senator in the city for a brief visit, with one objective to "touch base" with a reporter friend, offers one level. Two local figures who have announced that they will run against each other for the sheriff's job offers another.

A last variable—the reporter's own experience, education and subconscious prejudices and biases—also plays a part in determining what constitutes an adversary relationship.

A Natural Tension

It has been suggested that a natural tension exists between a government that exercises power and the press that reports, explains and criticizes the use of that power. Political scientist Ithiel de Sola Pool sees the tension stemming from the disturbing position in which the journalist is placed:

> To do his job he must grow close to politicians and win their trust, but his job is also to publicly expose them. To do his job, he must develop confidential relations with sources and protect those sources, but his job is also to strip the veil of privacy from everyone else's business.

The relationship creates conflict and tension within a shared system, Pool contends:

> The whole relationship of reporter and politician resembles a bad marriage. They cannot live without each other, nor can they live without hostility.

Another researcher, William L. Rivers, argues that too many reporters take on the role of "sweetheart," not only with federal officials, but with state and local public figures as well. Rivers lauds reporters who challenge what he calls "officialdom":

> The necessity for a challenging journalism does not spring primarily from the fact that officials lie. They do. But far more often, the public is misled because well-meaning, high-minded officials really believe in their policies and programs. They would not be likely to serve well if they did not believe. But believing as devoutly as many of them do, they approach the public interest through a narrow channel and from a narrow perspective. Such men cannot be expected to *really* serve the public interest because their perspectives are so narrow—unless they are called to account by an independent press.
>
> These facts have led me to the conclusion that the proper role of the political reporter is that of adversary. As George Reedy (press secretary to the late President Lyndon B. Johnson) said, the official views public communications in terms of help or hindrance toward a common goal; the reporter views public communications in terms of what he regards as reality. The divergence is inevitable. The politician will seek to promote his strategies and programs by preserving his options and by hiding most political frictions; he usually has a vested interest in tranquility. If he succeeds, decisions are often made without public debate.

There is no unanimity among political scientists. A different viewpoint is expressed by Irving Kristol, who sees the adversary relationship as a concept inappropriate to journalism:

> You cannot have an adversary procedure that works only one way. So, if media is an adversary to government, should the government be an adversary to media? I think it is as idiotic for the government to be an adversary to the media as for the media to be an adversary to the government.

These two dissimilar views point up the broad range of philosophies regarding the role of the press and raise further questions:

—Is there a limit to the pugnacity that a reporter should display in dealing with public officials? Is there a balance point on the spectrum of tension beyond which a journalist should not venture?

The adversary relationship, if it should exist at all, becomes a delicate balance of tact and antagonism, of cooperation and conflict. Not much is required to disrupt that balance.

As the late columnist Walter Lippmann suggested, if press and government have a common obligation to "provide a picture of reality on which men and women can act," does an adversary relationship in imbalance tend to distort the "picture" and make understanding more difficult for the public?

Leon V. Sigal sees reporters as important "allies" of public officials. In his book, *Reporters and Officials*, Sigal says,

> Their favorable treatment of information can aid an official's cause at some future date. Dispensing exclusives to a reporter increases the likelihood of such treatment because the exclusive or "scoop," the story he and only he obtains, enhances a reporter's reputation among his colleagues. One man's leak is the other's exclusive. Keeping reporters in their debt is a subsidiary motivation in most officials' disclosures.

Former Secretary of State Henry A. Kissinger, while recognizing the reality of some kind of adversary relationship, also sees it as having definite limits. In an address to the American Society of Newspaper Editors in 1976, Kissinger pointed to the need for compassion and understanding of the complexity of decision-making:

> I would like to stress that I believe we have gone through a decade of national trauma, and that sometimes in the relations between the press and the government the attitudes are those of generals who endlessly fight old battles over and over again.
>
> And while I recognize that the relationship of the press to government is importantly and healthily an adversary relationship, as Americans we are also partners in a common task, and we must never forget that the peace and progress of the world depends, finally, on American vision and on American constancy.

Kissinger, himself known as a master in coordinating news events, is not on record as commenting on the views of a White House reporter who in 1977 adopted what might be considered an "adversary stance" toward relationships with former President Jimmy Carter:

> Only five and a half weeks after taking office, Mr. Carter appeared to be adopting some of the attitudes of his predecessors about secrecy and news leaks. Saying he was "quite concerned" about the number of people who have access to this kind of information, Mr. Carter said he had been working closely with Congressional

leaders to try to reduce the overall number of people who have access to knowledge of covert operations.

Such a stance would indicate an element of hostility on the part of both media and government. Perceptive public officials are aware that the media has substantial power to shape government—both policies and leaders—through dissemination of all kinds of information, including some with questionable news value.

A presidential press secretary might decide to prohibit television cameras at news briefings because he believes it is in the best interests of his superior to do so. When President Carter's press secretary, Jody Powell, banned television cameras, American Broadcasting Co. correspondent Sam Donaldson offered his explanation for the decision:

> Powell believes that television is a "hot" medium, that television has an impact beyond the written word. Powell needs to do things in the press room, he believes, that he does not want to be seen doing. Powell dances and weaves, he backs and fills, he evades. And he does it very well.

This may not square with Lippmann's "picture of reality," but it does illustrate that an adversary relationship works both ways. George Reedy, former press secretary to President Johnson, explained the relationship this way:

> Any time a president gets into political trouble, he will have a bad relationship with the press. To people in the White House, the press comes to symbolize a president's troubles. They are a group of outsiders who ask a lot of nasty questions.

Is Some Hostility Beneficial?

Those supporting the adversary theory hold that some element of hostility is helpful to the system, since it serves as a defense against political alliances that might leave the public unprotected. The question remains, however: What degree of hostility is necessary? Does it become unhealthy and inimical to the public interest at some point, undercutting a reasonable expectation that legitimate national goals can be achieved?

Reporter Jules Witcover sees three basic responsibilities for the press in reporting affairs of government:

1. Reporting what the government says.
2. Finding out whether it is true.
3. Determining whether the policy will work, or whether it did or did not work.

This seems a simple and cogent formula; yet political scientist Pool raises the question that a further function of the press might be to create a consensus behind national policy, enabling the diverse elements in a nation of more than 200 million persons to assure that such a policy is carried out.

Can the press be both an agent of cohesion and at the same time serve as a source of criticism and even abuse?

The possibility exists that press support of non-divisive issues can be an instrument in helping create a national consensus, but opponents argue the line separating divisive issues from non-divisive ones is narrow.

Press coverage of the U.S. role in the Indochina war offers an excellent example. In 1968, the administration of President Lyndon Johnson was referring to the Tet offensive in Vietnam as a "major allied victory" which left the enemy, the Vietcong, "crippled and ineffective after an obvious suicide mission." Government officials bitterly criticized the press for insisting that the Tet offensive was actually a defeat for American military forces. Years later, after publication of the now famous *Pentagon Papers*, which detailed U.S. involvement in the Indochina war, the press and public learned what U.S. military leaders were saying privately:

> To a large extent, the Vietcong controls the countryside. His determination appears to be unshaken. His recovery is likely to be rapid, his supplies adequate. He has the will and capability to continue [the war].

While the Vietnam conflict was an example of government insistence that the war effort was supportive of peace, decency and freedom, millions of Americans believed otherwise. This genuine division of opinion was merely being reported by the media. This may be regarded as an easily definable "divisive" issue, but others not so divisive come to mind:

—To help control inflation, the government pleads with people not to hoard supplies, and the press takes up the plea.

—To reduce auto fatalities, the government urges people to fasten their seatbelts and observe federally mandated speed limits.

—To protect the environment, the government urges recycling of cans and paper and calls on the public to close water taps tightly.

—Smoky the Bear receives reams of publicity as the symbol for the need to protect the nation's forest resources.

—Bond drives to improve education facilities, library resources and a multitude of other worthy causes are supported by the press.

Whether or not these are "divisive" depends upon the perception of each of them by the public and segments of the public. Almost any bond drive, whose goal is to increase taxes on the property owner, is bound to be controversial, and the long-distance highway hauler will argue that the 55-mile-an-hour speed limit may save a few lives but is unrealistic and is costing him and the nation's buyers money.

So while it is clear that the press serves as a major instrument of communication in the policy-making process, its role as an agent of "cohesion" is open to question. Merely because an issue appears to be non-divisive is no reason for the press to support it. The sharp divisions of a decade ago over the conduct of the war in Vietnam remain, and new issues continue to crop up. Meanwhile, the argument over whether the press should be adversary or partner continues unabated.

Journalists themselves criticize the press. Patrick Buchanan, an important White House aide during the term of President Richard M. Nixon and whose writing is well known, argues that the press serves as "a cooperator, collaborator" with the institutions with which it agrees, maintaining an adversary relationship only "with the men and institutions with which it disagrees."

But Tom Wicker, a columnist for *The New York Times*, placed heavy emphasis on the need for an adversary relationship:

> It is often argued that government cannot function if its officers cannot deal with one another in confidence, but seldom if ever has it been so graphically demonstrated [by the *Pentagon Papers*] that when men are relieved of the burden of public scrutiny, uncomfortable though it may be, no other form of accountability takes place.

Other Reasons for Disagreement

In seeking limits, however broad, to the adversary relationship, journalists and public officials find little ground for agreement. Political scientist Paul Weaver attributes this partly to the basic literary form of the news story, placing it in the Aristotelian category of epidictic rhetoric, whose heart is praise and blame. Analysts utilize deliberative rhetoric, Weaver said, that aims at balancing costs and benefits of policy alternatives. Countering, journalists point to today's political rhetoric, which certainly lacks a deliberative tone, although its participants believe it does.

Kristol takes another approach. He believes that journalists lack specialized expertise (in which many appointed and elected public officials are similarly deficient) that would enable them to master analytic writing about highly technical government problems. "They turn instead to procedural matters that they can understand: who took what stand against whom in Congress debate, the course of an issue through the courts, who sides with whom on an issue." Because of this, Kristol suggests, the adversary stance replaces the "craft of getting the facts straight."

However, editor Harold Liston challenges Kristol, arguing that the adversary role of the press does not target government but, rather, those who staff the government, the policy-makers and administrators:

> Adversaries can share goals and beliefs. Lawyers often share goals while occupying adversary roles. In any event, I've never met one on either side of a case who did not claim justice and truth on his side.

Liston adds an important ingredient:

I have no love for the careless use of "adversary" to describe the press' role in dealing with government. But surely it does not mean hostility toward American institutions. However, something more than good-humored skepticism must be among the tools of a free press.

Liston's point makes sense. The reporter deals daily with the people who propel government, guide it, are entrusted with it and are responsible for making it work. Indeed, news accounts abound with proposals advanced and actions taken by such officials, personalities in themselves. Rarely do reporters return to enabling legislation covering a specific government function except for background purposes.

Seldom is the basic function of the Internal Revenue Service brought into question by the press, whereas rules, regulations and changes in them are constantly a source of news. The controversy over a new cabinet-level Department of Education, for example, is fueled by statements from proponents and opponents of the proposal rather than by the basic issue of education itself.

Many factors intrude to create a so-called adversary relationship. Even the manner in which a news story is written, the way in which it is edited and the play it is given in publication are open to question. Several years ago, a straightforward wire service story received wide front-page display with this lead:

> Washington—The Federal Trade Commission slapped price-fixing and other charges against the dental profession Friday, an action aimed at allowing Americans to shop around for tooth care.

The dictionary definition of "slap" suggests "putting, placing or throwing with careless haste or force" or "to assail verbally." Accordingly, some newspapers recast the lead to the story, placing the material in somewhat different perspective:

> The Federal Trade Commission accused the American Dental Association Friday of illegally restraining competition among dentists by prohibiting its members from advertising their services and engaging in price competition.

To impute some deep-seated hostility to the wire service reporter would be unfair, and most journalists pass off the incident as an effort to create readability. The risk remains, however, that the effort constitutes an unacceptable reporting approach for an enlightened public.

To further complicate this example, the information was released to the press late on a Friday afternoon, too late for Friday newspapers but designed for Saturday publication, normally the smallest newspaper package of the week. Was it the intention of the information givers at the federal level to minimize dissemination of the material? The complex tug-of-war between press and government inhibits a direct answer, but the result is to suggest that those tugs constitute a sort of adversary relationship.

The "Secrets" of Government

At what point does the intrusion of the press in government become unwarranted and thus an unacceptable adversary relationship? Some journalists contend that any information that "escapes" into the hands of a reporter is usable. This, they suggest, creates the adversary relationship between press and government.

Columnist Jack Anderson was awarded a Pulitzer Prize in 1970 for reporting the confidential details of meetings of the National Security Council in Washington. While the administration of President Richard M. Nixon professed to be neutral in the then sensitive dispute between India and Pakistan, Secretary of State Henry A. Kissinger privately directed the State Department to "tilt" toward Pakistan. Anderson was criticized for breaching national security in publishing the material.

It can be argued that Anderson was merely a courier in disseminating the information and that someone in government *willed* that the information be made public. When a government official "leaks" information, the reporter may merely be an instrument. Once in possesson of such material, it is impossible to return it to a state of secrecy.

—A Washington reporter has written for many months, based on assurances by government officials, that no war is in progress in a distant country. He has done so because U.S. officials, in what they perceive to be the nation's interest, have been lying about the "war." The reporter obtains fresh information that clearly indicates such a conflict is in progress, breaching the "secret." It is clearly impossible to return the "secret" to government; to continue reporting "there is no war in progress" as officials maintain would make the reporter an arm of government.

The knowledge that has "escaped" is thus usable and helps to create the adversary relationship between press and government.

Nowhere is this better illustrated than at the local level when a community attempts to acquire new industry in an effort to improve the economic climate of the area. Several cities may be bidding for location of a major new industry. The facility, which promises to employ up to 2,500 persons, has the potential for dramatically improving the living and working conditions of the city in which it decides to locate. The race is on among several cities to acquire the industrial plum.

Public officials argue that premature publication of the sensitive negotiations could jeopardize acquisition of the industry, and the reporter agrees to keep the "secret," awaiting the moment when officials are ready to make the announcement.

The information will deliberately remain unpublished until it "escapes" into the public domain, but not every such negotiation is a clear case of "hold the information and you will receive it exclusively from us." A nearby city has apparently lost out in the bidding, and the newspaper in that community, under no such constraints, publishes details of the affair, along with the information on cities remaining in the running for the acquisition. The "secret" is no longer a "secret," despite local officials' contention that publication would continue to endanger acquisition.

Other factors intrude to complicate this hypothetical negotiation. The 2,500 jobs envisioned for the facility might turn out to be only 200 because of automation. Positive effect on the economic climate might be minimal. In fact, prime industrial land might be put to better use. In short, the disadvantages of acquisition might then outweigh the advantages, but there has been no public debate.

With the public totally unaware of these factors because negotiations are "secret," the reporter risks the loss of objectivity and any adversary status. In this case, the community's economic health and the perceived need for stimulus constitute another of the variables that determine the degree of adversary relationship betwen the press and public officials.

How Far Is Too Far?

The public affairs reporter has engaged the mayor in a freewheeling prime time television conversation, touching on such non-controversial subjects as progress on the new sewage disposal plant, new snow removal policies and purchase of riverfront property for recreation expansion.

Now the reporter takes a different tack. Councilman Svoboda had resigned suddenly the previous week, citing press of business and family problems as his reasons. "Mr. Mayor," the reporter asks, "could you give us your thinking on the effect of the Svoboda resignation and a vote on the proposed city income tax?"

The mayor stiffens perceptibly. It is a politically sensitive subject. He responds carefully.

"That's something Council will have to work out, Bob. But I'd rather not get into it at this point, if you don't mind."

The reporter leaves the politically sensitive issue behind and turns easily to other subjects. But the question remains: At what point does the adversary relationship, seemingly non-existent at this stage of questioning, become an unjustified burden in the mechanics of governing?

No journalist will contend that this legitimate question about the resignation constitutes unwarranted pressure on the mayor. But what if the reporter had persisted, asking it again and prefacing the second question with the comment, "The people have a right to know, Mr. Mayor," Or even a third time, with still another comment to the public official: "I'm afraid we'll have to insist on a response, sir."

The amicable exchange even holds the potential for turning ugly at some point if the reporter wills it, effectively putting the relationship in permanent cold storage.

What if the reporter had turned to the vast television audience and said,

"You are looking at a public official who refuses to answer what the press sees as a question in the public interest."

Then he turns to the mayor and asks,

"Are you going to answer or not, Mr. Mayor?"

Long before he reached this extreme point, the reporter left the politically sensitive question hanging, but at any point farther along the line, pursuit could have been interpreted as being unfair to the public official.

In this case, the reporter, to assure a continuing and amicable relationship with the mayor, stopped short of fulfilling his mission to his audience—to provide further information on the resignation and its effects. He could have pursued the issue, but only at risk to himself.

The adversary relationship thus becomes a delicate balance of tact and antagonism, of cooperation and outright hostility.

In another example, the president of the Board of Education, who is also a local physician, finds the demands on his time excessive and limits his accessibility to the press to business hours. A reporter for the morning newspaper, however, believes the limitation is unreasonable and insists on rousing the school official at midnight with questions on a pending school issue. The public official and the reporter see totally different limits on the need for accessibility, with the official finally coming to look on the reporter and his publication as "adversary." It might have been a different relationship, however, had the publisher acceded to the official's demands and called off the reporter.

When *The New York Times* obtained a copy of the Defense Department study detailing U.S. involvement in Vietnam in 1971, the newspaper began publishing the hundreds of pages of top-secret material, so classified for reasons of national security. Attorney General John N. Mitchell sought and obtained an injunction temporarily barring the *Times* from further publication, on grounds that publication of the material compromised national security.

In this case, the government believed the press had exceeded its bounds and had to be restrained. Even some members of the press believed that the adversary relationship had been stretched too far by publication of the sensitive material, even though the study was years old by that time.

Although the Supreme Court ultimately upheld the right of the press to publish the *Pentagon Papers*, and the *Times* resumed publication, the issue remains. How far is too far in the adversary relationship?

The answer remains unknown, constantly shifting along the broad spectrum of decision-making between government and the media.

Allowing "Administrative Convenience"

The city hall reporter for a medium-sized newspaper learns that an important administrative position has opened through a resignation but that the position is not politically sensitive. The resignation story is written. The mayor wants to appoint a political ally but needs assurance that the party will accept. The mayor doesn't want the embarrassment of being forced to later offer the job to someone who will then know that he or she is second choice. The mayor prefers to make the offer and obtain a rejection—if one is forthcoming—in secret.

From the mayor's point of view, this course of action is defensible. But the reporter must ask questions: In allowing such administrative convenience to the mayor by withholding speculation on the nominee, is the reporter acting in the public interest? Is it important to the public to learn the identity of a potential administrator several days before the mayor plans to announce it publicly?

Other questions arise: How much energy should be devoted to prying out information that public officials will produce in the normal course of events? When the reporter decides to identify candidates before officials are ready to do so, does it constitute an unnecessary adversary relationship?

Some indication of the wide range of response comes from two *New York Times* editors, Max Frankel and James Reston. Frankel offers this observation on administrative convenience and its effect on the adversary relationship:

> Scotty Reston and I sometimes differed because when I was diplomatic correspondent, he thought one of the great things to do for the prestige of the newspaper was to report who would be the new ambassador to Moscow three days before it was announced. I used to say, "Scotty, I can find that out. It's easy. It's going to take me two days. In those two days I might learn something far more substantial, which we would never learn if I didn't invest the two days. But the ambassador to Moscow we will find out by the announcement." Is it important?
>
> He regarded me as insufficiently zealous for feeling that it isn't. Always want to be first, he argued, because vigilance resides in that instinct. He feels that if you get into the habit of waiting for government to tell you *when* it wants to tell you, you're going to lapse on more serious matters.

The Dangers of Cronyism

The downtown restaurant was filled with lunchtime small talk when the commissioner swept in, flanked by three associates. Stopping to shake a hand here, slap a shoulder there and laugh at a pale joke, the commissioner and his party worked their way toward a table at the rear of the restaurant.

But he took a moment to pause and cordially greet the reporter who was lunching with a friend, alerting the reporter to a new development in the marina project. It is one of the commissioner's favorites. "Stop by the office this afternoon, Joe, and we'll look at the plans." The camaradie swells and the reporter is subtly swept up in the excitement of a successful public figure's appearance.

How the public pat on the back, the friendly and highly visible exchange which transfers minute portions of the official's charisma to the reporter affects news coverage is open to question. But the subtle process raises legitimate questions about the relationships between those who report government and those who run it.

The reporter's raison d'être is to communicate the business of government to the public. In that daily employment, the reporter deals with powerful and well-known personalities at the local as well as the national level. What journalist is not affected when a charismatic (which is at least partly how men and women are elected in the first place) public figure singles him or her out for a special public greeting? The traditional press card is rarely necessary for the deference accorded reporters by officeholders and bureaucrats. It comes naturally, as night follows day.

Through this process, friendships between journalists and public officials develop, with reporters often engaging in tacit bargaining with those they cover. The process is subtle. By withholding from the public some of what they know (occasionally embarrassing information), reporters assure continued amiable contact and keep sources in their debt. Exposing a public official, or sometimes merely irritating him or her, endangers that channel of information forever to the reporter. So stories that might have that effect are handled cautiously.

The effect of these close relationships, at whatever level of government, serves to make the reporter a part of the system, with a continuing danger that he or she will feel a greater stake in supporting the system than by exposing abuses in it. The seduction is subtle, and good journalists will consciously take steps to minimize the danger. Washington correspondent James McCartney warns that a loss of independence leads to even more serious problems:

> Some reporters are so enthralled by authority that in the extreme form reporters become spokesmen for their news sources rather than dispassionate observers. They become sloppy about recognizing that alternative views may exist, and about digging out and including alternative views in their stories. Over a period of time, some may be press agents for those they are covering and, indeed, sometimes perform that role, or something very close to it.

The Weapons of "War"

In the face of possible problems involving inquisitive journalists, a public official has a number of weapons, including the offer of friendship and preferential treatment. Other weapons include censorship, where possible, extensive bars to information access and outright lying. Every clever public official worth his or her salt will develop methods for monitoring and controlling the flow of information.

The press, however, possesses its own arsenal, including its tradition for exposing and promoting news and events which public officials would prefer not to be identified. Inside this shared relationship, the reporter and public official engage in various levels of confrontation. Seldom is it at one end of the spectrum: nearly always it is near the center.

The late editor V. M. Newton believed strongly in a healthy adversary relationship, and he encouraged his staff to ferret out abuses in government. Sometimes, Newton warned, the latent hostility engendered by the diverse roles in the relationship breaks into the open:

> The politician seeks to lull the people with pleasantries of government. The journalist seeks the cold hard facts of government. Sometimes these don't jibe, whereupon the politician reaches for the microphone and assures the people that the journalist is the worst sort of skunk.

Inside this shared system, reporters often find themselves caught in the middle ground between public officials, whose policies and goals are not always parallel. Broadcast executive William Small warns:

> Congressmen are not altruistic or idealistic in sharing information. They share because it is self-serving to them and they share only that information which serves this end. Their goals, however, are often at variance with those of the administration and that is why they are a reporter's natural allies and most profitable source.

Herbert Gans sees a system of mutual obligation between reporter and decision-maker, which incorporates the journalist into the process by inviting him or her backstage, but with the requirement that the journalist subtly limit coverage of the actual government.

> The reporter learns all (or almost all), but cannot tell; the decision-maker tells all (or as much as he has to), but knows he will not learn about it in next morning's newspaper. The relationship is perhaps less a system than a tug-of-war, for the decision-maker is always trying to reveal as little as possible, and the reporter attempts to publish as much as he can without alienating his source.

Nowhere is this tug-of-war more pronounced than during political campaigns, although there is argument that the process is never ending, since officeholders are constantly under pressure from the electorate to maintain a mandate.

Editorial page criticism of a public figure often hinges realistically on the possibility that the official might one day soon be the choice of the newspaper's editorial board for re-election, despite that official's shortcomings. Criticism of the official might be further tempered with disclaimers that the criticism is merely "constructive." Even more subtle are the temperate reports in the news columns, sometimes reflecting the "pluses" in the officeholder's actions rather than the "minuses."

Human nature being what it is, the danger is always present that the journalist who is on a first-name basis with the public official will accept the thinly disguised propaganda in the form of press releases, publishing it with little or no reference to origin and with little or no editing. The excuse of the small-city editor is the rush to get the newspaper on the street by deadline. Far too many newspapers stand guilty of "letting things get by on a busy day," as one editor puts it. In this, there is danger that the press will become an unquestioning arm of government, no longer fully serving the public.

The journalist's most effective defense against cronyism lies in awareness of its dangers and refusal to allow any fragment of it to influence his or her judgment. New York *Times* editor James Reston, a proponent of the moderate view of this adversary relationship, puts it this way:

> When they (press and government) do their best work, they are allies with one another, and with the "remnant" in the nation that wants to face, rather than evade reality. Clever officials cannot "manipulate" reporters, and "clever" reporters cannot "beat" the government. From both sides, they have more to gain by cooperating with one another, and with the rising minority of thoughtful people, than by regarding one another as the "enemy."

Booster or Watchdog?

At the local level, the press is at its most effective in performing a multitude of functions in its community:

Reporter—providing a balanced and accurate account of news about government;

Watchdog—digging out evidence of incompetence, error and outright wrongdoing by officials who serve the public;

Critic—offering an independent assessment of government performance;

Forum—providing the vehicle to carry out an ongoing and open debate of public issues;

Ombudsman—assisting citizens in communicating with their government.

These functions are indisputable, but some journalists and political scientists often add another: *collaborator* or *cooperator* in the public interest, sometimes serving as *booster* in the community to promote what the press perceives as the public welfare.

However, the term "booster" implies a blind, Babbit-like approach, suggesting an overly supportive enthusiast who views the community only through rose-colored glasses, ignoring its blemishes and other imperfections. A more appropriate designation, in the view of some journalists, might be "community builder" or "responsible citizen."

No matter the designation, the intent of this popular function is that the press identify with the community, willing it to prosper because the future of the press is inextricably tied to it. It is seeking ways to encourage that prosperity. Unfortunately, this function does not always neatly jibe with the other functions listed.

The mayor of a small Florida city once told a young reporter: "We don't want a big town, son. We want a GOOD little town."

The response was delivered off the cuff in reaction to the state's proposal that a new and improved access highway be located nearby. The question: If most of the citizens of that community believed strongly as the mayor did, was there an obligation on the part of the press to fulfill its function so that the goal of the majority could be realized? Or was it more essential that the press independently analyze the proposal and come up with a reading at variance with that of most of the citizens? The answer depends on what the publication—and its employees—see as the publication's mission to the community.

In researching Levittown, New Jersey a number of years ago, Herbert J. Gans found that its citizens wanted a performance by the press that would give the outside world an idealized picture of the community. If an event reflected negatively on Levittown, many readers preferred to have it hushed up.

The danger of disruptive incidents that force the reporter and his or her editor to make difficult decisions is always present. The result is to often fulfill one function or the other: watchdog to the community or "responsible citizen." This is one example:

—The reporter covering the County Health Board is knowledgeable about its operation, and the public is receiving good coverage of the agency. The members of the board are concerned citizens intent upon assuring the community that the agency offers good service, mainly diagnostic.

The agency is sufficiently large to have several department heads, one who has served the agency with distinction for nearly 20 years. However, a private audit determines that the official has been quietly misusing some of the funds with which she has been entrusted.

Before details of the misuse of funds become public, the employee decides to reimburse the agency for the questionable funds, amounting to nearly $2,000, and take "early retirement." The board, after much private discussion, decides to accept this approach, merely establishing safeguards to protect against future incidents. It declines to discuss the matter with the press, preferring to drop the matter.

The reporter is left with the choice of insisting upon pursuit and publication of the story or allowing it to quietly fade away, justifying the decision by arguing that no purpose would be served by detailing the imperfections of the employee and agency.

Most journalists, of course, will insist upon a public accounting, arguing that the public has a right to know how its business is being handled. Others will take the approach that the money has been returned and that no prosecution was initiated; thus the matter is best left unpublished.

A survey published in *Public Opinion Quarterly* in 1971 indicated that the press is generally supportive of authority in a community. The community press, it found, "generally tends to protect community institutions rather than report the disruptive side of public life."

Even prize-winning newspapers sometimes fall into this trap. A Southern newspaper which consistently won national awards through the years with exposes of shocking jail conditions and discriminatory judicial practices in nearby communities rarely pursued such crusades inside its own, drawing substantial criticism from other members of the press in the state.

During Gans's research on Levittown, one local reporter told him:

> I would never publish anything nasty about C________. If he makes a mistake, either a political or a moral one, I tell him to watch out, but I don't put it in the paper.

"The reporter begins to identify with the community," Gans wrote, "omitting uncomplimentary items, and helping people and causes he thinks deserve publicity." Gans cited one editor who provided extra space to a local organization and kept out stories of its internal conflicts, because the organization provided a worthy community service.

Other editors, however, insist on a more thorough accounting of local events. In a much bigger city, Chicago, a reporter during the 1960s researched the thoroughly disruptive internal conflicts in a local cultural organization dependent upon local contributions, and the matter was duly aired in the news columns of his newspaper.

"If you are not a combination watchdog and booster, over a period of time you will disassociate yourself from your readership, alienate yourself and have no impact at all," said a Midwestern editor, but he warned, "You can't be a cynical watchdog all the time either."

Another warned that undue emphasis on the newspaper as "community builder" would also reap adverse dividends:

> If "booster" means running a story in the spring saying Mannington is a nice place in the spring, I see nothing wrong with that. But if it means covering up or ignoring a serious housing problem in the city for fear it might frighten away industry, that's absolutely out.

While pure "boosterism" has no place among the reporter's functions, it is important that the journalist develop an affinity for where he or she lives and works. No cut-and-dried formula exists for achieving this goal, but development of a philosophy that assesses the community and its people with some sensitivity is desirable. This, coupled with a professional approach and an awareness of the ethical considerations, will help to achieve the desired place on the spectrum.

In developing such a philosophy that will place the adversary relationship in desired perspective, the reporter might ponder the words of John Milton:

Give me the liberty to know, to utter, and to argue freely according to conscience, above all liberties. The liberty and not the right: the reader cannot demand knowledge, he can only demand the right to acquire it; the labour or learning must be his own.

And to know, not just to have opinions which may or may not be well based: if he wants knowledge, he must have the proper information, as full and accurate as can humanly be had.

This knowledge, further, is preliminary. Only when it is absorbed can there be utterance and argument. The reader, perhaps, asks no more than to know; it is already a considerable demand. But the writer, the journalist, asks also to utter and argue freely. *He must know and offer the same opportunity to others.*

So it is with today's journalist, who faces the barbs of outraged public officials and a demanding public. The public affairs reporter must be willing to endure the heat, as the late President Harry S Truman so aptly put it, or get out of the kitchen.

Suggested Readings

MAGRUDER, JEB, *An American Life* (New York: Atheneum, 1974). Recollections of a White House official during the Nixon years. Of special interest to reporters are the Prologue, Chapter IV, "Learning the Ropes," and Chapter V "The Office of Communications."

SAFIRE, WILLIAM, *Before the Fall* (Garden City, NY: Doubleday, 1975). Chapter 5, "The Press Is the Enemy."

DUNN, DELMAR D., *Public Officials and the Press* (Reading, MA: Addison-Wesley, 1969). Chapter 5, "Public Officials' Views of the Press."

SIGAL, LEON V., *Reporters and Officials* (Lexington, MA: Heath, 1973). "The Organization and Politics of Newsmaking."

SMALL, WILLIAM, *Political Power and the Press* (New York: Norton, 1972). Chapter VI, "When Politicians Seek to Seduce, Anticipate or Intimidate" and Chapter XI, "Whose Battle Is It—the Press's or the Public's?"

RESTON, JAMES, *The Artillery of the Press* (New York: Harper & Row, 1967). Chapter V, "The Influence of the Press" and Chapter VI, "What Can be Done?"

RIVERS, WILLIAM L., *The Adversaries* (Boston: Beacon, 1970).

DORSEN, NORMAN, and STEPHEN GILLERS, editors, *None of Your Business* (New York: Viking, 1974). Recommended is "The Secrets of Local Government" by M. L. Stein

CHAPTER 16
Investigative Reporting

—The reporter settled himself behind a clump of scrub palmettos, slapped at an errant mosquito and began a patient wait. A reliable source had tipped him off that one of the county commissioners was using county equipment to work on a private drive leading to his property. The surest way was for the reporter to check it himself.

—Another reporter sat in the office of his publishing company's comptroller, seeking advice in understanding the annual audit of the Hospital Authority. A source had confided that questionable transfers of funds were being made into medical staff "contingency" accounts.

—Still another reporter is entering her third week of laboriously checking Zoning Commission decisions in the county courthouse. Systematic extraction of information may show her a pattern of preferential treatment given to certain property owners in zoning decisions, resulting in inordinate increases in land values.

All these reporters are engaging in what has come to be known as investigative reporting. As Carl Bernstein, currently with ABC, has said, "All good reporting is investigative reporting." In that sense all reporters are basically investigators. However, the many levels of reporting public affairs has clothed the term with deeper and more dynamic implications.

Investigative reporting has come to denote uncovering information that some individual or group has willed should remain concealed.

With some small effort the reporter can gain access to state records to determine how much more the football coach is being paid than the university's president. But it will take far more persistence and substantially more time to obtain access to and research admission records to determine whether star athletes were admitted to the school under questionable conditions and without the minimum requirements.

The same qualities that determine a good reporter also define whether that person is capable of handling the demands of investigative reporting. Something extra is often required:

—Extraordinary patience, a person willing and able to follow a trail to a blank wall, then begin the trail again with the same painstaking effort.

—The instinct that something may be "rotten in Denmark" when information is concealed, a healthy skepticism that overrides the natural inclination to drop the matter.

—A strong conviction that the public has a right to know just about everything that affects it and for which it pays—either in the form of taxes, service fees, interest on loans or for goods themselves.

—A logical and careful thinker, who is willing to work hard and face the possibility that at the end of a three-month investigation, there may be no story at all.

There is still another aspect to investigative reporting, which makes it more demanding. An exposure in journalism tends to be an accusation, an inference or charge that something is wrong. The inherent inequality between accusation and reply places a heavy burden on the investigative reporter to assure a fair as well as a totally accurate report. People's reputations and livelihoods are at stake where wrongdoing is often exposed.

Public officials and government bodies constitute only a segment of the arena in which the investigative reporter operates. Business, industrial corporations and financial houses are legitimate subjects of scrutiny. So are political organizations and non-profit groups such as charities. An investigation is never restricted by the makeup of the subject.

Organizing for the Task

The telephoned message from the anonymous caller was brief, coming during the late shift when the newsroom was uncharacteristically quiet. Deadline time had come and gone, and except for the static of a police monitor, a sharp-eared editor could hear a pin drop.

The caller came right to the point. "You press guys ought to look into the old Dockman property. You might find something interesting—and funny." He refused to identify himself. "It'll be worth your while," he assured the reporter at the other end of the line.

Such tips from disgruntled parties to a transaction often trigger extensive searches of public records to determine whether fraud or other illegality has been concealed and should be exposed to public view. In this case, the tip merely leads in the direction of a story. Documentation follows logically.

—An ownership check on the Dockman property might reveal that it had indeed recently changed hands, that it lay on the edge of a potentially profitable industrial development site, and that it had routinely undergone a zoning change aided by a behind-the-scenes developer with the assistance of a city official who possessed a peripheral interest in the enterprise.

Whatever the information, its implications must first be thought through. Where might it lead? What kind of story will develop? What kind of research needs to be done? To what sources will the material take the reporter? How might the story be significant? What would be the impact on the community and the people involved? How long will it take to develop the story? What help might be needed?

Many of these questions will have to be answered before work begins on what could develop into a complex story. Tentative assumptions must be tested, and reporters often delineate in outline form the sources of possible information that will help to determine how and where the facts can be quickly acquired.

It often pays to identify the maximum and minimum story that might be yielded early in the investigation. The minimum story may be that a public official merely appropriated $2,000 for a questionable purpose; the maximum may be that the official systematically looted a public account over a period of time, creating the possibility of a serious misprision charge carrying a substantial fine and/or prison sentence.

Such a hypothesis sometimes can be bounced off the subject under investigation, who may come up with reasonable answers for the appropriation. The logical step is to check the official's answers to determine whether they are valid.

The reporter needs discipline to remain on the track, since complex investigations often lead in many different directions. A useful file should be maintained, and each reporter should construct a system that works for him or her. Many reporters use a card filing system with name, description of the information and cross-filing information at the bottom of the card leading to other pertinent information. Handling a file in alphabetical order enables the reporter to drop information on new cards into the file.

The reporter is a fount of information and knowledge, but he or she cannot be expected to know everything. Good organization implies the ability and desire to acquire technical information efficiently. Roger Hedges, a Gannett News Service correspondent, suggests that experts can serve as road maps to assist in gathering information:

> Suppose you're looking at the operations of a business and don't know the first thing about how that business should be working. Find a cooperative competitor, one you can trust, and let him walk you through the standard internal operations of a typical business in his field.

Hedges recommends asking a cooperative banker to lead the reporter through the labyrinth of high finance. "The same goes for stock brokers, lawyers and accountants. They're all specialists in their fields and many of them are happy to share their knowledge with outsiders who admit the gaps in their own knowledge."

Dealing with Sources

Triggers to successful investigative reports exist everywhere, not merely as anonymous calls to newsrooms. Whatever the source, the information provided rather than the identity is important. The reporter is going to test the information, whatever the source.

Information should be judged on its merits rather than on the motives of the person who conveys it. A disgruntled employee may have been passed over for promotion, has information that his or her employer has been tinkering with records and angrily "blows the whistle" on the employer. Or a career public employee may simply tire of seeing inefficiency or petty corruption in his or her department and decide to right some wrongs. An expert hired for his or her scientific or technological background may object to a political hack, with no discernible value to the organization, who is periodically milking a fund.

Journalist Bill Sloat offers an example:

> A veteran Florida traffic cop wandered into the newsroom at TODAY's Titusville bureau in 1972 and said he had a complaint about his police chief. The cop handed over Xeroxed duplicates of about 300 traffic tickets he said were taken from a locked drawer at the police station. All of the tickets had been marked "void" by high-ranking officers and the police chief. None of the recipients had gone to traffic court.

Using city directories, a reporter checked the identification and occupations of the names on the tickets, and Sloat reported,

> Surprisingly, the names on the voided tickets turned out to be city officials, politicians, bankers, members of the police chief's country club, and the children of many of these people. The action of the chief in ordering tickets voided wasn't illegal—but it was questionable.

Was it in the public interest? Was the action selective law enforcement? The story was written, and Sloat says, the chief lost his job a few months later.

People who sue for one reason or another often volunteer far more information than what appears on the court record. In the business world, a firm that believes lucrative government contracts are endangered because of petty bribery may tip off a reporter to information about a public official.

Sometimes information is offered by persons who merely like to gossip, not realizing that their information is providing the journalist with the basis of an exposé of their employer. People sometimes spill out information just to "get it off their chests." *They're* not involved, they assert with relish, but someone else is.

Others enjoy the idea of serving as "inside dopesters" and offer far-fetched tips that sometimes are based on fact. Having adopted the image of being an inside expert, they constantly seek information to sustain it. Unpaid, but highly motivated, such people can sometimes be approached to provide specific data not easily obtainable by outsiders. However, caution should be exercised, because material from such sources is often exaggerated.

Information sometimes comes from unlikely sources. An anonymous voice student at a Western university felt that she had been improperly pressured to spend hundreds of dollars in additional lessons by one of the professors in the School of Music. An investigation turned up highly improper procedures and payments, involving more than one teacher and many students.

Self-interest often triggers exchange of information. A recently fired or disgruntled employee is frequently a source. Election officials often set a reporter on the path to a good story, especially when questionable activity focuses on the other party. Partisan activities in politics often open informational doors. Leaks do not always pan out, but persistent rumors should be checked, based on the old saw that where there is smoke there is fire.

A surprising amount of information can be obtained from purchasing agents. Disgruntled officials of firms which did not get a contract often will point in the direction of questionable bidding procedures.

A reporter's investigation of bids taken for relocation contracts by a Housing and Redevelopment Authority in the Midwest uncovered illegalities. Three trucking firms which submitted the only bids were found to have close ties to one another. Records revealed that the firms were actually headquartered at the same address, and the officers all had close business ties. Before bidding with the agency, they had signed documents assuring that no price-fixing or other collusion was involved, with violation punishable by fines and prison sentences.

Grants from government agencies are another area that often yield valuable information. Thousands of such grants are awarded each year, with the insistence of the government that someone or some group is supposed to be helped through each. If no one is being helped, there is a story. Funds are designed to be used for a specific purpose. The reporter's question: were they?

Protecting Confidential Sources

Relationships with confidential sources are among the most sensitive areas of investigative journalism. While motives may or may not be important to the reporter, protection for sources is always a prime consideration. Any action that might risk identification should be avoided, and the risks attendant to giving of information should be clearly pointed out to sources.

No absolute right exists for confidentiality between journalist and source. In cases where confidentiality interferes with the constitutional insistence on a fair trial, the courts have increasingly ruled for disclosure, putting additional pressure on the reporter to disclose his or her sources.

Prosecutors and judges exercise broad discretion in the search for evidence, and it is wise for the reporter to be familiar with past judicial decisions requiring disclosure and general philosophy regarding press confidentiality. While shield laws permit limited protection in some areas, they should not be counted upon in sensitive cases.

The value of information gained in this manner should be carefully weighed against the consequences that might occur should the issue end in court action. The best approach is to always seek ways to limit the vulnerability of both reporter and source, and prime consideration should be given to documenting material through public records or other sources. Preliminary notes that might identify a source should be "sanitized" and code names used when there is danger to the source. Those who are aware of such leads in an investigation should be kept to a minimum.

The reporter risks a contempt of court charge if he or she destroys or tampers with notes after a subpoena has been issued for them. The best approach is to destroy sensitive information after the reporter has reproduced it in random form to eliminate possibility of successful identification.

Former reporter Clark Mollenhoff warns young reporters of the risks:

> Unless you are relieved of the responsibility of the confidential relationship, you should be prepared to serve a substantial jail term, to pay a fine, and to pay legal fees. Your publisher can pay your fine and your legal fees to uphold your pledge to confidentiality, but he cannot serve your jail term for you.

Coping with the Task

Investigative reporting often demands special effort. Information that a public official or private corporation has *willed* should be kept secret sometimes has to be pried loose. Since reporters do not possess subpoena powers, they must utilize other means to obtain information.

Successful reporters use many devices to dig up material that otherwise remains hidden. Part of their arsenal is the ability to convince sources that it is to the source's advantage to provide information. The reporter is not being unethical but is simply using all the persuasive power he or she possesses to collect needed information.

An assistant district attorney may be aware of the explosiveness of some information he possesses, but he hesitates to endanger his position by discussing it. The task of the reporter is to convince the official that the information can be verified elsewhere and not appear to come from within the department at all.

Good reporters play one source against another. Small bits of information can be dangled before an unwilling contact, with the suggestion that the reporter already knows much of the story, and it is to the foot-dragger's advantage to give his or her side of the story. The investigative reporter acts as though he knows exactly what he is looking for, even though he may be merely "fishing" for information.

It does no harm to adopt an authoritative air, with the implication that additional questions are being asked only in the interest of accuracy. Care should be taken, however, to show respect in searches such as these. Strong-arm tactics sometimes have a place in the reporter's armament, but they should be utilized cautiously.

Investigative reporting often calls for playing competing agencies against one another. This is not to suggest that the journalist should spend a career poking at snakes' nests with a sharp stick, but little love is generally lost between a city and county agency, and the reporter should take advantage of that fact. Each agency has its particular constituency, and the reporter is only capitalizing on the natural checks and balances in the system.

One advantage of breaking a story into print before it is fully developed lies in the potential for opening new sources of information. Author Robert Caro explained it this way:

> Investigative reporters quickly become aware of a phenomenon of their profession: information so hard to come by when they are preparing to write their first story in a new field suddenly becomes plentiful as soon as that first story has appeared in print. Every city agency has its malcontents and its idealists and its malcontent-idealists.

Experienced reporters quietly and efficiently make themselves available to a wide range of sources after the initial material has been made public.

It should be remembered that public documents and interviews with officials complement each other. By first analyzing a document, the reporter is capable of asking more knowledgeable questions. From another standpoint, records become a check on the veracity of the interviewee. Having scrutinized the record, the reporter knows a lie when he or she hears one.

There is always a danger, too, that a source, upon thinking it over, will attempt to retract or change his or her story. Public documents are important in holding informants' feet to the fire.

Robert Greene of *Newsday* suggests that the reporter make use of "a slowly encircling noose" in researching a story. Investigation should begin away from the main characters, with covert information gathering enabling the reporter to obtain large amounts of material before the subject or subjects realize they are under investigation.

Editor Kent Freeland once worked with a two-man reporting

team that meshed time and talent to uncover attempts by organized crime to secure vending machine rights and sanitation contracts in New York:

> Once the reporters had discovered a branch of the operation, the two would identify the principal characters, then time their questioning carefully to interview two sources at the same time in different places. They then would compare answers and bore in on the areas where they found discrepancies.

Depending upon the kind of information needed, however, enormous amounts of time can be saved by applying directly to the subject. Hours can be spent in tracking down the holdings of a major landowner in a community, while much of the preliminary information may be readily available in biographical form from vanity directories or even from the person's office. Important people like the public to know how important they are, and dates, names, directorships in corporations and other background material are often easily located. Much time can be saved for more important efforts.

It should be remembered that people who are being investigated will often disclose a lot of information but will attempt to place a different and perfectly legitimate interpretation on it. Should they admit something, it offers further verification, and the resulting information often sends the reporter to still other sources. The reporter should always return and give the subject the opportunity to reply fully to any allegations against him or her. The goal is gathering information, not "getting someone." Questionable material should always be checked with an attorney, whose legal assistance can be helpful in assuring that information is privileged or that no sign of malice is present.

Error should be absent too. Even the most minor miscalculation can result in hue and outcry from officials who have been otherwise fairly arraigned at the public bar. Investigative reporter Bill Sloat reported that a county commission paid $130,000 more for a park site than the county appraiser said it was worth, after it had the opportunity to purchase the property a year earlier for an even cheaper price. But Sloat noted a minor error in the story: "I wrote that the county commission 'bought' the land on a certain date, rather than saying they 'voted to buy' land on a certain date." The commissioners attacked the story on the basis of the minor error.

> Never mind the fact that the land cost the public $260,000 more in 12 months time, and that the decision to buy the property was made on June 15. The story was only as strong as its weakest link—which was the use of the word "bought" rather than "voted to buy."

It is an important lesson.

A Guide to Records

The actual process of sifting through mounds of dry, initially baffling, documents and statistics is tedious, admit prize-winning reporters Donald L. Barlett and James B. Steele. But public records reporting has a special appeal, they say:

> It fulfills one of journalism's traditional roles, that of acting as a watchdog over public officials. But secondly, and perhaps more important in this era of ever-greater governments, it enables reporters to monitor institutions which have such a profound effect on our lives.

Documents and the information they contain serve as the key to nearly every significant investigative report produced by the press. Whatever the level of government, whatever the corporate transaction, written details exist in some form and in some files that bind the tiles to create a full mosaic.

Investigating a private corporation at the federal level, the reporter might begin with the Securities and Exchange Commission, asking for a copy of Form 10K, which details important current developments within the XYZ Corp.

Valuable information available from this document includes changes in the company's business, competitive conditions in the industry, legal proceedings, securities transactions and specific financial information. Another public form, the 8-K, is filed with the SEC when there have been changes in control of a firm, acquisition or disposition of corporate assets in material amounts and defaults in payments.

Armed with this information, the reporter might move on to a state agency that enforces a uniform commercial code. The documents produced indicate whether the XYZ Corp. has borrowed against its assets and gives the identity of the debtor and party providing the security, a description of property used as collateral, and possibly the loan's maturity date.

Finally at the local level, the reporter ties the material together with a visit to the county clerk's office, where a mortgage agreement might be attached to an original real estate deed. Armed with this information, the reporter is in a position to approach corporation officers and financial houses with questions on the meaning of the series of transactions. No matter how reluctant corporation officials may be to provide details of their business operations, the persistent reporter can often get his or her information elsewhere. The same applies to public officials.

At the Federal Level

Every federal office offers the opportunity to add to the knowledge already possessed by the astute reporter, and even the Congress itself is a source of important information.

A congressional committee might have held hearings on a product or service, or investigated the practices of a company. It may have subpoenaed company records or court proceedings, and placed them in the public record. All sorts of witnesses may have testified.

There are two methods of determining whether such information is available: the Congressional Information Service Index, which publishes transcripts of hearings and is available in many libraries, and the House Bill Status Office, which identifies all legislation on a subject. Key words, such as land rights, pensions or manufacturers' warranties will send the reporter to the pertinent committee for transcripts of hearings held on the issue.

Some federal agencies have traditionally offered easy access to information and documents supporting it. Reporters generally find consumer-oriented offices cooperative. Other agencies have resisted information-gathering efforts, and the 1974 Freedom of Information Act, with its amendments and regulations, has served to open many files previously inaccessible to the press.

The key to effective information gathering at the federal level lies in the reporter's knowledge of what is available in the various agencies, and who can direct him or her to further sources. The Federal Trade Commission documents complaints and investigations by the agency and also provides economic reports and manufacturers' requirements. Other agencies offer similar material. The Maritime Commission collects reports of self-policing activity, complaints and how they are handled, and records of investigations into maritime carriers.

The Department of Housing and Urban Development operates an Office of Interstate Land Sales, which maintains files on principals of companies dealing in such land sales, property descriptions and financial reports. Federal legislation and scrutiny have curbed unscrupulous land developers, but some continue to slip through the nets. Alert reporters continue to mine the public records in efforts to expose them.

The Food and Drug Administration also investigates business and industry and maintains records of its investigations. Often there is overlap among agencies, and a second might provide information that the first did not possess. Failure to find documentation at the FDA might lead to the Consumer Product Safety Commission, which maintains a correspondence log, identification of product defects and petitions for agency action.

Pension trusts have been the subject of many investigations in recent years because of their sheer financial size and complexity. The Department of Labor's Pension Benefit Guaranty Corporation, a self-financing, wholly owned government corporation established to guarantee payment of insured benefits, collects copies of pension plans, annual reports of pension funds, documentation of lawsuits and records of termination of plans. Disgruntled pensioners have been known to trigger press investigations which lead to these federal agencies and to questionable investments by the huge pension funds as well.

Other agencies frequently approached by reporters include the National Labor Relations Board, which is a source of decisions and orders in cases of unfair labor practices, and the Environmental Protection Agency, which files comments on proposed legislation, impact statements, EPA guidelines and environmental orders to firms charged with violating them.

At the State Level

Growth of state government has been paralleled by the expansion of the record-keeping apparatus. It is useful for reporters, and state offices should not be overlooked as sources. For instance, out-of-state companies doing business within a state as franchisers must disclose information about their operations, and firms desiring to compete for state contracts must disclose substantial information to state agencies. Much of this is available as public record.

Several dozen different kinds of offices keep information about companies on file, with much of the data pertinent to the reporter trying to link facts. The secretary of state's office offers basic information about business, such as place and nature, names and addresses of directors, officers and incorporators, the firm's capitalization, and notices of consolidation and merger. Identity of the operators is difficult to hide.

As with its federal counterpart, the Department of Labor and Industrial Relations offers much information through inspections of workplaces for possible safety violations, penalties assessed and agency orders, and decisions on arbitration between municipalities and public employee unions.

Consumer protection agencies, sometimes operating out of the attorney general's office, record complaints about companies or products. A reporter might find difficulty in obtaining information about a pending case, but generally the records are available. Insurance companies must submit financial reports, including income statements, to a state insurance department, and the documents on file often include records of investigations of companies and agents.

The independent occupational and professional licensing boards maintain records showing the education and other qualifications of members of the professions practicing in the state. Records of investigations are also available. It is simple to determine the qualifications of any persons whose credentials are questioned.

In recent years, water and air pollution agencies have required permits to discharge pollutants, and monitoring reports are usually available to reporters. Records of complaints, violations and enforcement actions, and description of operations are also kept.

Every state office operates a purchasing department, which records contracts between state government and private industry. Some states maintain extensive files on contractors, which show financial strength, identification of officers and other data.

Reporters have frequently found the Department of Motor Vehicles useful for obtaining identification of owners of auto registration plates.

Food production, processing, labeling and distribution are also regulated in most states, with agencies collecting information regarding illegal or unethical practices and decisions by the agencies. Pharmaceuticals and cosmetics are also subject to state regulation, with decisions on their use public record.

At the Local Level

Local records are often pure gold to the investigative reporter. For one thing, they are at hand and accessible, in contrast to the federal records housed in Washington and state records stored in the capital. The reporter is more likely, with the assistance of a cooperative clerk, to find helpful information more quickly.

With few exceptions, local record-keeping is consistent from locality to locality, and the alert reporter should have little difficulty adjusting to local situations. Searching through a grantor-grantee index, which lists buyers and sellers of property, is as valid in one community as in another. Zoning designations may vary, but the effect of zoning is the same, and records will reflect the same kinds of action in Arizona as in New Jersey.

There is, however, a wide variance as to which records are considered public record and which ones are not, plus the additional problem of ready access to the records. The federal Freedom of Information Act that has opened many documents to public scrutiny does not apply at the local level, and the reporter must sometimes rely on ingenuity to gain access. Many states have passed specific open records legislation, which has served to smooth the path for the reporter and the public. However, some are vaguely worded and include so many exceptions as to make them difficult to utilize.

At the local level, access sometimes depends upon how the reporter approaches a clerk and the clerk's perception of the request. Entry to documents can be forced through lawsuits, but it is usually time consuming and sometimes impractical in sensitive investigations. It is always best to try to obtain the clerk's cooperation; that approach can have the additional advantage of tips to shortcuts that eliminate some of the time-consuming documentation.

Officeholders come and go, but clerks in public records offices generally are career public servants, sometimes seeing the press as a shield from demanding politicians and as an outlet for their own grievances. Usually they have nothing to hide and, within reason, should be cultivated.

Endless Sources

Seemingly mundane documents can yield valuable bits of information. Birth certificates, available in a health department or county clerk's office, are useful in establishing family ties and sometimes determine nepotisim in public departments. Death certificates are filed in a similar manner, sometimes with a state agency as well. Marriage and divorce records and local vehicular records can be useful in following a trail.

While the voting booth is private, investigation of voting records will tell a reporter whether a subject is registered in a specific precinct, and his or her stated address and whether a vote was cast. A person claiming a false address for some other purpose is often identified through the voting rolls.

Details of payroll activity constitute part of the public record, and audits can be used to substantiate relationships between officeholders and corporations or individuals doing business with an agency or other governmental unit. Specific salary schedules are available through budgets and the auditing process. A person's military records are available through federal government sources and can sometimes constitute a further personal check on other information. Personal records such as these are valuable guideposts to additional documentation.

Substantial legislation in recent years has placed candidates for public office on record for campaign contributions and expenditures. It is often worthwhile to compare contributors with records of those doing business with the government and with polticial appointments. Purchasing departments in an agency can provide information on such contractors.

One of the more sensitive areas for the investigative reporter is the local groups that serve the charitable needs of the community. Fraud is possible, even among the most worthy of these charities, but the motives of both reporter and newspaper will likely be questioned when the practices of a local institution are bared for all to view and discuss. Every action taken by the reporter should be justified in investigating such charitable groups.

All non-profit organizations must file income and expense records with the Internal Revenue Service, and those forms, known as 990s, are open to inspection by the public. Sometimes the activities of the charity are questionable; at other times there may be outright misapplication of funds. Money is sometimes spent for purposes other than those for which it was ostensibly raised, some funds are raised through deceptive practices, and some are raised but not reported.

Spot checks often help to assure the accuracy of the figures. There have been instances in which charities serve as thinly disguised "protection rackets," in which business people are coerced into paying off police, fire or political "charities." The IRS's records offer one means of checking on these unscrupulous operators.

The reporter should be alert to strange gaps in files, both in a newspaper library and among the clerk's documents. Missing years of coverage may signal a problem. At the conclusion of a highly publicized charity drive, reporters who covered it busied themselves with other issues. Another reporter later checking the files became curious about the long gap in news clippings and began checking the records. He found that the charities never received any funds and that there was questionable disposal of the funds that were raised.

Property: Who Owns It and Why?

Use of land ranks equally in importance with other aspects of community life. Where people live and under what conditions, how much it costs them, who makes use of the land around them and how, and their relationships with those persons and corporations provide an ever-changing tapestry of cooperation and conflict.

Old property records, some dating back hundreds of years, are constantly in a state of flux as new owners are identified, taxes adjusted, mortgage commitments added and land uses changed. They are an ever-renewable resource for the investigative reporter. While many county offices continue to store these records in the traditional oversized ledger books, other agencies have turned to computer storage and other sophisticated record-keeping devices that make the records even more accessible to the enterprising reporter.

One of the most lucrative places to begin is through the zoning process. A section of a political subdivision is restricted by law to a particular use to protect the value of property, such as homes, apartments and other rental units, businesses or many types of industry. Sometimes the restrictions are minimal, as in rural areas of a county; at other times, uses are rigidly enforced, such as establishment of a tavern or alcoholic beverage store near a church or a school.

Through changes in zoning by public agencies charged with this responsibility, the value of land can be made to rise and fall. Speculators amass fortunes through manipulation of zoning ordinances and acquisition of preliminary information about changes in land use. One area of a county may be zoned for agricultural use only, but a legal change to industrial use can boost the value of thousands of acres, with an accompanying decline in nearby residential property values. Farmland that went begging at $500 an acre is suddenly in demand at $3,000.

A reporter need only to investigate recent major changes in zoning to begin cutting through tall grass to a story. The activity may not always be illegal, but it certainly might be questionable to the reader.

Zoning variances are particularly susceptible to manipulation. Professional planners recommend basic zoning regulations, which have the force of law, but individuals and organizations often seek a different use for the property. They apply for a zoning variance which allows them to use the property in non-conformance with the property adjacent to it.

Variances may be simple: A property owner wants to construct a garage on his property, but zoning regulations restrict the structure to at least 12 feet from the property line. The owner wants to build the garage only nine feet from the line.

They may also be complex: Zoning regulations require only single-family dwellings in an area, but a homeowner wants to convert a series of huge old homes into Victorian-style apartments without destroying the appearance of single-family dwellings. The result could be to actually upgrade the appearance of the neighborhood. An industrial zone may permit only certain types of activity, and a developer wishes to establish a meat packing plant.

Variances forecast basic changes in zoning to the reporter, as well as raise legitimate questions of why the original zoning was adopted in the first place. Many questions must be answered. Who owns the property and who benefits from allowance of a variance? What board allowed the variance and what is its complexion? What might be the relationships with those who benefit from such changes? And who will be adversely affected by the variance?

In answering such questions, the reporter is fulfilling the legitimate investigative role to which he or she is assigned.

Future land use is important to most communities, and planning boards are the key to successful growth. But the process of planning for the future also creates a climate for manipulation and questionable actions which handsomely reward a few people. Proposed changes in land use often have tremendous impact on property values. A high-rise residential development may be the intent of a planning commission, but the final occupant of the land may turn out to be high-rise offices, which yield a more substantial return on an investment, or a sprawling shopping center, which yields an even more substantial return.

Planning commissions often operate at two levels: the decision-making commission itself, which includes appointed members of the community, and experts in land planning who are hired to study land use and make recommendations. Market value of land usually depends on the designation placed upon it by the experts, and the process becomes complicated as the commission deliberates its decision. Unscrupulous public officials sometimes benefit from inside knowledge of such actions.

Handling these zoning and planning stories requires caution on the part of the reporter. Land use symbols are complex, and change from area to area. While R1 may mean that a district is restricted to single-family dwellings, R1A and R1B may offer subtly different restrictions that could change the intent of a story completely. The reporter dealing with these land uses should possess complete familiarity with the various designations and what they infer.

As with records of zoning and planning decisions, property tax records offer similar yields of valuable information. The recorder's office or register of deeds should be familiar and comfortable territory to the investigative reporter. Real estate deeds, indexed by grantor and grantee, provide identities of buyer and seller, a description of the property including size and legal designation, and any mortgage agreements. Tax stamps affixed to the deed enable the reporter to determine the purchase price and date of purchase. Maps and plats in the recorder's office locate parcels of land. The complex legal descriptions come alive, but the reporter should be cautioned to double-check numbers. An error in a single number, for instance, could result in description of totally different property and persons involved.

It doesn't take much time to learn the intricacies of the property tax structure, including the difference between real value of land as opposed to its assessed value, which is the value placed upon it for tax purposes. Wide variations exist in the method for computing the assessed value, depending upon state law and local legislation, but equalization legislation is tending to remove these variations.

Usually the assessed value is a fixed percentage of the real value of the property. In some states, the percentage depends on the type of property; in others, all property is assessed at the same fraction of real value.

The tax assessor's office maintains record cards or sheets, which are the worksheets the assessor uses to determine property value for tax assessments. As with the register of deeds, this official's records list ownership, describe the parcel of property and give its size. Some offices provide an assessment roll, a printout of assessed values listed by parcel.

Building permit records are also useful in researching the history of property. Many offices maintain records showing legal history, including previous uses and building plans and specifications. By checking the cost of the permit, building value can be estimated.

It is difficult but not impossible to conceal ownership of property. When the public interest is at stake, the persistent reporter can obtain just about everything he or she requires to properly document the trail of ownership and property uses.

Using the Freedom of Information Act

The very presence of the 1974 Freedom of Information Act and its amendments have forced much previously hidden information into the public domain. More than that, however, the press is increasingly taking advantage of its provisions, despite the time-consuming correspondence and expense involved.

Amendments to the act outline information request procedures, appeal routes, and costs of search and duplication of material. In implementing the act, federal agencies have taken somewhat different paths. Some, such as the Justice Department, have set up specific search organizations to locate requested information and to determine whether its release is warranted. Other agencies maintain traditional procedures, leaving press offices to respond to information requests.

Under the act, anyone can request information, and many private individuals and organizations are joining the press in making use of the right. Uniform fee schedules are in force among the agencies, and with a small effort the reporter can determine the cost of information search.

A telephone call or visit to the agency is the first step. The reporter must be able to describe the information sought with sufficient specificity so that a clerk can identify the material. Sometimes a telephoned request will be rejected on the basis that the request be made in writing. Press offices are often more sympathetic to telephone requests than are other agency offices. At the least, however, the call should provide some idea of how long and expensive the search will be.

The act directs each agency to promulgate regulations specifying a uniform schedule of fees for searches, limited to "reasonable standard charges" for document search and duplication. To save time and duplication costs, some reporters inspect documents in person. Many agencies provide space in which reporters can work, including a typewriter, and sometimes they provide modest amounts of duplication of material at no cost.

The act has been given teeth, subjecting federal employees who arbitrarily deny information sought under the act to administrative penalties, including possible loss of salary. This has had the effect of opening files more freely, but it has also been the vehicle for having the decision passed along to officials higher up in the agency.

A waiver of search fees can be requested if the news agency believes they are too expensive, and the agency may waive the fees itself if it decides that release of the information is primarily in the public interest.

There is a provision for a formal request for information if there appears to be a reluctance to supply on the part of federal bureaucrats, and journalists can initiate action in federal district court should such a request be denied. The law calls for expedited treatment for court action, which means that it is given precedence over other pending litigation.

Not everything in the federal files is open to public scrutiny. The act specifically exempts some information, such as executive orders classified as secret "in the interest of national defense or foreign policy." The act specifies, however, that the courts will decide whether the claim of national security is justified, placing an additional burden on officials who so classify historical records or documents with obvious political repercussions.

Other exempt documents include those related solely to internal personnel rules and practices of an agency, trade secrets of private industry, personnel and medical files, and those specifically exempt from disclosure by statutes other than the Freedom of Information Act, such as Internal Revenue Service regulations.

Also exempt are records of investigations by law enforcement agencies, to the extent that their release would interfere with one in progress or deprive a person of a fair trial or adjudication of an action. However, the burden is on the government to prove that the documents were compiled for criminal or civil law enforcement purposes.

The detailed Freedom of Information Act, along with specific government agencies which deal with it, is published widely, including in the *U.S. Government Manual.*

Suggested Readings

MOLLENHOFF, CLARK R. *Investigative Reporting.* (New York: Macmillan, 1981).

DOWNIE, LEONARD, JR., *The New Muckrakers* Washington: New Republic, 1976). Especially "Scoop Artist," an account of reporter Seymour Hersh's efforts to track down Lt. William L. Calley Jr. for the story of My Lai.

NOYES, DAN, *Raising Hell, A Citizen's Guide to the Fine Art of Investigation* (San Francisco, CA: Foundation for National Progress)

DYGERT, JAMES H., *The Investigative Journalist, Folk Heroes of a New Era* (Englewood Cliffs, NJ: Prentice-Hall, 1976). Especially Chapter 2, "Washington's Master Watchdogs."

ANDERSON, JACK, *Washington Expose* (Washington: Public Affairs Press, 1967). A modern muckraker looks at some specific investigative stories.

WILLIAMS, PAUL N., *Investigative Reporting and Editing* (Englewood Cliffs, NJ: Prentice-Hall, 1978). The late Paul N. Williams interviewed many reporters and editors in gathering the material for this definitive look at investigative reporting procedures.

CHAPTER 17
Privacy and the Public's Right to Know

—An influential member of Congress, with many years of seniority on key committees, is known to be an alcoholic. Although this fact is common knowledge in the congressman's home district, it goes unreported by the press.

—The wife of another public figure undergoes extensive treatment for mental illness at a nationally known clinic. Following a reporter's interviews with two fellow patients, the information is made public.

—A family bereaved by the loss of a child in a street murder is photographed at a private funeral. The pictures are published.

—A reporter joins angry tenants in eavesdropping on a landlord they have charged with violating housing agreements. The reporter writes a news story from the resulting information.

—Another reporter attempts to interview a suspect being held in the county jail, and the details of his efforts are published.

Decisions such as these being made daily by journalists indicate the thin line drawn between the public's right to know, as defined by the U.S. Constitution, and the newly emerging right to privacy. Nowhere in public affairs reporting are constitutional issues more in conflict or more sensitive decisions to be made.

When is the legitimate right to be let alone compromised by the public's equally legitimate right to know the facts? The answers often lie in the perceptions of those involved.

The reporter may argue that the congressman forfeited his right to privacy when he ran for public office. A similar argument could be made for the wife of the influential public figure.

The editor may contend that politicians should generally be held accountable to an exacting standard because they are inclined to preach morality in one form or another, and so *their* morality then becomes the public's business. The civil rights advocate may argue that the right to privacy exists despite that fact and that many of the congressman's constituents will contend that he has the same right to privacy that they do.

The subjects themselves are increasingly turning to the courts as a means of determining the issues.

Beyond the courts, however, lie the ethical considerations. Journalistic codes uniformly mention the need for respect of the rights of persons involved in the news process and observance of common standards of decency on the part of the press.

But the subject of an "exposé" can argue with equal fervor that the press has traditionally failed to observe these common standards in publishing what is seen as questionable material.

Who Is a "Public Figure"?

Resolution of at least some of these questions lies in the definition of a "public figure." The U.S. Supreme Court has ruled that the determination of a public figure is always a factual one limited to two types:

1. Those persons who occupy positions of such pervasive power and influence that they are deemed public figures for all purposes, or those persons who are "intimately involved in the resolution of important public questions."

2. Those otherwise private individuals who have voluntarily thrust themselves into the vortex of a significant public controversy in order to influence the resolution of the issues involved.

The bereaved family, the landlord who has been "bugged," and the jailed suspect certainly cannot be cast in either of these molds, the courts have agreed. Their actions, conversations and records are in the public domain nevertheless.

The public affairs reporter actually confronts two problems in this sensitive area of privacy:

1. How and when should the press report on those who *are* legitimate public figures? Does a legislator have a right to several nips before a session, if that practice does not affect his handling of public affairs? Does the relative of a public figure have a right to some privacy, if only out of common

decency? Are the hours that a celebrity or a politician spends outside the public eye his or her own business?

2. How much should the press report on people *who may or may not* be legitimate public figures, and who may have a greater right to privacy? A person's position on a public payroll may not always make him or her a "public figure." A person caught up in a newsworthy event may have a legitimate right to privacy.

Two Sets of "Limits"

Compounding these two problems are two sets of "limits" with which the reporter must constantly grapple:

1. The legal limits, as defined by common law and statute, to the public's right to know and the individual's right to privacy.

2. The ethical limits to those rights, as defined by the public's perception of the limits and by the journalist's obligation to be fair and understanding, while observing the common standards of decency.

Some of the answers are to be found in the press's perception of its right to probe and publish confidential information. Other answers hinge on government, which in this country serves as a reflection of the public will. Still other answers depend on the public itself, which must often decide when privacy becomes secrecy. And some answers, of course, depend upon the judicial process, which is subject to constantly shifting opinions.

The Legal Limits

It is easier to draw a line between these great constitutional guarantees through the legal process. While it is too simplistic to argue that the public's right to know extends to anything that the press cannot be sued for, this approach tends to represent the practical application of privacy rights as they exist today.

If a reporter or editor believes that information lies in the public domain and is in the public interest to reveal, it is published. Then begins the process of determining through the courts whether the right to privacy actually exists in a specific area.

A newspaper publisher filed suit against a magazine writer several years ago, charging defamation of character in an article published in a national magazine. However, the publisher suddenly withdrew his action when the court, after due consideration, ruled that he was a public figure. The effect of that ruling was to generally place newspaper publishers in the role of public figures, and future actions will be decided on that premise.

In some cases, the journalist can successfully argue that some people become public figures unwillingly, through events that are thrust upon them. So members of the bereaved family, whatever the standards of common decency that may be ignored by the photographer, become public figures through an act of providence. Such figures cannot rely on the legal process to protect them; rather, they must rely on the standards of decency and good taste.

Public figures, on the other hand, are saddled with a much heavier burden of proof than are mere "private individuals." But it must be remembered that truth, generally a solid defense against libel for journalists, is not necessarily a defense in a lawsuit for invasion of privacy.

Growth of Privacy Claims

During the past 10 years, journalists have watched the U.S. Supreme Court grapple with the shifting laws of privacy, in an effort to reconcile them with the rights of the press. Communication lawyers Victor A. Kovner and Heather Grant Florence had warned in 1978 that increasing demands for privacy legislation would lead to an ever-growing number of civil claims against the press. Since that time, dozens of courts throughout the United States have been confronted with claims, some for the first time.

The growth of sophisticated communications has led to new interpretations of the right to privacy. In his book, *The Assault on Privacy*, Arthur R. Miller pointed to the inhibitions before the turn of the century:

> Snooping in the days before mass circulation newspapers, radio, television, computers, or even telephones, was inhibited by the natural limitations of the human eye, ear, voice and memory.

But the picture was changing dramatically:

> As larger amounts of information began to be gathered and circulated to wider audiences, the chances that those receiving it would have direct knowledge about the subject or be able to test the truth of what they heard or read decreased, while the likelihood that the printed or spoken word would be accepted as truth increased.

It is not surprising, Miller noted, that the law began to entertain second thoughts about recognizing a right to resort to the courts to protect individual privacy.

Development of Privacy Rights

Ironically, what was perceived as excesses on the part of the press prior to 1900 led to the idea that individuals have an interest in privacy, which the courts have some obligation to protect. Boston newspapers had taken to vividly describing parties given by socially prominent citizens of the city. Two young law partners, Samuel D. Warren and Louis D. Brandeis, who was later to become a justice of the Supreme Court, produced an article in the *Harvard Law Review* in

1890 complaining that the press had served "idle and prurient curiosity" in its accounts, overstepping the bounds of propriety and decency.

In the article, "The Right to Privacy," Warren and Brandeis argued that recognition of a right to privacy was essential in protecting private individuals from "mental pain and distress far greater than could be inflicted by mere bodily injury."

"To occupy the indolent," they wrote, "column upon column is filled with idle gossip, which can only be procured by intrusion upon the domestic circle." The article warned that recent innovations, particularly the development of photography and mass-circulation newspapers, presented grave new threats to personal privacy. "Gossip is no longer the resource of the idle and of the vicious, but has become a trade, which is pursued with industry as well as effrontery."

There was widespread support for the writers' contentions, but its acceptance through the statutory process was slow. Now, nearly a century later, only a handful of states have adopted legislation specifically protecting individuals, although nearly all the states recognize the right as common law. Only Nebraska and Rhode Island have specifically rejected the right to sue for invasion of privacy.

While the dimensions of protection vary from state to state, the law has become fairly standardized within clear boundaries.

The Present Common Law of Privacy

Invasion of privacy, and the slow growth of protection for the individual who considers himself or herself wronged by that invasion, has evolved in four basic areas: disclosure of truthful but embarrassing facts, placing a person in a false light, intrusion and misappropriation. Some of these areas are more important to the public affairs reporter than are others, but all are especially relevant to the press.

To many, the vast collections of records being maintained on individuals constitute the cause for gravest concern, one that spills over into the area of mass communication. In a comment on this country's diminishing right to privacy, California Judge Leonard M. Friedman noted,

> Our nation's current social developments harbor insidious evolutionary forces which propel us toward a collective, Orwellian society. One of the features of that society is the utter destruction of all privacy, the individual's complete exposure to the all-seeing, all-powerful state. Government agencies, civilian and military, federal, state, and local, have acquired miles and acres of files, enclosing revelations of the personal affairs and conditions of millions of private individuals. Credit agencies and other business enterprises assemble similar collections. Information peddlers burrow into the crannies of these collections. Microfilm and electronic tape facilitate the storage of private facts on an enormous scale. Computers permit automated retrieval, assemblage and dissemination. These vast repositories of personal information may easily be assembled into millions

of dossiers characteristic of a police state. Our age is one of shriveled privacy.

Leaky statutes imperfectly guard a small portion of these monumental revelations. Appellate courts should think twice, should locate a balance between public need and private rights, before deciding that custodians of sensitive personal files may with impunity refuse to investigate claims of mistaken identity or other error which threaten the subject with undeserved loss. The office of judges is to strike that balance rather than to pursue sentiments of sympathy. It is obvious, nevertheless, that an unwarranted record of conviction, even of arrest, may ruin an individual's reputation, his livelihood, even his life.

While privacy is a problem for each individual, it also constitutes a problem for the communications media. A misstep on the part of a reporter or photographer, whether unintentional or deliberate, can result in judicial action with expensive consequences. Growing pains in this area of law are constantly breaking new ground, and the wise journalist remains abreast of it.

DISCLOSURE OF TRUTHFUL BUT EMBARRASSING PRIVATE FACTS

Michael Virgil, a well-known sports figure, told a reporter for *Sports Illustrated* magazine about his hobbies—putting out lighted cigarets in his mouth, eating spiders and diving down flights of stairs to impress women. He later decided, however, that he did not want the information made public. The magazine went ahead and published an article about Virgil, and he sued for invasion of privacy.

In ruling against the surfer, the U.S. Court of Appeals said a publication cannot be found liable for publishing a truthful description of private facts about a person in the news because such facts are "newsworthy." However, the court warned, "the line is to be drawn when the publicity ceases to be the giving of information to which the public is entitled and becomes a morbid and sensational prying into private lives for its own sake, with which a reasonable member of the public, with decent standards, would say that he had no concern."

To be successful in bringing an action for invasion of privacy, a person must prove that the published material

1. would be highly offensive to a reasonable person, that is, embarrassing to that person;

2. is not of legitimate concern to the public, that is not newsworthy;

3. was published without the person's consent.

Many courts have also specified that public figures must also prove actual malice.

For the reporter, then, the problem is determining whether the material can be construed as being of legitimate public interest. Fortunately for the press, the courts have generally deferred to the media view of what constitutes newsworthy material or is in the public interest to disseminate.

And while truth is not a defense in a privacy issue, the existence of a public record has usually prevented recovery for invasion of privacy. If a matter is public record, such as a birth or marriage date, or an official court record, its publication usually escapes successful lawsuits against the publication.

Embarrassing facts about a public official, for example, might be defended on the basis that the official's place on the public payroll entitles the public to some information which might not be similarly considered if the individual were a private businessperson.

College athletes have been ruled public figures because their academic records directly affected their status as public figures and could be publicized with impunity. The *Washington Star* and the University of Maryland student newspaper were sued for $72 million for invasion of privacy because of articles the two papers published involving basketball players' academic problems. The private facts claim was dismissed by the court.

The question often hinges on whether a person is considered a "public figure." Merely being on the public payroll does not automatically place an individual in the public domain. That person must thrust himself or herself into the public limelight.

A public school teacher leads a private life but is suddenly thrust into the limelight through a sex change operation. A college professor is reasonably anonymous but decides suddenly to climb up on a soap box and deliver a jeremiad. The distinction quickly becomes clear in cases such as these, but others are more complex and not nearly so simple to categorize.

The key in making decisions in this area and assuring protection for the journalist is *care*. The protection of newsworthiness tends to vanish quickly if carelessness or deliberate misrepresentation can be proven.

FALSE LIGHT

Making individuals appear to be something they are not, even if it is not defamatory, is dangerous for a reporter or photographer. This area of privacy law, "putting the plaintiff in a false position in the public eye," has proven costly to many publications.

Identifying a person at a rally as a supporter of the political figure present, when in reality the person had merely stopped at the rally out of curiosity, would tend to put the person in a false light and create a climate for court action.

For a basic false light claim to be pursued, these factors must be present: the material in question must be proved false; the material has been published and done without the complainant's consent; and, in cases involving public figures, actual malice or reckless disregard for the truth has been shown.

False light is often confused with libel, but the two are distinguishable. Libel implies damage to a person's reputation, whereas false light does not. As in the case of the bystander at the political rally, an individual may be cast in a false light without being defamed.

A photograph of a woman taken in an Alabama funhouse with her skirt blown up over her head was accurate, but its context allegedly placed her moral character in question. Even the photographer who snaps pictures of young women jumping over rain puddles on a downtown street runs the risk of court action.

The emphasis of certain elements in a woman's suicide and the omission of others were held to constitute an invasion of privacy. The test of reckless disregard for the truth created an actionable suit.

INTRUSION

A third area of invasion of privacy is intrusion, which has generally been defined as "physical" invasion of an individual's privacy. There must be some kind of trespass without consent, but the area is a sensitive one for the journalist. If the reporter or photographer has successfully obtained someone's consent, or even the clear implication of consent, he or she should have no problem. The act of intrusion, rather than publication of the material, is the basis for this privacy claim, although some courts have not always made the distinction.

Modern technology has expanded the scope of lawsuits in recent years. Peeking into windows and hiding behind doors offer only the traditional concepts of intrusion. Surreptitious surveillance, such as use of sophisticated long-range telephoto lenses on cameras and electronic recording devices that can be carried in one's pocket, have brought intrusion claims. So has unauthorized use of private documents.

The courts have generally ruled that it is not an invasion of privacy to take a picture in a public place, but private property is another matter. Climbing a telephone pole to peer into a private window has been ruled an invasion of a person's privacy.

Taking microphones or other wiretapping equipment into a person's house without his or her consent is also considered intrusion. The reporter's job is further complicated in this area by state and federal statutes prohibiting wiretapping.

The courts have ruled that the press is protected when it publishes information obtained from someone else who invaded an individual's privacy, but the reporter who encourages or helps another to invade a private area without consent may also be held liable. The issue of trespass has been clouded by the reporter's physical presence on the scene. Columnist Drew Pearson was provided with copies of private documents by the staff of U.S. Sen. Thomas Dodd, and the material was subsequently published. Even though Pearson knew the documents were stolen, the publication of the material did not constitute action for trespass, because the journalist did not participate in the unlawful reproduction of the documents.

Despite the 1974 federal privacy act's protection of the confidential records of students, the suit against the *Washington Star* and the University of Maryland student newspaper for intrusion was dismissed on the ground that the material was gratuitously obtained from an unnamed source. The reporters had not inspected, solicited or authorized inspection of confidential files.

There is no unanimity on what is considered a "public place," where trespassing cannot be claimed, and jurisdictions have ruled differently. Neither is there unanimity on what constitutes a "private place." Some courts have given reporters protection when covering police raids on private property and in reporting fires and other disasters.

This issue was placed in somewhat clearer focus in 1977, when the Florida Supreme Court ruled in favor of a photographer who had been invited to join police officials in a tour of a burned house in which a young girl had died. While in the house, the photographer took several pictures, including one of a silhouette remaining on the floor after the body had been removed. The girl's mother sued for trespass after the picture was published, charging invasion of privacy and intentional infliction of emotional distress. The defendant, the Florida Publishing Co., claimed that its photographer was acting in accordance with press custom in covering a newsworthy event. While the court ruled in favor of the press, it noted that the customary right of entry vanishes when one is informed "not to enter at that time by the owner or possessor or by their direction." Left unanswered was the course of the action had the press been specifically directed by the distraught family not to enter the house.

In another trespassing suit, a New York state judge ruled against a television news crew after the crew without permission entered a New York City restaurant which was charged with city code violations. The judge ruled that "the right to publish does not include the right to break and enter, or the right to invade or otherwise to enter upon and trespass upon the property of these plaintiffs [the restaurant]."

The courts have also distinguished between private and public officials when surreptitious surveillance has been involved.

Secretly recording and photographing a "quack doctor" who was subsequently convicted for the unauthorized practice of medicine, with subsequent publication of the material in *Life* magazine, was held admissable in court on the question of damages.

However, a television reporter's secret filming of a police officer's undercover investigation of a massage parlor did not constitute intrusion in view of the public interest in the officer's conduct. The court carefully distinguished the police officer's role as a public official.

An invitation has often been held vital to the legality of what otherwise might be considered intrusion. While interviewing a defendant under a drug indictment, two *Louisville Courier-Journal* reporters who were working on a story on the local drug culture were told that the defendant understood that an attorney could "fix" her case for $10,000. The newspaper advanced the money to the defendant with the stipulation that she wear a concealed recording device to her next meeting with the lawyer. Although the recorded conversation produced denials by the lawyer that the case could be fixed, portions of the conversation were published. A claim of intrusion was denied, on the grounds that admission to the attorney's office was not fraudulently obtained.

MISAPPROPRIATION

Anyone who appropriates to his or her own use or benefit the name of likeness of another is subject to a suit for invasion of privacy. A variety of court cases in recent years suggests that the cause for action has moved substantially beyond the mere application of a person's name or likeness.

The four factors necessary for a successful appropriation claim include publication, identification, commercial gain and lack of consent. While advertisements using a person's name or picture without permission have been the most common basis for claims, news operations have become increasingly involved.

In one of the more significant cases, the U.S. Supreme Court ruled in 1977 that the First Amendment to the Constitution does not protect the press from liability for broadcasting a performer's act as a news report.

A Cleveland television station had filmed Hugo Zacchini, billed as the "Human Cannonball," being shot out of a cannon at a fair, and broadcast his entire 15-second act on the nightly news. Zacchini sued for invasion of privacy, charging that the broadcast had commercialized and appropriated "professional property." The court ruled that the broadcast of the performer's entire act posed a "substantial threat to the economic value of his performance."

On the other hand, an actress's claim that her photo on the cover of a magazine which contained a story about her invaded her privacy was dismissed. Another claim, that a private individual viewing a public parade as a spectator was entitled to damages because written consent was not obtained, was denied by the courts.

Former athlete Joe Namath lost an effort to recover damages from the magazine *Sports Illustrated* when the court held that use of Namath's photograph in advance advertising of the magazine was "merely incidental" to publicizing the magazine, which had carried accurate articles about the former football star.

Defenses for the Journalist

Difficult as it has been for the courts to define, the best defense in invasion of privacy cases continues to be the concept of newsworthiness. Two other useful defenses have emerged for the press:

1. Convincing the judiciary that a person is a legitimate public figure and thus newsworthy in his or her own right.
2. Consent by a person to have his or her privacy invaded.

Newsworthiness

No two journalists agree on the definition of newsworthiness, and the courts are in equal disarray. One court has defined news as "that indefinable quality of information which arouses public attention." Journalists have often insisted that news is whatever interests people. Within this loosely drawn concept, however, the courts have tended to give the media the judicial benefit of the doubt and have accepted journalists' definitions of news. Reliance upon this factor has saved many a newspaper and broadcast outlet from successful claims for invasion of privacy.

People who seek public office or any kind of celebrity status, willingly placing themselves in the public limelight, have generally been found by the courts to have given up to some extent their right to be let alone. Such persons—actors, politicians, athletes or explorers—have made themselves newsworthy and have given up their privacy.

Some, however, have been caught up in the news as unwilling participants, when they would prefer the anonymity of private citizens. In such cases, the courts have generally ruled that such persons cannot recover damages in cases of public interest and in which the accounts of the event have been accurate.

One case that set such a pattern involved Mrs. Lillian Jones, who unwillingly became a public figure on a Louisville, Kentucky street in 1929. Her husband was stabbed to death in Mrs. Jones's presence, and the *Louisville Herald-Post* published a picture of her, quoting her as saying of her husband's attackers, "I would have killed them." Mrs. Jones sued for invasion of privacy, but the court, while acknowledging the existence of a right to privacy, stated, "There are times, however, when one, whether willing or not, becomes an actor in an occurrence of public or general interest."

The courts have also ruled that persons who are essentially private figures lose their right to anonymity when they seek redress through the courts. Substantially accurate accounts taken from the public record have been ruled in the public domain as have pertinent photographic coverage and other details of the case.

Coverage by the *Minneapolis Times* of a sensational divorce trial and related child custody hearings brought a suit for invasion of privacy. In finding for the newspaper, a judge ruled that in the proceedings the plaintiff had departed from his "quiet peaceable life free from the prying curiosity and unmitigated gossip which accompanies fame, notoriety and scandal." In a sense, the plaintiff had become a quasi-public figure in the community.

The privilege of newsworthiness has occasionally been attacked in the courts on the basis that passage of time has eliminated the news element. While the event may have constituted legitimate news when it occurred years before, it is now out of the public limelight and thus a private affair. Used by itself, however, the time lapse argument has generally failed to stand up to the basic argument of newsworthiness.

Recent decisions of the Supreme Court, however, have tended to narrow the definition of a public figure who has been out of the public eye for a long time. The court ruled in 1979 that a reclusive plaintiff who had been convicted of contempt of court in 1958 was not a public figure for purposes of a 1974 court action. Some justices relied on the passage of time, finding that the plaintiff had acquired public figure status in 1958 but had lost it by 1974.

Since 1967, the courts have generally relied upon *Time, Inc.* v. *Hill* as a standard for the defense of newsworthiness. The case stemmed from a *Life* magazine article about a new play based on a book about a family held hostage in its home by escaped convicts. The article said the novel was inspired by the true-to-life ordeal of the James Hill family three years earlier.

Hill sued under New York State privacy statutes, alleging that the article was intended to give the impression that the play mirrored the Hill family's experiences. The magazine knew that this was false, Hill argued, but still referred to the play as a re-enactment of the Hill family ordeal. Although Hill won the suit, the magazine's appeal to the U.S. Supreme Court was successful.

The court ruled that the Constitution prevented applying the New York privacy statute in matters of public interest "in the absence of proof that the defendant published the report with knowledge of its falsity or in reckless disregard for the truth." The court ruled that Hill would have to prove that the magazine knew its story was false and showed a reckless disregard for the truth of the article.

However, the protection of newsworthiness can suddenly disappear if carelessness can be proven. *The Saturday Evening Post* published a story in 1967 about Mafia influence on gambling in the Bahama Islands. With the article appeared a photograph showing James Holmes and four other persons at a gambling table. The caption read:

> High-rollers at Monte Carlo have dropped as much as $20,000 in a single night. The U.S. Department of Justice estimates that the casino grosses $20 million a year, and that one-third is skimmed off for American Mafia "families."

Holmes sued for libel and invasion of privacy, arguing that the photo and caption placed him in a false light. While Holmes was not mentioned in the article, he was a focal point in the photograph. The court ruled that the libel and privacy issues would have to go to trial. The court said:

> Certainly defendant's caption is reasonably capable of amounting to a defamation, for one identified as a high stakes gambler or having a connection with the Mafia would certainly be injured in his business, occupation and/or reputation. As to plaintiff's action for privacy, there appears no question that if it were not for defendant's caption beneath plaintiff's photograph, this court would be justified in dismissing plaintiff's invasion of privacy cause of action.

Consent of Parties Involved

Invasion of privacy always places the reporter in a defensive posture and often on infirm legal ground. An important element of his or her defense is consent by the party involved.

For the defense to stand up, however, the consent must be proven by the defendant in an action, and the consent must be as broad as the invasion of privacy. A young man had consented to have his picture taken, ostensibly discussing the World Series. *Front Page Detective* magazine used the photograph, however, to illustrate an article entitled "Gang Boy." Courts allowed the photographed person to recover damages, ruling that consent to one thing is not necessarily consent to another.

The best rule is to obtain a signed release, something that many subjects are not always willing to provide to a reporter. Good intentions are not always a good defense, and a reporter may honestly believe that he or she had implicit consent from a person to invade that person's privacy. Without clear and specified consent, the danger will always be present and must be taken into account. The reporter should remember that the burden of proof will be on him or her to show just what the plaintiff in an action consented to.

Journalists should not take excessive comfort in the defenses of either newsworthiness or consent. Both remain dangerously subject to the perception of judge and jury.

The Ethical Limits

The legal limits to privacy are in a constantly changing state, but the ethical limits, which become much more subjective, depend on even shiftier sands. Often the limits depend simply on the reporter's perception of what is news, but more often the complex social fabric of society helps to determine those limits within which he or she must operate.

Ethics, the discipline dealing with what is good and bad and with moral duty, sets a special obligation on the journalist. His or her community will play an important part in setting the ground rules concerning privacy that are ultimately adopted and generally observed. So the reporter must think not only about the legal limitations in pursuing a sensitive story, but must also use an ethical yardstick in final decisions to produce material that invades a person's privacy.

—People *do* after all have a right to privacy.

—But the public *does* have a right to be informed about issues that concern it.

The basic questions then become

—Just what do people have a right to know? When do they have a right to know it? in What form should it be presented? How much do they have a right to know before it becomes merely a prurient interest in the affairs of others?

To draw from an example, a mayor is considered a public figure; yet many communities consider that he is entitled to at least some privacy. And while his public duties are subject to constant and often piercing scrutiny, his private life remains rather private. Yet at one point the mayor is reported to have been involved in a midnight altercation at an out-of-the-way tavern. Police were called but no charges were filed. While no one will discuss the incident "for the record," the persistent reporter is aware of the story. Does this public official have any right to privacy outside his public duties?

The line is difficult to draw, but some guidelines can be set down that will at least create a climate in which there is some assurance that both these basic rights are protected. The reporter can begin with these:

1. Anything that affects people should be reported.
2. Anything that can be legitimately considered news should be considered as publishable.
3. Anything that the press cannot be sued for publishing is at least worthy of consideration.
4. When there is danger that privacy becomes secrecy, the decision to publish becomes simpler.

An affirmative response to some or all of these guidelines offers solid ground for the reporter's decision to pursue the story.

Legitimate Public Figures

It is always somewhat easier to make such decisions on public figures, those who occupy the positions of pervasive power and influence or those who thrust themselves into the public limelight to influence events.

The press, however, has been ambivalent in its coverage of the purely personal affairs of such public figures. One powerful congressman's problems with alcoholism, for example, were well known for years but went unpublicized until after his death. Another congressman's well-known alliance with a nightclub entertainer was the subject of much talk in the nation's capital, but it did not break into print until a minor traffic infraction created news coverage that ultimately resulted in the official's resignation from office. The late President John F. Kennedy's personal friendships with a number of women were not unknown to many reporters, yet they went unreported until long after his death in 1963.

Author David Shaw asks a pointed question about public figures:

> Is it a legitimate news story when (actress) Doris Day's son files for divorce? Or when (former Vice President) Spiro Agnew's son is arrested as a peeping Tom? Or when Senator James Abourezk's son is given food

stamps? Or when Los Angeles Mayor Bradley's daughter or Pennsylvania Senator Hugh Scott's daughter or (comedian) Jerry Lewis' son is arrested on relatively minor drug charges?

He points out that respected newspapers printed these stories—but only because the stories involved the offspring of celebrities. "Stories on divorce, suicide, voyeurism and routine drug cases are rarely published if they involve the children of truck drivers and waitresses and bank tellers," Shaw writes.

Editors are beginning to question whether such celebrity stories constitute an unwarranted invasion of privacy for both parent and child, but there are no rules to go by. Almost every case, an ethics committee convened by the American Society of Newspaper Editors decided, had to be judged on its own merits. There was no broad consensus.

Who is qualified to decide whether a messy divorce, late-night partying, a child's misstep or psychiatric treatment in a private hospital facility affects a public official's fulfillment of his or her duties? The reporter may find it easier to make a case for publicizing an illness or a liaison that offers potential conflict of interest for an officeholder, but the difficult cases remain.

Questionable Public Figures

A professor at a public university may qualify as a public figure because he or she is on the public payroll, yet maintain a certain right to privacy because there is no effort to seek the limelight. The wife or daughter of a public official may not seek the limelight, and in fact may not even campaign for their relative, yet are considered to be public figures.

Excessive efforts to collect a private loan may give rise to notoriety for a person. When does he or she become a public figure? A person is suffering from a rare disease yet desires a certain amount of privacy in a hospital setting. When does he or she become a public figure?

Questionable public figures are far more difficult to quantify:

—A certified public accountant volunteered to perform accounting work for a political committee in 1971. An erroneous report that the accountant's firm had served as a "laundering agency" for political money, and tying the man to the story, resulted in a libel suit. However, the court quickly granted the defendant's request to drop the case, deciding that no malice was involved and that the accountant had thrust himself into the public eye by volunteering to assist the political committee.

The noted Firestone case has tended to narrow the court's protection of the press in the area of privacy:

—Mrs. Russel Firestone, wife of the heir to the tire fortune, had filed suit against *Time* magazine after the publication reported in 1967 that she had been divorced "on grounds of extreme cruelty and adultery." The magazine also noted, 'According to certain testimony in behalf of Mr. Firestone, extramarital escapades of Mrs. Firestone were bizarre and of an amatory nature that would have made Dr. Freud's hair curl."

After losing a $100,000 Florida court decision to Mrs. Firestone, *Time* appealed to the U.S. Supreme Court, contending that she was a public figure, which would obligate Mrs. Firestone to prove that the magazine was guilty of "actual malice" as well as inaccuracy. *Time* contended that Mrs. Firestone had held press conferences during the divorce proceedings and subscribed to a press clipping service, further enhancing her status as a public figure.

The court, however, decided for Mrs. Firestone, ruling that she had a right to sue *Time*, Inc. as a private person because she had merely exercised her privilege of going to court for a divorce. The Firestone case indicates the murkiness of the privacy waters for reporters trying to draw a line on legitimate privacy.

Purely private figures, such as businessmen and women, can often be construed as affecting the public interest in what they do. The industrialist who operates a huge plant in a city may become a subject of public debate when his actions in closing part of the operation affect the tax structure of the community. How far is the reporter justified in personally pursuing the industrialist to complete the story? The press can often make a good case for pursuit of persons operating in the private sector because of the involvement in the business, financial or industrial structure of the city.

Missoula: A Classic Argument

Nowhere has the confrontation between the public's right to know and a family's right to privacy been so delineated as in the Cindy Herbig story:

—In early 1979, *The Washington Post* developed a story on the life and death of Miss Herbig, the daughter of a prominent Missoula, Montana couple, who had been stabbed to death a week earlier on the streets of Washington, D.C. She was 20.

Miss Herbig, a talented but troubled student at the prestigious Radcliffe College in Cambridge, Massachusetts, had dropped out of school, returned to Missoula briefly, then went east with a man she had met in a bar. Police said the man had approached several local women in an effort to lure them into prostitution. In Washington, Miss Herbig was twice convicted on prostitution charges before she was murdered.

The *Post* story, which detailed these facts, was picked up and published by the hometown newspaper, *The Missoulian*, resulting in a storm of criticism from readers. Outraged subscribers denounced the newspaper's insensitivity to the dead child and her bereaved parents. Educator Jack Hart, who studied the aftermath of the publication of the story, wrote:

> The anguish the Herbig story brought to bear on all parties involved set into sharp focus the soft, treacherous ground between some news values and a growing public concern for the right to privacy.

In the wake of the controversy, journalists seized upon the *Post* story and the *Missoulian's* handling of it to examine their own ethical as well as news values. While reader surveys indicated that public opinion ran strongly against such publication, editors reached a consensus: A local newspaper faced with a similar story "would have to publish." However, management of the newspaper owed readers an explanation for its reasoning in invading the privacy of those involved.

As a direct outgrowth of the Herbig story, articles detailing the continuing recruitment by peripatetic pimps of dissatisfied young women for purposes of prostitution were published, resulting in greater public awareness of the dangers posed to young people.

The Herbig story suggests the continuing obligation on the part of reporter and editor to weigh the costs and benefits of decisions of this nature.

The Journalist's Responsibility

In the end, the responsibility for making such decisions rests with the reporter and editor, who must exercise good taste, judgment and restraint.

The statement of principles adopted by the American Society of Newspaper Editors places on newspaper people a "particular responsibility. Journalism demands of its practitioners not only industry and knowledge, but also the pursuit of a standard of integrity proportionate to the journalist's singular obligation."

Under a section on fair play, the statement places this additional responsibility on the reporter:

> Journalists should respect the rights of people involved in the news, observe the common standards of decency and stand accountable to the public for the fairness and accuracy of their news reports.

While these principles are non-specific, their use as guidelines is unquestioned. Such a yardstick can be helpful to the public affairs reporter in reaching the ethical decision and doing the right thing.

Privacy Legislation

While the concept of the individual's right to privacy has evolved through the common law, fewer than half a dozen states have enacted statutes protecting persons from invasion of privacy.

The main statutory thrust in the direction of individual rights has come at the federal level, mainly in the Privacy Act of 1974 and accompanying amendments which are designed to protect the privacy of students and parents in public schools.

The legislation (P.L. 93-579) was enacted by Congress to counter harm to individual privacy from the increasing use of computers and sophisticated information technology. The law gives an individual the right to inspect records maintained on him or her by most federal agencies through establishment of a code of fair information practices for use of government records.

Most federal agencies must now obtain written permission before releasing an individual's records for anything but "routine" use or to anyone other than officials of law enforcement agencies. Federal employees are subject to criminal penalties for releasing personal information or records without permission from the person in question. The act also placed limitations on the use of social security numbers as personal identifiers.

Later in 1974, the Congress enacted the Family Educational Rights and Privacy Act, commonly known as the Buckley Amendment because of the efforts of then Sen. James Buckley (R-N.Y.) to protect the privacy of parents and school children. The act generally insures access to school records by parents and students but denies such access to others. Written permission must be obtained from either the student or the parents to obtain access to information. There are exemptions—school officials of the institution where the records are maintained and those considering a student's application for financial aid.

Consent is not required to disclose information to groups conducting educational studies if the student will not personally be identified in conclusions reached or reports made. If it is necessary to protect the health and safety of the student or others, personally identifiable information may be disclosed. And student "directory information" may be provided to the press and public, unless the student or parent requests that it be withheld. This information includes the student's name, address, telephone number, date and place of birth, major field of study, participation in officially recognized activities, height and weight if an athlete, dates of attendance and awards received, and the most recent school attended.

While this kind of material can be useful to a reporter, the potential problems in obtaining other kinds of information can be easily identified. Athletes with academic problems, for example, may be threatened with suspension from teams; yet little or none of this kind of information may be officially supplied. While the legislation protects the privacy of individuals, it also has the effect of limiting access of the press to educational information.

Suggested Readings

SHAW, DAVID, *Journalism Today* (New York: Harper, 1977). Chapter 1 "Public Figures, Private Lives."

MILLER, ARTHUR, *The Assault on Privacy* (Ann Arbor, MI: University of

Michigan Press, 1971). The chapter, "The Law Relating to Privacy," is useful.

PRACTISING LAW INSTITUTE, New York City, *Communications Law.* An invaluable reference manual produced annually and designed to keep interested parties up to date in the field of communications law. Special sections on development of privacy law.

Index

Abraham, Henry J., 262
Adversary relationship, 386
Agricultural Marketing Service, 119
Agricultural Research Service, 118
Agricultural Stabilization and Conservation Service, 119
Agriculture, Department of, 118–19, 380
  state, 94
Air Force, U.S., 111
Alabama, 179
Alaska, 353
Alcohol, Tobacco and Firearms, Bureau of, 175, 244, 245
American Bar Association, 182
American Civil Liberties Union, 220
American Council on Consumer Interests, 379
American Federation of Labor, 311
American Federation of Labor–Congress of Industrial Organizations (AFL–CIO), 302
American Movers Conference, 339
American Political Science Review, 145
American Society of Newspaper Editors, 387, 434, 436
American Society of Planning Officials, 153
Anderson, Jack, 392
Arbitration, labor, 317
Army, U.S., 111
Assault on Privacy, The, 423
Attorney general, state, 86
Auditor, state, 68, 87
Authorities (*See* Special districts)

Banks, Louis, 332
Barker, Bernard, 251
Barlett, Donald L., 410
Baton Rouge, La., 15
Bernstein, Carl, 402
Berry, John M., 333
Better Business Bureau, 369, 379
Blackmun, Harry, 272
Bliss, George, 154
Bollens, John C., 38, 143
Border Patrol, 245
Boston, Mass., 15, 42, 145, 423
Brandeis, Louis D., 423–24
Brown, Edmund Jr., 281
Buchanan, Patrick, 390
Buckley, James, 437
Burger, Warren, 272
Burke, Edmund, 280
Business
  monitoring the community, 335
  state agencies, 95
Business pages, 326–30
Byrne, John A., 353

California, 183
Caro, Robert, 408
Carter, James Earl, 387–88
Caucuses, state party, 67
Census, Bureau of, 114
Center for Auto Safety, 366
Center for the Study of Responsive Law, 366
Changing Times, 379
Chase, Stuart, 364
Chatters, Carl H., 152
Chicago, Ill., 145, 363, 400
Chicago Sun-Times, 353
Chicago Tribune, 154
Cigar Makers Union, 312
City charter, 8
City clerk, 21, 30
City council (commission), 16
  operation of, 16–22
  ordinances and resolutions, 17
City managers, 12–14, 18
Civil Aeronautics Board, 109, 116, 177, 344
Closed shop, 319
Coast Guard, U.S., 102, 247
Cohen, Julius, 146
Colorado, 180
Commerce, Department of, 102, 113–14, 318, 347, 380
Commodity Credit Corporation, 119
Commodity Futures Trading Commission, 344
Common Cause, 71
Complaint
  civil, 192, 193–96
  criminal, 258
Comprehensive Education and Training Act, 108
Comptroller of the Currency, Office of, 347
Confidential sources, protecting, 406
Congress, U.S., 104–106
  and economic news, 348
Congress of Industrial Organizations, 312

Congressional Information Service Index, 411
Constitution
federal, 65
state, 64
Consumer Affairs, Office of, 366
Consumer News, 380
Consumer Product Safety Act, 366
Consumer Product Safety Commission, 379, 411
Consumer Reports, 379
Consumer Sourcebook, 380
Consumers
movement in United States, 361–62
historical background, 362–67
perception of marketplace, 367–68
Consumer's Arsenal, 380
Consumer's Bill of Rights, 365–66
Consumer's League, 363
Contempt of court, 168–69
Cordtz, Dan, 333
Corps of Engineers, U.S., 111–12
Courts, 163–210, 249–76
Civil action, 191–210
Answer, 196–98
Arrest and bail, 203
Calendar, 206
Certiorari, 205
Claim and delivery, 203
Complaint, 192–96
Consent decree, 199–200
Counterclaim, 199
Default judgment, 197
Demurrer, 198
Depositions, 200
Discovery, 200
Garnishment, 203
Habeas corpus, 203, 234
Injunction, 201–203
Interrogatories, 200
Mandamus, 204
Motions, 199
Plea in abatement, 198
Pretrial conference, 205
Prohibition, 205
Summary judgment, 199
Trial proceedings, 207–210
Writ of attachment, 203
Common law, 170
Contempt, 168–69
Criminal action, 249–76
Arraignment, 258
Arrest, 258
Complaint, 258
Demurrer, 264
Free press vs. fair trial, 271–72
Grand jury, 261, 262–64
Information, 262
Justice of peace, 58, 180–81
Kinds of crime, 254–58
Officers of the court, 266
Plea bargaining, 260–61
Courts [*cont.*]
Pleas, 259
Preliminary hearing, 261
Presentment, 263
Pretrial pleading, 264–65
Rights of the accused, 252–53
Trial procedure, 265–71
Defendant, 192
Different methods of coverage, 166
Federal, 173–79
Appellate courts, 177
Court of Claims, 177
Court of Customs and Patent Appeals, 177
Court of Military Appeals, 177
Customs Court, 177
District courts, 174
Supreme Court, 178, 271–72, 431, 435
General damages, 194
Judgment order, 192
Judicial process, 163–90
Jurisdiction, 172
Nominal damages, 194
Plaintiff, 192
Pleadings, 192
Prayer, 192, 196
Punitive damages, 194
Researching cases, 187–89
Reversals, 184
Special damages, 194
staffing, 181–87
attorneys, 186
bailiff, 187
clerk, 184
commissioners, 185
court reporter, 186
friend of court, 187
judge, 182–84
jury commission, 185
magistrate, U.S., 176–77
marshal, U.S., 177
masters, 185
referees, 185
state, 173, 179–87
Statutory law, 170
Substantive vs. procedural law, 171
County boards and agencies, 58–60
County officials, 51–58
agricultural agent, 56
assessor, 46, 55
attorney, 54
auditor, 55
clerk, 53
clerk of court, 57
coroner, 58
engineer, 55
health officer, 56
justice of peace, 58, 180–81
prosecuting attorney, 58, 262–63
purchasing agent, 56
recorder

County officials [*cont.*]
register of deeds, 53
sheriff, 57
surveyor, 55
treasurer, 54
Customs Service, U.S., 347
Cutlip, Scott, 351

Dade County, Fla., 15
Daley, Richard, 11
Defamation (*See* Libel)
Defense, Department of, 110–13, 394
Delaware, 66
Democratic National Committee, 251
Democratic Party, 251, 252
Denver, Colo. 42
District of Columbia, 251
Dodd, Thomas, 427
Donaldson, Sam, 388
Dorfman, John, 380
Dougherty, William P., 353
Drug Enforcement Administration, 175, 242, 245

Economic Development Administration, 99, 113
Education
Department of, 135
Office of, 115, 380
reporting, 122–42
budgeting process, 131–34
governing boards, 125
personnel matters, 129
powers of officials, 125
school board agenda, 128
school district, 124
state involvement, 88
Employment agencies, 318
Energy, Department of, 103, 347, 380
Energy Reporter, 380
Environmental Protection Agency, 98, 99, 248, 411
Equal Employment Opportunity Commission, 248
Equal Opportunity, Office of, 115
Extension Service, 118

Fair Labeling and Packaging Act, 366
Fair Labor Standards Act, 319
Farm Credit Administration, 118
Farm Economics Review, 379
Farmers Home Administration, 118
Federal Aviation Administration, 101, 102, 116, 244
Federal Bureau of Investigation, 108, 175, 216, 242, 251
functions of, 244
Federal Communications Commission, 177, 344, 346
Federal Contract Compliance, Office of, 316
Federal Crop Insurance Corporation, 119
Federal Highway Administration, 65, 116
Federal Home Loan Bank Board, 346
Federal judiciary (*See* Courts, federal)
Federal Mediation and Conciliation Service, 319–20
Federal Railroad Administration, 117
Federal Register, The, 121, 342, 379
Federal Reserve System, 344, 346
Federal Trade Commission, 248, 366, 379, 411
Firestone, Mrs. Russell, 434
Fish and Wildlife Service, U.S., 248
Florence, Heather Grant, 423
Florida Publishing Co., 428
Florida State Turnpike Authority, 155
Food and Drug Administration, 107, 242, 366, 380, 411
Food and Nutrition Service, 119
Ford, Gerald, 291
Forest Service, U.S., 101, 119
Foster, Jack, 368
Frankel, Max, 395
Fraternal Association of Steel Haulers, 323
Freedom of Information Act, 411, 413, 417–18
Freeland, Kent, 408
Friedman, Leonard M., 424
Front Page Detective, 432
FTC News, 379

Galveston, Texas, 12
Gannett Group, 368
Gannett News Service, 405
Gannett v. DePasquale, 271–72
Gans, Herbert, 397, 399–400
General Accounting Office, 111
General Services Administration, 119, 247
Geological Survey, U.S., 117
Gilbertson, H. S., 143
Gompers, Samuel, 312
Government
county, 38–61
budgeting process, 48
equalization board, 47
financing, 46
forms of, 41–42
organization, 52
taxes, 46
who governs?, 42–46
federal, 97–121
covering at the local level, 98–103
regulators, 107–109
structure, 109–120
municipal, 3–37 (*Also see* City)
audits, 24

Government [*cont.*]
budgeting process, 23, 28
charter, 8
conflict, 6
defined, 5
forms, 10
operating funds, 26
organization, 18, 27
personnel matters, 35
policy-making process, 33
pressure groups, 9, 31
taxes, 26
special district (*See* Special districts)
state, 62–96
agencies and departments, 87–95
constitutions, 64
executive branch, 80
governor, 83–85
institutions, 96
legislative branch, 66–80
officials, 85–87
politics, 84
powers, 64
pressure groups, 70, 82
Governor, 62, 67, 74, 83–85
Grand jury, 168, 261, 262–264
Greene, Robert, 408
Gulick, Luther, 151

Harper's magazine, 353
Hart, Jack, 436
Harvard Law Review, 423
Hazlitt, Bill, 236
Health, Education and Welfare, Department of, 110 (*See also* Health and Human Services, Department of)
Health and Human Services, Department of, 91, 114–15, 366
Health, National Institutes of, 115
Health
and safety standards, 95
state involvement, 90
Hedges, Roger, 405
Helicopter Association of America, 335
Herbig, Cindy, 435
Hill, James, 431
Holmes, James, 431
Home Appliance Manufacturers, Association of, 369
Home Furnishings Daily, 379
Housing and Urban Development, Department of, 102, 110, 380, 411

Immigration and Naturalization Service, 245
India, 392
Indian Affairs, Bureau of, 117
Indianapolis, Ind., 15
Industrial development, state, 95
Interior, Department of, 117
Internal Revenue Service, 102, 247, 414
Interstate Commerce Commission, 177, 339
Isaacs, Norman, 240
Izaak Walton League, 71

Jacksonville, Fla., 15
Johnson, Lyndon B., 388–89
Jones, Mrs. Lillian, 430
Judge (*See* Courts)
Judiciary (*See* Courts)
Jungle, The, 363
Jurisdiction (*See* Courts)
Justice, Department of, 110, 242, 251, 417
Justice of peace, (*See* Courts, criminal actions)

Kaufman, Irving, 166, 272
Kennedy, Donald, 120
Kennedy, John F., 365, 433
Kettleborough, Charles, 145
Kissinger, Henry A., 387, 392
Knights of Labor, Noble Order of, 311
Kovner, Victor A., 423
Kristol, Irving, 386, 390

Labor
coverage of, 301–25
covering disputes, 321–24
federal legislation, 318–21
historical background, 311–13
organization, 314–16
politics, 314
public employee unions, 304
state agencies, 95
state legislation, 316–18
Labor, Department of, 103, 110, 177, 302, 319, 320, 411
Labor-Management Reporting Act (Landrum-Griffin Act), 320
Labor Statistics, Bureau of, 337
LaGuardia, Fiorello, 11
Land Management, Bureau of, 117
Law enforcement, 211–248
booking register, 237
complaint board, 225
federal agencies, 244–48
guidelines for police, press, 237
homicide, 232
hospital coverage, 240–41
police blotter, 217, 223–25
police chief, 217–21
police department organization, 217–223
policy-making, 217
service bureau, 225
state agencies, 242–444
suicide, 232

Law enforcement [*cont.*]
to print or not to print, 238–40
Law Enforcement Assistance Administration, 247
League of Women Voters, 71
Lee, Richard, 288
Legislature, state, 66–80
calendar, 72
committee system, 71, 73
councils, 68
coverage, 74–80
floor debate, 73
law-making process, 69
lobbyists, 70
local legislation, 78
organization, 67
Levittown, N.J., 399, 400
Libel, 214, 228–29
Life magazine, 428, 431
Lippmann, Walter, 387–88
Liston, Harold, 390
Lloyd George, David, 145
Lobbyists, state, 70 (*Also see* Politics; Special interest groups)
Lockouts (*See* Labor, covering disputes)
London, Port of, 145
London Observer, 145
Louisville Courier-Journal, 428
Louisville Herald-Post, 430

McCartney, James, 396
Marine Corps, U.S., 111
Maritime Commission, Federal, 411
Maritime Administration, 113
Marshal's Service, U.S., 247
Martin, Roscoe C., 157
Maryland, University of, 426, 428
Mayor, 10–13
Mediation, labor, 317
Mencken, H. L., 279
Metropolitan government, 14
Meyer, Peter, 353
Miami, Fla., 15
Miller, Arthur R., 423
Milton, John, 400
Mines, Bureau of, 117
Mining Enforcement and Safety Administration, 247
Minneapolis Times, 430
Minnesota, 66
Minority Business Enterprise, Office of, 113
Missoula, Mont., 435
Missoulian, 435–36
Missouri, 183
University of, 352
Mitchell, John N., 394
Mohler, Harold S., 330
Mollenhoff, Clark, 407
Money, 379
Monitoring public opinion, 295–99
Moses, Robert, 151

Municipal court, 180
Municipal government (*See* Government, municipal)

Nader, Ralph, 366
Namath, Joe, 429
Nashville, Tenn., 15
National Association of Realtors, 335
National Bowling Council, 335
National Bureau of Standards, 113
National Commission on Product Safety, 366
National Guard, 85, 92, 243
National Highway Traffic Safety Administration, 380
National Labor Relations Act (Wagner Act), 319
National Labor Relations Board, 177, 319, 411
National Labor Union, 311
National Park Service, 117
National Railroad Passenger Corporation (Amtrak), 117
National Transportation Safety Board, 344
National Weather Service, 102, 113
Natural resources, state, 94
Navy, U.S., 111
Nixon, Richard M., 41, 251, 390, 392
Nebraska, 66, 424
Nebraska Press Assn. vs. Stuart, 271
Nessen, Ron, 291
Nevada, 349
New Hampshire, 66
New Jersey, 145, 153
New Jersey Highway Authority, 154
New Mexico, 349
New Orleans, La., 15, 42, 145
New York City, 15, 42, 145
New York Port Authority, 145, 146, 155
New York Post, 149
New York state, 150, 181, 428, 431
New York Times, 155, 156, 157, 394, 395, 398
Newark Star-Ledger, 155
Newsday, 408
Newsroom Guide to Polls & Surveys, 299
Newton, V. M., 397
North Carolina, 180
Nuclear Regulatory Commission, 344, 347

O'Brien, Lawrence, 251
Occupational Safety and Health Administration, 320
Occupational Safety and Health Review Commission, 344
O'Harrow, Dennis, 153
Ohio, 180
Ombudsman, 372

Onondaga (N.Y.) County Water Authority, 157
Open meetings laws, 127, 142, 156
Oregon, 349
Otwell, Ralph, 353

Pakistan, 392
Patterson, James D., 152
Pearson, Drew, 427
Pennsylvania, 152, 153, 353
Pentagon, 111
Pentagon Papers, 389, 392, 394
Personnel Management, Office of, 104
Pfretzchner, Paul A., 153
Philadelphia, Pa., 15, 42, 145
Planning and zoning, 413
Planning and zoning boards, 59
Police (*See* Law enforcement)
Political parties, 283–86
  and elections, 279–300
    backgrounding stories, 290
    caucuses, 287
    elections, 286–87
    ground rules, 292–94
    keeping confidences, 288
    selective perception, 288–90
Politics
  in education, 125
  in the judiciary, 182
  in labor, 314
  in municipalities, 31–33
  in special districts, 153
  at state level, 84
Polling (*See* Monitoring public opinion)
Pool, Ithiel de Sola, 386, 388
Porter, Kirk, 151
Portland, Ore., 145
Postal Service, U.S., 245, 246
Pottsville (Pa.) Republican, 353
Powell, Jody, 388
Precinct
  police, 217
  political, 284
Pressure groups (*See* Special interest groups; Politics)
Privacy, legal limits to, 424–29, 436–37
Privacy Act of 1974, 436–37
Property records, checking, 414–17
Public Buildings Service, 247
Public Citizen Inc., 366
Public figure, defined, 421
Public Health Service, 91, 115
Public information office, 350–52
Public Interest Research Group, 366
Public Officials and the Press, 288
Public Opinion Quarterly, 400
Public utilities, 92
Pulitzer Prize, 154, 155, 392
Purchasing Management, National Association of, 339

Reardon, Paul C., 238
Reardon rules, 238
Reclamation, Bureau of, 117
Reedy, George, 388
Rehnquist, William, 272
Reporters and Officials, 387
Republican Party, 252
Reston, James, 395, 398
Revenue sharing
  county, 49–50
  education, 135
  municipal, 26
Rhode Island, 42, 424
Richmond Newspapers vs. Commonwealth of Virginia, 272
Rivers, William L., 283, 386
Rockefeller, Nelson, 281
Rural Development Service, 118
Rural Electrification Administration, 118

San Francisco, 42
Saturday Evening Post, 431
Schlink, F. J., 364
Schools (*See* Education)
Secret Service, U.S., 246
Secretary of State, 85
Securities & Exchange Commission, 248, 344–45, 410
Shaw, David, 433
Shepard's Citations, 189
Sigal, Leon V., 387
Sinclair, Upton, 363
Sloat, Bill, 405
Small, William, 397
Social and Economic Statistics Administration, 114
Social Security Administration, 98
Soil Conservation Service, 118
South Carolina, 180, 349
Special districts, 143–59
  functions, 146–54
  origins, 145
  secretiveness, 156–57
Special interest groups, 82 (*See also* Politics)
Sports Illustrated, 425, 429
St. Petersburg Times, 155
State, Department of, 110, 392
State Abortion League, 71
State, County and Municipal Employees Union, 313
State militia (*See* National Guard)
Steele, James B., 410
Stevens, John Paul, 271
Stewart, Potter, 261
Strikes (*See* Labor, covering disputes)
Sunshine legislation, 16 (*See also* Open meetings laws)
Superintendent of Documents, 110
Supreme Court, U.S., 271–72, 431, 435

Taft–Hartley Act (Labor Management Relations Act), 319
Tamm, Quinn, 235
Taxes, municipal, 26
Taylor, Arthur R., 331
Teamsters, International Brotherhood of, 312, 323
Telecommunications, Office of, 113
Texas, 12
Time Inc. vs. Hill, 431
Time magazine, 342, 434
Transportation
  Department of, 116–17, 247, 380
  state, 93
Travel Service, U.S., 113
Treasurer, state, 87
Treasury, Department of, 102, 245, 246, 347
Trial balloons, 283, 307
Truman, Harry S, 401
Tucker, Carl, 332

Unemployment compensation, 317
United Farm Workers Organizing Committee, 312
United Mine Workers, 312
U.S. Chamber of Commerce, 334
United States Government Manual, 110, 242, 418
Unsafe at Any Speed, 366

Veterans Administration, 103, 120
Veto, governor's, 74
Vietnam conflict, 389, 394
Virgil, Michael, 425
Virginia, 42

Wager, Paul C., 40
Walker, Stanley, 350
Wall Street Journal, 379
Warren, Samuel D., 423–24
Washington Post, 251, 435
Washington Star, 426, 428
Wasserman, Paul, 380
Watergate case, 251
Waters, Barney, 370
Weaver, David H., 299
Weaver, Paul, 390
Weintraub, Tina, 152
Welfare, state, 90–91
Welles, Chris, 334
West Virginia, 290
West's Digest, 188
Whips, party, 68
Wicker, Tom, 390
Wilhoit, G. Cleveland, 299
Witcover, Jules, 388
Work stoppages (*See* Labor, covering disputes)
Workman's compensation, 317
World Traders Data Reports, 347

Your Money's Worth, 364

Zacchini, Hugo, 429
Zoning records, 413, 415
Zoning variances, 415